AF540964

MANAGING AND MEASURING PATIENTS' SATISFACTION

MANAGING AND MEASURING PATIENTS' SATISFACTION

By

Professor (Dr.) Parimal H. Vyas

Dean, Faculty of Commerce & Head
Dept. of Commerce & Business Management
The Maharaja Sayajirao University of Baroda
Vadodara (Gujarat)
(India)

&

Dr. Madhusudan N. Pandya

Faculty Member
Dept. of Commerce & Business Management
Faculty of Commerce
The Maharaja Sayajirao University of Baroda
Vadodara (Gujarat)
(India)

DISCOVERY PUBLISHING HOUSE PVT. LTD.

NEW DELHI-110 002

Published by:

Tilak Wasan

DISCOVERY PUBLISHING HOUSE PVT. LTD.

4383/4B, Ansari Road, Darya Ganj

New Delhi-110 002 (India)

Phone : +91-11-23279245, 43596064-65

Fax : +91-11-23253475

E-mail : discoverypublishinghouse@gmail.com

sales@discoverypublishinggroup.com

parul.wasan@gmail.com

web : www.discoverypublishinggroup.com

First Edition: **2013**

ISBN: 978-93-5056-277-2

Managing and Measuring Patients' Satisfaction

Printed at:

Aditi Fine Art Press

Delhi

The Success of Every Child is a Credit
To the Parents

With Lots of Love and
Hearty Salutations

I Dedicate this book

to My

Beloved Father

Sri K.S. SANTIAGO

Preface

Services are many times found slow to respond to users' demands about what services should be available, about when and where they should be provided, and about what standards of staff behaviour, information provision, accommodation and service outcomes are acceptable to the public. One would have thought that attempts to diagnose and solve this problem. By the mid 1980s, marketing departments has been established in most of the large healthcare organizations in West part of India. By early 1990s, market orientation at the level of the firm has been achieved to a substantial extent in the healthcare industry. However, the same has not been readily penetrated down into the customer orientation of the personnel involved in the provision of healthcare services. The importance of marketing in healthcare today is reflected by the fact that many health professionals are encouraged if not commended to become marketers of a sort. Today, thousands of healths professional with no marketing background are being asked to develop marketing plans for their healthcare units. There is no doubt that the concept of marketing requires knowledge about customers' satisfaction and healthcare is no exception to it.

The importance of customer satisfaction is well recognized by organizations involved in providing various services and they are continuously striving to maintain their base of satisfied customers. Such satisfied customers are profitable and generate revenue by purchasing more, and more often they recommend such service to new customers and as such they deserve special consideration from the service provider. Much attention has been given to this aspect in the literature and still many efforts to make in this area for further improvement in satisfying customers. The researcher took up the present study and has made an effort to determine the underlying dimensions of satisfaction in health care service especially in hospital services provided by Government Hospitals, Trust Hospitals and Private Hospitals. Based on empirical evidence the important underlying dimensions has been identified and presented in the book.

The subject matter of this book titles as "Managing and Measuring Patients' Satisfaction" is organized in eight chapters and brief sketch about the same is discussed below.

In Chapter 1 a brief review of health sector of India is made considering critical diagnosis of healthcare sector of India and public health planning in India considering history way back to Indus valley civilization, period of Ashoka, and in modern time Bhore Committee report etc. The review of National Health Care Policy (NHP) of India was also covered in this chapter. It also includes review of Gujarat Human Development Report: 2004 and review of "human development in south Asia, 2004 – the health challenge". At the end of the chapters highlights of Global Public Health is provided.

The Chapter 2 provides highlight of review of literature on patients' satisfaction which covers an important areas related to patients' satisfaction and its measurement such as, Patients' Satisfaction with Quality of Services; Patients' Satisfaction; Comparison of Patients' Satisfaction from Hospitals; Patients' Satisfaction and Customer Relationship Management; Measurement of Attitude of Patients; Patients' Expectations/Perceptions and Patients' Safety emerging issues and challenges.

Chapter 3 incorporates discussion on need for measurement of patients' satisfaction/service quality; factors influence patients' satisfaction measurement; critical aspect in patients' satisfaction measurement; key models for measurement for patient satisfaction/service quality.

Key success areas and challenges for patients' satisfaction and its measurement is discussed in Chapter 4, which includes areas such as Patients' Satisfaction Measurement: Hype or Hope!; Medico Negligence: A Key Disquiet For Patients' Protection; Patients' Safety, Emerging Issues and Using Information Technology [IT] For Improving Quality Of Healthcare Services.

Chapter 5 covers detailed information about the research methodology used in measuring patients' satisfaction and includes information about research design, objectives of the research study, sources of information, and sampling decisions.

Chapter 6 provide complete analysis of data for the research undertaken to measure patients' satisfaction in Government, Trust and Private Hospitals.

Chapter 7 and 8 cover the detailed information about findings of the research study and conclusion and suggestions of the research study separately for Government, Trust and Private Hospitals. It also covers details about the implications of the findings which will be helpful; to Government, Trust and Private Hospitals for understanding importance of measuring customers'/patients' satisfaction and developing their strategies for providing better healthcare services to their patients.

Aknowledgements

We sincerely express a deep sense of gratitude and respectfully acknowledge the contributions and publications offered by authors as specified in respective chapters of this book which has immensely helped us in the preparation of this publication. We are equally thankful also to the management and staff of the publisher of this book.

We welcome the esteemed readers to offer their comments and valuable suggestions on this publication.

We hope that fellow academia and the students shall certainly find this publication useful.

Authors

Contents

1

A Brief Review of Health Sector of India

The efforts of Government of India for providing the safer and healthy environment can be witnessed in form of an in the introduction of various Government programmes, policies, and legislations implemented from time to time.

An attempt to put forward a cursory overview on the health care sector of India is being made in this part on basis of available factual data concerning Health Care Indicators of India, Infrastructure for health, and Expenditure incurred for the Health Care Sector although in case of certain selected health indicators, India has improved substantially during 1951 to 2001.

One can find continuous improvement in various health indicators from the year 1951. To illustrate, life expectancy had reached to 64 years; the Infant Mortality Rate (IMR) has fallen to 63 per 1,000 Populations; Crude Birth Rate has declined to 25 whereas Crude Death Rate has fallen to 8.1. (J. Kishore, 2006). As per the Report "Macroeconomics and Health, 2005" of the National Commission, longevity in India had reached to 66 in the year 2004 whereas IMR has declined by over 70 per cent in the year 1990. Besides, the favourable changes were observed in case of selected diseases such as Malaria which has been contained at 20 lakh cases. Smallpox and Guinea-warm have been completely eradicated, and Leprosy as well as Polio has reached to nearly state of elimination. A significant improvement in the Quality of Health Care over the years becomes evident as shown in Table Number 01. Crude Birth Rate (Per 1000 Population) has induced from 40.8 in the year 1951 to 23.1 in the year 2007. Crude Death Rate (Per 1000 Population) has declined from 25.1 in the year 1951 to 7.4 in the year 2007. Similarly, Total Fertility Rate (Per Woman) had gone down from 6.0 in the year 1951 to 2.8 in the year 2006. IMR (Per 1000 Live Births) had reduced from 146 of the year 1951 to 55 in the year 2007. Child (0 to 4) Mortality Rate (Per 1000 Children) was 57.3 in the year 1972 which has reduced to 17.3 in the year 2006. The Life Expectancy at Birth for Males had increased from 37.2 in year 1951 to 62.6 during years 2002 to 2006. The Life Expectancy at Birth for Females had increased from 36.2 of the year 1951 to 64.2 during years 2002 to 2006.

(The Economic Survey, 2006-2007, 2007-2008 and 2008-2009). During years 2000 to 2005, over 1,00,000 deaths have been averted due to the up scaling of Directly Observed Treatment Short-Course (DOTS) (Ibid).

Table 1.1: Selected Health Indicators in India

Sl. No.	Selected Indicators	1951	1981	1991	Current level
01	Crude Birth Rate (CBR) (Per 1,000 Population)	40.8	33.9	29.5	**23.1 (2007)**
02	Crude Death Rate (CDR) (Per 1,000 Population)	25.1	12.5	9.8	**7.4 (2007)**
03	Total Fertility Rate (TFR) (Per Woman)	6.0	4.5	3.6	**2.8 (2006)**
04	Maternal Mortality Ratio (MMR) (Per 1,00,000 live births)	NA	NA	437 (1992-1993) NFHS	**254 (2001-2004)**
05	Infant Mortality Rate (IMR) (Per 1,000 live Births)	146 (1951-1961)	110	80	**55 (2007)**
06	Child (0 to 4) Mortality Rate (Per 1,000 Children)	57.3 (1972)	41.2	26.5	**17.3 (2006)**
07	Couple Protection Rate (In Percentages)	10.4 (1971)	22.8	44.1	**48.2 (1998-1999) NFHS**
08	Life Expectancy At Birth [8.1] Males	37.2	55.4 (1981-1985)	59.0 (1991-1995)	**62.6 (2002-2006)**
	[8.2] Females	36.2	54.7	59.7 (1991-95)	**64.2**

Source: *The Economic Survey 2006-2007, 2007-2008 and 2008-2009.*
NFHS: National Family Health Survey; NA: Not Available.

The progress has not only been observed in case of selected health indicators and diseases but the Indian health care is considered best at the global level. Indian doctors are comparable to the best in the world as they are technically proficient, and capable of performing sophisticated procedures and that too at a fraction of the cost available in the west (Ministry of Health and Family Welfare, 2005).

Further, one can also find significant improvement also in Health Care Infrastructure as shown in Table Number 02. One can find consistent increase in the total number of Dispensaries and Hospitals as well as Total Number of Beds in the Hospitals as well as Doctors and Nursing Staff (Ibid). The Rural Primary Public Health Infrastructure has recorded an impressive increase consisting of 1, 45,000 Sub-Centers as well as 23,109 Primary Health Centers, and 3,222 Community Health Centers, catering to a population of 5,000, 30,000 and 1,00,000 respectively as well as 3,000, 20,000 and 80,000 Populations in Tribes and Desert Areas respectively (Annual Report of Health and Family Welfare Report, 2005-2006).

Table 1.2: Trends in the Health Care Infrastructure in India (1951-2004)

Sl. No.	Particulars	1951	1981	2005	(Period/ Source)
01	SC/PHC/CHC	725	57,353	1,71,608	*
02	Dispensaries and Hospitals (All)	9,209	23,555	27,770	**
03	Beds (Private and Public)	1,17,198	5,69,495	9,14,543	(All types)**
04	Nursing Personnel	18,054	1,43,687	8,65,135	@
05	Doctors (Modern System)	61,800	2,68,700	6,56,111	@

Source: *Ibid.*

* RHS: Rural Health Statistics, 2006.

** Health information of India, 2004. @ National Health profile, 2005.

Public health is of crucial importance to any community and it needs to be given priority. If one considers, the Health Expenditure of India in view of prevalent trends on basis of the various Five Year Plans of India as shown in the Table number 03, it becomes evident that the priority to Health Sector of India showed declining trend in terms of Expenditure incurred on Health as a per cent of Total Development Plans of India. The amount spent on Health Sector of India in the First Year Plan (1951-1956) was 3.33 per cent that has been reduced to 2.09 per cent in the Tenth Five Year Plan in India (2002-2007).Therefore, there exist a need to enhance and broaden the Public Health Knowledge with new research activities and community based experiences.

Table 1.3: Trends in Health Expenditure of India (1951-2002): (Rupees in Millions)

Five-year Plans	Period	Amount	Total Plan Investment (All Development Heads)	Health (Central and States)	
				Outlay/ Expenditure	Per cent of Total Plan
First	**1951-1956**	**Actual**	**1,960**	**652**	**3.33**
Second	1956-1961	Actual	4,672	1,408	3.01
Third	1661-1966	Actual	8,576.5	2,259	2.63
Annual	1966-1969	Actual	6,625.4	1,402	2.12
Fourth	1969-1974	Actual	15,778.8	3,355	2.13
Fifth	1974-1979	Actual	39,426.2	7,608	1.93
	1979-1980	Actual	12,176.5	2,231	1.83
Sixth	1980-1985	Outlay	97,500	1,821	1.87
Sixth	1980-1985	Actual	1,09,291.7	20,252	1.85
Seventh	1985-1990	Outlay	1,80,000	33,929	1.88
Seventh	1985-1990	Actual	2,18,729	36,886	1.69
	1990-1991	Actual	61,518	9,609	1.56

...(Contd.)

...*(Contd.)*

	1991-1992	Actual	65,855	10,422	1.58
Eighth	1992-1997	Outlay	4,34,100	75,822	1.75
Ninth	1997-2002	Outlay	8,59,200	19,818.4	2.31
Tenth	2002-2007	Outlay	14,84,131.3	31023.3	2.09
Eleventh	**2007-2012**	**Outlay**	**36,44 ,718**	**–**	**–**

Source: *www.cbhidghs.nic.in* (1) GOI, 1997 (Adapted from Human Development in South Asia, 2004), and Central Bureau of Health Intelligence, Ministry of health and Family Welfare.

It becomes evident that the priority to health sector showed declining trend in terms of expenditure incurred on health as a per cent of total development plans of India.

The amount spent on health sector in the first plan (1951-1956) was 3.33 per cent that has been reduced to 0.6 per cent in the ninth five year plan in India. Further, the year wise details of expenditure by private and public sector on Medical Health and Sanitation are provided in Table number 1.4 as follows.

Table 1.4: Details of Year-wise Expenditure on Medical, Health and Sanitation in India

Year	Private Final Consumption Expenditure on Health	RVE on Medical, Health and Sanitation (both Central and State)	RVE Increase in Percentages	CPE on Medical, Health and Sanitation (Both Central and State)	CPE Increase in Percentages
Apr-1991	14698	4917.88	–	241.79	–
Apr-1992	16065	5429.15	10.396	296.5	22.627
Apr-1993	17557	6150.49	13.286	269.45	–9.1231
Apr-1994	19543	7234.48	17.624	282.9	4.9916
Apr-1995	27859	8119.05	12.227	391.35	38.335
Apr-1996	32923	7527.1	–7.291	344.62	–11.941
Apr-1997	37341	8693.69	15.499	415.78	20.649
Apr-1998	45899	9985.27	14.857	520.71	25.237
Apr-1999	65389	12203.01	22.21	584.56	12.262
Apr-2000	84359	13765.38	12.803	788.92	34.96
Apr-2001	99338	14872.68	8.0441	681.03	-13.676
Apr-2002	114413	15458.68	3.9401	717.37	5.336
Apr-2003	128303	16151.37	4.4809	779.64	8.6803
Apr-2004	146374	16837.91	4.2507	1095.27	40.484
Apr-2005	–	19821.67	17.72	1379.52	25.953
Apr-2006	–	22192.13	11.959	2054.47	48.926

{lval = level value (it gives growth value also); RVE = Revenue Expenditure; CPE =Capital Expenditure}

Source: www.cmie.com (Centre for monitoring Indian Economy-CMIE).

From Table 1.4 it is revealed that the private final consumption expenditure on health has increased continuously from Rs.14,698 Crores in April 1991 to Rs.1,46,374 Crores in April 2004. The revenue expenditure on medical, health and sanitation of both Central and State showed improvement of 10.39 per cent from April 1991 to April 1992. It further continued to improve by 13.28 percent in April 1993, and 17.62 per cent in April 1994. But, revenue expenditure has begun to reduce from April 1995 (12.22 per cent) to April 1998 (14.85 per cent). Once again, revenue expenditure had increased by 22.21 percent in April 1999 but after that it has declined continuously and percentage increased in revenue expenditure had reached to 4.25 per cent in April 2004. Revenue expenditure further increased by 17.72 per cent in April 2005 and again reduced to 11.95 per cent in April 2006.

This showed that Government of India had focused more in terms of revenue expenditure on medical, health and sanitation at both the levels that is Central and State during 1991 to 1993; from April 1997 to April 1999 and from April 2005 to April 2006. Similar was the case with Government approach towards capital expenditure on medical, health and sanitation that too showed similar trends.

The expenditure on health can also be compared with the total expenditure of Governments, and expenditure incurred on total social sector. Table number 1.5 provides data about trends of social sector expenditure by the Central and State Governments.

Table 1.5: Trends of Social Sector Expenditure by General Government (Central and State Government Combined)

Items	2001-2002 Actual	2002-2003 Actual	2003-2004 Actual	2004-2005 Actual	2005-2006 RE	2006-2007 BE
In Rupees Crore						
Total Expenditure	6,44,746	7,04,904	7,96,384	8,69,757	10,09,668	11,14,929
Expenditure on Social sector	1,37,843	1,45,226	1,56,893	1,77,016	2,22,210	2,47,572
Expenditure on Health	28,578	31,457	34,822	39,078	50,164	56.932
In Percentage						
As Percentage of GDP:						
Total Expenditure	28.26	28.77	28.85	27.82	28.30	27.19
Expenditure on Social sector	6.04	5.93	5.68	5.66	6.23	6.04
Expenditure on Health	1.25	1.28	1.26	1.25	1.41	1.39
As Percentage of Total Expenditure:						
Expenditure on Social sector	21.4	20.6	19.7	20.4	22.0	22.2
Expenditure on Health	4.4	4.5	4.4	4.5	5.0	5.1
As Percentage of Social sector Expenditure:						
Expenditure on Health	20.7	21.7	22.2	22.1	22.6	23.0

(RE -Revised Estimates, BE-Budgeted Estimates)

Source: Budget Documents of Union and State Governments/RBI (The Economic Survey 2006-2007).

In terms Governments expenditure on health as a percentage of Gross Domestic Product (GDP), it was 1.25 per cent in 2001-2002, 1.28 per cent in 2002-2003, 1.26 per cent in 2003-2004 and 1.25 per cent in 2004-2005. On an average, it remained near to 1.26 pr cent. But, it showed improvement in 2005-2006 as1.41 per cent and in 2006-2007 as 1.39 per cent respectively.

From the year 2005 onwards Government of India had put more emphasis on improvement of health of Indian population and a percentage of total expenditure on health expenditure had remained between 4.4 to 4.5 per cent from 2001-2002 to 2004-2005. But, it has showed improvement from 5.0 per cent of 2005-2006 to 5.1 per cent in 2006-2007. In terms of health expenditure as a percentage of social sector expenditure for the period from 2001-2002 to 2004-2005, it had remained at lower level of 20.7 per cent and at a higher level of 22.2 per cent. It too had showed improvement from 22.6 per cent of 2005-2005 to 23.0 per cent in 2006-2007 (The Economic Survey 2006-2007).

A CRITICAL DIAGNOSIS OF HEALTHCARE SECTOR OF INDIA

According to the Ernst and Young Healthcare Survey in the year 2007, the Indian Healthcare Industry is poised to grow at a Compounded Annual Growth Rate of 15 per cent. Nearly, 90 per cent of this growth in healthcare will come from the Private Sector. Further, Private Hospitals in India are expected to collect $35.9 Billion (Rs. 1,47,154.1 crores) in the year 2012 compared to $15.5 Billion (Rs. 63,534.5 Crores) of the year 2006. Correspondingly, along with a shift in emphasis from socialized to privatized healthcare, the share of the private sector in India's healthcare industry is set for a quantum increase in the decade of 2010.

In the early 2000s, healthcare was looked upon as a sunrise sector, three big corporate houses, Fortis Healthcare promoted by Ranbaxy Labs, Wockhardt Hospitals, and Max Healthcare announced its plans to set up hospital chains across India. Further, Mumbai-based Asian Heart Hospital and Global Hospitals and Care hospital in Hyderabad sprung up, which specialized in niche areas such as Cardiac Care, Eye Care, Orthodontics and Laparoscopy. The trend has since matured with Indian hospitals adopting many of the management practices and tools used by their counterparts in the West. With hospital chains being seen as a capital intensive business with long gestation periods, pressure has grown for greater transparency. Most private hospital chains now insist on sweating their assets to gain operational efficiencies.

An Ernst and Young and Business World undertook the very first of its kind of Survey to identify and define the Key Financial Operational Parameters and Benchmarks of the India's Healthcare Sector with critical perspectives of Business and Operational Efficiency revealed favourably on India's Healthcare Sector's growing business and operational maturity. It also highlighted new change-agents and drivers of this sector coupled with emergence of multi-specialty hospitals that have been successful in garnering the most revenues. One also witnesses on the crucial influence of Third-Party Players that is insurance companies pushing hospitals for greater financial and operational efficiency. The other major growth drivers of the India's Healthcare Sector are e.g., rising literacy levels; growing public health awareness; higher incidence of lifestyle-related diseases; this sector's recognition by Government of India as a Priority

Sector, and growth of Medical Tourism in India. The flip-side to this progress is the Private Investments which are way below the levels of its actual requirement needed to bridge the financial gap of growing India's Healthcare Sector's (www.businessworld.in). As per the Survey of the Ernst andYoung's on The Business of HealthCare: An Industry Diagnostic revealed that the boom in Indian economy has catapulted India's Healthcare Sector on to the evolutionary roadmap. Growth rates have been frenetic with both private players and the Government evincing keen interest to nurture the industry with a view to providing universal healthcare. The windfall began when one critically evaluates quality of selected medical services in select hospitals of India for less than half the prices paid in the West.

So, it is hardly surprising that healthcare is widely seen as being India's next big growth story. But, such a high investment trajectory in the health sector with the absence of any standard operational and financial benchmarks is a lacuna that needs to be addressed. As per the World Health Organization's (WHO) estimates, China had a ratio of two beds for every 1,000 people in the year 2002 compared to just a miniscule figure of 1.1 per 1,000 of India in the year 2006. To get to where China was in 2002, India needs six more years, subject to an addition of about 1.2 Million more beds and an investment of $90 billion (Rs 3,68,910 Crores, and a big portion of this investment would have to come from the private sector for the creation of Tertiary Care Infrastructure as the State increasingly focuses on the improvement of the India's Primary and Secondary Healthcare. In view of corporatizing of investment in healthcare and considering element of the profitability of existing hospitals various questions have become pertinent concerning financial records of hospitals that are not open to the public. Besides, very few healthcare companies of India have been listed on the stock exchanges which too make the task of its benchmarking of the business performance difficult of such hospitals.

The survey revealed that a majority of the hospitals are not generating operating margins close to a competing industry like hospitality. Private investors always seek higher profitability. While the primary reason for low profitability of some hospitals may be the lack of proven business models, the Indian hospitality industry, on the other hand, has clearly established business models that are globally aligned and more mature. The profitability of hospitals is also being affected by the increasing influence of Health Insurance Companies and Third Party Administrators (TPAs). Profitability is also impacted by issues such as utilization of high-end capital equipment, inadequate planning of capacity usage between various departments of hospitals, weak controls to arrest revenue leakages and the average length of stay. Finally, resource availability is the next frontier for India's healthcare industry.

With a low supply and high demand for doctors, nurses and paramedical staff, the war for talent is expected to intensify further, resulting in mounting payroll costs. Unlike the Hospitality Sector, where skills can be imparted in relatively shorter time-frames, it takes nearly six years before one can start practicing medicine and three years for the nursing staff to come on Board fully trained. Failing that, there will most likely be a deficit of 500,000 Doctors and a Million Nurses in India by the year 2012 (Ibid).

By making such allocation of funds, the Government of India had put efforts to improve the public health as the national health of India is one of vital component of global health and therefore, public health services provided to the population with the ultimate aim to prevent diseases and maintain good health. Planning of the public health in India thus has long history. An attempt to the public health history has been made as follows.

PUBLIC HEALTH PLANNING IN INDIA

National health planning is the orderly process of defining national health problems, identifying unmeet needs and surveying the resources to meet them, establishing the priority goals that are realistic and feasible and projecting administrative actions to accomplish the purpose of the proposed programme. A health plan is a predetermined course of action that is firmly based on the nature and extent of health problems from which priority goals are devised. Planning for public health services in India have long been a part of history way back to Indus valley civilization, period of Ashoka, and in modern time Bhore committee report etc.

The history of planning for public health in India is summarized as follows:

Bhore Committee (1943-1946)

In British India, an effort was made to improve public health in the form of opening of hospitals and medical colleges. A National Planning Commission was set up by the Indian National Congress in 1938. First time in India, in 1943, the British Government appointed the "Health Survey and Development Committee", with Sir Joseph Bhore as Chairman, and committee had submitted elaborate report in 1946.

It had offered various recommendations such as setting up of comprehensive primary health system based on smallest service unit for 10,000 to 20,000 population; setting up of 30 bedded hospitals for every two primary health units; formation of village health committee; doctors' should behave as 'social doctor'; formation of district board for each district as well as ensuring suitable housing, sanitary surroundings as well as safe drinking water supply, and elimination of unemployment with emphasis on preventive work.

But, after the Independence in 1947, the Government of India set up a Planning Commission in the year 1950 under Indian Constitution, and started Five Year Plans System of planning for socio economic development of India. Besides, the Five Year plans, the Government set up various committees from time to time to examine health situations or any important problem being faced by us to sought suggestions for necessary reforms.

Mudaliar Committee (1959-1961)

The Mudaliar Committee was set up under the chairmanship of Dr. A. Lakshmanswami Mudaliar to evaluate the medical and public health services since the submission of report of the Bhore Committee. It recommended for upgrading and strengthening of Public Health Centers (PBHC's); strengthening of district hospitals; offering of mobile service teams rural areas; levy of small fee except poor; long range health insurance policy all citizens; formation of central health cader; inclusion of Medical Colleges under University Grants Commission; Institute of National programs, and improving effectiveness of the Central Council of health.

Chadha Committee (1963)

A special Committee under the chairmanship of Dr. MS. Chadha, Director General, (Health Services) was appointed to recommend on details of the requirement related to PHC and maintenance of Malaria Eradication Program. It opined that the maintenance of malaria was the responsibility of the general health services. Its recommendations included vigilance through medical institutions; multipurpose domiciliary health services for all health programs including Malaria, Small-pox, and control of other Communicable Diseases, and emphasis on health education.

Mukherjee Committee (1966)

Under the chairmanship of Union Health Secretary a Committee was appointed to undertake the review of Family Planning (FP) Program in suggesting FP strategy. It recommended administrative set up at different levels from Primary Health Unit to the State Headquarters, and delinking of Malaria maintenance activities from Family Planning Program.

Kartar Singh Committee (1972-1973)

Kartar Singh Committee too was set up to study the Family Planning Program, It too recommended in favour of appointment of multipurpose workers for the delivery of health, family welfare and nutrition services. An appointment of one male health workers for a population of 6,000 to 7,000; one PBHC to serve 50,000 population covering 16 sub-centers as well as one female worker for a population of 10,000 to 12,000, and training for all workers in the field of health, family planning and nutrition.

Shrivastava Committee (1974-1975)

Under the chairmanship of Dr. J.B. Shrivastava, this Committee made various recommendations such as organization of the basic health services within the community; economic and efficient program of health services; creation of a National Referral Service, and creation of necessary administrative and financial machineries.

Bajaj Committee

This Committee acted as an Expert Review Committee for Health Manpower under the chairmanship of Shri J.S. Bajaj. It focused on health management and recommended several measures to improve the quality of medical education (J. Kishore, 2006).

Based on various recommendations of various committees, the Government of India took various Initiatives and important action plans.

An attempt has been made to describe in brief various initiatives of the Government of India as follows.

Initiatives of Government of India in Health Sector

The initiatives in India for the health sector were also based on events took place by events at global level for movement towards health improvement. Two major events for movement of economies in the world towards health improvement includes, Firstly, World Health Organization (WHO) conference in 1978 at Alma Ata and Second, Millennium Development Goals set up by United Nations Millennium General Assembly, based on the Millennium Summit in September 2000.

Alma Ata Declaration, 1978 focused on health enhancement resolution which stated that, "Health is a State of complete physical, mental and social well being and not merely the absence of disease or infirmity".

It is a fundamental human right and the attainment of the highest possible level of health is a most important world-wide social goal whose realization requires the action of many other social and economic sectors in addition to health sector" (Human Development in South Asia, 2004).

In September 2000, the world leaders from 189 countries attended the United Nations Millennium Summit to adopt the Millennium Development Goals [MDGs] to make collective efforts to overcome poverty, promote equality, peace, and to achieve sustainable development by the year 2015 or earlier. Its main focus area was poverty eradication and health. The MDGs are made up of 08 Goals, 18 targets, and 48 indicators. These 08 MDGs included (*i*) eradicating extreme poverty and hunger; (*ii*) achieving universal primary education; (*iii*) promotion of gender equality and empower women; (*iv*) reduction of child mortality; (*v*) improvement maternal health; (*vi*) combating Human Immunodeficiency Virus/Acquired Immunodeficiency Syndrome (HIV/AIDS), Malaria and other diseases; (*vii*) ensuring environmental sustainability, and (*viii*) setting up of a global partnership for development.

The first 03 MDGs are directly related to health whereas its 4th to 6th goals deals with basic issues such as maternal health, child mortality and communicable diseases viz., Malaria, Tuberculosis and HIV/AIDS. The 07th MDG focuses upon Environmental Sustainability to make provisions for safe and clean drinking water. Its 08th MDG centered on globally achieving of these MDGs (J. Kishore, 2006 and Human Development in South Asia, 2004).

An attempt has been made to outline in brief few initiatives of the Government of India as follows:

Increase Public Spending on Health

The Government of India is committed to raise public spending on health from the current 0.9 per cent to 2.3 per cent of GDP by the year 2010 with a focus on primary health care.

The plan allocation made was Rs. 2,908 Crore for the year 2005-2006 as against the budgeted estimates of Rs. 2,208 Crore for the year 2004-2005. A further step up is visualized in the allocation budgeted for 2006-2007 at Rs. 3328 Crore (Annual Report of Health and Family Welfare, 2005-2006).

India Health Vision 2020

It has been suggested to improve diagnostic services and treatment that can reduce the prevalence and incidence of Tuberculosis (TB) the year by 2020. About 2 million cases of Malaria are reported in India each year.

Restructuring of the "Malaria Workforce" and strengthening of health infrastructure can be helpful in reducing the incidence of TB up to 50 per cent by the year 2010. Another major cause of illness, Childhood Diarrhea is largely preventable through simple community action and public education. Deaths due to Diarrhea are to be eliminated by the year 2010. By projected improvement in living standards; food security;

improved educational levels as well as access to health care amongst all levels of population, and substantial progress too be made in reducing the prevalence of severe under nutrition in children by the year 2020 (J. Kishore, 2006).

Bridging the Gap between Infrastructure and Man Power

During the Tenth Five Year Plan (2002-2007), the main aim of the family welfare programme was to supplement strengthening of infrastructure for service delivery of health programme and bridging the gap in essential infrastructure and manpower.

National Population Policy 2000

The Government of India has brought out the National Population Policy, 2000 which provided a policy framework and the expected level of achievements by the year 2010. Its little achievement included, (*i*) reduction in IMR to below 30 per 1000 live births; (*ii*) reduction in Maternal Mortality Rate (MMR) below 100 per 100000 live births; (*iii*) and achieving of 80 per cent institutional deliveries and 100 per cent deliveries by trained persons.

National Rural Health Mission (NRHM)

The NRHM was launched on 12th April, 2005, by Honourable prime Minister of India and it is being overanalyzed from the financial year 2005-2006.

The major purposes of NRHM includes, (*i*) To provide accessible, affordable, accountable, effective and reliable primary health care facilities for poor section; (*ii*) To bridge the gap in rural health care services through creation of a cadre of Accredited Social Health Activities (ASHA); (*iii*) To provide overarching umbrella to the existing programmes of health and family welfare; (*iv*) To address the related issues of health such as sanitation and hygiene, nutrition, safe drinking water etc.; and (*v*) To build greater ownership of the health programme among the community through involvement of Panchayati Raj institutions, Non-Government Organisations (NGOs) and other stakeholders at National, State, District and Sub-District level.

The outlay of NRHM for the year 2005-2006 was Rs. 6,731 Crore and the Department of Health and Family Welfare have been merged in to a single department by Government of India to implement this mission.

Pradhan Mantri Swasthya Suraksha Yojna (PMSSY)

In order to correct the imbalances in availability of affordable and reliable tertiary level healthcare services, in India in general and to augment facilities for quality medical education in the underserved States the PMSSY in particular was approved in March 2006.

An attempt has been made to describe in brief various Disease Control Programmes of the Government of India as follows.

Disease Control Programmes Mainly Includes Following:

National Vector Borne Disease Control Programme (NVBDCP)

Since 2003, in order to prevent and control the vector borne disease such as, Malaria, Filarisis, Kalaazar, Dengue/Dengue hemorrhagic fever, and Japanese Encephalitis, the NVBDCP programme was initiated. Its aim was to reduce mortality on account of

Malaria, Dengue, and Japanese encephalitis by 50 per cent and elimination of Kalaazar by 2010 and of Lymphatic Filarisis by the year 2015.

National Leprosy Eradication Programme (NLEP)

The National Health Policy, 2002 has kept the goal of Leprosy elimination by the year 2005 through setting up of target as prevalence rate less than 1 case per 10,000 populations. The prevalence rate declined from 57.6 in 1981 to 1.34 in the year 2005 and further came down to 1.07 lakhs giving prevalence rate of 0.95 cases per 10,000 populations in December 2005.

Revised National TB Control Programme (RNTCP)

The RNTCP was implemented in a phased manner since 1997, by using Directly Observed Treatment Short course (DOTS) strategy. By October 2005, 1065 million that is 95 per cent of India's population has been covered and more than 49 lakh patients were placed on DOTS treatment which saved about 8.8 lakhs additional human lives.

National Programme for Control of Blindness

An action plan was been prepared during the10th Five-year Plan to implement National Programme for Control of Blindness which focused on development of comprehensive eye care services.

National Cancer Control Programme (NCCP)

The NCCP has aimed to revamp the geographical imbalances in the availability of cancer treatment facilities with the recognition of new Regional Cancer Centers, and strengthening of existing centers.

National Mental Health Programme

The National Mental Health Programme was launched by the Government of India during the 10th five year plan under which 50 new districts were covered in the year 2004-20005 and 94 districts in the year 2005-2006.

Integrated Diseases Surveillance Project

To develop capacity for early identification of important communicable diseases such as, Cholera, Typhoid, Polio, Malaria, TB, HIV/AID, Ministry of health launched Integrated Common Non-Communicable Disease to cover Road traffic accidents in all States and UTs in a phased manner.

National AIDS Control Programme (NACP)

The NACP was started in the year 1992 and the Government of India adopted the National AIDS Prevention and Control Policy in April 2002. The budgeted provision was Rs. 259 Crore in the year 2004-2005; Rs. 533 Crore in the year 2005-2006 and the total project cost of NACP phase II was Rs. 2,064.65 Crores (Annual Report of Health and Family Welfare 2005-2006).

Above mentioned Government Initiatives and Public Health Programmes called for successful implementation in form of laws which shall provides coercive power to the Central and State Governments of India. The Government of India needs to make sufficient provisions for protection, promotion and growth of every individual, worker, group and vulnerable population in relation to their health. To achieve these fundamental goals of protection, promotion and growth of every individual various legislations and policies were drafted by the Government of India. Such legislations were introduced for variety of purposes such as, to improve and maintain high standards in the medical education and services; to assess for public registration to mortality and enumeration of population; to prevent public health problems; to achieve Maternal Health and to empower women; to safeguard the children and young; to prevent drug addiction; to protect workers and to provide social security; to protect environmental, and to promote voluntary work.

The list of important Indian Legislation related to health covers, viz., The Indian Medical Council Act, 1956 and Regulations 2002; The Indian Nursing Council Act, 1947; The Dentist Act, 1948; The Pharmacy Act, 1948; The Rehabilitation Council of India Act, 1992; The Indian Medicine Central council Act, 1973; The Consumer Protection Act, 1986; The Registration of Births and Deaths Act, 1969; The Census Act, 1948. the other laws were viz., The Delhi Antismoking and Nonsmoking Health Protection Act, 1996; The Transplantation of Human Organ Act, 1994; The Prevention of Food Adulteration Act, 1954; The Indian Air Craft (Public Health) Act, 1934, and Rules, 1954; The Medical Termination of Pregnancy Act, 1971; The Maternity Benefit Act, 1961; The Prenatal Diagnostic Techniques (Regulation and Prevention of misuse) Act, 1994; The Infant Milk Substitutes, Feeding Bottlers and Infant Foods (Regulation of Production, Supply and Distribution) Act, 1992;

The Persons with Disabilities (Equal opportunity, protection of Rights and Full Participation) Act, 1995; The Mental Health Act, 1987; The Narcotic Drugs and Psychotropic Substances Act, 1985; The Drugs and Cosmetics Act, 1940; The Drugs (Control) Act, 1948; The Drugs and Magic Remedies (Objectionable Advertisements) Act, 1954; The Environment (Protection) Act, 1986;The Biomedical Waste (Management and Handling) Rules, 1998; The Municipal Solid Waste (Management and Handling) Rules, 2000; The Hazardous Waste (Management and Handling) Rules, 1989; The Air (Prevention and Control of Pollution Act, 1981; The Water (Prevention and Control of Pollution) Act, 1974; The Atomic Energy Act, 1962; The Insecticides Act, 1988; The Delhi Municipal Corporation Act, 1957; The Motor Vehicle Act, 1988; and The Red Cross Society (Allocation of Property) Act, 1936.

The Government of India under the Constitutional provisions owes its populations social security, health services, safety, environmental protection, equal opportunity, and justice. The methods adopted by the Government of India to deliver these services are framing policies. A few important National Policies include, National Policy and Charter for Children Draft; National Health Research Policy Draft; National Policy on Education; National Water Policy; National Conservation Strategy and Policy Statement on Environment and Development- 1992, National Nutrition Policy- 1993; National Housing and Habitat Policy-1998; National Policy for Old Person-1999; National Population Policy-2000; National policy for the Empowerment of Women-2001; National Blood Policy-2002; National AIDS Prevention and Control Policy-2002, and National Health Policy-2002 (J. Kishore, 2006).

REVIEW OF NATIONAL HEALTH CARE POLICY (NHP) OF INDIA

An attempt has been made to review in brief the National Health Care Policy as follows:

Various healthcare policies have evolved over a period of time. An attempt to describe it in brief has been made as follows:

National Health Policy: 1983

In India, the National Health Policy was formulated in 1983 which gave a general exposition of the policies and important policy initiatives under the NHP 1983, its major initiatives were as follows:

(*i*) Time-bound programme, in different phases under the hope to provide health to all, for comprehensive primary health care services, designed on the ground reality that elementary health problems can be resolved by the people themselves;

(*ii*) intermediation through health volunteers having appropriate knowledge, simple skills and requisite technologies;

(*iii*) establishment of Referral System to ensure that higher levels hierarchy patients, Who afford to pay more, do not become burdened at the decentralized level, where lower level patients are treated; and

(*iv*) encouragement of integrated net-work of speciality and super-speciality services through private investments for patients who can pay, so that the Government's facilities remain limited to those entitled to free use (www.mohfw.nic.in).

Government of India's initiatives in the public health sector have recorded some noteworthy successes over time, which are reflected in the progressive improvement of many demographic, epidemiological, and infrastructural indicators as follows.

Table 1.6: Achievements in Demographic/Epidemiological/Infrastructural Indicators of Public Health Sector in India

Sl. No.	Selected Indicators	1951	1981	2000
A	Demographic Changes			
01	Life Expectancy	36.7	54	64.6(RGI)
02	Crude Birth Rate	40.8	33.9(SRS)	26.1(99 SRS)
03	Crude Death Rate	25	12.5(SRS)	8.7(99 SRS)
04	IMR	146	110	70 (99 SRS)
B	Epidemiological Shifts			
01	Malaria (Cases in Million)	75	2.7	2.2
02	Leprosy Cases Per 10,000 Population	38.1	57.3	3.74
03	Small Pox (No of Cases)	>44,887	Eradicated	
04	Guinea worm (No. of Cases)	>39,792	Eradicated	

...(*Contd.*).

...(Contd.).

05	Polio	29709	265	
C	Infrastructural Indicators			
01	SC/PHC/CHC	725	57,363	1,63,181 (99-RHS)
02	Dispensaries and (All) Hospitals	9209	23,555	43,322 (95-96-CBHI)
03	Beds (Private and Public)	117,198	569,495	8,70,161 (95-96-CBHI)
04	Doctors(Allopathy)	61,800	2,68,700	5,03,900 (98-99-MCI)
05	Nursing Personnel	18,054	1,43,887	7,37,000 (99-INC)

Source: National Health Policy 2002, www.mohfw.nic.in.

It becomes evident from the table number 06 that smallpox and Guineaworm diseases have been eradicated from India and Polio is on the verge of being eradicated. Leprosy is expected to be eliminated in near future. Despite the impressive public health gains, the morbidity and mortality levels in India are still high.

Out of the communicable diseases Malaria, more deadly Falciparum Malaria, Tuberculosis (TB), and the common water-borne infections such as Gastroenteritis, Cholera, and some form of Hepatitis, have shown significant decline amongst the community. Since the declaration of the NHP 1983, a new and extremely virulent communicable disease "HIV/AIDS" has emerged on the health, and as there is no existing therapeutic cure or vaccine for this infection, the HIV/AIDS constitutes a serious threat to public health and also to economic development of India. Incidence of macro and micro nutrient deficiencies among women and children is another area in public health domain. The financial resources and public health administrative capacity was possible to marshal by NHP 1983, which was far short of the necessity to achieve such an ambitious and holistic goal of health for all especially for poor and under privileged people of India.

National Health Policy, 2002

The changed circumstances relating to the health sector of India have generated a situation in which it felt necessary to review the field, and to formulate a new National Health Policy, 2002.

The NHP, 2002 was an attempt to set out a new policy framework to accelerate achievement of the public health goals considering the socio-economic circumstances of India (Ibid).

Ministry of Health and Family Welfare, Government of India promulgated the National Health Policy (NHP) 2002 after a gap of 18 years. The reason behind recognizing the need to make changes in the National Health policy was related with the demographic changes, epidemiological transition including newer public health challenges; technological advancements, rising aspirations of the community and increasing globalization.

The main broad objective and emphasis of NHP, 2002 were viz., to achieve an acceptable standard of good health amongst the general population of the country; to increase access of the people to the decentralized public health system by establishing new infrastructure in deficient areas, and by upgrading the infrastructure in the existing institutions; emphasis given to increasing the aggregate public health investment through an increased contribution by the Central Government which further strengthens the capacity of the public health administration at the State level; emphasis on enhancing the contribution of the private sector in providing health services, for the population group which can afford to pay for services, and emphasis laid on rational use of drugs within the allopathic system and increased access to tried and tested systems of traditional medicine.

Within these broad objectives, the NHP 2002 was endeavor to achieve the following time-bound goals given as below.

Table 1.7: Time Bound Goals to be achieved under NHP by 2000-2015 in India

Sl. No.	Particulars	Year
01	Eradicate Polio and Yaws	2005
02	Eliminate Leprosy	2005
03	Eliminate Kala Azar	2010
04	Eliminate Lymphatic Filariasis	2015
05	Achieve Zero level growth of HIV/AIDS	2007
06	Reduce Mortality by 50 Per cent on Account of TB, Malaria and Other Vector and Water Borne Diseases	2010
07	Reduce Prevalence of Blindness to 0.5 Per cent	2010
08	Reduce IMR to 30/1000 And MMR to 100/Lakh	2010
09	Increase Utilization of Public Health Facilities from Current Level of <20 to >75 Per cent	2010
10	Establish an Integrated System of Surveillance, National Health Accounts and Health Statistics.	2005
11	Increase Health Expenditure By Government As a Per cent of GDP From The Existing 0.9 Per cent to 2.0 Per cent	2010
12	Increase Share of Central Grants to Constitute at Least 25 Per cent of Total Health Spending	2010
13	Increase State Sector Health Spending From 5.5 Per cent To 7 per cent of The Budget Further Increase To 8 Per cent	2005 2010

Source: *Ibid.*

The major prescriptions of the NHP, 2002 against scenario before NHP, 2002 are described as follows.

The public health investment in India over the years as a percentage of GDP had declined from 1.3 per cent in the year 1990 to 0.9 per cent in the year 1999. The aggregate expenditure in the health sector was 5.2 per cent of the GDP. The Central Budgetary allocation for health, during the period of 1990 to 1999, as a percentage of the total central budget, was stagnant at 1.3 per cent, while at the state level it had declined from 7.0 per cent to 5.5 per cent. Under the constitutional structure, the responsibility and principal contribution for the funding of public health services is to be from resources of the States with some supplementary contribution about 15 per cent from Central resources.

The key policy provisions of the NHP 2002 were as follows:

To overcome the difficult fiscal position of State Government, the emphasis was laid down on role of Central Government in augmenting public health investments. Under the policy, the plan was to increase the health sector expenditure to 6 per cent of GDP with 2 per cent of GDP being contributed as public health investment by the year 2010. The State Government was expected to increase their commitment to health sector by the year 2005 in the first phase of their resources to 7 per cent of the budget and by the year 2010, in the second phase, to 10 per cent of budget. In case of public health investment Central Government contribution shall rise to 25 per cent from the existing 15 per cent by the year 2010.

Despite the focus of centralized planning in the development process was on an equitable regional distribution. The following Table 1.8 indicates the attainment of health indices which is uneven across the rural-urban divide.

Table 1.8: Differentials in Health Status Among States

Sl. No.	Sector	Population BPL (Per cent)	IMR (infant Mortality)/ Per 1000 Live Births (1999-SRS)	<5 Mortality per 1000 (NFHS II)	Under Weight For Age-per cent of Children Under 3	MMR/ Lakh (Annual Report 2000)	Leprosy cases per 10000 population	Malaria +ve Cases in year 2000 (in Thousands)
A	**India**	**26.1**	**70**	**94.9**	**47**	**408**	**3.7**	**2200**
01	Rural	27.09	75	103.7	49.6	–	–	–
02	Urban	23.62	44	63.1	38.4	–	–	–
B	**Better Performing States**							
01	Kerala	12.72	14	18.8	27	87	0.9	5.1
02	Maharashtra	25.02	48	58.1	50	135	3.1	138
03	TN	21.12	52	63.3	37	79	4.1	56
C	**Low Performing States**							
01	Orissa	47.15	97	104.4	54	498	7.05	483
02	Bihar	42.60	63	105.1	54	707	11.83	132
03	Rajasthan	15.28	81	114.9	51	607	0.8	53
04	UP	31.15	84	122.5	52	707	4.3	99
05	MP	37.43	90	137.6	55	498	3.83	528

Source: Ibid.

It becomes clear that the attainment of health indices has been very uneven across the rural urban divide and it also brought out the wide differences between the attainments of health goals in the better performing states as compared to the low - performing States. The public health systems have been very uneven between the better endowed and the more vulnerable sections of society. The health indices on account of socio-economic inequality are given as follows.

Table 1.9: Differentials in Health Status Among Socio-Economic Groups

Sl. No.	Selected Indicators	Infant Mortality/ 1000	Under 5 Mortality/ 1000	Percentages of Children Underweight
A	**India**	**70**	**94.9**	**47**
B	**Social Inequity**			
01	Scheduled Castes	83	119.3	53.5
02	Scheduled Tribes	84.2	126.6	55.9
03	Other Disadvantaged	76	103.1	47.3
04	Others	61.8	82.6	41.1

Source: Ibid.

The key policy prescriptions of NHP, 2002 indicated that in order to reduce the various types of inequalities and imbalances, in the inter-regional; across the rural-urban divide; and between economic classes, the NHP, 2002 Policy set out the most cost-effective method which suggested to increase allocation of 55 per cent of the total public health investment for primary health sector, 35 per cent for secondary and 10 per cent for tertiary health sectors. The policy projected that the increased aggregate outlays for the primary health sector will be utilized for strengthening existing facilities and also for opening additional public health service outlets.

In terms of delivery of National Public Health Programmes, the scenario before introduction of NHP, 2002 is discussed in brief as follows.

In view of wide variety of socio-economic settings in India, National Health Programmes need to be designed with enough flexibility to permit the State public health administrators to craft their own customized programme. The technical and managerial expertise belonging to Central Government shall be gainfully utilized in designing of national health programmes for its implementation across the various States. Over the last decade, that is from the year 1990 to 1999 for the major disease programmes, the Government of India had relied upon a vertical implementation structure and was able to make a substantial dent in reducing the burden of specific diseases. But, such structure requires independent manpower for each diseases programme, is expensive and difficult to sustain. It is a wide spread perception that the rural health staff has become a vertical structure exclusive for the implementation of family welfare activities. The outcome is that there is no identifiable service delivery system for these public health programmes where there is no separate vertical structure.

The key policy prescriptions of NHP 2002 indicated the key role of the Central Government in designing National programmes with the active participation of the State Governments. The policy highlighted the need for developing the capacity within the state public health administration for scientific designing of public health projects, suited to the local situation (Ibid).

REVIEW OF GUJARAT HUMAN DEVELOPMENT REPORT: 2004

An attempt has been made to review in brief the Gujarat Human Development Report, 2004 as follows:

Various attempts have been made over a period of time by State Government of Gujarat. An attempt to describe it in brief has been made as follows:

Health and Human Development

Health is important in the process of human development and the member's country of WHO has also given importance at global level in the Alma-Ata Conference in 1978. Since the Alma-Ata Conference of 1978, it declared health as a fundamental human right, health and nutrition have been accepted as important national concern by developed and the developing countries. Another important event at global level was the declaration adopted by 189 countries at U.N. Millennium Summit in September 2000, in which world leaders promised to meet concrete targets for advancing development and reducing poverty by the year 2015 or earlier. The Major eight goals which were agreed upon amongst world leaders included viz., Goal 1: eradicate extreme poverty and hunger; Goal 2: achieve universal primary education; Goal 3: promote gender equality and empower women; Goal 4: reduce child mortality; Goal 5: improve maternal health; Goal 6: combat HIV/AIDS, malaria, and other diseases; Goal 7: ensure environmental sustainability; Goal 8: develop a global partnership for development. Three of these goals are directly health-related to health.

Goals four, five and six were expected to deal with basic health issues like maternal health, child mortality and communicable diseases like malaria, tuberculosis and HIV/AIDS. Even the first goal of eradication of poverty and hunger lead to better health of an individual as the poor health is both a cause and result of poverty and hunger. For achieving these goals of human development, the public action by the Government of India related to its social sectors which include health, nutrition, education, public distribution system, social welfare system and other social services (Human Development Report 2003). In the Indian Federal System, health is the concern of State Governments, though some of the important health programmes are funded by the Central Government of India (Gujarat Human Development Report 2004).

Government Expenditure on Social Sectors

For achieving higher levels of human development public action is an important component. The size and composition of public expenditure, particularly the expenditure on social sectors, determine the nature and extent of human development and is likely to influence the status of human development in several ways. There is a need to analyze how public spending on human development can be designed and monitored (Ibid).

In order to analyze and measure public expenditure on human development the Human Development Report 1991 (UNDP 1991) had suggested four expenditure ratios in order to enable monitoring and planning of the public spending on Human Development. The four ratios were: viz., First, Public Expenditure Ratio (PER) that is, percentage of national income that goes into public expenditure. Second, Social Allocation Ratio (SAR) that is, percentage of total expenditure earmarked for social services. Third, Social Priority Ratio (SPR), that is, percentage of social expenditure devoted to human priority concerns, such as elementary education, preventive healthcare (water supply and sanitation), and nutrition. Fourth, Human Expenditure

Ratio (HER), that is, percentage of national income devoted to human priority concerns. It is expressed as the product of the three previous ratios. According to the HDR 1991, HER should be around 5 per cent if a country wishes to do well in human development. This can be achieved if PER is around 25 per cent, SAR around 40 per cent, and SPR more than 50 per cent (Human Development Report, - UNDP-1991).

Expenditure Ratios in the State of the Gujarat

Prabhu and Chatterjee (1993) had computed the four ratios for the 15 major States of India for four years, 1974-1975; 1980-1981; 1985-1986, and 1990-1991. The performance against Public Expenditure Ratio (PER), found a good amount of progress at all India level, with the ratio increased from 15.29 in the year 1974-1975 to 24.79 in the year 1990-1991, but the ratio was still below the norm of 25.00. The performance of Gujarat was less than satisfactory with the ratio increased from 18.23 in the year 1974-1975 to 22.18 in the year 1990-1991. The performance against Social Allocation Ratio (SAR) it was found that there was marginal improvement at the All-India level, from 31.56 in the year 1974-1975 to 32.99 in the year 1990-1991, still, lower than the norm of 40. In Gujarat, there was an overall decline from 33.51 in the year 1974-1975 to 31.40 in 1990-91, only three States–Kerala, Bengal, and Tamil Nadu met the norm of 40.00 in the year 1990-1991 and Gujarat was ranked 9th among the 15 large States of India. The performance against Social Priority Ratio (SPR) was found that for the most States and for the country, SPR had remained far below the norm. There was only a marginal increase during the period 1974-1975 to 1990-91 (from 36.83 to 38.39). Gujarat's performance had been slightly better than that of the country, the value increased from 31.26 in the year 1974-75 to 38.79 in the year 1990-1991.

The performance against Human Expenditure ratio (HER) it was found that the India as a whole did show improvement in HER from 1.79 in the year 1974-1975 to 3.21 in the year 1990-1991. Gujarat State showed relatively less improvement, with the ratio moved up from 1.91 in the year 1974-75 to just 2.70 in the year 1990-91, a 42 per cent improvement (Gujarat Human Development Report 2004).

The ratios did not show any radical improvement in the post-reform period. The data of expenditure ratios in the State of the Gujarat from the year 1990-1991 to the year 2001-2002 are given in Table 1.10.

Table 1.10: Expenditure Ratios in the State of the Gujarat

Year	PER	SAR	SPR	HER
1990-1991	22.18	31.70	38.79	2.72
1991-1992	29.80	25.84	40.74	3.13
1992-1993	25.02	24.61	41.09	2.53
1993-1994	23.70	26.94	41.71	2.66
1994-1995	20.08	30.16	41.04	2.48
1995-1996	21.86	31.21	41.95	2.77
1996-1997	19.48	27.92	50.26	2.73

...(Contd.)

...(Contd.)

1997-1998	20.08	29.52	46.95	2.78
1998-1999	21.44	30.78	–	–
1999-2000	24.85	30.69	35.24	2.69
2000-2001	33.81	28.19	36.61	3.49
2001-2002	62.78	13.02	25.05	2.05
HDR 1991 norms	25.00	40.00	50.00	5.00

PER - Public Expenditure Ratio, SAR - Social Allocation Ratio, SPR - Social Priority Ratio, HER - Human Expenditure Ratio.

Source: Ibid.

As per Table 1.10, PER shows wide year-to-year fluctuations and a long term increasing trend from 22.18 in the year 1990-91 to 62.78 in the year 2001-02. SAR also showed wide fluctuations as this ratio declined from 31.70 in the year 1990-1991 to 13.02 in the year 2001-2002. SPR showed an increasing trend up to 1996-1997 (ratio reached the norm of 50.00). But, after that the ratio has declined sharply to 46.95 in the year 1997-1998. HER had remained almost constant with figures going slightly above or below 2.70 against the norm of 5.00 till the year 1999-2000. The Gujarat state has not met any of the norms set up by the UNDP with regard to social sector and public expenditure ratios either before or after the reforms.

What kind of priority was given to social services in the Five-year Plans in the State of the Gujarat? There was a clear decline from in the Fourth Plan. Although in the Fifth Plan, an increase was observed. In the Sixth and Seventh Plan, once again, there was a decline. However, some improvements were observed in the Eighth Plan with social services get a share of 19.00 per cent. Finally, in the Ninth Plan serious efforts towards social development were observed, with an increase in the outlay to the social sector. Composition of actual expenditure on various components of the social sector was very useful and the proportions of expenditure on health and education sectors were provided in Table 1.11.

Table 1.11: Trends in Expenditure on Health and Education in the State of the Gujarat

Year	As a Percentages of Expenditure on Social Services			
	Health		Education	
	Revenue	Capital	Revenue	Capital
1986-1987	30.66	3.94	48.14	1.70
1990-1991	25.49	2.78	56.75	4.92
1995-1996	21.82	2.62	59.79	11.51
1996-1997	22.07	3.41	59.90	5.18
1997-1998	27.32	6.64	54.00	6.19
1998-1999	23.45	7.61	57.47	3.36
1999-2000	26.38	5.68	54.47	2.76
2000-2001	35.61	2.41	47.59	1.17
2001-2002	44.97	1.60	42.19	0.63

Source: *Ibid.*

From the above mentioned, it can become evident that the health sector expenditure showed a consistent decline in terms of its percentage share. In the case of expenditure on education, one did not observe any clear increase in capital account, as there were year-to-year wide fluctuations. In the case of the health sector the composition of expenditure had changed in such a way that a relatively higher amount was spent on medical side given in Table 1.12.

Table 1.12: Expenditure Pattern in Health Sector of the State of the Gujarat

Year	Percentages of Expenditure on			
	Medical	Public Health	Water and Sanitation	Family Welfare
1985-1986	41.40	16.30	24.80	17.60
1990-1991	51.10	11.60	24.60	12.70
1995-1996	53.65	15.19	17.86	13.29
1996-1997	56.50	15.51	15.64	12.34
1997-1998	57.22	14.10	22.06	06.62
1999-2000	37.48	08.31	41.32	12.89
2000-2001	30.39	05.70	57.04	06.87
2001-2002	49.17	09.34	32.73	08.76

Source: Ibid.

It was found that the pattern of composition of expenditure in health sector focused more on medical side i.e. 41.40 per cent in the year 1985-1986 to 49.17 per cent in the year 2001-2002, which was higher than the expenditure on public health, water and sanitation and family welfare. Expenditure on public health as a percentage of total health budget showed a noticeable decline while expenditure on family welfare had drastically decreased. The share of water and sanitation in the health sector has increased, which was a very welcome development. The pattern of expenditure on the social sector in the State of the Gujarat did not reflected consistency in proportionate allocations to the components of this sector. The normative level of expenditure is a necessary, but not sufficient, condition for improving social sector development.

There is no doubt that the allocation to public health showed a less emphasis but health is a fundamental right and has been accepted as important national concerns in the developing countries (Ibid).

Health Status of the State of the Gujarat

The IMR in the Gujarat State came down from 145 to 63 deaths per thousand live births during the year 1973-1999. However, the state was far behind Kerala whose IMR was 14. Maternal Mortality Rate (MMR) in the state was 3.89 in the year 1992-1993, which was high as compared to Kerala's figure (0.87) per 1000. Total Fertility Rate (TFR) had declined from around 6 to 3 during 1951-98. The population policy intends to bring it down to 2.1 by the year 2010. The Couple Protection Rate (CPR) had increased from 10.4 per cent to 44 per cent in the year 1999. Gujarat's performance was compared against all India aggregates with regard to important Health indicators, which is given in Table 1.13.

Table 1.13: Health Status Indicators of the State of the Gujarat and India

Sl. No.	Health Status Indicators	Gujarat	India
01	Crude Birth Rate, 2001*	24.90	25.40
02	Crude Death Rate, 2001*	07.80	08.40
03	Maternal Mortality Rate1992-1993*	03.89	04.58
04	Infant Mortality Rate, 2001*	60.00	66.00
05	Life Expectancy at Birth,1996-2001-Male*	61.53	62.36
06	Life Expectancy at Birth,1996-2001-Female*	62.77	63.39
07	Neo-natal Mortality Rate 1998**	44.00	45.00
08	Peri-natal Mortality Rate1998*	38.00	42.00
09	Post Neo-natal Mortality Rate1998**	21.00	27.00
10	Child Mortality Rate (0-5 years) 1998*	85.10	94.90
11	General Fertility Rate 1998*	98.70	106.50
12	Total Fertility Rate 1998*	03.00	03.20
13	Gross Reproduction Rate 1998*	01.40	01.50

Note: Data given by the health department of Government of Gujarat.
Source: Ibid.

Gujarat's performance was better than all India aggregates with regard to important Health indicators. IMR had dramatically declined in India and Gujarat during the year 1971 and the year 2001. In the case of India, it had declined from 200-225 per 1000 live births at the time of Independence to 129 in the year 1971 and to 66 in the year 2001. In the case of Gujarat, it had declined much faster, from 145 in the year 1971 to 60 in the year 2001.

Inter State comparison puts Gujarat State in the middle order among the major 15 States as far as important health indicators are concerned, are given in Table 1.14.

Table 1.14: Interstate Comparison of Health Status of India

Sl. No.	States	CBR, 2001			CDR, 2001			IMR, 2001		
		Total	Rural	Urban	Total	Rural	Urban	Total	Rural	Urban
01	Kerala	17.2	17.4	16.6	06.6	06.8	06.1	11.0	12.0	09.00
02	Maharashtra	20.6	21.0	20.1	07.5	08.5	05.9	45.0	55.0	27.0
03	Punjab	21.2	22.1	18.7	07.0	07.2	06.4	51.0	55.0	37.0
04	Tamil Nadu	19.0	19.6	17.8	07.6	08.4	06.0	49.0	54.0	35.0
05	Karnataka	22.2	23.6	19.0	07.6	08.2	06.4	58.0	69.0	27.0
06	**Gujarat**	**24.9**	**26.6**	**21.5**	**07.8**	**08.8**	**05.6**	**60.0**	**67.0**	**42.0**
07	West Bengal	20.5	22.8	13.8	06.8	07.0	06.4	51.0	53.0	38.0
08	Haryana	26.7	27.8	22.8	07.6	07.6	07.4	65.0	68.0	54.0
09	Andhra Pradesh	20.8	21.3	19.6	08.1	08.9	05.6	66.0	74.0	39.0

...*(Contd.)*

...(*Contd.*)

10	Assam	26.8	27.8	18.5	09.5	09.8	06.6	73.0	76.0	33.0
11	Madhya Pradesh	30.8	32.8	23.0	10.0	10.8	07.2	86.0	92.0	53.0
12	Rajasthan	31.0	32.3	24.7	07.9	08.3	06.2	79.0	83.0	57.0
13	Orissa	23.4	23.9	19.6	10.2	10.7	06.8	90.0	94.0	60.0
14	Uttar pradesh	32.1	33.2	27.0	10.1	10.6	07.8	82.0	86.0	62.0
15	Bihar	31.2	32.3	23.4	08.2	08.5	06.3	62.0	63.0	52.0
16	**INDIA**	**25.4**	**27.1**	**20.2**	**08.4**	**09.0**	**06.3**	**66.0**	**72.0**	**42.0**

CBR-Crude Birth Rate, CDR-Crude Death Rate, IMR-Infant Mortality Rate.

Source: Ibid.

It becomes evident that Gujarat State stood ninth with respect to CBR (24.9) in 2001 as against 25.4 in India. Gujarat State was ranked seventh in the overall IMR, with IMR at 60 in 2001. It ranked seventh in rural IMR (67) and ninth in urban IMR (42). It was worth noting that though the Gujarat State was at the top on urban Crude Death Rate (CDR), it ranked far below at ninth rank in the urban IMR among the large states. Information of some of the health indicators by districts in the Gujarat state that were available mainly based on the 1991 Census showed that there was a high disparity among the districts in the State of the Gujarat given in Table 1.15.

Table 1.15: Morbidity Indicators in the State of the Gujarat

Sl. No.	Morbidity Indicators	Gujarat	India
A	Morbidity Rate Per 1000 Population (Rural)		
01	- Total	75.8	106.7
02	- Male	71.6	105.5
03	- Female	80.8	108.1
B	Morbidity Rate Per 1000 Population (Urban)		
01	- Total	84.3	103.0
02	- Male	95.0	098.2
03	- Female	74.5	108.4
C	Prevalence Of Illness by Type (Rural)		
05	- serious communicable diseases	21.0	015.6
06	- Acute Illness	49.6	077.9
07	- Chronic Illness	05.2	013.2
D	Prevalence Of Illness by Type (Urban)		
01	- Serious Communicable Diseases	18.8	014.0
02	- Acute Illness	52.8	070.6
03	- Chronic Illness	12.7	018.4

Notes: Reference period is one year. All India figures include State/Union Territories of Goa, Meghalaya, Puducherry, Chandigarh and Delhi Rural.

Source: Ibid.

The Morbidity Rate per 1000 Population in both rural and urban areas was high in India Compared to Gujarat State. The prevalence rates of serious communicable diseases were rated higher in Gujarat (Rural Rate 21.0 and Urban Rate 18.8) compared to All India Rate (Rural Rate 15.6 and Urban Rate 14.0), and that of Acute diseases and chronic diseases were lower in Gujarat than the respective rates for rural and urban areas in India as a whole.

Further, the data on different diseases reported in Gujarat over time were collected by the Health Commissionerate are given in Table 1.16.

Table 1.16: Year-wise Cases of Different Diseases in the State of the Gujarat

Year	Diseases							
	Gastro Enteritis	Scabies	Tuber-culosis	Cataract	Hepatitis	Leprosy	Malaria	Cholera
1988	69615	48127	139435	83425	7793	11249	460683	1207
1989	23096	30944	145272	93793	11939	11782	598653	274
1990	23413	44843	139863	94001	8095	9697	515926	144
1991	25071	53548	157303	112239	6817	11082	404735	107
1992	32389	59675	158928	124898	4407	11338	348532	246
1993	33600	132789	159471	153255	8825	13911	304109	265
1994	42035	–	165254	187332	7701	10278	248624	572
1995	25164	–	149376	229596	4780	11514	191028	65
1996	33173	–	153872	248681	6282	14303	143817	200
1997	23081	–	103621	274243	5824	15567	159652	49
1998	30966	–	126769	291030	5523	12778	106825	121
1999	24067	–	137494	–	–	–	64130	81
2000	37481	–	197910	–	–	–	36712	181
2001	33858	–	62779	–	–	–	84131	118

Source: *Ibid.*

It becomes evident that from the year 1988 to the year 2001 the most widely prevalent disease in Gujarat State was Malaria. The second most prevalent disease was Tuberculosis. Scabies too was widely prevalent.

Sanitation

Sanitation facilities are also considered as important factor affecting Health Status of People. The Census of India has brought out two publications in the year 1981 and the year 1991 on housing, electricity and toilet facilities. While the 1981 Report provided information for urban areas, the 1991 Report was for both urban and rural areas. National Sample Survey (NSS) Survey in 1998 estimated rural sanitation coverage in the State of the Gujarat to 20 per cent and urban coverage at 79 per cent. Mahadevia and Sarkar (2003), using NSS data, observed that in the year 1998 (NSS 54th Round which was on facilities), 17.4 per cent of households in urban areas in the State of the Gujarat had no access to drainage facility, while this figure for all India was 20.6 per cent (Ibid).

The Government of Gujarat had introduced the Gokul Gram Yojana, by realizing the importance of sanitation, under which individual latrines are constructed in Gokul Grams villages. The Gujarat Municipalities Act, 1963, prescribed that each municipality shall provide latrines and urinals in municipal limits for public use.

Though per capita healthcare expenditure in the State is much lower than that for the country, the Gujarat State had much higher level of health facilities given in Table 1.7.

Table 1.17: Health Facilities in Rural and Urban Gujarat and India

Sl. No.	Facilities Per lakh Population	Gujarat	India
01	Hospitals - Total	04.34	01.32
	- Rural	00.70	00.57
	- Urban	11.26	03.51
02	Dispensaries - Total	15.22	03.25
	- Rural	09.33	01.86
	- Urban	17.78	05.38
03	Primary Health Centers	03.24	03.55
04	Sub-Centers	26.41	20.90
05	Beds - Total	145.76	78.70
	- Rural	31.34	22.26
	- Urban	363.95	241.96
06	Doctors	52.98	47.19
07	Nurses	59.00	36.88

Source: Ibid.

The number of hospitals and dispensaries in 1991 in the State of the Gujarat (4.34) as per lakh population was more than three times the national average (01.32). But, the difference between the State of the Gujarat and India was not high when the health sub-centres (26.41 in Gujarat and 20.90 in India), per lakh population and doctors (52.98 in Gujarat and 47.19 in India) and nurses (59.00 in Gujarat and 36.88 in India), per lakh population were to be considered. With respect to Primary Health Centres (PHCs), Gujarat's (3.24) performance was lower than national average (3.55). Thus, Gujarat's performance was better in high order health facilities, which were generally located in urban areas. Urban-rural difference in high order health facilities was quite high in the State compared to all-India figures. The number of hospitals per lakh population in urban areas for the State of Gujarat (Urban 11.26 and rural 0.70) was 16 times higher than in rural areas. For India (Urban 3.51 and Rural 0.57) the difference was only near to six times. With respect to beds per lakh population, urban-rural difference was that urban facilities were 11 times more for the State of the Gujarat as well as for India (Ibid).

A study conducted by National Council of Applied Economic Research (NCAER) in 1994 on utilization of health care facilities in the State of the Gujarat, compared the utilization of health facilities in India given in Table 1.18.

Table 1.18: Utilization of Health Facilities, Gujarat and India

Sl. No.	Particulars		Gujarat		India	
			Public	Private	Public	Private
A	Out patient Treatment					
01	Rural	Male	36.8	62.2	40.2	54.4
	Female	36.7	59.8	43.3	50.8	
02	Urban	Male	38.7	57.7	34.7	58.9
	Female	31.6	63.2	33.2	60.9	
B	Hospitalisation					
01	Rural		32.2	67.8	62.0	38.0
02	Urban		27.2	72.8	60.1	39.9

Source: Ibid.

It was found that people, both males and females, depended more on private facilities in rural and urban areas. Dependence on the private sector for hospitalization cases was a common feature in the Gujarat State. This was contrary to the all India trend as well as the general understanding about the utilization of health care facilities. Hospitalization involved higher expenditure than outpatient treatment. For outpatient treatment, people were likely to reject public facilities. Long waiting period, non-availability of medical staff on time, and non-availability of quick treatment in Government hospitals and dispensaries discourages people from using public facilities. They, therefore, turned to the private sector. Dependence on public facilities was likely to be high in cases of prolonged treatment of chronic illnesses as well as for hospitalization that was expensive in private hospitals. The higher use of private hospitals in the State of the Gujarat can be explained by the fact that Gujarat probably has a large number of charitable trust hospitals providing hospitalization at reasonable prices, which makes them more popular than Government owned hospitals. One reason for the low utilization of public health care facilities in the State of the Gujarat was the large number of staff vacancies in Community Health Centers (CHCs), Public Health Centers (PBHCs) and Sub Health Centre (SHCs). At the lower end, with respect to paramedical staff, there was not much difference between the staff required and position sanctioned, but there was a significant gap in the case of doctors between positions sanctioned and positions filled (Ibid).

The State of the Gujarat had improved its performance vis-à-vis India in the long run. In the early 1970s, the situation was very bad, but the Gujarat State had made better progress. IMR was lower than that for the country but far behind that of Kerala. Expenditure on health as a proportion of total budgetary allocations had improved since the year 1997-1998 and in the year 2000-2001 and the year 2001-2002, there was a marked improvement. However, a large part of the population uses private health care facilities in rural and urban areas. In spite of increased expenditure on the health sector, the poor and specific sections of the marginal population remained outside the purview of public health facilities. An emerging area of concern for health problems in the State of the Gujarat includes, first of all, Gujarat faced the problem of groundwater in quantitative as well as qualitative terms.

Excess salinity, excess fluoride, and excess nitrite are responsible for diseases like fluorosis, leprosy, trachoma, and conjunctivitis. Leprosy and scabies were also very common in Gujarat. Conjunctivitis erupts during certain seasons. Industrialization in the State of the Gujarat was dominated by pollution-prone industries such as chemicals and petrochemicals, dyes and pharmaceuticals, etc. Many of the chemicals used or produced in the State are hazardous. The health impact of chemical pollution has not yet been investigated much and needs to be taken seriously (Ibid).

For this, monitoring of environmental health problems is essential. Gujarat is under the threat of diseases such as HIV/ AIDS, since it is a migrant receiving state.

Spending of People of Gujarat on Health

The survey titled 'How Indian earns, Spends, and Saves' carried out by Max New York Life Insurance (MNYLI) and National Council of Applied Economic Research (NCARE) covered 342 towns and nearly 2,000 villages across 250 districts and 2,255 wards. The sample size included 63,016 households equally divided between rural and urban areas. The findings indicated that burgeoning health expenditure are severely denting household income in the Gujarat State as people are incurring nearly 24 per cent of their annual income on health related expenses. The Gujarat State stood at number five in medical expenditure ranking with a health index of 0.70 slightly higher than National Index Score of 0.547. Among the households in the Gujarat State those faced major sickness, 63.0 per cent had exhausted their own life savings and 22.9 per cent had depended on loans from family and friends. The overall percentage of households having health insurance was found to be just 3.64 percent. With the growing incidence of diseases were due to largely changes in lifestyle, health insurance is recognized as one of the primary protection needs for all the members of the family. The financial preparedness to deal with health issues in India is low and health expenses continue to be a major source of stress for Indian households. A large section of households spend borrow money to take care of their major medical expenditure. This can change if health insurance becomes an essential aspect of financial planning for individuals across the country.

There exist the need for financial literacy in India which showed that Indians, whether urban or rural, poor or rich, primarily save money out of their household income for emergencies, to educate children, to cater for old age to buy a house, however, the instruments they choose to save is not appropriate.

While 36 per cent of the Indian households keep their savings at home and 51 per cent in bank deposits. Also health expenses were clubbed with emergencies and not addressed separately. A focused approach to improve awareness and financial literacy to improve protection for health problems is urgently needed today (The Economic Times, 13th September, 2008).

REVIEW OF REPORT - "HUMAN DEVELOPMENT IN SOUTH ASIA, 2004, THE HEALTH CHALLENGE"

The founder of UNDP Human Development Report Dr. Mahbub Ul Haq had developed "Mahbub Ul Haq Development Centre (MHHDC)" in November 1995 in Islamabad, Pakistan. This review was divided in to four major groups, viz., conceptual framework for the challenge of health in South Asia; state of South Asia Health, health and health care in India; and its overview.

A Conceptual Framework for the Challenge of Health in South Asia

Right to live is the most basic human right. In order to prepare a conceptual framework it was necessary to consider some rigid facts about South Asia region. As per the Report "Human Development in South Asia, 2004, The Health Challenge", the facts of South Asia included viz., (1) the life expectancy at birth of South Asian is 63 years, which was lowest in the world after that of Sub-Saharan Africa; (2) 92 out of 1,000 children under the age of five died in South Asia; (3) the Maternal Mortality Ratio in South Asia was 516 per 1,00,000 live births; (4) around 30 per cent of children in South Asia still were not fully secured from infection against preventable childhood diseases; (5) around one-third of South Asians lived in absolute poverty and were unable to afford quality healthcare; (6) 46 per cent of children under-five were under weight; (7) two- third of South Asians lacked access to sanitation facilities, and (8) more than Five Million people in South Asia were infected with HIV/AIDS due to low awareness (Human Development in South Asia, 2004).

Table 1.19 provides an overview of the current status of some of the most important determinants of ill health.

Table 1.19: Fundamental Determinants of Ill-Health in South Asia

Sl. No.	Fundamental Determinants of Ill-Health (other than lack of health services)	Percentages of South Asia's Populations (In Percentages)
01	Adult Illiteracy Rate, 2002	43.0
02	Population Below Poverty Line ($ 1 a Day), 1990-2002.	32.3
03	Population Without Access to Safe Water, 2000	14.1
04	Population Without Access to Sanitation, 2000	65.4
05	Malnourished Children (Underweight), 1995-2002.	46.0

Source: Ibid.

One can understand from the above table that under right to health people should be provided health care services but it is not enough to eliminate the root of the problems of ill health. As a determinant of health the poverty; illiteracy; lack of safe drinking water; sanitation, and the magnitude of malnourishment are undoubtedly connected with health. Another equally important aspect is implementation of health related human rights. The normal procedure for implementing human rights exists at two levels.

The first level included Government efforts to promote human rights by providing special assistance to marginalized communities and vulnerable groups, or by drafting policies that are guided by human rights.

In South Asia the Government had met failure because policymakers were often not concerned about extending human rights to marginalized sections of society. The second level included protection of human rights through a network of national and international mechanisms for monitoring and judging and documenting Governments on the status of human rights in the country.

The performance of healthcare system in various countries against two major indicators Immunization coverage and births attended by skilled staff are given in Table 1.20 follows.

Table 1.20: Proxies for the Extent of Healthcare System in South Asia

Sl. No.	Selected Countries	Immunization Coverage Rate for Measles (In Percentages of the Children Aged 12-23 Months, 2002)	Births Attended by Skilled Staff (In Percentages of Total, 1995-2000)
01	India	67	43
02	Pakistan	57	20
03	Bangladesh	77	12
04	Nepal	71	11
05	Sri Lanka	99	97

Source: Ibid.

Sri Lanka was the only country in the South Asia region where the healthcare system seemed to be adequate. The expenditure on healthcare in South Asia was inadequate. Per capita spending by South Asian countries are as follows (Table 1.21).

Table 1.21: Per Capita Spending on Health in South Asia, 2001

Sl. No.	Selected Countries	Per Capita Spending on Health (In $)
01	India	24
02	Pakistan	16
03	Bangladesh	12
04	Nepal	12
05	Sri Lanka	30

Source: *Ibid.*

Lower - income countries needed $ 30 to $ 45 as the minimum per capita sum. A vast gap existed between required expenditure and the current expenditure on health.

The developing countries, on an average, spent $ 47 per capita on health compared to high income countries which spend $ 2,841 on healthcare per capita. Per capita spending on health in South Asia ranges from $ 12 in Nepal and Bangladesh to $ 30 in Sri Lanka. Public expenditure on health in South Asian countries was 1 per cent of GDP compared to the developing countries average of 2.7 per cent and developed countries average of 6.3 per cent.

The low level of public sector service utilization reflects that public was not satisfied with these services. In case of India and Pakistan, as a part of South Asian region, the share of public sector in outpatient services was only 20 per cent.

Despite the public sector services are cheaper than private sectors, the damage is caused to the performance of the public sector provisions due to certain problems, viz., inadequate health infrastructure; inadequate provisions of medicines; inadequate trained health personnel; inadequate attention in public sector to individual case; perceived low quality of public healthcare services, and preoccupation of Governments with vertical projects which utilizes the same health personnel that provide other basic services.

In South Asian countries, the private sector dominates the healthcare provisions as it is completely unregulated and private sector has moved to fill inadequate provisions by public sector. In case of India and Pakistan as a part of South Asia the share of private sector in outpatient services was extremely high, about 80 per cent. The majority of public expends for private health services were through out-of-pocket payments as it was very expensive. The private services were not only expensive but such services were often very poor in quality; medicine practitioners were not properly qualified; exploitation of people due to majority was illiterate etc. Despite the low quality of health care provisions, there are excellent high quality corporate hospitals in urban centers in most countries, but, that are extremely expensive and out of reach for the vast majority of people.

In order to make the healthcare system of South Asia more suitable for poor people, revitalization of healthcare system is necessary by certain interventions, viz., and increase in public funding for health and its proper channelizing; enhance public health infrastructure; lower burden of out-of-pocket expenditures for poor clients; regulation of private sector; increase donor funding; curtail user fees for public sector case; effective public-private partnerships, and empower local Governments to implement services.

State of South Asia in the Health

In case of South Asia, health is biggest challenge and constraint for human development and facing a burden of communicable and non-communicable diseases, and the challenges of new and resurging diseases like HIV/AIDS, Tuberculosis etc. About 27 per cent of the estimated cases of TB in the World occur in South Asia and had highest percentage of underweight, dismayed and tired out children less than five years of age in the World. Malnutrition is one of the important causes of high rates of Mortality and Morbidity among children. Only 35 per cent of the population in South Asia had access to improved sanitation facilities, while 86 per cent have access to improved water resources. Uneven progress has taken place in South Asia. Overall, the health sector in South Asia suffers from lack of funds, inadequate infrastructure, inefficient management of health system and inadequate political commitments to provide healthcare for the masses (Ibid).

The necessary detail about the expenditure in various regions of the world is given below (Table 1.22).

Table 1.22: Health Expenditure by Various Regions of the World, 2002

Sl. No.	Selected Regions	Total Health Expenditure as Percentages of GDP	Public Expenditure on Health as Percentages of GDP	Public Expenditure on Health as Percentages of Total	Health Expenditure Per Capita (US $)
01	East Asia and Pacific	4.9	1.9	38.8	48
02	Europe and Central Asia	5.8	4.3	72.4	123
03	Latin America and Caribbean	7.0	3.4	48.0	255
04	Middle East and N. Africa	4.9	2.8	59.3	166
05	South Asia	4.8	1.0	21.6	22
06	Sub-Saharan Africa	6.0	2.5	41.3	29
07	High Income Countries	10.8	6.3	62.1	2,841
08	Europe EMU	9.3	6.8	73.5	1,856

Source: Ibid.

South Asia's the total expenditure on health as a percentage of GDP averaged to 4.8 per cent, and public expenditure as a percentage of GDP averaged only 1 per cent, which were lowest compared to other regions in the world. Further the details about health expenditure within the countries of South Asia Region are given in Table 1.23.

Table 1.23: Health Expenditure in South Asia, 2001

Sl. No.	Selected Countries	Total Expenditure on Health as Percentages of GDP		General Government Expenditure on Health as Percentages of Total Expenditure on Health		Private Expenditure on Health as Percentages of Total Expenditure on Health		Health Index (Rank)
		1997	2001	1997	2001	1997	2001	
01	India	5.3	5.1	15.7	17.9	84.3	82.1	140
02	Pakistan	3.8	3.9	27.2	24.4	72.8	75.6	147
03	Bangladesh	2.9	3.5	33.7	44.2	66.3	55.8	146
04	Nepal	5.4	5.2	31.3	29.7	68.7	70.3	162
05	Sri Lanka	3.2	3.6	49.5	48.9	50.5	54.1	79
06	Bhutan	3.6	3.9	90.4	90.6	9.6	9.4	132
07	Maldives	6.5	6.7	81.9	83.5	18.1	16.5	78
08	South Asia	–	4.8	–	22.1	–	77.9	–

Note: General Government Expenditure on Health is defined as public expenditure on health.
Source: Ibid.

To illustrate, Maldives is the only country, within the South Asia, that spent more than six per cent on health as a percentage of GDP. The major failure of the health systems in South Asia is due to lack of access of people to water, sanitation, health facilities, and the availability of health services and health provider. The required detail about access to water and sanitation by various regions in the world, in 2000 is given in Table 1.24.

Table 1.24: Access to Water and Sanitation by Region, 2000

Sl. No.	Selected Regions	Population with Access to improved Sanitation (In Percentages)	Population with Access to improved Water Source (In Percentages)
01	Arab States	83	86
02	East Asia and The Pacific	48	76
03	Latin America and Caribbean	77	86
04	South Asia*	35	86
05	Sub-Saharan Africa	53	57
06	Developing Countries	51	78

Note: *The aggregate average calculated by MHHDC used here differs from UNDP calculations as it refers to only seven South Asian countries excluding Tran and Afghanistan.

Source: *Ibid.*

Only 35 per cent of the population of South Asia had access to improved sanitation which was very low compared to other regions, whereas 86 per cent of South Asian population had access to improved water source which was competitive with the other regions. In south Asia, in terms of water coverage, 61 per cent in 1993 increased to 86 per cent in 2000; an additional 145.9 million had access to safe drinking water source. Although, the percentage of South Asian total population having access to sanitation had increased from 30 per cent (361 million) in the year 1993 to 35 per cent (491 million) in the year 2000. The total number of people without access to sanitation had increased from 830 million in the year 1993 to 835 million in the year 2000. In seven years (1993-2000), 175 million were added to South Asia's population which had resulted in increase in the number of people without sanitation. The Table 29 provides details about access to water and sanitation in South Asian in general and also by urban and rural areas, for the year 1990 and the year 2000 as follows.

The estimates of medical costs in India and United States are given in Table 1.25

Table 1.25: Estimated Medical Costs in India and the US

Sl. No.	Nature of Costs	India	United states
01	Magnetic Resonance	$ 60	$ 700
02	Hip Resurfacing	$ 5,000	$ 21,000
03	Total Cost of Surgery	$ 10,000	$ 2,00,000
04	Malpractice Insurance for Heart Surgeons	$ 4,000	$ 1,00,000
05	Death Rate for Coronary Bypass	0.8 per cent	2.35 per cent

Source: Ibid.

Further the surgeons in India's private hospitals are mostly trained in the developed countries and returned to India. Even in the United States, there is hardly a hospital without a doctor of Indian origin and nobody question the capability of these medical professionals. It is estimated that Indian's medical industry could yield as much as $ 2.2 billion annual revenue by the year 2012 but it would go a long way in addressing some of the challenges that the health sector faces in India.

A Measurement of South Asia's Health and Health Index of South Asia

The data obtained by UNDP and World Bank are used and health index of 177 countries was prepared and out of these the Health Index for South Asia, 2002 (Table 1.26).

Table 1.26: Health Index for South Asia

Sl. No.	Selected Countries	Health Index Value	Status Index	Infras-tructure Index	Limita-tions Index	Human Develop-ment Index	Rank Among 177 Countries
01	Maldives	0.751	0.830	0.704	0.769	0.752	78
02	Sri Lanka	0.751	0.892	0.618	0.875	0.740	79
03	Bhutan	0.544	0.743	0.417	0.596	0.536	132
04	India	0.476	0.708	0.310	0.575	0.595	140
05	Bangladesh	0.458	0.733	0.332	0.435	0.509	146
06	Pakistan	0.458	0.701	0.283	0.565	0.497	147
07	Nepal	0.379	0.681	0.275	0.285	0.504	162

Note: Data obtained from UNDP 2004 and World Bank 2004 used in calculating Indices.

Source: *Ibid.*

In one compare the health Index of South Asian Countries, the result of South Asian Countries were poor. The performance of South Asian countries was poor and the most common factor among all South Asian countries for such poor performance included, poor health infrastructure, high maternal mortality, undernourishment, poverty, illiteracy, and lack of sanitation.

Health and Health Care Sector of India

India is not only diversified in terms of language religion, food, cultural, geography but also diversity in terms of health performance. The key details about comparison of health, manpower and hospital beds as on 1990-1998 is given in Table 1.27.

Table 1.27: International Comparisons of Health, Manpower, and Hospital Beds, 1990-1998

Sl. No.	Particulars	Physician per 1000 Population	Nurses per 1000 Population	Midwifes per 1000 Population	Hospital Beds per 1000 Population
01	Indian Public Sector	0.2	-	0.2	0.4
02	India Total	1.0	0.9	0.2	0.7
03	World	1.5	3.3	0.4	3.3
04	Low Income Countries	1.0	1.6	0.3	1.5
05	Middle Income Countries	1.8	1.9	0.6	4.3
06	High Income Countries	1.8	7.5	0.5	7.4

Note: Income category is defined by per capita Gross National Product (GNP) in 1999; low income countries < $ 755; middle-income countries $ 756-9265; high-income countries > $ 9265. Country income averages are unweighted. Table is reproduced from World Bank 2001c.

Source: Ibid.

The comparison of India's healthcare with the performance of countries at international level was made and it became evident that India fell below the low income countries in terms of personnel and facilities for health care. India's performance was not only poor in terms of healthcare infrastructure but the utilization of these healthcare facilities was also poor shown in Table 1.28.

Table 1.28: International Comparisons of Health Service Utilization and Disability Adjusted Life Years (DALYs) Lost Per 1000 Population

Particulars	Inpatient Admissions per capita per year (Percentages)	Average length of inpatient stay (days)	Outpatient visits per capita per year	DALYs (per 1000 population)
Indian Public Sector	0.7	14.0	0.7	-
India Total	1.7	12.0	3.9*	274
World	9.0	13.0	6.0	234
Low Income Countries	5.0	13.0	3.0	256 **
Middle Income Countries	10.0	11.0	5.0	-
High Income Countries	15.0	16.0	8.0	119

Note: Income category is defined by per capita Gross National Product (GNP) in 1999; low income countries < $ 755; middle-income countries $ 756-9265; high-income countries > $ 9265. Country income averages are unweighted. * Includes all visits to health providers, regardless of system of medicine. ** Estimated for low and middle income countries combined. Table is reproduced from World Bank 2001c.

Source: Ibid.

It became evident that utilization of healthcare facilities in India was lower than other low-income countries.

Health Scenario of India

Health scenario of India can be viewed on the basis of certain indicators, viz., Infant and Child Survival; Sex Ratio; Maternal health; Reproductive health; Communicable diseases; Nutrition, and Financing of Healthcare expenses. So far as Infant and Child Survival is concerned the difference in Infant Mortality rate can be measured at viz., National level; State level; Rural and Urban level; differences among marginalized social groups, and Under Five Mortality Rate (U5MR) in India.

So far as sex ratio is concerned, the average female to male ratio was 990 per 1000 male. In Western Europe the ratio was 1064 female per 1000 male; in Africa it was 1015 female per 1000 male and in Asia the ratio was 953 female per 1000 male. In India the sex ratio has declined over the years as shown in the Graph 1.1.

Graph Number 1.1: Trends in Female to Male Ratio in India, 1961-2001

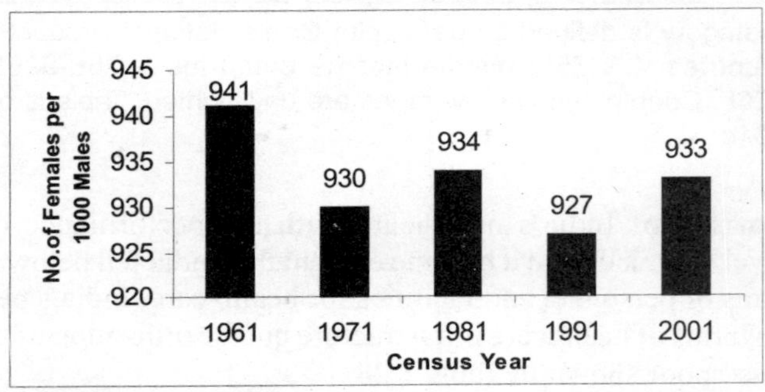

Source: *Ibid.*

The sex ratio showed little improvement to 933 but overall it was less than 1961 Census. India along with her close neighbours viz., Pakistan, Bangladesh, China, and South Korea appeared to form an art of anti - female countries that cuts across religious and nationalities.

The Maternal Mortality Ratio (MMR) is given in Table 1.29.

Table 1.29: MMR in Selected Developed Countries, 2000
(Per 1,00,000 Live Birth)

Sl. No.	Selected Countries	MMR*
01	Korea Rep.	20
02	Sri Lanka	92
03	Malaysia	41
04	China	56
05	Pakistan	500
06	Indonesia	230
07	India	540
08	Bangladesh	380
09	Nepal	740

* Values adjusted for under- reporting and misclassification for the year 2000.

Source: Ibid.

So far as Maternal Health is concerned the Maternal Mortality Ratio (MMR) in India was high as compared to some selected countries. The performance of India in terms of burden of diseases compared to high, low and middle income countries are given in Table 1.30.

Table 1.30: Burden of Diseases in India, High, Low and Middle Income Countries, 1998 (In Percentages)

Sl. No.	Selected Countries	Injuries	Communicable Diseases	Non-Communication Diseases
01	India	17	50	33
02	Low and Middle income countries	16	44	40
03	High income countries	12	7	81

Source: Ibid.

It appeared from the table number 1.30 that compared to high, middle and low income countries, the burden of communicable diseases in India accounted for 50 per cent of the total burden of diseases in India compared to only 7 per cent in high income countries. The data on burden of diseases revealed that India has to control the communicable diseases on the top priority basis.

So far as financing of health care expenses are concerned, the India's mobility and Mortality rates were higher not only due to widespread hunger and poverty but also due to low public investment in health. In terms of total five years plan expenditure, the health expenditure had declined as a proportion of total plan expenditure from 3.3 per cent in the first plan to 0.6 per cent in the ninth plan. With least ability to pay, the poor have the greatest need for health services and they bear the highest proportion of health care costs.

Profile of Diseases

The death due to communicable diseases was as high as 42 per cent of the total deaths. These were also responsible for 2.5 million child deaths below the age of five years and an equal number of deaths among young adults. The preventive incidence of various Non-Communicable Diseases (NCDs) for 1998 has been estimated and given in Table 1.31.

Table 1.31: Estimated Number of Cases of Selected NCDs in India, 1998

Sl. No.	Diseases	Prevalence/ Incidence	Number of Cases (In Million)	Percentages of total Population
01	All cancers	Prevalence	02	0.2
02	Heart Diseases	Prevalence	65	6.6
03	Respiratory Diseases	Prevalence	65	6.6
04	Diabetes mellitus	Prevalence	13	1.3
05	Injuries	Incidence	07	0.7

Source: *Ibid.*

It revealed that about a fifth of the population would have at least one of those selected NCDs. In addition to NCDs, it was estimated that the prevalence of major mental illness in India was one to two per 1000 while minor mental illness occurred in five to ten per cent of the population. The levels of suicides were estimated to occurred at a rate of 11 per 1,00,000.

Healthcare Provision

With the major health programme, the public sector provides a range of health services and private sector continues to dominate and accounts for a significant proportion of National Health expenditures.

Provision of Health Care through Public Sector

In 1980, the Government of India appointed a working group on population policy. The committee suggested differential interventions in different states in terms of health and family welfare programmes. India consisted of three-tire primary healthcare delivery system for rural areas, with Sub-Health Centre (SHCs), Primary Health Centers (PHCs), and Community Health Centers (CHCs), and District Hospitals, Sub-centers, catering to a population up to 5000, are the most peripheral points of contact between the healthcare system and the community. The clinics of Ayurveda and Unani also provide proved medical care. There are various research and training centers. But, with all these the system facing any problems viz., poor-staffing, absence of staff, absence of simple consumables etc. Such absence of adequate care in the primary health care system often forces the people to get the treatment from exploitative private sector. The PHC system is unable to bring about reduction in infections and communicable diseases. The PHC provides a range of preventive and promotive services through its healthcare programmes. Few of such programes are outlined in brief as follows.

National Malaria Control Programme

Due to high morbidity and mortality caused by malaria, the Government of India commenced a National Malaria Control programme in the year 1953. Due to initial success of the programme, it was converted into the Malaria Eradication Programme in the year 1958 aimed at eradicating Malaria in India by the year 1966. But, in 1966 the programme run into problems and from the year 1974 deaths due to malaria also began to show an increase and reached to 6.47 million in the year 1976. The modified plan of operation was launched in 1977 but despite this the year 1994 once again witnessed high rate of mortality.

National Tuberculosis Control Programme

A National Sample Survey conducted during 1955-1958 revealed that 1.8 per cent of the population suffered from TB and it had affected rural and urban areas evenly. A review of National Tuberculosis Programme in the year 1992 revealed that only in 40 per cent of cases the treatment was completed due to inadequate budget and a chronic shortage of drugs. The Revised National TB Control Programme (RNTCP) was formulated with DOTs (Directly Observed Treatment Short-Courses) strategy. Although the DOTs programme had revealed impressive results, the sustainability of programme was questioned. The Tenth Plan acknowledged poor coverage due to gaps in primary healthcare infrastructure and manpower.

National Leprosy Elimination Programme

The Government of India commenced a National leprosy Control programme in the year 1954, which was converted into the National Leprosy Elimination Programme in the year 1965. Diseases elimination stage has been reached in ten states and nearly 8.9 million persons were cured.

National AIDS Control Programme

The single largest infectious diseases and the fourth leading cause of death in the world is HIV. New infections are largely among the under-25 age group including a large proportion of women. The first case of HIV infection was detected in India in the year 1986 in the state of Tamil Nadu. As on date there were more than 5 million HIV cases detected in India. The Government of India responded soon after the first case was reported in the year 1986, and initial AIDS prevention efforts were confined to Maharashtra, Tamil Nadu, Manipur and some big cities. Since 1992, the World Bank has been funding India wide National AIDS Control Project. The first phase of this project (1992-1999), with an International Development Assistance (IDA) credit of US $ 84 million, focused on strengthening blood banks, sexually transmitted diseases clinics, Surveillance Systems and increasing awareness. The second phase of the project was launched in the year 1999 with in IDA credit of US $ 191 million.

Reproductive and Child Health

In 1950s, India commenced separate programmes for Family Planning and Maternal Child Health (MCH) services. Since the 1960s the focus had been largely on population control. The programme was renamed as Family Welfare Programme including MCH services. The expanded programme of Immunization was launched in the year 1979, and the universal immunization programme in the year 1985, integrated into the child survival and safe motherhood programme in the year 1990, but MCH services have frequently been crowded out by Family Planning (Ibid).

Provision of Healthcare through Private Sector

The private sector in India comprised of a large and heterogeneous group of actors and institutions. There exists a corporate hospital in urban localities that even the middle classes find difficult to access. On the other hand, there were vast numbers of ill qualified individual practitioners who provide the bulk of curative care in the country, and primary level care in particular. Between these two extremes there were range of non-profit NGOs, Trust, and Charitable and Religious Institutions that provide Medical and Healthcare. It was estimated that 93 per cent of hospitals and 64 per cent of hospital beds in India were in the private sectors as shown in the table number 1.32.

The share of private hospitals had shown a dramatic increase from 18.6 per cent share in the year 1974 to 68.1 per cent share in the year 1996. On the other hand, the public hospital share had decreased from 81.4 per cent share in the year 1974 to 31.9 per cent share in the year 1996.

Table 1.32: Growth and Share of Private Sector Hospitals and Beds, 1974-1996

Year	Hospitals			Hospital Beds		
	Public	Private	Total	Public	Private	Total
1974	2,832 (81.4)	644 (18.6)	3,176 (100)	2,11,335 (78.5)	57,550 (21.5)	2,68,885 (100)
1979	3,735 (64.7)	2,031 (35.3)	5,766 (100)	3,31,233 (74.2)	1,15,372 (25.8)	4,46,609 (100)
1984	3,925 (54.6)	3,256 (45.4)	7,181 (100)	3,62,966 (72.5)	1,37,668 (27.5)	5,00,628 (100)
1988	4,334 (44.1)	5,497 (55.9)	9,831 (100)	4,10,772 (70.1)	1,75,117 (29.9)	5,85,889 (100)
1996	4,808 (31.9)	10,289 (68.1)	15,097 (100)	3,95,664 (63.4)	2,28,155 (36.6)	6,23,819 (100)

Note: Figures in parentheses denote percentage share

Source: *Ibid*.

Management of Health Care

As per constitution of India, the healthcare is the responsibility of Central and State Governments. The Central Government finances some public health programmes through centrally sponsored schemes, viz., Family Welfare Programme; The Universal programme for Immunization, and the AIDS control programme. The Central Government also bears the responsibility for running a large number of Research and Training Institutes.

The State Government bears the major responsibility in implementation of programme and in financing of the rest of the health care budget, which comes to about 75 per cent of the total health expenditure. With the inefficiencies of health care system in both public and private sectors, the management of health care in India has not received the attention. First, reason is that public health is not a high priority for policy makers which are reflected in shortage of financial commitment. Second, India lacks a cadre of trained public health personnel to address health care needs. Third, lack of political commitment; and fourth reason is inappropriate development of human power, that is, India are producing more doctors they required while other staff, such as nurses and paramedical workers, are in short supply. The fifth reason is that there is not only shortage of manpower but there is also shortage of drugs and this has driven the patients, especially poor, in to the arms of the private sector.

Health Sector Reforms

Variety of methods in India have been employed for health sector reforms, aimed at improving efficiency, effectiveness and quality of healthcare by public health care services, and such reforms includes contracting, public-private partnership, user fees, and privatization. For improving the efficiency of services in public health sector, the contracting has emerged as new mechanism.

In contracting system, all aspects of health facilities and functions can be contracted out to private parties, including clinical, Para-medical, and administrative functions. Contracting leads to a reduction in costs, introduces greater flexibility in the use of labour, and can be utilized to provide services in areas that were previously under serviced. The contracting in India has been integrated in to the blindness programme and the AIDS Control Programme, and franchising arrangements have been set up with private providers under the RNTCP. Many non-clinical support services in public hospitals have been contracted out. A future possibility suggests that NGOs can be contracted to provide primary health care services in rural areas. Considering the problems faced by the health sector of India, there is need to systematically review the experience before extending it to other areas.

Another way out is to create the provision of a range of incentives to the private health sector through the provision of land at throw away prices, grant of customs duty exemptions for import of sophisticated medical technology and loans from financial institutions. These incentives have been provided to profit and Non-profit institutions, but, study need indicated that it was utilized primarily by urban-based institutions that did not always provide free medical services to the poor. Another alternative source of health financing is levying of user charges. But, experience of countries in Latin America and Africa have indicated that user charges had not generated adequate resources and has failed to increase efficiency and effectiveness and had proved to exclude the poor and neediest.

With varying degree of opposition the user charges have been implemented over the 1990s in the States such as Andhra Pradesh, Maharashtra, West Bengal, Madhya Pradesh, Orissa and Uttar Pradesh. But, with weak infrastructure in most public institutions and their poor outreach, user fees also tend to push more people to the private health sector.

By reviewing the cluster of projects that could be termed public-private partnership in health care, the Tenth Plan noted that many of these efforts were unsuccessful. Thus, contractual appointments of healthcare staff and hiring of private practitioners have not been able to fill the posts in urban-served areas. Earlier with a significant indigenous production of drugs the India characterized by low costs of drugs and pharmaceuticals. Over the 1990s the India had witnessed a sharp increase in medial care costs. India has also witnessed a greater connection of drugs production, a large role for multinational, a higher proportion of imported drugs and unbelievably steep rise in the costs of drugs. Costs of both outpatient and inpatient care had increased sharply in both rural and urban areas of India. In mid-1990s, compared to mid-1980s, Private outpatient costs have increased by 142 per cent as against 77 per cent in the public sector in the rural areas. In urban areas, private outpatient costs increased by 150 per cent compared to 124 per cent in the public sector. The increase in costs in inpatient care was even more striking, that is, average costs rose by 436 per cent in rural and 320 per cent in urban areas.

Any effort to improve public health in India must not only emphasis the important determinants of health but also the salient role of public spending. There is a common assumption that India is characterized by widespread State presence but, it is not the case with health sector.

Along with a weak State sector, an unregulated and powerful private healthcare sector raises several issues of universal care, comprehensive care and issues related with equity in health care. Larger macro-economic changes have increased regional, rural-urban and class inequalities that have compounded the problem (Ibid).

Highlight of Global Public Health

Countries in the world are pursuing the Millennium Development Goals and health of the people in the country is given more weightage so that healthy people contribute more in the output of the country and leads to economic growth of the country.

In this rest decade of the 21st century, immense advances in human well-being co-exist with extreme deprivation. In global health the benefits of new medicines and technologies are witnessed. Buf, there are unprecedented reversals such as, Life expectancies collapsed in some of the poorest countries, ravages of HIV/AIDS in parts of sub-Saharan Africa and to more than a dozen failed states. The world community had sufficient financial resources and technologies to tackle most of these health challenges; yet, today many national health systems are weak, unresponsive, inequitable - even unsafe.

To implement national plans, developing capable, motivated and supported health workers is essential for overcoming bottlenecks to achieve national and global health goals (World Health Report, 2006). The highlights of global public health by considering major health areas are given as follows.

Progress towards MDG 5: Maternal Mortality

As per the Millennium Development Goal 5 (MDG 5) target for maternal mortality requires a decline in the maternal mortality ratio of around 5.5 per cent each year. The latest estimate, developed by World Health Organization (WHO), United Nations Children's Fund (UNICEF), and the World Bank, was that 5,36,000 women died in the year 2005 as a result of complications of pregnancy and childbirth, and that 400 mothers died for every 1,00,000 live births. This is the "Maternal Mortality Ratio", the main indicator of the safety of pregnancy and childbirth. The MMR was 9 per cent in developed countries, 450 in developing countries and 900 in sub-Saharan Africa. This means that 99 per cent of the women who died in pregnancy and childbirth were from developing countries. No region in the world has achieved this result. Globally, the MMR showed a total fall of 5.4 per cent in the 15 years between the year 1990 and 2005, an average reduction of 0.4 per cent each year.

Gaps in Coverage Range From 20 Per Cent to Over 70 Per Cent

Coverage, defined as the percentage of people receiving a specific intervention among those who need it. The Coverage Gap is an aggregate index of the difference between observed and "ideal" or universal coverage in four intervention areas viz., family planning, maternal and neonatal care, immunization, and treatment of sick children. Estimates from the most recent surveys showed that the mean overall gap across all 54 countries was 43 per cent, with values for individual countries ranging from more than 70 per cent in Chad and Ethiopia to less than 20 per cent in Peru and Turkmenistan. In 18 of the 54 countries, the gap was 50 per cent or more; it was between 30 per cent and 49 per cent in 29 countries and less than 30 per cent in the remaining 7 countries.

HIV/AIDS Estimates are Revised Downwards

Estimates of the size and course of the HIV epidemic are updated every year by UNAIDS and WHO. The number of people living with HIV worldwide in 2007 was estimated at 33.2 million. The new data and improved methods used in 2007 also led to a substantial revision of the estimates for the year 2006 and before. For instance, the new best estimate for the year 2006 was now 32 million and not 39.5 million as published in the year 2006. In fact, the number of people who become infected every day (over 6800) was greater than the number who dies of the disease (around 6000). Worldwide, 0.8 per cent of the adult population (aged 15-49 years) was estimated to be infected with HIV, with a range of 0.7-0.9 per cent.

Progress in the Fight against Malaria

Malaria is endemic in many of the world's poorest countries. The MDG target aims to have halted and begun to reverse the incidence of the disease by the year 2015. In Africa, where 80 per cent of the global burden of malaria occurred, new data from household surveys and research analysis based on surveillance data allowed one to assess changes in intervention coverage in the fight against malaria in the region. Insecticide-Treated Nets (ITNs) are a cheap and highly effective way of reducing the burden of malaria. Though, the pattern is not consistent across Africa, In the majority of the 21 African countries with data from at least two national surveys, the proportion of children sleeping under ITNs increased five to ten times within five years.

Reducing Deaths from Tobacco

The use of Tobacco is the single largest cause of preventable death in the world. Based on the WHO Report on the Global Tobacco Epidemic, 2008, total tobacco-attributable deaths from ischemic heart disease, cerebrovascular disease (stroke), chronic obstructive pulmonary disease, and other diseases projected to rise from 5.4 million in the year 2004 to 8.3 million in the year 2030, almost 10 per cent of all deaths worldwide.

More than 80 per cent of these deaths will occur in developing countries. However, nearly two thirds of the world's smokers live in just 10 countries: Bangladesh, Brazil, China, Germany, India, Indonesia, Japan, the Russian Federation, Turkey and the United States, which collectively comprise about 58 per cent of the global population.

Cancer, Mortality and Screening

Globally, cancer is one of the top ten leading causes of death. It was estimated that 7.4 million people died of cancer in the year 2004 and, if current trends continue, 83.2 million more will die by the year 2015. Among women, breast cancer is the most common cause of cancer mortality, accounting for 16 per cent of cancer deaths in adult women.

Projections by UNAIDS, WHO and World Bank stated that globally, deaths from cancer was to increase from 7.4 million in the year 2004 to 11.8 million in the year

2030, and deaths from cardiovascular diseases was to rise from 17.1 million to 23.4 million in the same period. Deaths due to road traffic accidents were to increase from 1.3 million in the year 2004 to 2.4 million in the year 2030. By the year 2030, deaths due to cancer, cardiovascular diseases and traffic accidents will collectively account for 56 per cent of the projected 67 million deaths due to all causes. This increase in deaths from noncommunicable diseases will be accompanied by large declines in mortality for the main communicable, maternal, perinatal and nutritional causes, including HIV infection, tuberculosis and malaria (World Health Statistics, 2008).

According to World Development Report, 2006 the inequalities in health gets translated into inequalities in other dimensions of welfare and Demographic and Health Survey (DHS) data from 60 countries, indicated that, Infant Mortality Rates vary markedly from a low of around 25 per 1,000 live births in Colombia and Jordan, to more than 125 in Mali, Niger, and Mozambique. But, the figures for children whose mothers had a secondary education or higher were dramatically lower. Further, infant mortality rates were also sharply differentiated across population groups defined by rural-urban residence and economic status. Extreme Stunting was another dimension of health which also varied across the countries. Overall rates were as high as 30 per cent in Pakistan and the Republic of Yemen, but, negligible in Trinidad and Tobago and very low in Jordan, Armenia and Kazakhstan. The difference between children born in rural and urban areas can be dramatic. In Guatemala stunting rates for children in urban areas were around 10 per cent, but in rural areas they were much as three times higher. So far as access to immunization was concerned, children born in families whose asset ownership places them in the top quintile of the distribution of economic status had a high probability of access to health services, having received at least one of three key childhood vaccinations (Bacille Calmette Guetrin, Diptheria, Pertussis and tetanus or measles).

So far as high-impact health services are concerned, the poor were considerably less likely than the non-poor to have access to high impact services, such as, skilled delivery care, antenatal care, and complementary feeding etc. DHS data further indicated that disabled people were much more likely to be poor. It has been argued that the social inequalities can be argued to be detrimental to individual health outcomes. The income inequality at the group level does not matter independently for individual health. Thus, the main inequalities that affect health may not be the income. The other dimensions of inequality are land ownership, women's agency (health and fertility in India), and democratic rights (in England in the 1870s and in the U.S. south in the 1960s). In general, an individual's rank in the relevant hierarchy has been found to be important to health (World Development Report, 2006).

The large inequalities in health care use and health outcomes in many developing countries did not reflect different preferences or needs but they arose from constraints on the ability of individuals to achieve good health. Income is one important constraint and low-income people around the world had worse health and use fewer health services. Ethnicity, race, and location also influenced outcomes.

Infant Mortality Rates among blacks in South Africa were 5.5 times higher than those among whites; life expectancy among the rural Chinese was almost 6 years lower than among urban dwellers, while the life expectancy gap between China's richest and poorest provinces was 10 years. A lack of knowledge about hygiene, nutrition, available services, and treatment options, particularly among the uneducated, lowers demand for health services. Health clinics (hospitals), especially in poor and remote areas, were often inaccessible, have high rates of absenteeism and low quality and responsiveness to clients. There are various ways to attain good health viz., by (i) boosting people's knowledge about basic health practices and services, (ii) expanding their access to affordable care, and (iii) enhancing the accountability of providers (Ibid).

The hospitals are significant in the sense that hospital takes a large part of health care budget. Hospitals policies and practices have an enormous impact on health care and put the hospitals at the position of apex body of the healthcare system. In the light of the expectation in new millennium, all healthcare enterprises will be required to seek best governance practices to act as guidelines and shall reflect priorities of healthcare providers. Such guidelines will enable, encourage and energizes them to manage the interface between national health policies, unique local needs, availability of local economic realities and performance challenges of local hospitals (Ibid).

REFERENCES

Annual Report of Health and Family Welfare (2005-06); Ministry of Health and family Welfare; (www.mohfw.nic.in).

Centre for Monitoring Indian Economy, (CMIE), www.cmie.com.

Gujarat Human Development Report 2004; Mahatma Gandhi Labour Institute, Ahmedabad, 2004, pp. 61-66, 115-146.

http://www.cbhidghs.nic.in, Retrieved on 16/09/2009.

Human development in South Asia, 2004 (2005); Published for the Mahbubul Haq Human Development Center; Oxford University press, 2005.

Human Development Report (1991); United Nations Development Progamme (UNDP); Oxfprd University Press, New York, 1991, p. 39.

Human Development Report 2003; United Nations Development Progamme (UNDP); Oxfprd University Press, New York, 2003, pp. 1-2.

J.Kishore (2006); "National Health Programs of India - National policies and legislation Related to Health"; 6th edition, 2006, Century publications, New Delhi.

Ministry of Health and family Welfare (2005); "Report of the National Commission on Macroeconomics and Health", New Delhi, 2005.

Ministry of Health and family Welfare (2005); "Report of the National Commission on Macroeconomics and Health", New Delhi, 2005.

The Economic Survey, 2006-2007 and 2007-08 (http://indiabudget.nic.in).

The Economic Survey, 2006-2007, 2007-08 and 2008-2009 (http://indiabudget. nic.in).

The Economic Times (2008); Survey Conducted by Max New York Life Insurance (MNYLI) and National Council of Applied Economic Research (NCARE); "Gujaratis Spending 4th of their Income on Health"; The Economic Times, 13th September, 2008.

The World Health Report 2006; Working together for health; World Health Organization, 2006 Geneva (http://www.who.int/whr).

World Development Report (2006); 'Equity and Development'; A copublication of The World Bank and Oxford University Press, 2006.

World Health Statistics 2008; World Health Organization 2006 (http://www.who.in / healthinfo/statistics/programme/en/index.html).

www.businessworld.in.

www.mohfw.nic.in. (Ministry of Health and Family welfare).

2 Review of Literature on Patients' Satisfaction

An attempt has been made by the research scholar to collect various kinds of information and data from the available Books, Journals, Business Newspapers, Reports published by various State and the Central Government of India as well as by Expert Agencies and the researcher has also downloaded material using various websites and search engines.

REVIEW OF LITERATURE ON PATIENTS' SATISFACTION

A brief outline of literature on patients' satisfaction has been given as follows:

In the healthcare industry, hospitals provide similar kind of service, but they do not provide the same quality of service. Furthermore, consumers today are more aware of alternatives offerings and rising standards of service have increased their expectations. Measurement of patients' satisfaction with services provided by the concerned hospital is therefore, important as the patients constitute the hospital's direct business. The effectiveness of the hospital relates to provision of good patient care as intended. The patient satisfaction is the real testimony to the efficiency of hospital in to providing hospital services. As the hospital service can also be considered as similar to other service sectors, the same criteria can be applied for determining the patients' satisfaction based on the quality of services provided by hospitals.

The review of literature on patients' satisfaction has been classified as follows:

(1) Patients' Satisfaction with Quality of Services (2) Patients' Satisfaction (3) Comparison of Patients' Satisfaction from Hospitals (4) Patients' Satisfaction and Customer Relationship Management (5) Measurement of Attitude of Patients (6) Patients' Expectations/Perceptions (7) Patients' Safety.

Patients' Satisfaction with Quality of Services

A model of service quality was developed through an exploratory research by Parasuraman, Zeithaml, and Berry (1985), in four services categories, such as, retail banking, credit card, securities brokerage, and product repair and maintenance, conducted with the help of total 12 focus group interviews. It revealed that the criteria used by consumers in assessing service quality fit in potentially overlapping dimensions. These dimensions were reliability, responsiveness, competence, access, courtesy, communication, credibility, security, understanding/knowing the customer, and tangibles (A. Parasuraman, *et al.*, 1985).

An another study by them focused on conceptualization and operationalisation of the service quality construct that described the development of 22 items instrument called as SERVQUAL used for assessing customers' perceptions of service quality in service and retailing organisations. The original 10 dimensions of service quality measurement were combined in to five distinct dimensions called tangibles, reliability, responsiveness, assurance, and empathy.

The assurance dimensions contains five original items of earlier study of Parasuraman, Zeithaml and Berry (1985) viz., communication, credibility, security, competence, courtesy, as well as empathy dimension. Empathy dimension contained two original items of the same study as first understanding/knowing customers and access. Therefore, while SERVQUAL has only five distinct dimensions, they captured facets of all 10 originally conceptualized dimensions (A. Parasuraman, Valarie A.Zeithaml, and Leonard L. Berry, 1988).

Parasuraman Zeithaml and Berry (1991) also undertook a follow up study to redefine the SERVQUAL. In this study, the customer assessments of service quality were measured for three types of services viz., telephone repair; retail banking, and insurance). In the original study of 1988, the SERVQUAL was considered as generic instrument with good reliability, validity and broad applicability even after this study they continued to feel confident of usefulness of SERVQUAL (A. Parasuraman, Valarie A.Zeithaml, and Leonard L. Berry, 1991).

De Dennis McBride *et al.* (2002/2003) conducted survey of consumers and visitors at Western State Hospital (WSH), Washington to gain their perspective on the quality of care, services, and hospital environment. Their major findings suggested that, consumers and visitors at WSH were generally satisfied with their hospital experience. (De Dennis McBride, Jonathan Lindsay and Morgan Wear, 2002/2003).

Pauy Cheng Lim and Nelson K.H. Tang (2000) conducted study at Singapore hospitals to determine the expectations and perceptions of patients. They considered total six dimensions and an analysis covering 252 patients revealed that there was an overall service quality gap between patients' expectations and perceptions, thus, improvements were required across all the six dimensions. It became clear that assurance and responsiveness were the critical dimensions of Singapore hospitals' service quality. However, it was found that services, as perceived by the patients failed to meet expectations in all the six dimensions (Pauy Cheng Lim 7 Nelson K.H. Tang, 2000).

Mik Wisniewski and Hazel Wisniewski (2005) undertook study at the Scottish Colposcopy Clinic between October 2000 and 2001 aimed to measure service quality using both the gap concept and service quality dimensions using SERVQUAL instrument developed by Parsuraman *et. al.,* (1985) that was modified by Anderson and Zwelling (1996). Their findings revealed that largest service quality gap was observed for the reliability of services and the need for improved premises (Mik Wisniewski and hazel Wisniewski, 2005).

Anne E. Tomes and Stephen Chee Peng Ng (1995) carried out study in the medical wards of a NHS large general hospital in the East of England over a period of three months in 1993, to develop a measurement scale to assess the quality of service provided in NHS and NHS trust hospitals and to identify the basic constructs underlying patients perceptions of quality of service provided by these hospitals. The two questionnaires were piloted on 20 patients. The final questionnaire were prepared consisting of 49 statements and major 8 dimensions emerged, in which six dimensions were relating to Intangibles viz., empathy/understanding, relationship of mutual trust, commutations, reliability courtesy and dignity and two related to tangibles viz., food, and physical environment. The study also identified seven factors relating to the service quality with respect to in-patient care five Intangible factors that is empathy, relationship, of mutual respect, dignity, understanding, religious needs and two tangible factors-food and physical environment (Anne E. Tomes and Stephen Chee Peng Ng, 1995).

Ambuj Bharadwaj *et al.,* (2001) conducted study to assess the spectrum of expectations people had from health care services and the variation in their expectations among different demographic and socio economic strata. It further aimed at studying the marketing orientation of a selected private hospitals located at Delhi and the consumer's perspective of perceiving the quality of health care delivered in terms of the satisfaction/ dissatisfaction with different attributes of the service delivered and such attributes were Quality of accessibility/tangibles and facilities; interpersonal relationship; technical care; continuity of services, and administrative services. An exploratory study was conducted by contacting 80 patients and the findings revealed that the reason for choice of hospital follow the preference in the order own choice due hospital's image; suggested by friends and relatives of the patient, and referred by their family physician. Further, patients had selected this hospital as per the perceived image and various other attributes which includes highly qualified doctors; advanced investigation facilities; large hospital cleanliness; courteous behavior of the hospital staff, and easy accessibility. The crux of this study was that in order to be successful in today's competitive health care environment, the health care provider should deliver the services tailored to consumer needs and must actively review the changes in their demands and expectations in context to time and the socioeconomic strata of the community being served (Ambuj Bharadwa, *et. al.,* (2001).

David Camilleri, Mark O'Callaghan (1998) applied the SERVQUAL model and also used Donabedian's framework to compare and contrast Malta's public and private hospital care service quality, through the identification of six dimensions such as catering; hospital environment; professional and technical quality; patient amenities; service personalization, and accessibility, which includeed 16 service quality indicators and the use of a Likert-type scale, Two questionnaires were developed to measure patients' pre-admission expectations for public and private hospital service quality. It also measured patients' perceptions of provided service quality and their results showed that both private and public hospital service users considered the professional and technical care quality as well as the degree of personal attention given to them as the two most important aspects of the service product. Private sector users considered price as that factor having least importance, On the other hand, public service users considered price as second only to the quality of core services.

The study also showed that private hospitals were expected to offer a higher quality service, particularly in the hotel services, but it was the public sector that was exceeding its patients' expectations by the wider margin (David Camilleri, Mark O'Callaghan, 1998).

Joseph C.H. Wong (2002) undertook a project to evaluate quality of service provided for ambulatory clients at the Bone Densitometry Unit in the Royal Brisbane (Austria) Hospital using the SERVQUAL dimensions of service quality viz., tangibles, reliability, responsiveness, assurance and empathy. Total number of 102 patients out of 140 completed the 12 items covering five dimensions during the six-month period. The findings showed high satisfaction ratings with both perception scores and expectation-minus-perception gap scores. Of the five dimensions, responsiveness, assurance and empathy factors were more important predictors of overall service satisfaction (Joseph C. H. Wong, 2002).

Christopher Johns and Stephen Bell (1995) of UK with the assistance of the clinical audit and quality facilitator attempted to discover the reasons why the day hospital was ineffective. The main findings highlighted some issues such as there was no policy for referral of patients or policy in use was ineffective; patients were not regularly reviewed; 50 per cent of patients attending the day hospital were there for purely social reasons. The medical audit facilitator met with the charge nurse of the day hospital and together they designed a questionnaire that was completed by the nursing staff on all 68 patients attending the day hospital. The main change implemented as suggested by the audit facilitator and charge nurse, a result of the findings included that quality team need to be established to look at all aspects of the day hospital; admission criteria are to be designed for selection of patients for admission (Christopher Johns and Stephen Bell, 1995).

Yves Eggli, Patricia Halfon (2003) viewed that most of the conceptual frameworks used for hospital quality management exhibit shortcomings, terminology barriers or too much complexity, and proposed a simple model specific to hospitals based on four entities viz., Patients; activities; resources, and effects, and six levels viz., representations; priorities; measures; standards; evaluation, and accountability, which can be plotted against the four entities in order to measure the development of quality (Yves Eggli, Patricia Halfon, 2003).

James Agarwal, (1992) examined the usefulness of the SERVQUAL scale for assessing patients' perceptions of service quality in a mid-sized hospital in the Southern part of the United States using 5-point Likert scale with 15 statements relating to patients' expectations on the quality of the service that hospitals should offer and 15 corresponding items relating to their perceptions of the quality of service actually delivered. The scale was tested on fundamental principles such as reliability; underlying dimensionality; and convergent; discriminant, and nomological validity. Items for each subscale that is, tangibles; reliability; responsiveness; assurance, and empathy were subjected to reliability assessment.

It was concluded that practical insights such as recognition and reward system will improve an employee's attitude on the responsiveness dimension of service quality. The scale provided hospital administrators a tool for identifying low scores on any of the dimensions, which could, however, be symptomatic of a deeper problem (James Agarwal, 1992).

Cem Canel, Elizabeth A. Anderson Fletcher, (2001) analyzed the quality of service provided by a university Health Care Center at the University of North Carolina at Wilmington's (UNCW) Students' Health Center. Students' expectations and perceptions of the centers services were identified and another survey was also administered on the employees of the Center to compare student's perceptions to those of the employees. The SERVQUAL instrument, as modified for health care by Mangold and Babakus (1991), was administered to 500 UNCW students and all 14 employees of health center. As per the findings, the employees felt that students valued the dimension of reliability most of all and followed by assurance, empathy, responsiveness and tangibles. The students' responses supported the findings of Parsuraman *et. al.*, (1985) and the order of service quality determinants viz., reliability; responsiveness; assurance; empathy, and tangibles. Both groups listed reliability as the most important determinant and tangibles as the least important determinant of service quality in a University Health Care Center. The most important outcome of this study was the linking of students' perception of service quality to resource allocation decisions (Cem Canel, Elizabeth A. Anderson Fletcher, 2001).

Mahmoud M. Yasin, Jafar Alavi (1999) conducted study in order to illustrate how the Constant Market Share (CMS) Model can be utilized to show the competitive benefits of TQM. They used fictitious data for the period of 1988-1990 for patients' admittance to the three hypothetical hospitals A, B, and C operating in a Metropolitan Area where hospital A was the largest and B was the second largest, and C was the smallest. Several hospital administrators were interviewed and consulted during the data generation process to ensure as much realism in the data as was possible. They assumed that hospital implemented TQM on all of its operational units. Hospital B, however, did not take any quality initiatives. Hospital C implemented TQM only in its cardiac unit. The results clearly showed that hospital A benefited the most in terms of patient admissions during this period, hospital B was very disappointing, but not surprising since this hospital did not apply TQM in any of its units, and Hospital C performance was better than hospital B. Based on the results of this study, it was concluded that the fears of some healthcare administrators are unfounded. Not only that TQM does not compromise organizational effectiveness, but it actually improves it, as it contributes to increasing market share (Mahmoud M. Yasin, Jafar Alavi, (1999).

Clare Chow-Chua, Mark Goh (2002) presented a research paper on knowledge-based framework for evaluating the performance of a hospital using a model based on the Singapore Quality Award (SQA) criteria and the Balanced Score Card (BSC) approach.

A specific case study of a public sector hospital in Singapore was used to illustrate how the SQA and the BSC can be integrated to help a public sector hospital to implement and manage performance-based programs. The preliminary results suggested that hospitals can also use this approach to their advantage, yielding sustainable improvement in patients' satisfaction and better inter-departmental communication. Through this framework, hospitals can make better quality decisions based on structured measurement and knowledge (Clare Chow-Chua, Mark Goh, 2002).

C. Potter, P. Morgan and A. Thompson, (1994) initiated research project with the help of by Cardiff Business School for National Health Service (NHS) in Wales, U.K., to investigate how an approach to continuous quality management might be facilitated in a hospital setting. Three departments were selected for consideration, because of their service orientation to the rest of the unit that included medical records; operating theatres; and X-ray. Its results aroused out of staff brainstorming sessions and an observation, concerning ways to improve the quality of service to patients included important aspects. Patients appeared quite well and found as satisfied with the service received as far as courtesy and consideration was concerned. Medical records staff should, therefore, be encouraged to continue to pursue their work in the professional manner in which they were performing. Informally or formally to maintain and enhance the service and the gains, feedback from patients should continue to be encouraged. Some explanation for the delays (waiting time) should be given, so that patients should be aware about delays. If patients were unabie to see the doctor of their choice some explanation should be given to patient (C. Potter, P. Morgan and A. Thompson, 1994).

Judith H. Hibbard, Jean Stockard, and Martin Tusler, (2005) conducted study to assess the long-term impact of a public hospital performance report on both consumers and hospitals. In the study the Alliance, a large employer purchasing cooperative in Madison, Wisconsin, sponsored the public report on hospital quality and safety. The report, Quality Counts, compared performance on twenty-four hospitals in South Central Wisconsin. The experimental design included two intervention groups and one control group. The primary intervention group was the twenty-four hospitals in South Central Wisconsin and the other ninety-eight general hospitals in Wisconsin were randomly assigned to either the secondary intervention or the control group. The findings provided substantial evidence that making performance information public stimulates long-term improvements beyond those stimulated by private reports. The improvements appeared to be linked to quality improvement efforts that began immediately after the report's release. Its findings suggested that the mechanism by which public reporting affects improvement was more likely to be with concerns about reputation than with concerns about market share (Judith H. Hibbard, Jean Stockard, and Martin Tusler, 2005).

Kathleen L. McFadden (1996) analysed the proposed policy changes in patient care, along with a total restructuring plan of a hospital's obstetrics ward, aimed at to improve overall operational efficiency. The study was conducted, in conjunction with a large Texas hospital, USA, in its maternity section as it was the largest revenue generating area of this hospital, with the intent of the proposed changes in patient flow is to improve quality of service and operating efficiency.

The hospital under study altered the existing health care facility by constructing 15 Labour; delivery, and recovery (LDR) room suites, and incorporated the proposed policy changes in patient movement. These modifications increased overall operating efficiency and patient satisfaction. The hospital had also seen a reduction in average length of stay. It demonstrated how quantitative models can be used to evaluate the cost-effectiveness of hospital programmes. Based on this study, the application of operations management techniques proved useful in improving decision making with regard to the hospital's alternatives (Kathleen L. McFadden, 1996).

Raduan Che Rose, Mohani Abdul, and Kim Looi Ng, (2004) considered six quality dimensions viz., technical, interpersonal, amenities/environment, access/waiting time, costs, outcomes and religious needs identified from the literature. This study provided a more holistic comprehension of hospital service quality prediction. In total, 491 usable questionnaires were collected on the spot that is 247 from the public hospitals and 244 from the private hospitals in Malaysia. Its findings suggested that the technical quality factor was the most important determinant of service quality for the two hospitals. Although, 79 percent of variation was explained, other than technical quality the impact of the remaining factors on quality perception was far from constant and socio-economic variables further complicated unpredictability. Contrary to established beliefs, the cost factor was found to be insignificant. Hence, to manage service quality effectively, the test lies in how well healthcare providers know the customers they serve. It is not only crucial in a globalized environment, where trans-national patients' mobility is increasingly the norm, but also within homogeneous societies that appears to converge culturally (Raduan Che Rose, Mohani Abdul, and Kim Looi Ng, 2004).

Eitan Naveh, Zvi Stern (2005) conducted study at the hospital level by including all acute care hospitals in Israel and data was collected from 16 of the country's 23 hospitals., It compared hospital performance before and after implementation of the Quality Improvement (QI) program. It aimed to brought an empirical evidence to support the hypothesis that a QI program in a general hospital, a special context of the health care delivery system did not necessarily lead to better overall organizational performance results. Its findings showed that QI created meaningful improvement events. In addition, the research supported the hypothesis that increasing the number of QI activities (items) included in the QI program brought about more improvement events. The results did not supported the hypothesis that high, rather than low, intensive implementation of QI activities leads to more improvement events (Eitan Naveh, Zvi Stern, 2005).

Mike Hart (1995) undertook a pilot study, the aims of which were to determine a baseline for waiting times and to establish a sound methodological base for further measurement work. The study actually used three different methods to calculate an average waiting time viz., time between appointment time and the start of the consultation, time between arrival time and the start of the Consultation, and waiting time estimated periodically throughout the clinic. The data were collected by nursing staff for each patient in the clinic. Its findings suggested that patients will differs in their approach to waiting times depending on their domestic, work and other commitments. Most patients would like a degree of predictability in the time spent in an out-patient department so that other commitments related to work; child-care arrangements and so on can be coordinated (Mike Hart, 1995).

Mike Hart (1996) presented the results of a monitoring programme instituted to comply with the objectives laid down in The Patients' Charter (U.K.) aimed to assess the quality of out-patient clinics by the use of single, simplistic indicators such as a waiting time. It examined the ways in which total quality management was deployed in a health-service context and also to incorporate more user-centered approaches into evaluations of quality in the National Health Service, such as the patient satisfaction survey based on the application of the SERVQUAL. It concluded that the import of TQM philosophies and techniques into the National Health Service (NHS) cannot be an easy process. (Mike Hart, 1996).

David M. Williams and Janet M. Williams, (1994) worked on the project which identified patients' problem areas viz., waiting times in clinic; availability of case notes; clinic management; medical records; and patient information. The Project's achievements had made real changes to the quality of the out-patient service viz., queues at the Out-patient department desk have been eliminated; number of patients waiting less than 30 minutes has increased; number of out-patients' clinics starting on time has increased; case note availability has now reached 99.9 per cent at the start of each clinic; all patients have individual appointment times; an out-patient information booklet has been produced; and doctors received monthly feedback in league table format of their clinic start-time records and the average wait of patients in their clinics (David M. Williams and Janet M. Williams, 1994).

Keith Stevenson *et. al.,* (2004) conducted the project to test a method for involving patients in setting quality indicators locally for their primary care providers. The study was carried out at East Lindsey Primary Care Group (PCG) during May 2001 to October 2002. A sample of 92 UK patients voluntarily participated in focus groups that discussed about elements important of local primary care provision to them. While the creation of the patient generated quality indicators was one aim of the study another was to gain practices' acceptance of the indicators so that they would assess themselves against them and carry out changes to their service provision to better meet the needs of patients. The patient generated quality service indicators included 18 indicators and based on five dimensions viz., accessibility; consultation; referral; prescriptions, and communication (Keith Stevenson *et. al.,* 2004).

James Agarwal, (1992) undertook a study to develop multiple risk-adjusted measures of hospital outcomes using available data sources and then to determine whether or not these measures were correlated. However, rather than adopting positive outcome indicators, they considered adverse events, namely inpatient mortality indices (Risk-Adjusted Mortality Index- RAMI), unscheduled readmissions (Risk- Adjusted Readmission Index- RARI), and complications (Risk- Adjusted Complication Index-RACI). The rationale in doing so was the ready availability of data from hospital abstract and billing information. The relationship among the three indices was tested by using a Spearman rank-order correlation, which revealed that no relationship between a hospital's rankings on any of these indices. The hospitals high on one index were not necessarily high on either of the other two measures. It was concluded by commenting that the three indices should not be combined into a uni-dimensional measure of quality, at least at the hospital level of analysis (James Agarwal, 1992).

Ronald L. Zailocco, (1992) conducted a national telephone survey amongst the Voluntary Hospitals of America of 20,000 household heads in 40 separate markets representing 20 States, during 1984 to 1988. Respondents were asked to rate local hospitals, identified by name, in comparison with other area hospitals. Ratings were analyzed against 16 variables from four general areas viz., community; institutional; quality and cost, and control. It found that consumers believed that they can differentiate between high and low quality hospitals and were willing to pay more for higher quality hospitals. Patients' relations; medical staff; nursing staff; convenience, and technology were identified as factors defining a level of quality. Hospitals rating highest in quality had the characteristics viz., nonrural larger; tertiary care;, teaching, higher patient census, better staffed; lower mortality rates; higher average employee salaries, and more costly (Ronald L. Zailocco, 1992).

E. Joseph Torres, Kristina L. Guo (2004) described several approaches for implementing quality improvement initiatives to improve patients' satisfaction, which enabled health-care organizations to position themselves for success. (E. Joseph Torres, Kristina L. Guo, 2004).

Christine Lapointe, Jan Watson, (2004) reported that while making educational presentations, the refractive laser companies found question related with Clinical and surgical staff, that is, how to modify everything from record-keeping to payment to patient flow to satisfy' patient-customer expectation, and made several recommendations. It included areas which the refractive surgery staff had to learn and restructure in their practice, which included take a time for preparation and organisation to anticipate any possible patient situation; proper communication standardized forms so that all patients and staff are getting and giving required information; accountability and commitment for all staff members; use efficiency and foresight for the surgery; and serventhood must be the primary driver which ensure excellent care of patient (Christine Lapointe, Jan Watson, 2004).

C. Jeanne Hill, *et. al.,* (1989) conducted study to examine the importance of nineteen selected criteria consumer might use in their choice of a professional service provider. Factor analysis reduced the variables to five factors which included knowledge; comfort; time, social reputation, and accessibility. The result presented strong implications for competitiveness of professional service providers, with knowledge and comfort items representing as the most important to individuals (C. Jeanne Hill, *et. al.,*1989).

James H. McAlexander *et. al.,* (1994) examined the efficacy of four models for measuring service quality and concluded that SERVPERF methods were superior to SERVQUAL methods. Their study found that dental patients' assessments of overall service quality were strongly influenced by assessments of provider performance. Furthermore, an examination into the causal order between perceptions of overall service quality and patients' satisfaction revealed such strong reciprocal influences that it's impossible to conclude that one empirically precedes the other. Finally, the study also found that purchase intentions are influenced by both patients' satisfaction and patients' assessments of overall service quality (James H. McAlexander *et. al.,* 1994).

Stephen J. O'Connor, *et. al.,* (1994) conducted study that included the entire medical staff (81), administrative staff (51), patient-contact (non physician) employees (382), and established adult patients (2,069) which showed that doctors in a multispecialty clinic rated patient expectations of reliability;, responsiveness; assurance, and empathy lower than did administrators, patient-contact personnel, and, most significantly, the patients themselves. Health care marketers need to educate doctors on the importance patients place on certain issues and how to address them. (Stephen J. O'Connor, *et. al.,*1994).

Katherine McKinnon, Paul D. *et. al.,* (1998) undertook study in which the patients were asked to comment and to evaluate how satisfied they were and some of the aspects of outpatient which showed that high levels of patients' satisfaction with the quality of their consultations and the attitude shown to them by medical staff. Patients' feedback showed that despite the introduction of the Patients' Charter, waiting times from referral to appointment, and delays in clinics were the main areas for improvement. Its findings showed that patients were, however, remarkably tolerant and understood the pressures and demands placed upon outpatient staff (Katherine McKinnon, Paul D. *et. al.,* 1998).

Kui-Son Choi, Hanjoon Lee *et. al.,* (2005) conducted study to investigate the structural relationships between out-patient satisfaction and service quality dimensions and an examination of the estimated path coefficients showed that the pattern of relationships between service quality and patient satisfaction was similar across the gender, age, and service type subgroups. Its results also revealed that the level of satisfaction, was not the same for subgroups when divided by age and the types of services received (Kui-Son Choi, Hanjoon Lee *et. al.,* 2005).

Fenghueih Huarng, Mong Hou Lee, (1996) explained about use of a computer simulation model that was developed to show how changes in the appointment system, staffing policies and service units affected the observed bottleneck. Its results showed that the waiting time was greatly reduced and the workload of the doctor was also reduced to a reasonable rate in the overwork and overcrowding periods (Fenghueih Huarng, Mong Hou Lee, 1996).

Fiona Payne, (2000) provided information about how out-of-hours services were used by those with mental health problems. It highlighted some clear patterns in how out-of-hours services were used for mental health problems. It was useful in helping providers to plan their services more appropriately. The study also brought some of the problems in collecting routine data of this nature (Fiona Payne, 2000).

David Sinreich, Yariv Marmor (2005) recognized that in order to provide quality treatment to all the patient types, Emergency Department (ED) process operations have to be flexible and efficient. They examined one major benchmark for measuring service quality, patient turnaround time. The analysis revealed that waiting time comprises 51-63 per cent of total patient turnaround time in the ED and its major components included, time away for an x-ray examination, waiting time for the first physician's examination, and waiting time for blood work (David Sinreich, Yariv Marmor, 2005).

Anthony J. Avery *et. al.,* (1996) addressed some issues concerning the use of general practice and Accident and Emergency (A and E) services outside normal surgery hours. They found marked differences in the distribution of problems that patients presented to the two types of service that is General Practices and Accident and Emergency services. (Anthony J. Avery *et. al.,* 1999).

Research Studies Relating to Patients' Satisfaction

Robert Rosenheck *et. al.,* (1997) undertook study to examine patient and facility related determinants of satisfaction with inpatient mental health services. It concluded that the strongest and most consistent predictors of satisfaction were older age and better self reported health. Patients' characteristics associated for more of the variance in satisfaction than did facility characteristics. Older and healthier patients reported greater satisfaction with mental health care services (Robert Rossenbeck , Nancy J. Wilson,and Mark Meterko, 1997).

R.D. Sharma and Hardeep Chahal, (2000) conducted a research study to understand the extent of patient satisfaction with diagnostic services. The study was conducted in 3 reputed hospitals of Jammu city during April 1996 to March 1997, with 81 statements questionnaire having five point scale, and data were collected from pre-tested questionnaire, and finally analyzed responses of 220 patients. The study has constructed special instrument for measurement of patients' satisfaction and captured information from patients about behaviour of doctors; behaviour of Paramedical staff; quality of administration, and atmospherics / environment of hospital and also considers role of patients' demographic characteristics. Demographic characteristics like gender, occupation, education and income etc. Their results of pretesting of questionnaire were found satisfactory. The results revealed that in choosing a hospital patients gave first preference to the efficiency of doctors followed by prior-family experience, and recommendations of friends and relatives. The findings identified several non-medical aspects of some of the service encounteres that were responsible for producing increased satisfaction, and major items included knowledge; cooperation; interpersonal warmth; adequate and timely information; prompt services; efficiency of the staff, and convenience etc. Professional ability was ranked amongst the top three factors influencing overall patients' satisfaction with regard to doctors and medical and paramedical staff (R.D. Sharma and Hardeep Chahal, 1999).

Prasanta Mahapatra, Srilatba S. Sridbar P. (2001) conducted a survey in 25 District or Area Hospitals managed by the Andhra Pradesh Vaidya Vidbana Parishad (APVVP) during May to July 1999 from 1179 persons, and found that overall level of patients' satisfaction was about 65 per cent. The patients' assessment of hospital services showed the major dimensions viz., access-availability-convenience; communication; financial aspect; general satisfaction; interpersonal aspects; technical quality; and time spent with doctor. Corruption appeared to be very highly prevalent and was the top cause of dissatisfaction among selected patients. Other important areas of hospital services contributing to patients' dissatisfaction were poor utilities like water supply, fans, lights etc., and poor maintenance of toilets and lack of cleanliness, and poor interpersonal or communication skills (Prasanta Mahapatra, Srilatba S. Sridbar P., 2001).

Talluru Sreenivas, G.Prasad (2003) carried out an empirical study to find out an answer to the question as to how far the high technology hospitals had attained their organisational goals. The study evaluated patients' satisfaction as a vital tool to measure efficiency of three large hospitals, at Hyderabad city managed by Government viz., Osmania General Hospital 240 patients, Quasi Government (Nizam's Institute of Medical Sciences 240 patients), and Corporate Sectors (Deccan Hospitals Corporation Limited - 90 patients), who are providing tertiary care and are considered as high-tech hospitals. Patients' need services considered the only reason for a hospital's existence, which are reasonably accessible and readily available at all times. It was concluded that out of three sample hospitals, Deccan that runs along corporate lines was satisfying the needs of the patients considerably. Though, it stood first in the analysis, these hospitals were not away from the problems such as, Doctors are unable to come out from their own psychological set up; Paramedical staff is becoming strong and envious of doctors and Institution and unable to come up to the expectations of the top administration; cost of medical care (Talluru Sreenivas, G.Prasad, 2003).

Arpita Bhattacharya *et. al.,* (2003) evaluated the perception of Patients and found that Very high levels of satisfaction were expressed on doctors' work. The technical aspects of nursing care were satisfactory to 88 per cent of patients. Moderate levels of satisfaction were recorded regarding the general attitude of nurses and ward servants. 37 percent of patients felt the treatment facilities could be better (Arpita Bhattacharya *et. al.,* 2003).

Sharon E. Riley *et. al.,* (2005) assessed parent satisfaction with children's mental health services with instrument called the "Youth Services Survey for Families (YSSF)". Its results interpreted as providing support for the reliability of the YSSF in evaluating children's mental health services in Community Mental Health Centers (CMHCs) (Sharon E. Riley *et. al.,* 2005).

Venkatapparao Mummalaneni *et. al.,* (1995) empirically investigated, by obtaining total 2,340 responses, two proposed models of patients' satisfaction the Mediational model and the Moderator model. In the Mediational model, sociodemographic characteristics such as sex; age; employment status; occupation; education, and income were viewed as mediators in the relationship between healthcare attributes and patients' satisfaction, and in Moderator model patients' satisfaction was influenced by both characteristics of the delivery system and patient sociodemographics. Six major dimensions of satisfaction were considered viz., access; financial aspects; availability of resources; continuity of care; technical quality, and the interpersonal manner of the physician. The results indicated that a huge proportion of the variance in consumer satisfaction was accounted for by the delivery system characteristics. Income was the only sociodemographic variable that appeared to have much influence on satisfaction, but it would have relevance only if providers were targeting a specific income group (Venkatapparao Mummalaneni, 1995).

D. Andrew Loblawa *et. al.,* (2004) conducted study and respondents completed two questionnaire (t1 and t2) packages. The first package (t1) was completed in the clinic and also included demographic information on age; gender; education; marital status; primary cancer site, and whether the patient had immigrated to Canada. Patients were instructed to complete the second package at home between 3 to 5 days later and to return it by mail. Of the 149 eligible patients we approached, 92 (62 per cent) agreed to participate and 80 (87 per cent) outpatients at a Canadian Cancer Center provided data at both t1 and t2. Exploratory factor analysis extracted two factors, labeled 'physician disengagement' and 'perceived support,' with average coefficient alpha values of 0.93 and 0.90. Test-retest reliability was 0.83 and 0.73, respectively, for the two factors. The two (t1 and t2) questionnaire was a brief, valid and reliable questionnaire that taps two complementary facets of patient satisfaction (D. Andrew Loblawa *et. al.,* 2004).

Iris Gourdji *et. al.,* (2003) examined the patients' satisfaction and importance of ratings of quality in an outpatient oncology center by collecting data from a convenience sample of 96 patients from an oncology outpatient center completed a 26-item patients' satisfaction questionnaire (SEQUS). Overall satisfaction ratings indicated that patients were satisfied with their care. Patients' perception of waiting time and lack of questioning regarding their medications by the pharmacist were identified as two areas needing improvement. Their findings suggested that by identifying what was most important to patients, nurses can readily modify the care environment to enhance patients' satisfaction and quality of care. The patients indicated three areas that were rated by them as low in satisfaction and high in importance which included cleanliness of the washrooms in the waiting area; limited pharmacist inquiry into patient; medication regimen, and length of waiting time (Iris Gourdji *et. al.,* 2003).

Rob Baltussen, and Yazoume Ye (2006) compared perceived quality of care of 853 pairs of Users and Non-Users of modern health services with an aim to Nonusers were matched to users on age, sex, occupation of the head of the household and distance to health post. Questions were structured according to four dimensions of quality of care. Its findings suggested that both users and non-users were relatively favourable about health personnel practices and conduct (77 Per cent versus 70 Per cent of the maximum attainable score), and about health care delivery (77 Per cent versus 74 Per cent). The conclusion of the study was that in order to remove barriers to increase utilization, policy makers may do good to target their attention to improve financial accessibility of modern health services and improve drugs availability. These factors seemed most persistent in decisions of ill people to stay with home-based care and/or traditional medicine, or go to consult modern health services (Rob Baltussen, and Yazoume Ye, 2006).

Martha T. Ramirez Valdivia *et. al.,* (1997) proposed alternatives to achieve the timeliness customer service standard for United States Veterans', and thus try to enhance the hospital's efficiency by improving the quality of its services. The research study presented a new methodology, called as the Simulation Service Quality System (SSQS), developed in order to improve operating performance measures in the light of customer preferences. The results suggested that in order to reduce the waiting time to be seen by a doctor, it was necessary to reduce the check-in time window. For this, it was necessary that the clinic's administration developed procedures to educate its patients to check-in more closely to their scheduled appointment times. The results obtained by applying the SSQS methodology had successfully reduced the waiting of clinic patients and, hence, had achieved the original timeliness standard goal. It was believed that achieving this goal would increase patients' satisfaction (Martha T. Ramirez Valdivia *et. al.,*1997).

Mohamed M. Mostafa (2005) investigated how patients perceived service quality in Egypt's public and private hospitals and also tested the SERVQUAL dimensions in hospitals within an Arab, non-Western context.

The results highlighted a three-factor solution for the SERVQUAL instrument with 67 per cent of variance explained. Their result did not supported the five-component original SERVQUAL. The model was found to be significant in explaining patients' choice of the type of hospital. The major implication of the study was that the use of quantitative methods alone is valuable in establishing relationships between variables, but is considered weak when attempting to identify the reasons for those relationships. Patients may have a complex set of important beliefs that cannot be captured in the questionnaire (Mohamed M. Mostafa, 2005).

Neil Drummond *et. al.,* (2001) examined relationships between the macro-levels, meso-levels (healthauthority level), and micro-levels in the National Health Services (NHS) at the end of the fundholding period and considered its contemporary implications for Primary Care Groups (PCGs) and Local Health Care Co-operatives (LHCCs). Their findings suggested that Fundholding achieved some success in challenging the way in which services were provided at the micro-level ([illegible] practice), but had a less marked effect in terms of changing services provision at the health authority (meso - health authority level) level or in developing collaborative working with trusts and health authority in strategic decision making. Fundholding had an impact on service configuration and delivery in different ways which includes, it had small effects on overall (macro- and meso- health authority level) service provision in most areas; it made a difference to the care offered to some patients, in terms of access to specialist consultations or to professional allied to medicine (micro-level); and while it was accused of undermining the equity of health care at local level, its overall impact on equity is likely to have been modest because it achieved relatively little change (at meso-level) in service provision (Neil Drummond *et. al.,* 2001).

Prof. (Dr.) Parimal H. Vyas and Shri P.D. Thakkar (2005) conducted an empirical study and reported on selected patients' satisfaction who were drawn from Government Hospitals (GHs); Trust Hospitals (THs); as well as Private Hospitals and Dispensaries (PHs) located at Baroda during the year 2001-2002, and they had offered Comparative Market Performance Analysis of selected type of hospitals that is GHs, PHs, and THs to reflect upon its performance with regard to delivery of patients' satisfaction. Overall, it was found that patients' most favourably reported their own decision as the most important reason followed with suggestions by relatives, family doctors and non-availability of such hospital. Majority of the patients of the selected hospitals had rated performance as 'Good' in case of staff service attributes, but in case of GHs quickness was rated as Fair.

The patients' of GHs revealed dissatisfaction on majorities of the selected health care service features whereas mixed feelings were inferred by patients' in THs and PHs the patients of PHs were found relatively better satisfied followed with THs than GHs (Prof. (Dr.) Parimal H. Vyas and Shri P.D. Thakkar, 2005).

Stephen A. Kapp, Jennifer Propp (2002) attempted to addressed a gap in the literature regarding the satisfaction of parents with children in foster car, for the purpose of examining the current system of gathering information on customers' satisfaction about the foster care services provided by private service contract agencies, and using these information to develop a more effective consumer satisfaction survey and protocol, based on the voices of consumers. Eight focus group were developed and data were collected and themes that emerged includes concern related to service provider viz., communication; availability; respect; parent caregiver involvement rights, and satisfaction survey comments. Theses themes that emerged relate not only to the development of a satisfaction instrument and protocol, but to the experience of having a child in the foster care system (Stephen A. Kapp, Jennifer Propp, 2002).

Robert J. Casyn *et. al.,* (2003) conducted study in which involved participants suffered from severe mental illness and were homeless at baseline, investigated on some major questions. It concluded that when two choices were nearly equal in attractiveness respondents experience the greatest amount of freedom, and consequently the greatest amount of personal responsibility for their choice. It indicated that positive expectancies and the alternative choice variables were fairly independent of each other. Thus, a client can simultaneously have positive expectancies about the chosen program, and still be attracted to another program (Robert J. Casyn *et. al.,* 2003).

Yvonne Webb *et. al.,* (2000) evaluated patients' experience using the Your Treatment and Care assessment tool that showed that many patients did not have a copy of their care plan and had not been involved in the care planning procedure. Many reported shortcomings in their experience of their key worker and their psychiatrist. However, there was substantial variation in experience across services. It showed good internal reliability was acceptable to users and appeared to be able to access actual experiences better than a traditional satisfaction item (Yvonne Webb *et. al.,* 2000).

Syed Saad Andaleeb (1998) proposed a study to test a five-factor model that explained considerable variation in customers' satisfaction with hospitals and included factors such as communication with patients; competence of the staff; their demeanour (act or behave in a specific or cheap way); quality of the facilities, and perceived costs. The results indicated that all five variables were significant in the model and explained 62 per cent of the variation in the dependent variable.

The findings suggested that hospital customers accord great importance to the demeanour (act or behave in a specific or cheap way) of the staff, a multi-attribute construct that must be instilled and inculcated, much like an attitude, among the staff (Syed Saad Andaleeb,1998).

An Emergency Nurses Association (ENA) Board of Directors (2005) discussed the customer service and satisfaction in the Emergency Department of health care service provider. Increasing numbers of Emergence Department (ED) patient visits, delays at discharge; longer ED stays; overcrowding, and diversion to other ED facilities might have lead to decreased quality of care and patients' dissatisfaction. In the ENA National Benchmark Guide the Emergency Departments, 1,380 ED managers reported that 88 per cent of their patients rated their satisfaction with the ED as good to excellent. (ENA Board of Directors, 2005).

Jill Murie, Gerrie Douglas-Scott (2004) summarised five years' experience of patient and public involvement in primary care, citing examples from the Lanark practice and Clydesdale Local Health Care Co-operative (LHCC) in Lanarkshire, Scotland. It also provided an overview of some of the challenges to and opportunities for meaningful patient and public involvement. It described initiatives which involved patients and the public in the design, delivery and quality of local health care. By adopting principles derived from clinical governance significant event analysis; audit, and risk management; needs assessment surveys; consultation and health promotion lifestyle change; community development; effective dialogue between health professionals, patients, and the public had been established. The Positive outcomes reported were effective dialogue between health professionals, patients and the public, service developments and quality improvements (Jill Murie, Gerrie Douglas-Scott, 2004).

C.Renzi, D.Abeni *et. al.,* (2001) examined factors associated with patients' satisfaction with care among dermatological outpatients in which participants were recruited during at the out-patient clinics of the Istituto Dermopatico dell'Immacolata (IDI) (Rome, Italy). 396 completed the study and overall satisfaction was reported by 60 per cent of patients and the likelihood of overall satisfaction increased by the physician's ability to give explanations and to show empathy for the patients' condition, and by the older age of patients. The likelihood of satisfaction also increased with increasing disease severity, but decreased with symptom-related poor quality of life. The lowest level of satisfaction was found among patients whose symptom-related quality of life was worse than the clinical severity rated by the dermatologist. Improving the physician's interpersonal skills can increase patient satisfaction, which is likely to have a positive effect on treatment adherence and health outcomes. Dermatologists succeeded better in establishing a good relationship with clinically more severely affected patients than with patients who were clinically mildly affected despite their quality of life being impaired (C.Renzi, D.Abeni *et. al.,* 2001).

Christina C. Wee *et. al.,* (2002) examined whether obesity is associated with lower patients' satisfaction with Ambulatory Care among 2,858 patients seen at 11 academically affiliated Primary Care Practices in Boston and completed a telephone survey during August 1996 to October 1997.

Obesity is associated with only modest decreases in satisfaction scores with the most recent visit, which were explained largely by higher illness burden among obese patients (Christina C. Wee *et. al.,* 2002).

Michel Perreault *et. al.,* (2001) verified whether information on services would appear as a distinct dimension of satisfaction in a multidimensional scale. The findings suggested that not only it was important to consider information as a distinct dimension of satisfaction but it was equally important to examine three categories, consisting of satisfaction with information on; patients' problems/illness; distinct treatment components such as medication and psychotherapy; and patients' treatment progress (Michel Perreault *et. al.,* 2001).

Senga Bond, Lois H Thomas (1992) assessed patients' satisfaction with the care they received assumed greater importance and satisfaction with nursing was no exception. With the introduction of consumer - orienentated recommendations, the emphasis on measuring patient satisfaction with health care delivery is unlikely to decrease. Furthermore, there is a need for nursing to ascertain how it affects patient outcomes, of which patient satisfaction was the most frequently measured. (Senga Bond, Lois H Thomas, 1992).

Karin Braunsberger, Roger H. Gates, (2002) investigated whether there existed any relationship between patient health status and satisfaction with care, and found those who perceive system performance to be high and those with lower levels of system usage were more satisfied with both their healthcare and health plan than their opposite counterparts. (Karin Braunsberger, Roger H. Gates, 2002).

Dawn R. Deeter-Schmelz, Karen Norman Kennedy (2003) investigated the role of one component of team dynamics that is cohesion of the people to stick together and remain united in the pursuit of its objectives. The research revealed a strong link between team cohesion and the quality of patient care, which in turn associated with patients' satisfaction. (Dawn R. Deeter-Schmelz, Karen Norman Kennedy, 2003).

Ingrid Hage Enehaug (2000) considered to evaluate whether patients' participation with health care service provider requires a change of attitude or not? Partnership founded on equality and mutual respect. In the health care the balance of power between the patient and the healthcare professional rarely observed. By focusing on interpersonal relationship health partner ship can be created. To understand the system and be able to change the system healthcare professionals look at it from the patients' point of view that is, change of attitude in healthy care. Healthcare providers need to select, plan, and execute their own behavioural changes; create a system based on the premises of the consumers; establishing a patient/ relative panel for creating an arena for building partnerships with patients. By combining professional knowledge with systematic input from experienced consumers the hospital organization can get access to valuable knowledge and insight to improve the care for the patients (Ingrid Hage Enehaug, 2000).

Janice Nicholson, (1995) examined the concept of patient-focused care and how it fits into Hospital Process Re-Engineering. The conclusion was made that patient-focused care was as an important development process which helped hospitals to redesign the care processes. Patient-focused care and hospital process reengineering are both about a fundamental change in culture and attitude. (Janice Nicholson, 1995).

Douglas Amyx *et. al.,* (2000) examineed the relationship between the patients' freedom to choose a physician, the outcome of treatment and the patients' satisfaction.

The study yielded four major findings. First, patients who experienced a good health outcome were significantly more satisfied than patients who received a bad health outcome. Second, patient satisfaction ratings differed significantly only in the bad outcome condition, suggesting an outcome bias. Third, patients who were given the freedom to select a physician but did not receive their chosen physician were least satisfied. Fourth, there was no difference in satisfaction between patients who had a choice of physician and those who did not. The results indicated that the freedom to choose a physician may not be as important to patients as originally thought. Patients did not discriminated between having or not having a choice of physician (Douglas Amyx *et. al.,* 2000).

Beach MC *et. al.,* (2005) undertook study which included 59 primary care physicians and 65 surgeons. A total of 1265 office visits were audio taped and evaluated for statements that described a physician's personal experience that had medical or emotional relevance for the patient. Self-disclosure- that is, sharing a personal story with patients - is perceived favorably by patients of surgeons but less so by patients of primary care physicians. In this non-randomized study in which physicians occasionally self-disclosed, patients' perceptions of their physician's warmth and friendliness, reassurance and comfort, and their degree of satisfaction with their visit increased with disclosure by surgeons but decreased with disclosure by primary care physicians (Beach MC *et. al.,* 2005).

Benjamin G. Druss *et. al.,* (1999) examined the association between administrative measures and quality of care at both an individual and a hospital level. The results revealed that at the patient level, satisfaction with several aspects of service delivery was associated with fewer readmissions and fewer days readmitted. Better alliance with inpatient staff was associated with higher administrative measures of rates of follow-up, promptness of follow-up, and continuity of outpatient care, as well as with longer stay for the initial hospitalization (Benjamin G. Druss *et. al.,* 1999).

Ingemar Eckerlund *et. al.,* (2000) analyzed the preferences, satisfaction and actual cost-benefit valuation of provided health care services as they were explicitly perceived by the patients. The results obtained from the empirical survey pointed out at improvements where both the satisfaction and the willingness to pay were strong.

It was seen that most of the major improvements proposed in the health personnel - patient relationship were more expensive to implement than the patients were willing to pay for (Ingemar Eckerlund *et. al.,* 2000).

Viroj Tangcharoensathien *et. al.,* (1999) compared patients' perceptions of quality of inpatient and outpatient care in hospitals of different ownership in order to explore how patients' payment status affected patients' perception of quality. Its results indicated that clear and significant differences emerged in patient satisfaction between groups of hospitals with different ownership. Non-profit hospitals were most highly rated for both inpatient and outpatient care. For inpatient care public hospitals had higher levels of satisfaction amongst clientele than private for-profit hospitals. For both inpatient and outpatient care the private non-profit hospitals were highly appraised, but whereas public hospitals were generally better thought of than private for-profit hospitals for inpatient care, the reverse was true for outpatient care. The only dimensions in which private for-profit hospitals out-performed public hospitals for inpatient care was with respect to the amenities available, such as comfort of surroundings, availability of chairs etc. (Viroj Tangcharoensathien *et. al.,* 1999).

The Department of Defense (DoD) in US was concerned about how well military medical treatment facilities in the military health system performed. The proposed theoretical model for a patients' satisfaction attitude consisted of three main components that is, the individual patient, the object of the care itself and associated beliefs as well as the situation in which the care occurs. The overall level of perceived satisfaction was good over the years surveys were used. The model demonstrated the use of examining demographic and attitudinal components of patient satisfaction in military medical facilities (A. David Mangelsdorff, Kenn Finstuen, (2003).

Claire Batchelor *et. al.,* (1994) examined how consumer evaluation studies of health-care services should best be undertaken both to elicit patients' views adequately and to provide information that managers can act on. It proposed appropriate methodological guidelines and provided suggestions for the conduct of future research. (Claire Batchelor *et. al.,* 1994).

Joby John, (1992) established that prior experience with health care had a significant influence on patients' evaluative outcomes in a subsequent health care experience: on perceived quality, on satisfaction with that health care experience, and on behavioral intentions after that future health care experience. Because these patients' evaluations were influenced significantly by prior experiences through patient expectations, the hospital must attempt to condition patient expectations before and during the hospital experience (Joby John, 1992).

Daniel Simonet, (2005) reviewed patients' satisfaction and they described the US history of managed care and its effect on the satisfaction of several patient categories including the general population, vulnerable patients and the elderly. Much information available on patient satisfaction with their insurers and most surveys indicated the lack of choice of a provider which was to be considered as a major source of discontent. Therefore, patients' protection laws are necessary to avoid abuse. Patients have little ability or are not willing to rely on the information available when selecting a provider. Increased media attention may boost public confidence in utilizing rankings and evaluation of health care providers (Daniel Simonet, 2005).

Carobne Haines, Helen Childs, (2005) developed and implemented a user friendly, evidence-based survey tool that addressed the key concerns of parents who accessed the Pediatric Intensive Care (PIC) service. Respondents provided suggestions. for service development, particularly regarding information, communication and preparation for the transition from PIC to ward environments (Carobne Haines, Helen Childs, 2005).

Kathryn Frazer Winsted (2000) examined behaviors of doctors that influenced patients' evaluation of medical encounters. It examined such behaviors in both the USA and Japan. Behaviors were grouped, using factor analysis from consumer surveys, into four dimensions in the USA viz., concern; civility; congeniality, and attention and five dimensions in Japan viz., concern; civility; congeniality; communication, and courtesy. Despite many differences in the cultures of these two countries and their medical delivery systems, many similarities were found in how consumers evaluated medical services in these two countries. Measures included some concepts including conversation; genuineness; attitude, and demeanor. These dimensions and constituent behaviors provided a framework for future research and medical training and management. Clearly, there is vast similarity between the behaviors that most relate to satisfaction in these two countries, but, there are some differences also. For the USA encounters, the top three behaviors in terms of correlation to satisfaction were caring, sincere, and pleasant. For the Japanese encounters, the behaviors most related to satisfaction were pleasant, nice and attentive. The Japanese seemed much more concerned about speed of service than the Americans (Kathryn Frazer Winsted, 2000).

Gregor Hasler *et. al.,* (2004) investigated the influence of diagnosis, type of treatment, and perceived therapeutic change on patients' satisfaction following psychiatric treatment for non-psychotic, and Non-substance-related disorders. The results showed that patients' with somatoform, eating, and personality disorders were less satisfied than patients with affective, anxiety, and adjustment disorders. Symptom reduction and changes in the interpersonal domain were important outcomes associated with patients' satisfaction.

Although, pharmacotherapy itself was not related to patients' satisfaction, patients who perceived improvements in pharmacotherapy as one of the most important treatment outcomes were less satisfied than others. Preliminary evidence showed that coping with specific problems and symptoms is associated with satisfaction among male patients (Gregor Hasler *et. al.,* 2004).

A. Breedart *et. al.,* (2003) reported on a cross-cultural comparison of the Comprehensive Assessment of Satisfaction with Care (CASC) Response Scales. They investigated what proportion of patients wanted care improvement for the same level of satisfaction across samples from oncology settings in France, Italy, Poland and Sweden, and whether age; gender; education level, and type of items affected the relationships found. Across country settings, an increasing percentage of patients wanted care improvement for decreasing level of satisfaction. However, in France a higher percentage of patients wanted care improvement for high-satisfaction ratings whereas in Poland a lower percentage of patients wanted care improvement for low-satisfaction ratings. Age and education level had a similar effect across countries (A. Breedart *et. al.,* 2003).

Amina T. Ghulam *et. al.,* (2006) assessed patients' satisfaction with the preoperative informed consent procedure in obstetrics and gynecology. Most of the patients considered the written and oral information to be good or excellent, and more than 80 per cent did not desire further written Information. Forty-five percent had preferred to receive the structured information the same day the decision to undergo an invasive procedure was made, and more than half of the patients were reassured by the information provided. The combined written and oral preoperative information presented was well adapted to patients' informative wishes and needs; it allowed for a structured conversation, facility of documentation, and offering valid legal proof that adequate information has been provided (Amina T. Ghulam *et. al.,* 2006).

Cathy Shipman *et. al.,* (2000) compared patients' satisfaction with co-operative, General Practitioner (GP) practice-based and deputizing arrangements within one geographical area 15 months after a co-operative had become established; and with telephone, Primary Care Centre and Home Consultations within the co-operative. There were no significant differences between organizations in terms of overall satisfaction, but patients using practice based arrangements were significantly more satisfied with the waiting time for telephone consultations; and more satisfied with waiting times for home visits than deputizing patients. Within the co-operative, overall satisfaction, satisfaction with the doctor's manner and with the process of making contact was greater among those attending the primary care centre, and satisfaction with explanation and advice received greater than for patients receiving telephone consultations alone (Cathy Shipman *et. al.,* 2000).

Jafar A. Alasad, Muayyad M. Ahmed (2003) investigated patients' satisfaction with nursing care at a major teaching hospital in Jordan. The findings showed that patients in surgical wards had lower levels of satisfaction than patients in medical or gynecological wards. Gender, educational level, and having other diseases were significant predictors for patients' satisfaction with nursing care (Jafar A. Alasad, Muayyad M. Ahmed, 2003).

Ruth Belk Smith *et. al.,* (1986) conducted study for the American College of Obstetricians (OB) and Gynecologists (GYNS) by a commercial marketing research firm. Its results showed that patients seemed quite satisfied with scheduling of appointments; helpfulness of the staff; received sufficient information on billing and insurance procedures; thought fees charged were reasonable. Where as Open-ended responses indicated, however, that a number of patients had to wait too long to get an appointment and requests were made for more varied hours as well as for receptionist to inform by telephone and in person if the doctor was running far behind schedule; less satisfaction with the staff, requesting more respect, friendliness, and more satisfactory information; fees were considered too high in relation to the short amount of time spent with the physician (Ruth Belk Smith *et. al.,* 1986).

Giuseppina Majani *et. al.,* (2000) assessed patients' satisfaction about everyday life. In Satisfaction profile (SAT-P), 732 patients were asked to evaluate their own satisfaction level on 32 daily life aspects concerning their last month experience. The factor analysis extracted 5 factors viz., Psychological functioning; physical appearance; type of work; social functioning. test-retest reliability; pearson's coefficients were used and all together with the user friendly structure, the brief administration and scoring time, the simple graphic representation, suggested to consider the SAT-P a useful complementary tool in Health Related Quality of Life (HRQOL) assessment (Giuseppina Majani *et. al.,* 2000).

Nancy Gregory, Dennis O. Kaldenberg (2000) developed and illustrated a psychometrically sound survey that measured patients' satisfaction with a facility's billing process. The data for this study were based on responses from 496 patients representing both inpatient and out patient experiences. The survey included questions about bills received; interaction with business office staff; billing procedures followed, and personal issues dealing with the patients' understanding of the billing process and explanations given by staff. Factor analysis generated a relatively clean, five-factor solution and these factors were labeled as yiz., bills for services, staff, procedures, personal issues, and other ratings (Nancy Gregory, Dennis O. Kaldenberg, 2000).

Joanne Coyle, Brian Williams (1999) clarified concept of dissatisfaction by examining what studies of patients' satisfaction can and cannot tell us about dissatisfaction. The resources directed towards satisfaction surveys may not be well spent. The lack of conceptual clarity and inadequate theorization are the key problems facing patients' satisfaction research. This led to a number of unwarranted assumptions being made about the concept of satisfaction and to the neglect of dissatisfaction.

Many people may willingly express dissatisfaction, and yet not make any form of complaint. The aim of review was to question the implicit assumptions made about dissatisfaction in patients' satisfaction research and, to move towards a definition of dissatisfaction. It was argued that researchers should not assume that dissatisfaction and satisfaction are the opposite ends of the same continuum; the expression of dissatisfaction represents a negative evaluation of health care; and dissatisfaction results from the failure to meet expectations. Instead dissatisfaction considered to be subjective transformation, complicated and involves the crystallization of a strong, undifferentiated, vague, negative emotion experienced immediately into a more stable negative interpretation of the experience. Further, categories such as power, control, attributions, and personal value/worth are complex variables which intervene between the experience of untoward events and the expression of dissatisfaction (Joanne Coyle, Brian Williams, 1999).

Patrick M. Baldasare (1995) conducted focus group interviews among the members of Mercy Health Plan in 1994 to understand what Medicaid patients meant by the term quality of care. Two surprising themes emerged in the research. First, it was found that issues related to empathy, and respect dominated the focus group discussions. Second, even issues that were not typically related to respect were interpreted in light of the respect issue. In addition to the technical quality of care, these patients reckoned with a larger issue that is, seeking respect, equal treatment, and empathy from the care provider (Patrick M. Baldasare, 1995).

M.A.A. Hasin (2001) attempted to determine an element of customers' satisfaction, by collecting information through survey, using both written questionnaire and interview, and then statistically determining correlation between factors and elements of dissatisfaction. It was found that though the hospital had a good level of overall service, there were many areas that needed attention for further improvement of the hospital services. Some of the factors which were found necessary at this specific hospital, were viz., change in attitude of employees; training at all levels; breaking of the departmental barrier, and absence of policy that was needed to be resolved (M.A.A. Hasin, 2001).

Dawn Bendall-Lyon *et. al.,* (2004) linked satisfaction with structure and process attributes to global satisfaction and behavioral intentions. The authors developed and presented a Structural Equation Model that encompasses these relationships based on a survey of 635 consumers of healthcare services who received inpatient medical services at a teaching hospital affiliated with a Carnegie I extensive research university. The results indicated that satisfaction with both structure and process attributes had a significant impact on global satisfaction. Global satisfaction was found to directly influence both intention to recommend and intention to return to the healthcare service provider. Its results indicated that structure is as important as process, and satisfaction with service delivery had influenced equally in case of both of these elements (Dawn Bendall-Lyon *et. al.,* 2004).

Dawn Bendall Lyon *et. al.,* (2003) evaluated an impact of mass communication and the passage of time on consumer satisfaction and loyalty in a high-involvement service setting. The study was based on a survey of two groups of individuals, who received inpatient medical services at a teaching hospital affiliated with a Carnegie Level One Research university. First group included a short-time lag group consisted of individuals who were surveyed immediately after receiving a service and one year letter. A long-time lag group consisted of individuals who were surveyed immediately after they received a service and two years later. Satisfaction and loyalty decreased from the initial time of the service encounter for both the short-time and long-time groups. While satisfaction and loyalty declined over time for both groups, the results revealed no difference in the change in satisfaction between the two groups. In addition, exposure to mass communication did not influence the change in satisfaction and intention to return over time (Dawn Bendall Lyon *et. al.,* 2003).

Jessie L. Tucker, (2002) determined whether the patients' socio-demographic, health status, geographic location, and utilization factors predict overall patient satisfaction with health care in military facilities at Department of Defense (DOD) in USA. Its findings suggested that patient-specific factors predicted patients' satisfaction after controlling for factors depicting patients' evaluations of health system characteristics (control variables). Patient specific factors provided added, although very minimal, explanatory value to the determination of patients' satisfaction (Jessie L. Tucker, 2002).

Karin Newman, *et. al.,* (2001) examined the complex issue of nurse recruitment; retention; healthcare quality, and patients' satisfaction for UK National Health Services (NHS). The study described a generic conceptual framework or chain derived from a review of the literature on nurse recruitment and retention; service quality and human resource management. The patients' satisfaction chain was made up of components which included, NHS and Trust; conditions and environment (internal quality); service capability; nurse satisfaction; nurse retention; quality of patient care; and patient satisfaction. Its key findings indicated that customer service was a pre-requisite for customer satisfaction; employees play a key role in the provision of service; employees influence the quality of, and delivery of products and services; evidence of a positive relationship between employee satisfaction and customer satisfaction (Karin Newman, *et. al.,* 2001).

Mayo, Harrah (2004) provided their views on keeping very satisfied customers by following the notion 'The Customer is always Right'. The company policy, a rule, that never bended to consider the customer or patient comes first in all consideration. Such slogan provided an opportunity not merely as an advertising slogan. Staff in the hospital must be clean and immaculately presented down to the minor details because the hospital and their brand. Hospital creators should insist on backing up extensive medical knowledge and up to the minute healthcare with constant visual and experiential clues.

Hospitals should be never considered by a patient a nice place to visit, and so make every effort to put patients at ease within their surroundings before they even see a physician. (Mayo, Harrah, 2004).

Suzanne C. Tough *et. al.,* (2004) made an attempt to describe the demographic and lifestyle characteristics of women who had recently delivered a live-born infant. It also determined if satisfaction with prenatal care was related to self-reported emotional health prior to pregnancy. The study concluded that patient assessment of satisfaction with prenatal care may be related to both self-reported emotional health and delivery of medical care. Identifying and addressing emotional health of prenatal patients may improve compliance with medical recommendations, ultimately improving health outcomes (Suzanne C. Tough *et. al.,* 2004).

Charles Zabada *et. al.,* (2001) pointed out the growing importance of the concept of patients' satisfaction, and suggested that one of the ways to improve patients' satisfaction rating was to put more emphasis on the use of appropriate Information Technology in the delivery of healthcare. A framework through which improvement can happen is designed to help managers conceptualize the process. They had developed four-category classification, which offer dimensions that can provide managers with a framework well amenable to Information technology, includes, interaction evaluation, competence evaluation, financial transaction evaluation, and facilitating factor evaluation (Charles Zabada *et. al.,* 2001).

Mary Draper, Sophie Hill, (1995) reported on the feasibility of national benchmark questions for patients' satisfaction surveys. The substantive intent here was to reflect on consumers' perspectives within the exercise of setting National Quality Benchmarks. The purpose for undertaking consumer feedback activity needs to be articulated and owned by hospitals as part of their overall organisational strategy. There are several related issues which emerged from the consumer research included, such as communication; being treated with respect, and being involved in decision-making. For some people, access to hospital care was important which included the cost of, or the lack of public transport; they were not informed about waiting; they did not get in for some reason. Patient satisfaction surveys need to be undertaken in a context that goes beyond comparison of results to a context where hospitals use benchmarking, or other approaches, to establish what the processes are that lead to good practice (Mary Draper, Sophie Hill, 1995).

James A. Hill (1969) explored the therapeutic perspectives of patients and therapists by determining the cluster dimensions of therapist goals, patient wants, and patients' satisfactions, and investigated the influence and interaction of the intention factors on the satisfactions patients reported receiving from psychotherapy. Analysis of the averages of these ratings over time revealed that patients' satisfaction was uninfluenced by patient wants, but significantly paralleled the therapist's goal-setting behavior (James A. Hill, 1969).

Robert J. Wolosin, (2005) provided data that indicated general satisfaction with care provided by family physicians. Physicians themselves obtained the highest ratings, followed by nurses. Patients were less satisfied with access to care issues; items pertaining to waiting for the physician were rated the least satisfactory of all. Patient gender affected ratings of several survey items; women were more satisfied with physician-related items than were men; men were more satisfied with process-related issues than were women. If family physicians want more satisfied patients, they should show more respect for patients' time (Robert J. Wolosin, 2005).

Fayek N. Youssef (1996), measured patients' expectations before admission, recorded their perceptions after discharge from the hospital, and then attempted to close the gap between them across five broad dimensions of service quality viz., tangibility; reliability; responsiveness; assurance; and empathy. Its results recorded the average weighted NHS Service Quality Score overall for the five dimensions as significantly negative. A striking result was that reliability was considered by far the most important dimension. Empathy was the second most important dimension, and was closely followed by responsiveness. Tangibility was considered the least important amongst the selected five SERVQUAL dimensions (Fayek N. Youssef, 1996).

A survey on patients' satisfaction ratio at SMHS Hospital, Srinagar was conducted by Waseem Qureshi *et.al.,* (2005) for inpatient services. The results concluded that the hospital administrators should be aware of the needs and expectations of the public as per the feedback of the public relations department and accordingly take policy decisions. (Waseem Qureshi *et. al.,* 2005).

Comparison of Patients' Satisfaction Amongst Hospitals

Naceur Jabnoun and Mohammed Chaker (2003), compared the service quality rendered by private and public hospitals. It found significant difference between private and public hospitals in terms of overall service quality and the four dimensions of empathy; tangibles; reliability, and supporting skills. (Naccur Jabnoun and Mohammed Chaker, 2003).

David Camilleri, Mark O'Callaghan (1998) applied the principles based on the SERVQUAL model and along with Donabedian's framework to compare and contrast Malta's public and private hospital care service quality, through the identification of 16 service quality indicators which were classified under six dimensions viz., catering; hospital environment; professional and technical quality; patient amenities; service personalization; accessibility. In Malta, the private hospital service was regarded as being of superior quality to that provided by the public sector; especially in terms of quality sentinels reflecting the augmented ("hotel") service product, but it was the public sector that was exceeding its patients' expectations by the wider margin.

Both the private and the public hospital services were exceeding the corresponding customers' expectations. In this respect, it is apparent that the expectations/ perceptions gap for the public sector is wider than that for the private sector (David Camilleri, Mark O'Callaghan, 1998).

Penelope Angelopoulou *et. al.,* (1998) conducted study to determine how do physicians and patients perceive the quality of medical services offered in the private and public sector. On the basis of a survey interesting characteristics were identified. Patients in the public sector attribute greater importance to resources of a medical and technical nature and did not seem particularly concerned about the contextual or environmental features of a hospital. Private patients were expecting a more holistic approach to their treatment and expected some attention to be directed to their emotional needs. Private surgeons were worried about the limited basic resources in private hospitals and their inability to satisfy the non-clinical needs of their patients (Penelope Angelopoulou *et. al.,* 1998).

Sandra K. Smith Gooding, (1995) explored the links between perceived quality, perceived sacrifice, and perceived value in the hospital choice scenario. The findings have implications not only for hospital strategic planning and marketing, but also for public policy makers who want to involve consumers in the health care decision-making process and determine what information they need. Suggestion based on findings included quality concerns carry significantly less weight with consumers for minor treatment than for major care; similarly, monetary and other sacrifice concerns are significantly more important for minor care than for major treatment. However, local hospitals cannot afford to dismiss the importance of perceived quality and must address any negative consumer perceptions while also emphasizing the value of location; Likewise, regional hospitals should promote the quality perception of the entire institution and its specialties while minimizing the sacrifice of longer travel times, etc. in consumer messages (Sandra K. Smith Gooding, 1995).

Patients' Satisfaction and Customer Relationship Management

B.Krishan Reddy, G.V.R.K. Acharyulu (2002) conducted the study aimed at presenting some of the CRM concepts and elements to formulate CRM strategy in order to take proactive measures towards customer-centric business in a corporate hospital to improve customer satisfaction by building up better customer relationships leading to increase in revenues. This study focused on the Master Health Check (MHC) Packages, profile of customers, and their behaviour and finally determined the relationship factors to design CRM strategy. It found that the reason for maximum number of customers opting for MHC and Executive Health Check were due to Heart Check and Well Women

Check were specialized packages confined to only specific purpose; Master health Check is highly demanded because it provided the customers with a list of comprehensive tests and it was also economical (Rs. 1700) compared to the other package; and Executive Health Check was a package that is directed only to the office going people and the executives not recommended for all (B.Krishan Reddy, G.V.R.K. Acharyulu, 2002).

Markus Orava, Pekka Tuominen (2002) analysed the quality of a professional surgical service process, and revealed the main elements that constitute excellence in the experience of the surgical service of a private hospital. Empirical research was conducted in private hospitals and its results indicated that, in private surgical services, the surgical procedure itself was the single most important element, but that it must be supplemented by quality dimensions in both output and process throughout the whole surgical service process combined with deep patient-staff interaction, elements of professional expertise and pleasantness, and versatile supporting services and physical features. The need for relationship marketing was evident in private hospitals because empirical findings heavily underlined the importance of patient-staff interactions and the trusting nature of doctor-patient relationships (Markus Orava, Pekka Tuominen, 2002).

Beth Hogan Henthorne *et. al.,* (1994) described process for providing an enhanced level of service that is, the adoption and implementation of a Patient Advocacy Program. Prior to the introduction of the advocacy program, they conducted care satisfaction/complaining behavior surveys for both patient and clinic staff. Based on the findings of the initial patient and staff surveys, a three-month pilot plan was developed for a patient-oriented support service and after three months it revealed generally poor usage of patient representatives by clinic staff. Continued administrative concern about the appropriate use of the patient representatives led to further refinement of the system which includes, A permanent in-house site was established for program representatives; A plan was developed to re-sensitize staff to patient needs and aspects of patient satisfaction through additional staff in-service; A new patient letter was developed with a brief questionnaire to assess the patients' satisfaction with his or her recent clinic visit. Even though an increase in patients' satisfaction was a long-term goal of the advocacy program, the more immediate goal was to set in motion a system that addressed existing dissatisfaction in the health care environment (Beth Hogan Henthorne *et. al.,* 1994).

Measurement of Patients' Attitude

Nimma Satynarayana, *et. al.,* (2004) measured the patients' attitude towards payment an opinion survey through a structured questionnaire for a period of 2 months, with a total sample of 85 cases at the hospitals at Hyderabad. Its Findings suggested that more number of rural patients, particularly from nuclear family with mean income of Rs. 3,102.56 with male preponderance (74 per cent) attended the hospital. It also showed that white card holder (income <6000 per annum) dominates (52 per cent) the patient profile; and employed patients accounted for 61 per cent. It was surprising to note that 70 per cent patients were able to pay but unwilling to pay the hospital bills. The key finding of the study was that, contrary to expectation of attracting paying (middle income group) patients, the hospital was getting low income group/referral patients. In order to attract the paying patients' medical insurance policy should be considered (Nimma Satynarayana, *et. al.,* 2004).

Stephen Todd *et. al.,* (2002) investigated the perceptions and attendant behavioural attitudes of stakeholders, including patients and visitors, to the built environments and supporting facilities provided by Salford Royal Hospitals NHS Trust, U.K. the study had used variety of methodologies to collect empirical dat which included, extensive literature survey and research review, one-to-one patient interviews, a large questionnaire survey, patients' picture stories. The empirical evidence examined suggested that the notions of patients-friendly environments held by participants in the study were based upon three conceptual visions of the role and function of the built environments of health-care facilities, which includes notions of homeliness, notions of movement and accessibility through transitional spaces, and notions of supportive environments (Stephen Todd *et. al.,* 2002).

Patients' Expectations/Perceptions

Dr Sona Bedi *et. al.,* (2004) conducted a patients' expectation survey among 230 patients who visited the outpatient departments of two Government hospitals at Delhi. Its findings suggested that in both hospitals, waiting time in physicians' queues and duration of consultation time appear to be potentially dissatisfaction causing factors. Hospital administrators of both hospitals were expected to devise strategies to mitigate the effect of these factors. Both hospitals needed to have a strategy of improving communication skills of physicians (Dr Sona Bedi *et. al.,* 2004).

Eugene C. Nelson *et. al.,* (1992) conducted study based on 51 General Medical/ Surgical hospitals owned by the Hospital Corporation of America (HCA). The findings suggested that measurable improvements in patients' judgments of hospital quality might translate into better financial performance. Its analysis confirmed that patient perceptions of quality were associated with hospital financial performance. The factor analysis revealed four clear and distinct dimensions of hospital quality which included, medical/billing; nursing/daily care; admissions, and discharge. It clearly demonstrated that meeting inpatients' expectations was associated with the financial strength of hospitals in this investor-owned health care system (Eugene C. Nelson *et. al.,* 1992).

Li-Jen Jessica Hwang *et. al.,* (2003) conducted a survey utilizing a modified SERVQUAL instrument measured on a seven-point Likert scale was carried out on-site at four National Health Service (NHS) acute trust for evaluating the perceptions and expectations of meal attributes and its importance in determining patient satisfaction. The results of factor analysis found three dimensions i. e. food properties; interpersonal service, and environmental presentation. The food dimension was found to be the best predictor of patient satisfaction among the three dimensions, while the interpersonal service dimension was not found to have any correlation with satisfaction (Li-Jen Jessica Hwang *et. al.,* 2003).

Stefanie Naumann, Jeffrey A. Miles, (2001) conducted study based on 195 patients who visited the urgent care department of a rural hospital in Central England.

The study examined the effects of three elements of process control on patients' fairness and satisfaction perceptions with the triage process means a process in an urgent care department, and such elements included viz., allowing patients to have a voice in the waiting process; informing patients the expected waiting time, and keeping patients occupied while they wait for treatment. The results demonstrated that patients who believed they had a voice in the triage process had higher fairness perceptions and waited a shorter period of time than those who believed they did not have a voice in the triage process. In addition, patients' who were told the expected waiting time and were kept busy while waiting had higher satisfaction perceptions (Stefanie Naumann, Jeffrey A. Miles, 2001).

James M. Carman (2000) designed the study to provide answers to the question of how patients evaluated the quality of hospital care. It provided empirical evidence on the relative importance of the various dimensions of care and how these evaluations interacted with one another.

The study showed that consumers evaluated the technical dimensions of nursing care; physician care, and outcome as more important than the accommodation functions; accommodation, discharge and food of hospital care, and there were significant interactions among the technical dimensions. Both sets of dimensions were important and significant, but technical quality evaluations were not influenced by the perceived quality level of the affective attributes (James M. Carman, 2000).

Alan Baldwin, Amrik Shoal (2003) conducted study using research methodology based upon the SERVQUAL instrument to identify service quality perceptions of dental patients. Its results suggested facets of service quality emerged as priorities for dental patients as fear and anxiety, Punctuality, waiting times, collaborative treatment planning, and opening times (Alan Baldwin, Amrik Shoal, 2003).

M. Sadiq Sohil (2003) examined and measured the quality of services provided to 186 patients (out of which 150 were used for analysis) by five private hospitals across Malaysia in the first quarter of 2001. Its results indicated that patients perceived value of the services exceed expectations for all the variables measured. A comparative analysis with similar studies in other countries such as Hong Kong and Turkey, Malaysian health-care providers seemed to be doing better job in achieving customer satisfaction with regard to service quality (M. Sadiq Sohil, 2003).

Patients' Safety/Complaints

Thomas V. Perneger, (2006) have discussed various examples of studies on patients' safety as field of research area. Patient safety is to be considered as global problem that calls for global solutions. In-depth studies of errors, mishaps, and patient safety incidents; epidemiologic studies of incidents and errors identification of risk factors for patient safety events; research on human factors; patient involvement in safety; development of patient safety indicators; and evaluation of interventions to improve safety have been described as rich field of research.

It offers exciting opportunities to researchers of many disciplines. The impetus to patient safety research that will be given by the World Alliance and other governing bodies is a welcome development (Thomas V. Perneger, 2006).

Didier Pittet, Liam Donaldson (2006) advocated that improving the safety of patient care shall be considered as an issue which affects health systems in both developed and developing countries. To co-ordinate and accelerate improvements in patient safety, the World Health Organization (WHO) has supported the creation of the World Alliance for Patient Safety was launched in October 2004. The six action areas of the alliance were patients for patient safety; taxonomy; research; solutions for patient safety; reporting and learning, and a biennial global patient safety challenge. (Didier Pittet, Liam Donaldson (2006).

Kathleen L. McFadden *et. al.,* (2006) explored the use of Patient Safety Initiatives (PSIs) at the US hospitals which included such approaches as open discussion of errors, education and training, and system redesign. (Kathleen L. McFadden et.al., 2006).

Rachel Javetz, Zvi Stern (1996) agreed that patients provide important feedback to health-care providers and policy makers by voicing their complaints and requests. The unavoidable involvement of the customers' feedback role as a contributing factor in the endeavour for continuous quality improvement in the health-care system was emphasized. (Rachel Javetz, Zvi Stern, 1996).

Sophie Y. Hsieh *et. al.,* (2005) explored and evaluated how hospital staff responds to patients' complaints made against hospitals. It was revealed that: complaint handlers were not sufficiently empowered, information sharing was limited within the organization, communication among professional staff and with management was inadequate, the physical safety of workers had been threatened, and improvements could not be sustained. It became evident that the hospital did not use patient complaints as a source of learning that could have promoted higher standards of care. The case study revealed some of the constraints and identified requirements for appropriate use of information and feedback from patients. The study showed that hospitals need to establish clear policies and mechanism to improve their performance in complaints handling. Second, complaint handlers have to be sufficiently empowered to be able to deal with a variety of patient complaints. Third, an effective communication network between departments is essential to follow up the procedure of complaints handling and further to enhance monitoring any improvement activities occurred within the department (Sophie Y. Hsieh *et. al.,* 2005).

REFERENCES

Alan Baldwin, Amrik Shoal (2003); "Service Quality Factors and Outcomes in Dental Care"; Managing Service Quality, MCB UP Limited, Vol. No. 13, No. 3, 2003, pp. 207-216.

Ambuj Bharadwaj, D.K. Sharma, R.K. Sharma, P.C. Chaubey (2001); "Expectations of people from Quality Health Services in Metropolitan city of Delhi and to Propose a Sound Health Care Marketing Strategy for Private/Corporate Hospitals in Delhi";

Journal of the Academy of Hospital Administration; Vol. 13, No. 2 (2001-07-2001-12).

Amina T. Ghulam; Margrit Kessler; Lucas M. Bachmann, Urs Haller, Thomas M. Kessler (2006); "Patients' Satisfaction With the Preoperative Informed Consent Procedure: A Multicenter Questionnaire Survey in Switzerland" Mayo Clinic Proceedings, Vol. No. 8l (3, March 2006, pp. 307-312.

Anne E. Tomes and Stephen Chee Peng Ng, (1995); "Service Quality in Hospital Care: The Development of an In-patient Questionnaire"; International Journal of Health care Quality Assurance, MCB University Press, Vol. 8 No. 3, pp. 25-33.

Anthony J. Avery, Lindsay Groom, Daphne Boot, Stephen Earwicker and Robin Carlisle (1999); "What Problems Do Patients Present With Outside Normal General Practice Surgery Hours? A Prospective Study of The Use of General Practice and Accident and Emergency Services"; Journal of Public Health Medicine, Faculty of Public Health Medicine, Printed in Great Britain, Vol. No. 21, No. 1, pp. 88-94.

Arpita Bhattacharya, Prema Menon, Vipin Koushal, K.L.N. Rao (2003); "Study of Patient Satisfaction in a Tertiary Referral Hospital"; Journal of the Academy of Hospital Administration, Vol. 15, No. 1, Jan-June 2003.

B.Krishan Reddy, G.V.R.K. Acharyulu (2002); "Customer Relationship Management (CRM) in Health Care Sector-A Case Study on Master Health Check"; Journal of the Academy of Hospital Administration, Vol.No. 14, No. 1, January to June 2002.

Beach MC., Roter D., Rubin H., Frankel R., Levinson W., Ford DE. (2005); "Patient Satisfaction Affected by Physician Self-Disclosure"; The Journal of Family Practice, Vol. No. 54, No. 1, January 2005.

Benjamin G. Druss, Robert A. Rosenheck, Marilyn Stolar, (1999); "Patient Satisfaction and Administrative Measures as Indicators of the Quality of Mental Health Care"; Psychiatric Services, Vol. 50 No. 8, August 1999, pp. 1053-1058.

Beth Hogan Henthorne, Tony L. Henthorne, John D. Alcorn (1994); "Enhancing the Provider/Patient Relationship: The Case for Patient Advocacy Programs"; Journal of Health Care Marketing, Vol. No. 14, No.3, Fall 1994, pp. 52-55.

Breedart, C. Robertson, D. Razavi, L. Batel-Copel, G. Larsson, D. Lichosik, J. Meyza, S. Sch raub, L. Von Essen, And J.C.J.M. De Haes (2003); "Patients' Satisfaction Ratings And Their Desire for Care Improvement Across Oncology Settings From France, Italy, Poland And Sweden"; Psycho-Oncology, Vol. No. 12, 2003, pp. 68-77.

C. Jeanne Hill, S.J. Garner, and Michael E. Hanna (1989); "Selection Criteria For Professional Service Providers"; The Journal of Services Marketing; Vol. 3 No. 4 Fall, 1989, pp. 61-69.

C. Potter, P. Morgan and A. Thompson (1994); "Continuous Quality Improvement in an Acute Hospital: A Report of an Action Research Project in Three Hospital Departments"; International Journal of Health Care Quality Assurance, MCB University Press Limited, 1994, Vol. 7 No. 1, pp. 4-29.

C.Renzi, D.Abeni, A.Picardi, E.Agostini, C.F.Melchi, P.Pasquini, P.Puddu, And M.Braga (2001); "Factors Associated With Patient Satisfaction With Care Among Dermatological Outpatients"; British Journal of Dermatology, 2001, pp. 617-623.

Carobne Haines, Helen Childs (2005); "Parental Satisfaction With Pediatric Intensive Care"; Pediatric Nursing; Vol. No. 17, No. 7, September 2005, pp. 37-41.

Cathy Shipman, Fiona Payne, Richard Hooper and Jeremy Dale (2000); "Patient satisfaction with out-of-hours services; how do GP co-operatives compare with deputizing and practice-based arrangements?"; Journal of Public Health Medicine, Faculty of Public Health Medicine, Vol. 22, No. 2, pp. 149-154.

Cem Canel, Elizabeth A. Anderson Fletcher (2001); "An Analysis of Service Quality at a Student Health Center"; International Journal of Health Care Quality Assurance, MCB University Press Limited, 2001, Vol., 14/6, pp. 260-267.

Charles Zabada, Sanjay Singh, George Munchus (2001); "The Role of Information Technology in Enhancing Patient Satisfaction"; British Journal of Clinical Governance, MCB University Press, Vol. No.6, No. 1, 2001, pp. 9-16.

Christina C. Wee, Russel S. Phillips, Francis Cook, Jennifer S. Haas, Ann Louise Puopolo, Troyen A. Brennan, Helen R. Burstin (2002); "Influence of Body Weight on Patients' Satisfaction with Ambulatory Care" J Gen !ntern Med, Vol, 17, Feb 2002, pp. 155-159.

Christine Lapointe, Jan Watson (2004); "Welcoming Elective Surgery Patients"; Review Bottom Line, Review of Ophthalmology, September 2004, pp. 28-34.

Christopher Johns and Stephen Bell (1995); "A Multidisciplinary Team Approach To Day Hospital Patient Care"; Health Manpower Management, MCB University Press, 1995, Volume 21, Number 4, 1995, pp. 28-31.

Claire Batchelor, David J. Owens, Martin Read and Michael Bloor (1994); "Patient Satisfaction Studies: Methodology, Management and Consumer Evaluation"; International Journal of Health Care Quality Assurance, MCB University Press Limited, Vol. No. 7, No. 7, 1994, pp. 22-30.

Clare Chow-Chua, Mark Goh (2002); "Case Study framework for Evaluating Performance and Quality Improvement in Hospitals"; Managing Service Quality, MCB University Press Limited, Vol., 12, No. 1, 2002, pp. 54-66.

D. Andrew Loblawa,B Andrea Bezjaka, P. Mony Singhc, Andrew Gotowiecd, David Jouberte, Kenneth Mahe And Gerald M. Devins (2004); "Psychometric Refinement Of An Outpatient, Visit-Specific Satisfaction With Doctor Questionnaire"; Psycho-Oncology 13: PP. 223-234. [Published online 27 May 2003 in Wiley InterScience (www.interscience.wiley.com). DOI: 10.1002/pon.715]

Daniel Simonet (2005); "Patient Satisfaction under Managed Care"; International Journal of Health Care Quality Assurance, Emerald Group Publishing Limited, Vol. 18 No. 6, 2005, pp. 424-440.

David Camilleri, Mark O'Callaghan (1998); "Comparing Public And Private Hospital Care Service Quality"; International Journal of Health Care Quality Assurance, MCB University Press, Vol No. 11/4 (1998) pp. 127-133.

David Camilleri, Mark O'Callaghan (1998); "Comparing Public and Private Hospital Care Service Quality"; International Journal of Health Care Quality Assurance, MCB University Press, Vol. No. 11/4, 1998, pp. 127-133.

David M. Williams and Janet M. Williams (1994); "Improving the Quality of Service in an Out-Patient Department" International Journal of Health Care Quality Assurance, MCB University Press Limited, Vol. 7, No. 2, 1994, pp. 16-18.

David Mangelsdorff, Kenn Finstuen (2003); "Patient Satisfaction in Military Medicine: Status and an Empirical Test of a Model"; Military Medicine, Vol. No. 168, September 2003, pp. 744-749.

David Sinreich, Yariv Marmor (2005); "Ways To Reduce Patient Turnaround Time And Improve Service Quality In Emergency Departments"; Journal of Health Organization and Management, Emerald Group Publishing Limited, Vol. No.19 No. 2, 2005, pp. 88-105.

Dawn Bendall Lyon, Thomas L. Powers (2003); "The influence of Mass Communication and Time on Satisfaction and Loyalty"; Journal of Services Marketing, Emerald Group Publishing Limited, Vol. No. 17, No. 6, 2003, pp. 589-608.

Dawn Bendall-Lyon, Thomas L. Powers (2004); "The Impact of Structure and Process Attributes on Satisfaction and Behavioral Intentions"; Journal of Services Marketing, Emerald Group Publishing Limited, Vol. No. 18, No. 2, 2004, pp. 114-121.

Dawn R. Deeter-Schmelz, Karen Norman Kennedy (2003); "Patient Care Teams and Customer satisfaction: the Role of Team Cohesion"; Journal of Services Marketing, MCB UP Limited, Vol. No. 17, No. 7, 2003, pp. 666-684.

De Dennis McBride, Jonathan Lindsay and Morgan Wear (2002/2003); "Western state Hospital Consumer and Visitor Satisfaction Survey"; University of Washington School of Medicine Division of Psychiatry and Behavioral Sciences, Survey of The year 2002/2003.

Didier Pittet, Liam Donaldson (2006); "Challenging the World: Patient Safety and Health Care-Associated Infection"; International Journal for Quality in Health Care, Published by Oxford University Press, Vol. No.18, No. 1, 2006, pp. 4-8.

Douglas Amyx, John C. Mowen, Robert Hamm (2000); "Patient Satisfaction: A Matter of Choice"; Journal of Services Marketing, Mcb University Press, VOL. No.14, No. 7, 2000, pp. 557-572.

Dr Sona Bedi, Dr Sanjay Arya, Prof RK Sarma (2004); "Patient Expectation Survey-A Relevant Marketing Tool for Hospitals"; Journal of the Academy of Hospital Administration; Vol. No. 16, No. 1, January to June 2004, pp. 15-22.

E. Joseph Torres, Kristina L. Guo (2004); "Quality Improvement Techniques To Improve Patient Satisfaction"; International Journal of Health Care Quality Assurance, Emerald Group Publishing Limited", Volume 17, No 6, 2004, pp. 334-338.

Eitan Naveh, Zvi Stern (2005); "How Quality Improvement Programs Can Affect General Hospital Performance"; International Journal of Health Care Quality Assurance, Emerald Group Publishing Limited, 2005,Vol. No.18 No. 4, pp. 249-270.

ENA Board of Directors (2005); "Customer Service and Satisfaction in the Emergency Department"; Top Emerg Med, Uppincott Williams cand Wilkins, Inc., Vol. No. 27, No. 4, pp. 327-328.

Eugene C. Nelson, Roland T. Rust, Anthony Zahorik, Robin L Rose, Paul Batalden, and Beth Ann Siemanski (1992); "Do Patient Perceptions of Quality Relate to Hospital Financial Performance"; Journal of Healthcare Marketing, December 1992, pp. 6-13.

Fayek N. Youssef (1996); "Health Care Quality in NHS Hospitals"; International Journal of Health Care Quality Assurance, MCB University Press, Vol. No. 9/1, 1996, pp. 15-28.

Fenghueih Huarng, Mong Hou Lee (1996); "Using Simulation in Out-Patient Queues: A Case Study"; International Journal of Health Care Quality Assurance, MCB University Press, Vol. No 9/6, 1996, pp. 21-25.

Fiona Payne (2000); "Utilization of Out-of-Hours Services By Patients With Mental Health Problems"; Journal of Public Health Medicine, Faculty of Public Health Medicine, Printed in Great Britain, Vol. No.22, No. 3, pp. 302-306.

Giuseppina Majani, Antonia pierobon, Anna Giardini, Simona Callegari (2000); "Satisfaction Profile (SAT-P) in 732 Patients: Focus on Subjectivity in HRQoL Assessment"; Psychology and Health; Vol. No. 15, pp. 409-422.

Gregor Hasler, Hanspeter Moergeli, , Rosilla Bachmann, , Evelina Lambreva,, Claus Buddeberg,, Ulrich Schnyder (2004); "Patient Satisfaction With Outpatient Psychiatric Treatment: The Role of Diagnosis, Pharmacotherapy, and Perceived Therapeutic Change"; The Canadian Journal of Psychiatry; Vol No. 49. No 5. May 2004, pp. 315-321.

Ingemar Eckerlund, Jan A. Eklof, Jorgen Nathorstboos (2000); "Patient Satisfaction and Priority Setting in Ambulatory Health Care; Total Quality Management; Vol. No. 11, No. 7, pp. S967- S978.

Ingrid Hage Enehaug (2000); " Patient Participation Requires a Change of attitude in Health Care"; International Journal of Health Care Quality Assurance, MCB University Press, Vol. No. 13/4, 2000, pp. 178-181.

Iris Gourdji, Lynne McVey, Carmen Loiselle (2003); "Patients' Satisfaction and Importance Ratings of Quality in an Outpatient Oncology Center"; Journal of Nursing care Quality; Lippincott Williams and Wilkins, Inc. Vol. No. 18, No. 1, 2003, pp. 43-55.

Jafar A. Alasad, muayyad M. Ahmed (2003); "Patients' satisfaction with Nursing Care in Jordan"; International journal of Health Care Assurance, MCB UP Limited, Vol. NO. 16/6, 2003, pp. 279-285.

James A. Hill (1969); "Therapist Goals, Patient Aims and Patient Satisfaction in Psychotherapy"; Institute for Juvenile Research, Chicago; 1969; pp. 455-459.

James Agarwal (1992); "Adapting the SERVQUAL Scale to Hospital Services: An Empirical Investigation"; Journal of Health Care Marketing, Vol. 12, No. 3 (September 1992).

James Agarwal (1992); "Measuring Outcomes of Hospital Care Using Multiple Risk-Adjusted Indexes," Journal of Health Care Marketing, Vol. No. 12, No. 3, September 1992.

James H. McAlexander, Dennis 0. Kaldenberg, and Harold F. Koenig (1994); "Service Quality Measurement-Examination of dental practices sheds more light on the relationships between service quality, satisfaction, and purchase intentions in a health care setting"; Journal of Health Care Marketing, Vol. 14, No. 3, Fall 1994, pp. 34-39.

James M. Carman (2000); "Theoretical Papers Patient Perceptions of Service Quality: Combining the Dimensions"; Journal of Management in Medicine, MCB University Press, Vol. No.14 No. 5/6, 2000, pp. 339-356.

Janice Nicholson (1995); "Patient-Focused Care and its Role in Hospital Process Re-Engineering"; International Journal of Health Care Quality Assurance, MCB University Press Limited Vol. No. 8, No. 7, 1995, pp. 23-26.

Jessie L. Tucker (2002); "The Moderators of Patient Satisfaction"; Journal of Management in Medicine, MCB UP limited, Vol. No. 16, No. 1, 2002, pp. 48-66.

Jill Murie, Gerrie Douglas-Scott (2004); "Developing an Evidence Base for Patient and Public Involvement"; Clinical Governance: An International Journal, Emerald Group Publishing Limited, Vol. No. 9, No. 3, 2004, pp. 147-154.

Joanne Coyle, Brian Williams (1999); "Seeing the Wood for the Trees: Defining the Forgotten Concept of Patient Dissatisfaction in the Light of Patient Satisfaction Research"; International Journal of Health Care Quality Assurance incorporating Leadership in Health Services, MCB University Press, Vol. No. 12/4, 1999, pp. i-ix.

Joby John (1992); "Research in Brief: Patient Satisfaction: The Impact of Past Experience"; Journal of Healthcare Marketing; Vol. No. 12, No. 3, September 1992, pp. 56-64.

Joseph C. H. Wong (2002); "Service Quality Measurement in a Medical Imaging Department"; International Journal of Health Care Quality Assurance, Vol. 15/5 (2002), pp. 206-212.

Judith H. Hibbard, Jean Stockard, and Martin Tusler (2005); "Hospital Performance Reports: Impact on Quality, Market Share, and Reputation"; Health Affairs , Data Watch, Vol. 24, No. 4, pp. 1150-1160.

Karin Braunsberger, Roger H. Gates (2002); "Patient/Enrollee satisfaction with Healthcare and Health Plan"; Journal of Consumer Marketing, MCP UP Limited, Vol. No. 19, No. 7, 2002, pp. 575-590.

Karin Newman, Uvanney Maylor, Bal Chansarkar (2001); "The Nurse Retention, Quality of Care and Patient Satisfaction Chain"; International Journal of Health Care Quality Assurance, MCB University Press Limited, Vol. No. 14/2, 2001, pp. 57-68.

Katherine McKinnon, Paul D. Crofts, Rhiannon Edwards, Peter D. Campion, and Richard H.T. Edwards (1998); "The Outpatient Experience: Results Of A Patient Feedback Survey"; International Journal of Health Care Quality Assurance, MCB University Press, Vol., 11/5, 1998, pp. 156-160.

Kathleen L. McFadden (1996); "Hospital Policy Changes in Obstetric Patient Movement"; International Journal of Operations and Production Management, MCB University Press, Vol. 16,No. 3, 1996, pp. 28-41.

Kathleen L. McFadden, Gregory N. Stock, Charles R. Gowen (2006); "Implementation of Patient Safety Initiatives in US Hospitals"; International Journal of Operations and Production Management, Emerald Group Publishing Limited, Vol. No. 26, No. 3, 2006, pp. 326-347.

Kathryn Frazer Winsted (2000); "Patient Satisfaction With Medical Encounters: A Cross-Cultural Perspective"; International Journal of Service Industry Management, MCB University Press, Vol. No.11 No. 5, 2000, pp. 399-421.

Keith Stevenson, Paul Sinfield, Vince Ion and Marilyn Merry (2004); "Involving Patients to Improve Service Quality in Primary Care"; International Journal of Health Care Quality Assurance, Emerald Group Publishing Limited, Vol. No. 17, No. 5, 2004, pp. 275-282.

Kui-Son Choi, Hanjoon Lee, Chankon Kim, and Sunhee Lee (2005); "The service quality dimensions and patient satisfaction relationships in South Korea: comparisons across gender, age and types of service"; Journal of Services Marketing, Emerald Group Publishing Limited, Vol. No. 19/3, 2005, pp. 140-149.

Li-Jen Jessica Hwang, Anita Eves, Terry Desombre (2003); "Gap Analysis of Patient Meal Service Perceptions"; International Journal of Health Care Quality Assurance; MCB UP Limited, Vol. No., 16/3, 2003, pp. 143-153.

M. Sadiq Sohil (2003); "Service Quality in Hospitals: More Favourable Than you Might Think"; Managing Service Quality, MCB UP Limited; Vol. No. 13, No. 3, 2003, pp. 197-206.

M.A.A. Hasin, Roongrat Seeluangsawat, M.A. Shareef (2001); "Statistical Measures of Customer Satisfaction for Health Care Quality Assurance: A Case Study"; International Journal of Health Care Quality Assurance, MCB University Press, Vol. NO. 4/1, 2001, pp. 6-13.

Mahmoud M. Yasin, Jafar Alavi (1999); "An Analytical Approach to Determining The Competitive Advantage of TQM In Health Care"; International Journal of Health Care Quality Assurance, MCB University Press, Vol. No. 12/1, 1999, pp. 18-24.

Markus Orava, pekka Tuominen (2002); "Curing and caring in Surgical Services: A relationship Approach"; Journal of Services Marketing, MCB UP Limited, Vol.No. 16, No.7, 2002, pp. 677-691.

Martha T. Ramirez Valdivia, Thomas J. Crowe (1997); "Achieving Hospital Operating Objectives in t he Light of Patient Preferences"; International Journal of Health Care Quality Assurance, MCB University Press, Vol. No.10/5, 1997, pp. 208-212.

Mary Draper, Sophie Hill (1995); "The Role of Patient Satisfaction Surveys in a National Approach to Hospital Quality Management"; Report Funded by Faculty of Social Sciences and Communications Royal Melbourne Institute of Technology for Department of Human Services and Health, October, 1995.

Mayo, Harrah (2004); "The Personal Touch: Keeping Loyalty in Hand"; "Strategic Direction, Emerald Group Publishing Limited", Vol. No. 20, No. 1, 2004, pp. 21-23.

Michel Perreault, Theodora E. Katerelos, SteÂphane Sabourin, Pierre Leichner, Julie Desmarais (2001); "Information as a Distinct Dimension for Satisfaction Assessment of Outpatient Psychiatric Services"; International Journal of Health Care Quality Assurance, MCB University Press, Vol. No. 14/3, 2001, pp. 111-120.

Mik Wisniewski and hazel Wisniewski (2005); "Measuring Service Quality in a Hospital Colposcopy Clinic"; International Journal of Health care Quality Assurance, Emerald Group Publishing Ltd., Vol. 18 No. 3,2005, pp. 217-228.

Mike Hart (1995); "Improving Out-Patient Clinic Waiting Times: Methodological And Substantive Issues"; International Journal of Health Care Quality Assurance, MCB University Press Limited, Vol. 8 No. 6, 1995, pp. 14-22.

Mike Hart (1996); "Improving The Quality of NHS Out-Patient Clinics: The Applications and Misapplications of TQM"; International Journal of Health Care Quality Assurance, MCB University Pres, Vol. No. 9/2, 1996, pp. 20-27.

Mohamed M. Mostafa (2005); "An Empirical Study of Patients' Expectations and Satisfactions In Egyptian Hospitals"; International Journal of Health Care Quality Assurance, Emerald Group Publishing Limited, Vol. 18 No. 7, 2005, pp. 516-532.

Naceur Jabnoun and Mohammed Chaker (2003); "Comparing the Quality of private and Public Hospitals"; Managing Service Quality, MCB UP Limited, Vol. 13 No. 4, pp. 290-299.

Nancy Gregory, Dennis O. Kaldenberg (2000); "Satisfaction with the Billing Process: Using a Patient Survey to Identify Opportunities for Process Improvement"; Hospital Topics: Research and Perspectives on Healthcare; Vol.No. 78, No. 3, Summer 2000, pp. 20-25.

Neil Drummond, Steve Iliff, Sandra McGregor, Neil Craig, and Moria Fischbacher (2001); "Can Primary Care be Both patient-Centered and Community-Led?"; Journal of Management in Medicine, MCB University Press, Vol. No. 15, No. 5, 2001, pp. 364-375.

Nimma Satynarayana, K Padma, G.Vijaya Kumar (2004); "Patient Attitude towards Payment at Super Specialty Hospital in Hyderabad" Journal of the Academy of Hospital Administration; Vol. No. 16, No. 2, July-December, 2004.

Parasuraman, Valarie A.Zeithaml, and Leonard L. Berry (1985); "A Conceptual Model of Service Quality and its Implications for Future Research"; Journal of Marketing, Vol. 49 (Fall 1985). pp. 41-50.

Parasuraman, Valarie A.Zeithaml, and Leonard L. Berry (1988); "SERVQUAL: A Multiple-Item Scale for Measuring Consumer Perceptions of Service Quality"; Journal of Retailing, Vol, 64, No. 1, Spring 1988, pp. 12-40.

Parasuraman, Valarie A.Zeithaml, and Leonard L. Berry (1991); "Refinement and Reassessment of the SERVQUAL Scale"; Journal of Retailing, Vol, 67, Spring No. 4, Winter 1991, pp. 420-450.

Patrick M. Baldasare (1995); "Should Marketers Care About Satisfying Medicaid Patients?"; Journal of Health Care Marketing, Vol. No. 15, No. 4, Winter 1995.

Pauy Cheng Lim 7 Nelson K.H. Tang (2000); "A study of Patients' Expectations and Satisfaction in Singapore Hospitals"; International Journal of Health care Quality Assurance, MCB University Press, Vol. 13/7, pp. 290-299.

Penelope Angelopoulou, Peter Kangis, George Babis (1998); "Private And Public Medicine: A Comparison of Quality Perceptions"; International Journal of Health Care Quality Assurance, MCB University Press, Vol. No. 11/1, 1998, pp. 14-20.

Prasanta Mahapatra, Srilatba S. Sridbar P. (2001); "A Patient Satisfaction Survey in Public Hospital"; Journal of Academy of Hospital Administration, Vol. No. 15, No. 2, July- Dec. 2001. pp. 11-15.

Prof. (Dr.) Parimal H. Vyas and Shri P.D. Thakkar (2005); "Market Performance Analysis and Measurement of Patients' Satisfaction in Healthcare Services"; "The Indian Journal of Commerce", Vol. 58, No.1, January-March, 2005, pp. 150-161. (Quarterly Publication of the Indian Commerce Association, School of Management Studies, IGNOU, New Delhi).

Prof. R.D. Sharma and Hardeep Chahal (1999); "A Study on Patient Satisfaction in Outdoor Services of Private Health Care Facilities"; Vikalpa the Journal for Decision Makers; Indian Institute of Management, Ahmedabad, Vol. 24, No. 4 , October-December 1999, pp. 69-76.

Rachel Javetz, Zvi Stern (1996); "Patients' Complaints as a Management Tool for Continuous Quality Improvement"; Journal of Management in Medicine, MCB University Press, Vol. No. 10 No. 3, 1996, pp. 39-48.

Raduan Che Rose, Mohani Abdul, and Kim Looi Ng (2004); "Hospital Service Quality: A Managerial Challenge"; International Journal of Health Care Quality Assurance, Emerald Group Publishing Limited, Volume 17, No. 3, 2004, pp. 146-159.

Rob Baltussen, and Yazoume Ye (2006); "Quality of Care of Modern Health Services as Perceived by Users and Non-Users in Burkina Faso"; International Journal for Quality in Health Care 2006; Vol. No. 18, No. 1, pp. 30-34.

Robert J. Casyn, Gary A. Morse, Robert D. Yonker, Joel P. Winter, Kathy J. Pierce, Matthew J. Taylor (2003); "Client Choice of Treatment and Client Outcomes"; Journal of Community Psychology, Wiley Periodicals, Inc., Vol. No. 31, No. 4, 2003, pp. 339-348. [Published online in Wiley Inter Science (www. interscience. wiley.com). DOI: 10.1002/jcop.10053].

Robert J. Wolosin, (2005); "The Voice of the Patient: A National, Representative Study of Satisfaction with Family Physicians"; Quality Management in Health Care, Lippincott Williams and Wilkins, Inc., Vol. 14, Issue 3, July-September 2005, pp. 155-164.

Robert Rosenheck , Nancy J. Wilson,and Mark Meterko (1997); "Influence of Patient and Hospital Factors on Consumer Satisfaction with Inpatient Mental Health Treatment"; Psychiatric Services, December 1997, Vol. 48 No. 12, pp. 1553 to 1561.

Ronald L. Zailocco (1992); "The Public's Perception of Quality Hospitals II: Implications for Patient Surveys," Journal of Health Care Marketing, Vol. 12, No. 3, September 1992.

Ruth Belk Smith, Paul N. Bloom, Kelley Sonon Davis (1986); "Research On Patient Satisfaction Potential Directions"; Advances in Consumer Research; Vol. No. 13, 1986, pp. 321-326.

Sandra K. Smith Gooding (1995); "Quality, Sacrifice, and Value in Hospital Choice"; Journal of Health Care Marketing, Vol. No. 15, No.4, Winter 1995, pp. 24-31.

Senga Bond, Lois H Thomas (1992); "Measuring Patients' Satisfaction with Nursing Care"; Journal of Advanced Nursing, Vol. No. 17, 1992, pp. 52-63.

Sharon E. Riley, Arnold J. Stromberg, James Clark, (2005); "Assessing Parental Satisfaction with Children's Mental Health Services with the Youth Services Survey for Families"; Journal of Child and Family Studies, Vol. 14, No. 1, March 2005, pp. 87-99.

Sophie Y. Hsieh, David Thomas, Arie Rotem (2005); "The Organisational Response to Patient Complaints: A Case Study in Taiwan"; International Journal of Health Care Quality Assurance, Emerald Group Publishing Limited, Vol. No. 18 No. 4, 2005, pp. 308-320.

Stefanie Naumann, Jeffrey A. Miles (2001); "Managing Waiting Patients' Perceptions: The Role of process Control"; Journal of Management in Medicine, UCB University Press, Vol. No.15, No.5, 2001, pp. 376-386.

Stephen A. Kapp, Jennifer Propp (2002); "Client satisfaction methods: Input from Parents with Children in Foster Care"; Child and Adolescent Social Work Journal, Human Sciences press, Inc., Vol. No. 19, No. 3, June 2002, pp. 227-245.

Stephen J. O'Connor, Richard M. Shewchuk, and Lynn W. Carney (1994); "The Great Gap- Physicians' perceptions of patient service quality expectations fall short of reality"; Journal of Health Care Marketing, Vol. 14, No. 2, Summer 1994, pp. 32-39.

Stephen Todd, Andrew Steele, Cal Douglas, Mary Douglas (2002); "Investigation and Assessment of Attitudes to and perceptions of the Built Environments in NHS Trust Hospitals"; Structural Survey, MCB UP Limited, Vol. No. 20, No. 5, 2002, pp. 182-188.

Suzanne C. Tough, Christine V. newborn-Cook, Alexandra J. Faber, Deborah E. White, Nonie J. Fraser-Lee, Corine Frick (2004); "The Relationship Between Self-Reported Emotional Health, demographics, and Perceived Satisfaction with Prenatal Care"; International Journal of Health Care Quality Assurance, Emerald Group Publishing Limited; Vol. No. 17, No. 1, 2004, pp. 26-38

Syed Saad Andaleeb (1998); "Determinants of Customer Satisfaction With Hospitals: A Managerial Model"; International Journal of Health Care Quality Assurance, MCB University Press, Vol. No. 11/6, 1998, pp. 181-187.

Talluru Sreenivas, G.Prasad (2003); "Patient Satisfaction-A Comparative Study"; Journal of the Academy of Hospital Administration, Vol. No. 15 No. 2, July-Dec. 2003, pp. 19-27.

Thomas V. Perneger (2006); "A Research Agenda for Patient Safety"; International Journal for Quality in Health Care, Published by Oxford University Press, Vol. No. 18, No. 1, pp. 1-3.

Venkatapparao Mummalaneni, Pradeep Gopalakrishna (1995); "Mediators vs. Moderators of Patient Satisfaction"; Journal of Health Care Marketing, Vol. 15, No. 4, winter 1995, pp. 16-22.

Viroj Tangcharoensathien, Sara Bennett, Sukalaya Khongswatt, Anuwat Supacutikul, Anne Mills (1999); "Patient Satisfaction In Bangkok: The Impact of Hospital Ownership and Patient Payment Status"; International Journal for Quality in Health Care, International Society for Quality in Health Care and Oxford University Press, Vol.No. 11, No. 4, 1999, pp. 309-317.

Waseem Qureshi, Nazir A. Khan, Ajaz A. Naik, Shabnam Khan, Arshid Bhat, G. Q. Khan, Gh. Hassan, Shahid Tak (2005); "A Case Study on Patient Satisfaction in SMHS Hospital, Srinagar"; JK-Practitioner, Vol. No.12(3), 2005, pp.154-155.

Yves Eggli, Patricia Halfon (2003); "A Conceptual Framework for Hospital Quality"; International Journal of Health Care Quality Assurance, MCB UP Limited; Vol., 16/1, 2003, pp. 29-36.

Yvonne Webb, Paul Clifford, Vanessa Fowler, Celia Morgan, Marie Hanson (2000); "Comparing Patients' Experience of Mental Health services in England: A Five-Trust Survey"; International Journal of Health Care Quality Assurance, MCB University press, Vol. No. 13/6, 2000, pp. 273-281.

3 Models for Measurement for Patients' Satisfaction/ Service Quality

One of the significant trends in the development of modern healthcare is the involvement of patient/clients in the management of their care and treatment. A people centered health system identifies and responds to the needs of individuals; can be planned and delivered in a coordinated way; and it helps individuals to participate in decision making to improve their health.

NEED FOR MEASUREMENT OF PATIENTS' SATISFACTION/SERVICE QUALITY

Feedback from patients/clients can influence the whole quality improvement agenda and provide an opportunity for organizational learning and development. It provides crucial information on what the patients/clients expectations are and how they perceive the quality of care, which may be different from that of all staff providing that care. There is need for people-centered health care system which possess dynamic, integrated structures, which can adapt to the diverse and changing health needs of society generally and of individuals within it. These structures will empower people to be active participants in decisions relating to their own health.

As techniques to measure the quality of healthcare reproduce and improve, health professionals are beginning to accept that patient/clients and their families hold unique vantage points as expert witnesses of care and that they should plan their services to reflect the needs of patient/clients. Patient/client satisfaction is now a critical variable in any calculation of quality or value and therefore in the assessment of corporate/ individual accountability. It is a legitimate and important measure of quality of care. Patients/clients are rightly becoming more involved in their own healthcare and are being encouraged to do so. The movement to include patient/client evaluations of care is growing as more providers/organizations realize that patient/client satisfaction measurement is a cost effective, non invasive indicator of quality of care. Giving the patient/client an opportunity to voice their opinions about the care they receive can be seen as part of a broader commitment to public and patient/client participation in healthcare service planning and delivery. The increasing cost of the health services and the need for better use of available resources is a concern for healthcare providers. Consequently, it is evident that there is a need to measure the efficiency of health care to determine if proper use of available resources is being made.

FACTORS INFLUENCE PATIENTS' SATISFACTION MEASUREMENT

When including patient satisfaction mechanisms in health care systems, the options should take account of the capacity of users to understand what is being asked of them and to communicate their opinions and feelings effectively. Important factors influencing patients/clients in this regard include literacy levels, intellectual and physical/sensory disability levels and difficulties with language proficiency or ethnic and cultural diversity. Social elements within our society must be considered as they can very often dictate whether the consumer will provide feedback and express their satisfaction or otherwise, e.g., financial status, educational status, demographics (urban/rural), technology.

Satisfaction is, however, a relative measure may be influenced by many factors that should be considered.

Patients'/Clients' Expectation

The meetings of patient/client expectations are assumed to play a role in the process by which an outcome can be said to be satisfactory or unsatisfactory. Expectations are an important influence on the patient/client's overall measurement of satisfaction with a health care experience. Patient/client satisfaction is influenced by the degree to which care fulfils expectation. It can also however be suggests that a link between satisfaction and fulfillment of patient/client expectations is not necessarily the case, since it is possible that the patient/client's evaluation of a service may be largely independent of actual care received.

Age

Older respondents generally record higher satisfaction and the possible explanations include lower expectations of health care and reluctance to articulate their dissatisfaction.

Illness

While some studies have found that sicker patient/clients and those experiencing psychological stress are less satisfied, with the possible exception of some chronically ill groups, distinguishing between the experience of sickness or experience of health service treatment or other factors as causes of dissatisfaction has proven difficult.

Prior Experience of Satisfaction

Patients' satisfaction can be linked to prior satisfaction with health care and granting patient/clients' desires for acquiring treatment for their future illness.

Patients/Clients-Professional Relationship

One can observe the most important health service factor affecting satisfaction is the patient/client-practitioner relationship, including information and technical competence.

Choice of Service Provider

Choice of service provider is associated with higher satisfaction. Care provided under fee-for-service arrangements generates greater satisfaction than that delivered with prepaid schemes. Gate keeping organizations, where patient/clients have little or no choice in their treatment or are assigned treatment, score relatively poorly on satisfaction.

CRITICAL ASPECT IN PATIENTS' SATISFACTION MEASUREMENT

A critical aspect in the patient satisfaction's measurement is that models and instruments sometimes reflect the providers' perspective rather than the patients' one. For example, the patient capability to evaluate health services and professionals' skills is frequently questioned, even when these items receive high satisfaction rates. Patients are less capable of judging technical competence because of a real informative asymmetry and in any case they are more reserved in expressing critical comments with regard to the abilities of doctors. As a consequence, the high satisfaction scores observed may depend on the confidence in doctors' capabilities.

It has been argued that well designed questionnaires allow assessing both the technical competence and interpersonal skills of health professionals. The patient satisfaction measurements have been generally used in order to provide researchers, health managers and professionals with valuable information for understanding patients' experience, promoting patient's compliance with treatment, identifying the weaknesses in services and evaluating health service performance. Although the debate on the use of patient satisfaction as an outcome measure is never ending it has been observed that satisfied patients are more compliant and more likely to participate in their treatment. In fact, a satisfied patient is more aware of his care pathway and more willing to follow the physician prescriptions.

The level of satisfaction depends on several and different elements. For instance, healthy people tend to be more satisfied when they receive general information on health services and on their quality; on the contrary, people with a chronic condition may be more satisfied if involved in the decision-making process. Thus, the improvement of patient compliance requires adopting different actions depending on the patient's profile. The assessment of patient satisfaction with the process of care is an important measure of the care quality and it allows identifying the phases of the process to be improved. Questionnaires using report style questions allow observing how the care is delivered. Some studies have highlighted that satisfaction strongly increases when care is provided in accordance with the clinical standard procedures. Furthermore, the patients' point of view may help managers to evaluate activities such as the purchase of new technologies or the test of new medical treatments (Anna Maria Murante, 2009/2010).

KEY MODELS FOR MEASUREMENT FOR PATIENT SATISFACTION

A major problem in the measurement of Patients' satisfaction is the lack of an adequate theory/model to explain the meaning of satisfaction, and hence how it should be measured and how the findings are interpreted. Because of the lack of a fully developed theory, when developing patients' satisfaction questionnaires for use in general practice, several model can be considered for the same which are related with service quality measurement or patients' satisfaction measurement.

An attempt has been made to provide a brief explanation of models which provide an idea about model and dimensions involved in it.

GRÖNROOS PERCEIVED SERVICE QUALITY MODEL (1988)

According to Grönroos, the service quality experienced by a customer has two dimensions; namely technical quality and functional quality. Functional quality describes how the service is delivered and technical quality describes what the customers received during a service delivery. For example, a patient will judge the services of a hospital not only on the basis of cure element (technical quality) but on care element (functional quality) as well. The model is shown in following figure.

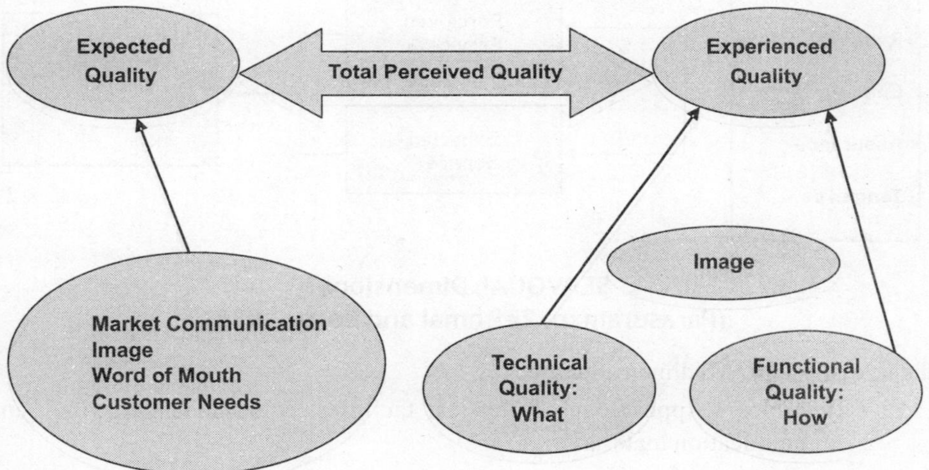

Grönroos Perceived Service Quality Model (1988)

Grönroos postulated that as long as the outcome or the technical quality is acceptable, the process dimension, or functional quality, frequently may be more critical to consumer's overall quality perception. Also, in certain cases the technical quality or the outcome may be difficult for the customers to judge and in such cases the quality perceptions will be based to a large extent on functional quality.

The quality perception process includes much more than just the two dimensions of service quality. If the experienced quality is good, the total perceived quality may still be low, if the expectations of the customers are very high or unrealistic. Conversely, the total perceived quality may be high even if experienced quality is not very good, if the customer has very low expectation. The image of the company doesn't only have an impact on the expected quality but also on perception of the quality experienced. It works as a filter i.e. if the image of the service provider is good in the minds of the customer, minor errors or mistakes are likely to be overlooked and conversely if the image is negative the impact of a mistake is likely to be greater than it otherwise would be. The expected quality depends on a number of factors like market communication, image, word of mouth communication, corporate image and customer needs, few of which are directly under firm's control and others only indirectly controlled. Gronroos, C., 1988).

SERVQUAL MODEL

Over the past few decades in the services marketing sector, much work has been undertaken to evaluate the consumer's perception of service quality, and a number of service models have been developed, with the gap model (Parasuraman et al., 1985) and its accompanying SERVQUAL (Parasuraman et al., 1988) having offered significant advances to the understanding and measurement of perceived service quality.

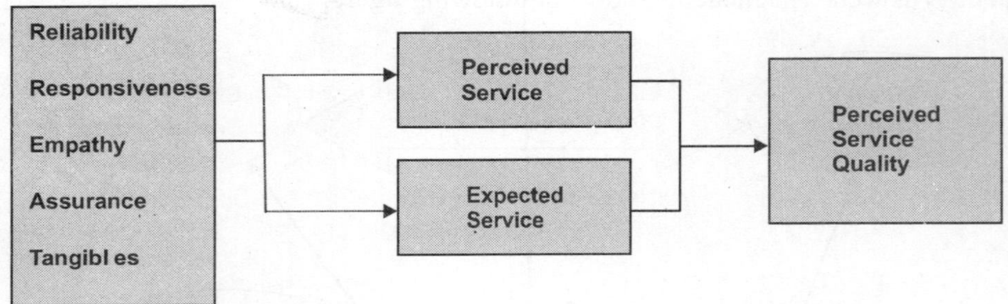

SERVQUAL Dimensions
(Parasuraman, Zeithmal and Berry-1988)

The five SERVQUAL dimensions are

- Tangibles - Appearance of physical facilities, equipment, personnel, and communication materials.
- Eligibility - Ability to perform the promised service dependably and accurately.
- Responsiveness - Willingness to help customers and provide prompt service.
- Assurance - Knowledge and courtesy of employees and their ability to convey trust and confidence.
- Empathy - Caring, individualized attention the firm provides its customers.

Not All Dimensions Are Equal. All dimensions are important to customers, but some more than others. Service providers need to know which are which to avoid majoring in minors. At the same time they can't focus on only one dimension and let the others suffer. SERVQUAL research showed dimensions' importance to each other by asking customers to assign 100 points across all five dimensions.

GARVIN'S 8 DIMENSIONS IN [PRODUCT] MANAGING QUALITY (1988)

The eight dimensions proposed by Garvin are given below:

(01) Performance (02) Features (03) Reliability (04) Conformance (05) Durability (06) Serviceability (07) Aesthetics (08) Perceived Quality.

The eight dimensions of product quality according to Garvin

1. Performance or the primary operating characteristics of a product or service.
2. Features or the secondary characteristics of a product or service.
3. Conformance or the match with specifications or pre established standards.
4. Durability or product life.
5. Reliability or the frequency with which a product or service fails.
6. Serviceability or the speed, courtesy and competence of repair.
7. Appearance/aesthetics or fits and finishes.
8. Image/perceived quality or reputation (Garvin D., 1988).

JCAHO DIMENSIONS [JOINT COMMISSION ON ACCREDITATION OF HEALTHCARE ORGANIZATIONS (1996)

Definitions of the JCAHO dimensions of quality are given below.

Efficacy

Efficacy "of the procedure or treatment in relation to the patient's condition. The degree to which the care of the patient has been shown to accomplish the desired or projected outcome(s)."

Appropriateness

Appropriateness "of a specific test, procedure, or service to meet the patients' needs. The degree to which the care provided is relevant to the patient's clinical needs, given the current state of knowledge."

Efficiency

Efficiency with which services are provided. The relationship between the outcomes (results of care) and the resources used to deliver patient care."

Respect and Caring

Respect and Caring "with which services are provided. The degree to which the patient or a designee is involved in his or her own care decisions and to which these providing services do so with sensitivity and respect for the patient's needs, expectations, and individual differences."

Safety

Safety of the patient (and others) to whom the services are provided. The degree to which the risk of an intervention and risk in the care environment are reduced for the patient and others, including health care provider.

Continuity

Continuity of the services provided to the patient with respect to other services, practitioners, and providers and over time. The degree to which the care for the patient is coordinated among practitioners, among organizations, and over time.

Effectiveness

Effectiveness with which tests, procedures, treatments, and services are provided. The degree to which the care is provided in the correct manner, given the current state of knowledge, to achieve the desired or projected outcome for the patient.

Timeliness

Timeliness with which a needed test, procedure, treatment, or service is provided to the patient. The degree to which the care is provided to the patient at the most beneficial or necessary time.

Availability

Availability of a needed test, procedure, treatment, or service to the patient who needs it. The degree to which appropriate care is available to meet the patient's needs (Joint Commission on Accreditation of Healthcare Organizations, 1996); Accreditation Manual for Hospitals, Volume Il. Oakbrook Terrace, IL: Author, 1996.

RICHARD BAKER'S PRAGMATIC MODEL OF PATIENTS' SATISFACTION (1997)

The model was pragmatic in that it linked together available empirical evidence about patients' satisfaction without recourse to more general social or psychological theories of behaviour, other than to define satisfaction as an attitude.

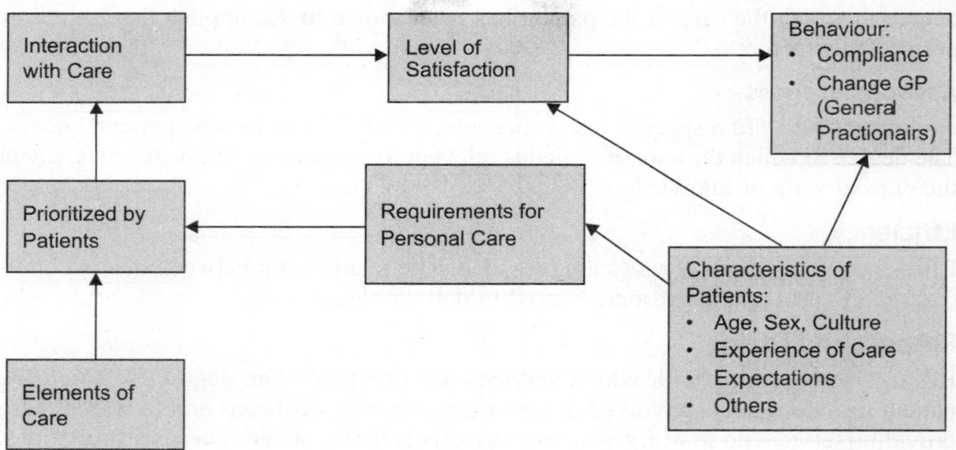

PRAGMATIC MODEL OF PATIENTS' SATISFACTION

Patients' characteristics may influence their attitudes towards care, and also the importance they assign to different elements of care. In the model, patients' characteristics are shown as influencing the priorities they assign to different elements of care and to their attitude or level of satisfaction after an interaction with the healthcare system. Some patients may allocate the highest priority to continuity; others may prefer readily available appointments. Patients' characteristics that may be influential include age and sex, past experience of care, expectations, health, cultural factors, mood, and others. Satisfaction can influence patients' future behavior such as compliance with advice or whether they change doctors. The model also argues that satisfaction influences some subsequent behaviour of patients. The only behaviour investigated was that of changing general practitioner without a change of home address. Patients who changed had lower levels of satisfaction with their previous general practitioner (Richard Baker, 1997).

KEY QUALITY CHARACTERISTICS ASSESSMENT FOR HOSPITALS (KQCAH-2001)

The primary objective of Research Study conducted by Victor Sower (2001) was to develop a valid and reliable instrument that will support hospital management's strategic and operational decision making. KQCAH is a multi-item scale that can provide valid and reliable information to hospital administrators so that they can be responsive to their present-day market-oriented environment. Both strategic and operational decision-making are enhanced by the information provided by the KQCAH, and its empirical dimensions are given below.

- Respect and Caring
- Effectiveness and Continuity
- Appropriateness
- Information
- Efficiency
- Effectiveness-Meals
- First Impression
- Staff Diversity

On the operational level, KQCAH is beneficial to benchmarking efforts since the assessment instrument

can be used to track the level of quality provided by various hospitals. An administrator can judge how his or her hospital is performing in relation to its competitors. A hospital company with multiple units will find KQCAH a useful way to compare the quality among its own units (Victor Sower, et. al., 2001).

CONSUMER MODEL IN A HEALTH CARE SYSTEM (2001)

The consumer model support in evaluating health care system, by studying the relationship between four variables i.e. expectations, perceived degree of fulfillment, satisfaction and changing of physicians.

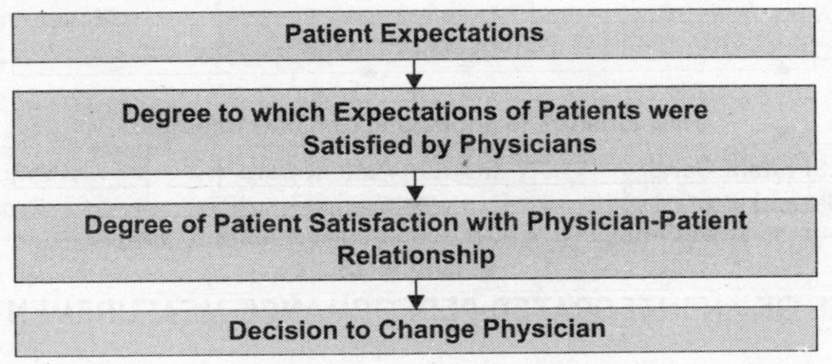

CONSUMER MODEL IN A HEALTH CARE SYSTEM

In this model, the assumption is that patients have expectations of the visit to the physician and that the degree to which these expectations are fulfilled can be measured and there is a clear relationship. The higher the perceived fulfillment of the expectation is, compared to the expectation, the higher the satisfaction is. When fulfillment is lower than the expectations the greater the gap and the lower the satisfaction. When fulfillment is higher than the expectation the greater the difference and the higher the satisfaction. When expectations are low, clearly they will be more easily met and a high level of satisfaction maintained. However, if patient expectations are high, the physician will have a harder task meeting these expectations and satisfaction is likely to be lower. According to the consumer model, patient satisfaction is also correlated with the patient's reported intention to change physician. Identifying these variables and the correlation between them may help evaluate the quality of the health care provider services (Orna Baron-Epel, Marina Dushenat And Nurit Friedman, 2001).

CONCEPTUAL MODEL OF AN INTEGRATED PERFORMANCE-MEASUREMENT SYSTEM FOR HEALTHCARE ORGANIZATIONS

Model of an Integrated Performance-Measurement Systems provided a means to align strategic objectives and market requirements, it coordinate the effective use of organizational resources, and monitor progress toward predefined strategic objectives.

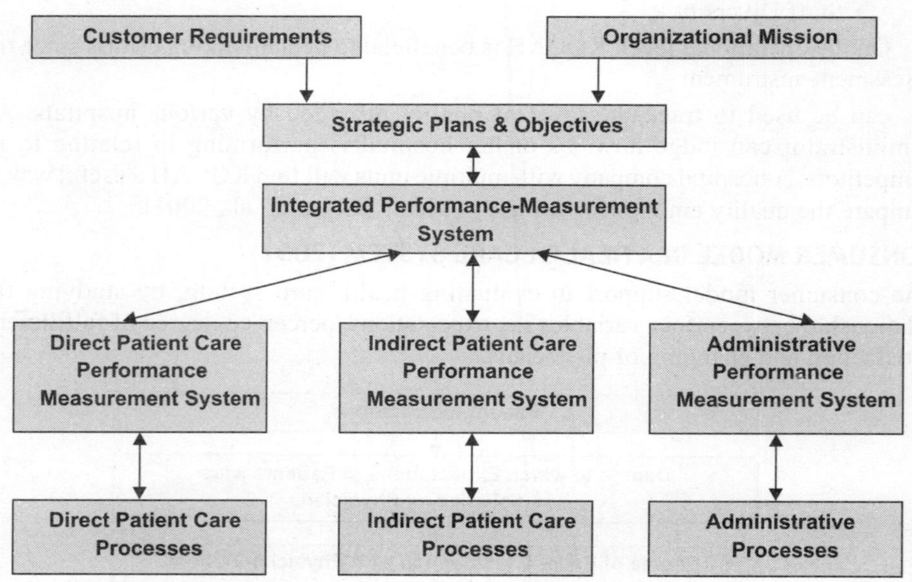

MODEL OF AN INTEGRATED PERFORMANCE-MEASUREMENT SYSTEM

Performance-measurement systems are composed of three elements: performance criteria, performance measures, and performance standards. Performance criteria are the relative elements used to evaluate performance. Performance measures are the actual results achieved in relation to the performance criteria over it specified period. Performance standards are the acceptable measures of performance for each criterion.

This model views direct patient care, indirect patient care, and administration as the three primary, aggregate functions of a healthcare organization that need to be linked. Direct patient-care services include physician consultations, treatment, and nursing services. Indirect patient care encompasses various services related to the diagnosis, treatment, and maintenance of patients that routinely involve minimal direct patient contact.

Administration includes those processes that support and maintain the organization's overall mission, human resources, and physical plant. These processes include strategic planning, operational budgeting, employee relations, accounting, and building maintenance.

The use of an integrated performance-measurement system is essential to ensure that the provider's day to-day clinical and administrative activities support its long-term strategic objectives.

An integrated performance-measurement system model exists for linking performance measurement of the three primary, aggregate, business functions (finance-, resource-, and customer-Oriented functions) and their corresponding business processes for accomplishing a firm's strategy.

This information is used as the basis for determining continual improvement opportunities in existing service delivery processes and developing new processes to further enhance patient and payer satisfaction (By Louis J. Stewart, and Archie Lockamy, 2001).

PERNEGER TV (2004) A THEORETICAL MODEL OF PATIENT VIEWS

Perneger TV (2004) proposed a theoretical model of patient views which was considered as detailed model for case-mix adjustment of satisfaction scores or patient report scores.

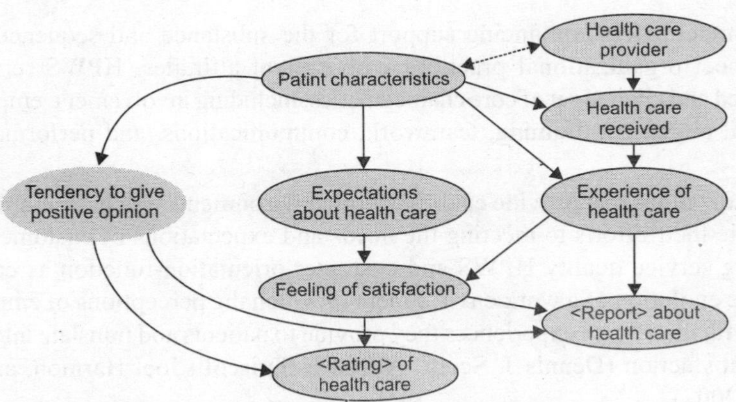

Perneger TV (2004) Model of Patient Views

Patient characteristics are associated with the type of health care received, how care is experienced by the patient, expectations regarding care, and a global tendency to give a positive or negative opinion. These intermediate variables influence ratings or reports of health care (T. V. Perneger, 2004).

HIGH-PERFORMANCE WORK SYSTEMS (HPWS) MODEL (2007)

Healthcare managers must deliver high-quality patient services that generate highly satisfied and loyal customers. HPWS model examined how a high-involvement approach to the work environment of healthcare employees may lead to exceptional service quality, satisfied patients, and ultimately to loyal customers.

HPWS was linked to, employee perceptions of their ability to deliver high-quality customer service, both directly and through their perceptions of customer orientation; employee perceptions of customer service are linked to customer perceptions of high-quality service; and perceived service quality is linked with customer satisfaction. Model is given below.

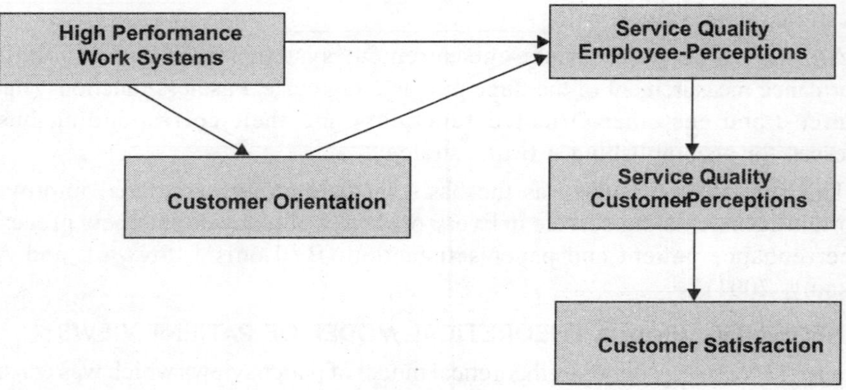

HIGH-PERFORMANCE WORK SYSTEMS (HPWS) MODEL

HPWS model offers convincing support for the substance and sequence of events that connect organizational practices with patient attitudes. HPWS represents an interrelated and aligned set of core characteristics, including involvement, empowerment, trust, goal alignment, training, teamwork, communications, and performance-based rewards.

Organizations that provide enabling work environments will have employees who can devote their efforts to meeting the needs and expectations of customers, thereby improving service quality HPWS and customer orientation-function as engines that propel the evolution of a work environment in which the perceptions of employees are aligned with the service experiences they provide to patients and translate into enhanced patient satisfaction (Dennis J. Scotti, Alfred E. Driscoll, Joel Harmon, and Scott J. Behson, 2007).

DAGGER ET AL. (2007) SERVICE QUALITY MULTIDIMENSIONAL MODEL

Dagger et al. (2007) have proposed service quality as a multidimensional, higher order construct, with four overarching dimensions (interpersonal quality, technical quality, environment quality and administrative quality) and nine sub-dimensions.

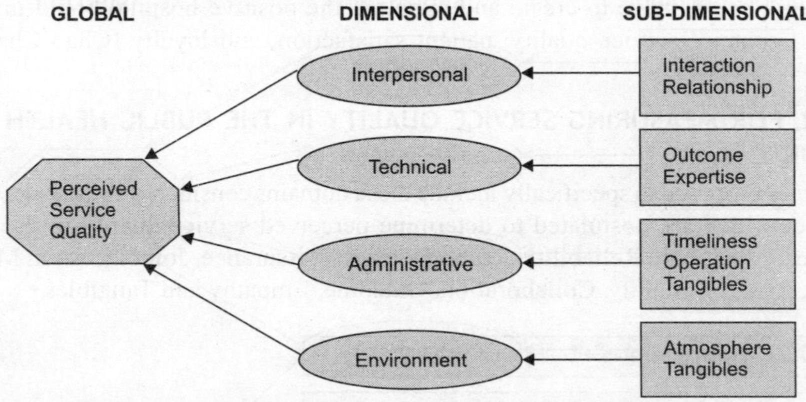

Dagger *et. al.,* (2007) Service Quality Multidimensional Model

Source: Dagger *et al.* (2007)
Source: Liz Gill and Lesley White (2009)

They suggested that consumers assesses service quality at a global level, a dimensional level and at a sub-dimensional level, with each level influencing perceptions as shown in above Figure. From their work with private oncology patients, Dagger et al. (2007) had also shown that their model reflects the private patient's service quality perceptions, and they have developed and tested a scale for measuring perceived private healthcare service quality. Yet this work has had little impact, as the study and measurement of patients' satisfaction continues to be the key target for consumer research in the health sector (Liz Gill and Lesley White, 2009).

MODEL TO MEASURE RELATIONSHIP AMONG HOSPITAL BRAND IMAGE, SERVICE QUALITY, PATIENT SATISFACTION, AND LOYALTY (2011)

This model suggested that positive hospital brand image not only increases patient loyalty directly, but it also improves patient satisfaction through the enhancing of perceived service quality, which in turn increases the re-visit intention of patients.

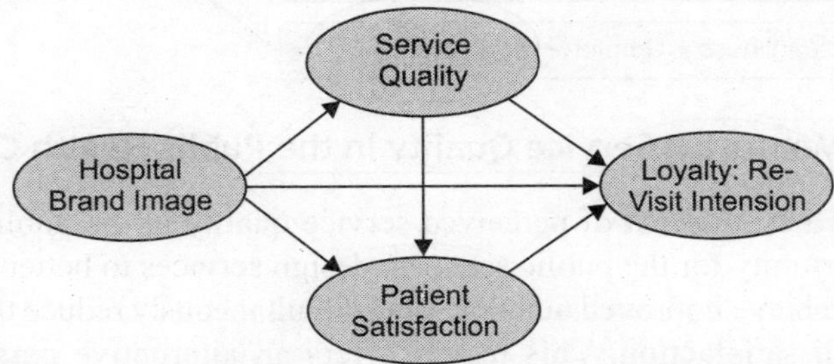

Model to Measure Relationship Among Hospital Brand Image, Service Quality, Patient Satisfaction and Loyalty (2011)

Hospital brand image indeed serves as a lead factor in enhancing service quality, patient satisfaction, and patient loyalty. In addition, the model take it granted that that the path from service quality to patient satisfaction is a key avenue for the impact of hospital brand image on patient loyalty. Consequently, this model proposed that hospital managers should strive to create and maintain the positive hospital brand image in order to enhance service quality, patient satisfaction, and loyalty (Chao-Chan Wu, 2011).

MODEL FOR MEASURING SERVICE QUALITY IN THE PUBLIC HEALTH CARE SECTOR

A model is proposed to specifically include those domains considered as the independent variables which are postulated to determine perceived service quality in the public health care sector are Reliability, Responsiveness, Assurance, Joint Decision Making, Caring, Risk, Continuity, Collaboration, Outcome, Empathy and Tangibles.

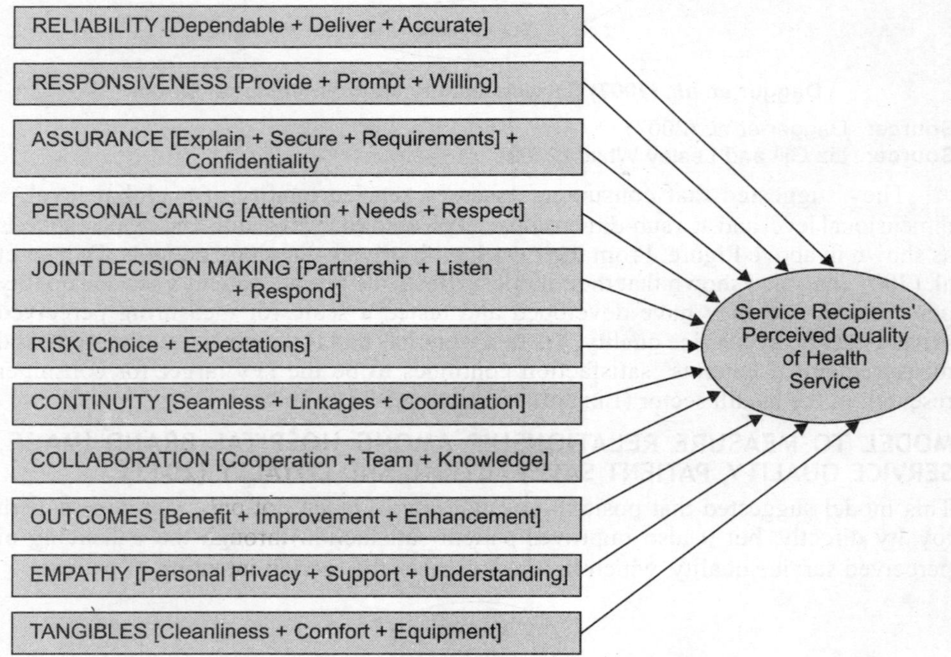

Model for Measuring Service Quality in the Public Health Care Sector

The targeted assessment of perceived service quality in the public health sector offers the opportunity for the public sector to design services to better meet the needs of consumers, achieve improved outcomes and simultaneously reduce the costs created by consumer dissatisfaction. This model offers an alternative perspective to the measurement of health service quality, through specifically targeting criteria essential to the successful delivery of a quality health service.

REFERENCES

Anna Maria Murante (2009/2010); Thesis on "Patient satisfaction: a strategic tool for health services management"; (http://www.phdmanagement.sssup.it/documenti/awarded/murante_thesis.pdf, Accessed on 15/08/2011.).

By Louis J. Stewart, and Archie Lockamy (2001); "Improving Competitiveness Through Performance Measurement Systems"; Healthcare Finance Management, 2001, pp. 45-50 "(http://www.bschool.howard.edu/programs/undergradprograms/accounting/documents/HealthcareIntegratedPerformanceMeasurement.pdf).

Chao-Chan Wu (2011); "The Impact of Hospital Brand Image on Service Quality, Patient Satisfaction And Loyalty"; African Journal of Business Management; 18 June, 2011; Vol. 5(12), pp. 4873-4882, (Available online at http://www. academic journals.org/AJBM, ISSN 1993-8233 ©2011 Academic Journals).

Dennis J. Scotti, Alfred E. Driscoll, Joel Harmon, and Scott J. Behson (2007); "Links Among High-Performance Work Environment, Service Quality, and Customer Satisfaction: An Extension to the Healthcare Sector"; Journal of Healthcare Management; BookComp/ Health Administration Press; Vol. 52, No. 2/Page 109-125 (http://view.fdu.edu).

Garvin D. (1987); "Competing on the Eight Dimensions of Quality"; Harvard Business Review; Vol 65/6, 1987, pp. 101-109 (http://elsmar.com/Forums/showthread.php?t=4529).

Gronroos, C. (1988) : Service Quality : The Six Criteria of Good Service Quality, Review of Business 3, p. 12. (Adapted from IGNOU Study Material of Marketing of Service MS-65 Unit-8, "Service Quality", pp.1-23)

Joint Commission on Accreditation of Healthcare Organizations (1996); Accreditation Manual for Hospitals, Volume II. Oakbrook Terrace, IL: Author, 1996; (http://isbndb.com/d/book 1996_accreditation_protocol_for_subacute_ programs. html).

Liz Gill and Lesley White (2009); "A critical review of patient Satisfaction"; Leadership in Health Services; Emerald Group Publishing Limited, 1751-1879, DOI 10.1108/17511870910927994; Vol. 22 No. 1, 2009; pp. 8-19.

Orna Baron-Epel, Marina Dushenat And Nurit Friedman (2001); "Evaluation of the Consumer Model: Relationship between Patients' Expectations, Perceptions and Satisfaction with Care"; International Journal for Quality in Health Care; 2001; Volume 13, Number 4: pp. 317-323 (http://intqhc.oxfordjournals.org/content/13/4/317.full.pdf).

Parasuraman, Valarie A.Zeithaml, and Leonard L. Berry (1985); "A Conceptual Model of Service Quality and its Implications for Future Research"; Journal of Marketing, Vol. 49 (Fall 1985). pp. 41-50.

Parasuraman, Valarie A.Zeithaml, and Leonard L. Berry (1988); "SERVQUAL: A Multiple-Item Scale for Measuring Consumer Perceptions of Service Quality"; Journal of Retailing, Vol, 64, No. 1, Spring 1988, pp. 12-40.

Richard Baker (1997); "Pragmatic Model of Patient Satisfaction in General Practice: Progress Towards A Theory"; Quality in Health Care, 1997; Vol No. 6; pp.201-204 (http://www.ncbi.nlm.nih.gov/pmc/articles/PMC1055494/pdf/qualhc00026-0025.pdf).

T. V. Perneger (2004); "Adjustment for Patient Characteristics in Satisfaction Surveys"; International Journal for Quality in Health Care; Volume 16, Number 6: pp. 433-435.

Victor Sower, JoAnn Duffy William Kilbourne, Gerald Kohers, and Phyllis Jones; (2001); 'The Dimensions of Service Quality for Hospitals: Development and Use of the KQCAH Scale'; Healthcare Management Review; Aspen Publishers, Inc., 2001, Vol. 26 (2), pp.47- 59 (http://www.shsu.edu/~mgt_ves/KQCAH.pdf).

4 Key Success Areas and Challenges for Patients' Satisfaction and it's Measurement

PATIENTS' SATISFACTION MEASUREMENT: HYPE OR HOPE!

Prologue

Patients are the foundation of all medical practices and therefore, it is very obvious that patients' must be satisfied with kind of services provided. Patients have two kinds of expectations from medical services, first, Medical or Clinical expectations which relates to accurate diagnosis and treatment that depends on the medical core competence. Second, those expectations that are related with Non-Medical aspects such as physical facilities and functional components of services. Satisfying patients is difficult as they are of varying kinds. To illustrate, some Patients are demanding, some Patients are annoying and difficult to deal with whereas some Patients are desirable, easy going and accommodating, and some Patients are timid questioning and uncertain about their requirement, but, healthcare service providers have to handle and satisfy all types of patients because Patients' satisfaction pays in terms of greater profitability; improved patient retention and patient loyalty; increased patient referrals; improved compliance; improved productivity, and better staff morale.

Patients' satisfaction measurement stands to play a crucial role amongst the health care providers. As physicians and hospitals have begun to experience increased pressure for the delivery of quality of hospital or medical services as well as enhancement of the patients' safety at an affordable cost which calls for greater attention and accountability amongst the health care professionals. The concept, philosophy and application of the patients' satisfaction measurement need to be further integrated into an overall measure of its clinical quality. Variation in Patients' satisfaction measurement tools, however, is an obstacle considering aspect of instrument's reliability part of the quality equation. At present, data on patients' satisfaction is gathered by various entities, for different purposes and at different levels in the health care system for designing of health plans, hospitals and medical practices.

The most commonly and largely used method for patients' satisfaction measurement is conducting of customized surveys to assess and improve its hotel-motel functions for ensuring delivery of a better medical or hospital service to maintain an apt stance in competitive health care market. The patients' satisfaction measurement is mainly based on improvement services, and use of available patients' discharge information for selection of a sample supported with use of focus group in few cases used to develop better insight on it. In few cases, a consultant division also keeps abreast of any changes in the medical or healthcare industry that might warrant alterations as data on patients' satisfaction measurement can play crucial role in the strategy formulation and in application of business tactics by the medico professionals and hospitals in designing and delivering of medical or hospital services to patients.

In a competitive health care environment, patients' want and expect better health care services than they did in the past, and medical centers are concerned about maintaining their overall image. The results of patient satisfaction surveys are used by hospitals to arrive at benchmarks for best practices across hospitals within the health system, using the data to make adjustments in areas such as efficiency of the admissions process, managing admission of patients' to a clinical unit or bed, and maintaining sensitivity to the needs of patients'. Information on patient satisfaction can also be for quality monitoring and improvement efforts at its clinical practices (Christopher Guadagnino, 2003).

Issues Confronting Standardization of Measurement of Patients' Satisfaction

An attempt has been made to reflect on various issues and its implications concerning standardization in patients' satisfaction measurement considering its three pioneering questions viz., Is patient satisfaction worth measuring? How can it best be measured? And how are we to use the results?

- **Is Patient Satisfaction Worth Measuring?**

  On one side the worried alliance of consumer advocates, marketing specialists, and proponents of patient-centered care favour the activities of measuring patient satisfaction. On the other side are skeptics who believe that focusing on patients' satisfaction diverts attention from what ought to be healthcare providers principal concerns in an era of resource constraints: inappropriate care; under use of necessary care; and clinical outcomes such as morbidity, mortality, and health status.

  These critics argument have a point in a sense that compared with measures of technical quality, data on patient satisfaction are easy to collect, and many health care organizations have surrendered to the temptation to stop there. Nevertheless, helping patients' achieve their goals is a fundamental aim of medicine. Because patients' goals and values vary widely, and are not predictable on the basis of demographic and disease factors alone, and are subject to change, the only way to determine what patients' want and whether their needs are being met is to ask them. From this perspective, viewing care through the patient's eyes is an ethical and professional imperative. Individual clinicians, medical groups, hospitals, and health plans all have reason to be interested in patient satisfaction, and not only because satisfied customers add to the bottom line. Indeed, arguments over the place of patient ratings usually turn not on whether measuring patient satisfaction is important, but on whether satisfaction can be measured reproducibly and meaningfully (Richard Kravitz, 1998, www.ncbi.nlm.nih.gov).

- **How Can Patient Satisfaction be Measured Best Way?**

  If patient satisfaction is to take its place alongside morbidity, mortality, and functional status, several critical measurement issues must be addressed that are outlined in brief as follows.

- **Scale Development Dilemma**

  First, scale developers and end-users need to be clear about what they are measuring. Patient satisfaction is not a unitary concept but rather a refinement of perceptions and values. Perceptions are patients' beliefs about occurrences that echo what has happened. Values are the weights patients' apply to these occurrences that demonstrate their desirability, expectation, and necessity. Most contemporary measures of patient satisfaction employ hybrid questions that assess perceptions and values simultaneously. Such hybrid questions have the virtue of linguistic economy but make it difficult to distinguish perceptions from values. Given these semantic vagaries, a patient who receives poor care but has low standards may report the same satisfaction as a patient who receives good care but whose standards are unreasonably high. If in the instrument developed patients' are asked about "Did the provider explain what to do if problems or symptoms continued, got worse, or came back?" Responses to questions of this type are not readily summed or averaged, and, nevertheless, what is lost in scalability is gained in interpretability (ibid).

- **Significance of Questionnaire Instrument in Patient Satisfaction Measurement**

  Patients' satisfaction measurement with medical care is not forthright. One approach is to use qualitative methods, but these are difficult to use for routine large scale service evaluation. Another alternative is to use a quantitative questionnaire which must be reliable, consistent, valid and with minimum errors of responses (Robert K McKinley *et. al.,* 1997.

- **Relationship Between Patient Satisfaction, Process of Health Care and its Outcomes**

  Another issue relating to patients' satisfaction measurement is with regard to the relation between patient satisfaction, process of care, and health outcomes. The association between patients' satisfaction and health status represents a tendency for healthier patients' to report greater satisfaction, rather than a tendency for patients' whose health has improved due to medical care to report greater satisfaction (Richard Kravitz, 1998).

- **Use of Results of the Patient Satisfaction Measurement**

  The real issue is concerning use of results of the patients' satisfaction measurement as many satisfaction batteries can reliably distinguish between physicians who are great communicators and those who are interpersonally challenged. It is also related to a variety of downstream outcomes, such as the propensity to change health plans, or to sue for malpractice. These results are clearly of interest to healthcare managers and marketers, but their relation to clinical quality improvement is weak. Separating patient perceptions from patient values and using questions that focus on potentially variable behaviors, of persons and of organizations, would help. If patient satisfaction measurement is not to be dismissed as one more health care fad, many challenges, like philosophical, empirical, and practical must still be addressed (Ibid).

- **Modification in Patients' Satisfaction Measurement Surveys**

  The variations in the patients' satisfaction measurement are an impediment to make it a reliable part of the quality equation. Even if variation of patient satisfaction measurement can be minimized to permit meaningful comparisons across providers, questions remain as to adapt to patient satisfaction surveys with appropriate modification so it can fulfill an expanded role of quality of healthcare measurement (Christopher Guadagnino, 2003).

- **Lack of Comparability of Information in Patients' Satisfaction Measurement**

  Lack of comparability of patient satisfaction data, however, remains another hindrance in its expanded use. The biggest single methodological obstacle to expanding the use of surveys to targeted groups of patients is the ability to collect a large enough sample from each group to yield valid results (ibid).

A Need for Standardization in Patients' Satisfaction Measurement in Hospital Services

In a competitive world, striving for excellence in every sphere for marching towards 21st century the standardization become essential which help in getting recognition to organization's practices and procedures. With the changing trends in medicine in the healthcare sector, the increasing awareness of the patients regarding quality medical services, and quest for patient satisfaction, healthcare/hospital services providers begun to realize the advantages of adopting a systematic way of functioning through standardization. The development of quality standards can bring about uniformity and consistency in practices and documentation of systems in use in healthcare organization. However, many officials in hospitals are still a bit nervous and skeptical, about introducing standardization activities in medical practices as they are still not convinced about impact of standardization on improving the running of hospital efficiently. But, still no one can deny the fact that the standardization helps to render better hospital services to patients as shown in Figure 4.1 below.

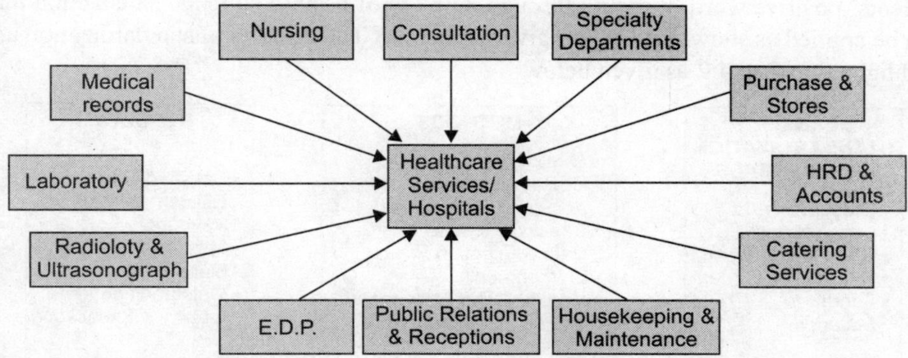

Fig. 4.1: Area Needs Standardization in Healthcare/Hospital Services

Source: http://mdrf-eprints.in/

To illustrate, there are plethora of laboratories in and around many hospitals giving varied results for the same sample. Being service oriented does these service providers do not have a major responsibility to ensure that the results generated by them are absolutely precise and reproducible. These standards can be developed and achieved by ensuring that equipment should be systematically inspected and regularly calibrated to obtain accurate and reliable results. Periodical validation of results to avoid Inter and Intra observer variations, and avoiding breakdown costs through regular preventive maintenance supported with compulsory calibration of all equipment and maintenance of such calibration records. Further cleanliness and hygiene must form part of quality of health care in the hospitals. Hospital-acquired infection can further aggravate the patient's difficulty. A major source of such infection is haphazard disposal of excrement, urine and other body fluid resulting in high risk of cross infections that may occur due to contact with such infectious wastes, splash of these body fluids and airborne infectious aerosols contaminating utensils, test tubes etc., that are used without proper cleaning. An efficient cleaning with high impact washing water followed by most steam heat destroys any pathogens remaining on the test tubes and other surfaces. The closed system disposal equipment that is incinerator need to be installed, and Needle tips must be incinerated through the needle burner/cutter and then packed separately, labeled and handed over to the cleaners.

Medical records are the folders which hold information regarding diagnosis and treatment. In many cases these records are not handled with the required care resulting in incomplete records, missing forms, illegible handwriting, unclear and unaccountable statements and improper filling. For this uniform methods and standards should be brought in to practice for keeping Medical Records. It is remarkable that even examination done by doctors can be standardized, thus avoiding wrong interpretation, missing diagnosis and unnecessary variation in patient care practices. So, standardization and continuous interaction with patients shall enable healthcare service providers to solve problems of both patients and hospital service providers that would be helpful also in developing quality-oriented technologies, procedures, and systems, which can earns patients' positive word of mouth through delivery of desired patients' satisfaction that can be applied as shown in a figure given as below.. The benefits of standardization are highlighted in Fig. 4.2 as given below.

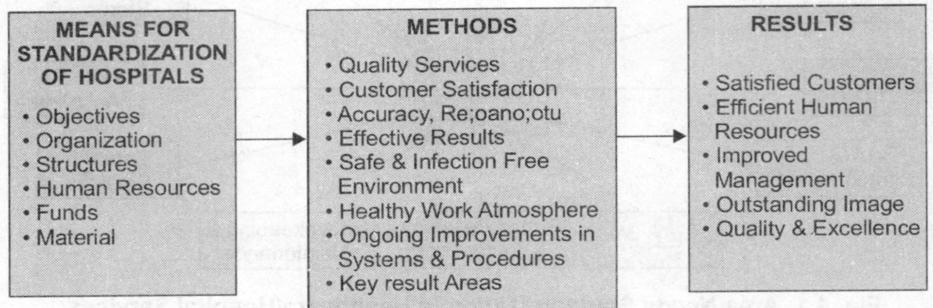

Fig. 4.2: Results of Standardization in Hospital Services

The Quality Diamond Model of Patient Satisfaction

Patients' satisfaction measurement is a complex task relating to hospital Services as provided by different types of hospitals which are significant from two perspectives. First, patients constitute the hospital's direct clientele. The patients' overall satisfaction is crucial aspect of the hospital service apart from other dimensions like technical quality of medical care, and effectiveness of medical treatment. Second, it provides an indirect measure of many other dimensions. It is usually correlated with effectiveness of medical treatment. The service quality of medical services too is multifaceted and its assessment requires manifold measures of process viz., response times, prescription, and admission rates combined with measures of outcome such as health status and patients' satisfaction.

Low patient satisfaction might be a result of poor obedience of procedures, waste of resources and suboptimal clinical outcome. Thus, Patients' satisfaction should be one of the key objectives of all medical services and need be included as an outcome measure.

The continual improvement in service quality of medical services is therefore fine tuned with measurement of patients' satisfaction. Customers have general expectations form hospital services which increase the complexity in providing satisfaction to patients to have clinical core competence.it implies that cure rate does matter, and lavish physical facilities can not substitute good clinical methods; rational therapy; display of confidence, and evidence based practices Customers expect that medico professionals must honor the appointments which must be accurate and flexible supported with communication in commonly used local language instead of use of medical jargons by doctors. It is essential that doctors patiently listen to patients' problems and give them sufficient time. Customers want that doctors should display personal concern with befitting body language towards the patients, and should possibly explain the lot about their illness and treatment. The Para-Medical staff should be well-equipped with adequate health education and display concern, courtesy, promptness, responsiveness, and empathy towards patients in their behavioural patterns. They need to keep positive attitudes and should preferably be flexible in handling patients in person and in case of telephonic conversations; promptness in all responses, and emergency case, admissions etc. should be focused. Customers anticipate that they are provided with reasonably good physical facilities in both types of treatment situations that are outdoor as well as indoor, and location of the hospital should be approachable with good parking facilities, clean with adequate hygienic sanitary facilities. It should be preferably supported with child friendly environment, recreation facilities with adequate space for movements.

Customers expect proper documentation with legible prescriptions; detailed discharge summary certificates, prompt issue of papers for Mediclaim, and clear explanation for administration of medicines to ensure compliance. Customers want that they should be provided with hospital information brochure and hospital should display informative sign boards.

They expect transparency in financial matters, which is one of the major causes for dissatisfaction; proper display of routine consultation and indoor charges. The patients should be properly informed about the expected expenditure before any procedure or admission. Customers wish that the hospital should make use of modern (information) technology, and adapt it with new diagnostic and therapeutic methods. The patients desire to have easy flow between various services to save time. Thus, the healthcare service providers consider factors affecting customers' expectations which include nature of medical illness; past experience in the same set up; experience at other set up; financial and social standing; level of education etc.

A diamond model of quality for its delivery for patients' satisfaction is given in Fig. 4.3.

CUSTOMER TYPES

- Difficult to deal: Demanding, annoying, unrealistic, loud and objectionable
- Desirable: pleasant, easygoing, intelligent, accommodating and knowledgeable
- Others: timid, questioning, unprepared, lacking in knowledge and uncertain about what they want or need

CUSTOMERS' EXPECTATIONS

- Medical (Clinical) expectations: These relate to accurate diagnosis and treatment. This is dependent on the medical core competence.
- Non-Medical expectations: These relate to physical facilities and functional components of services.

Quality Medical Care

CONTINUITY

- Develop method for ensuring continuous, consistent, ever-improving and never ending service quality.
- Search the ways and means of measuring, evaluating and monitoring the progress.
- Ensures that services get better day after day.
- Benchmarking that is looking beyond to other setups for better services and customer satisfaction.

COMMITMENT

- Emotional and intellectual pledge to a course of action
- 100% Commitment to qualitative services.
- Participative Leader
- Statement of Vision & Mission
- Recruit High Performance Staff
- Build a Team Committed to Quality
- Empower Employees
- Ensure Staff Satisfaction & Motivation
- Accreditation by Some Regulatory Authority

Fig. 4.3: The Quality Diamond Model of Patient Satisfaction

Source: www.iapindia.org

Conclusion Remarks

Given the push toward increased provider accountability and health care quality improvement initiatives, there is no question that the attention and weight given to patient satisfaction is going to increase. Patients' satisfaction data represents real events that transpire between providers and patients, and that it needs to be seen as equivalent to clinical indicators as a parameter of quality of care. The patient is the final arbiter of what the experience of care has been, and if healthcare service provider does not pay attention to it at some level, they will not understand how their processes can be improved so that the patient can walk away with an experience that is multidimensionally okay.

Satisfaction is related to the overall effectiveness of communication between physician and patient, which is necessary for achieving good outcomes, while ineffective communication can lead to poor quality. Satisfying the patient and addressing their concerns is an outcome of it as the patient is the best judge of whether their needs are being met. The changing philosophy of medicine has led to an increased sensitivity to patient satisfaction, and it focuses on quality health care, that is safe, equitable, evidence-based, timely, efficient and patient-centered healthcare services.

Hospital surveys have made physicians much more aware of patients' expectations of service quality as a separate component of quality of care. An increased focus on enhancing relationships with patients can result in a reduction in medical errors, and more satisfied patients are less likely to file medical malpractice lawsuits.

Patients' Satisfaction Survey expansion also raises the question whether patient satisfaction measurement should broaden its focus beyond quality of service and begin to measure perceptions of clinical outcomes. Some believe that patient surveys should add more specific questions about clinical quality to open a new window on provider care practices and further drive quality improvement, while others see fundamental barriers to integrating perceptions of service and clinical quality. While satisfaction measurement is still being used primarily to monitor and improve service excellence, some hospitals are beginning to ask more sophisticated, clinically-oriented patient satisfaction questions, such as whether a person felt safe during hospitalizations and whether they observed a medical error occur.

As patients become more sophisticated in their understanding of healthcare service provider, outcomes and complications rates, their perceptions of clinical quality should increasingly become part of their evaluation and satisfaction ratings.

There is going to be some movement in the healthcare industry toward asking patients more direct questions about the perceived level of the quality of care delivered, such as whether they were given the wrong medicine, whether the provider made the diagnosis accurately, and whether the patient got better.

But such a trend has limitations, that is, patient perception data about clinical processes and outcomes may lack validity, and not many tools currently exist to measure what is going on inside a hospital or a physician's office. There is also a belief that patient satisfaction measurement is best kept to the quality of service side rather than become integrated with quality of care issues. The importance and limitations of expanded patient satisfaction measurement can be expressed as "The perfect health care delivery is a perfect outcome and a perfectly happy patient".

The very process of measuring patient satisfaction reinforces a philosophy of quality by alerting patients' satisfaction that physicians are held accountable and showing physicians that patients' are pleased with the quality of care they receive.

The physician ratings tend to be the highest scores of any category on the surveys, which continues to reinforce for physicians the positive relationships they foster with patients', who in turn encourage other patients' to seek care at same hospital. Quality improvement feedback mechanisms are more useful in addressing provider-related concerns, such as the complaint and grievance process, and provider access and availability review. Healthcare Parishioners use the surveys to retain patient populations and attract more market share, to verify patient satisfaction results, and to assess and measure specific initiatives taken by healthcare service providers.

Practices that do wish to audit patient perceptions can acquire customized surveys to identify issues specific to the nuances of their practice, to identify services that they may need to add to the practice, to reinforce areas of excellent performance and to substantiate suspected problems. Patient satisfaction data are also valuable for staff training, morale-building and creative marketing.

patients' satisfaction measurement and interaction with patients would be unable to solve their problems and help to develop quality-oriented technologies, procedures and systems. This can reduce healthcare costs while providing customer satisfaction. A satisfied customer is an image builder of a healthcare organization/hospital. Undoubtedly, the healthcare organization/hospital not only builds its own image and good-will but also develops its services through quality standardization. The hospital thus earns customer loyalty because it aims to continuously satisfy their customers.

MEDICO NEGLIGENCE: A KEY DISQUIET FOR PATIENTS' PROTECTION

The Doctor patient relationship in India has undergone a sea change in the last decade and a half. The lucky doctors of the past were treated like God and people revered and respected them. We witness today a fast pace of commercialization and globalization on all spheres of life and the medical profession is no exception to these phenomena. As a result, the doctor-patients relationship has deteriorated considerably. Indian healthcare system, both public and private, still needs to improve their capabilities and its regulation enough to provide assurance on quality of healthcare delivered and protecting the interest of healthcare service users. In Fact, Medical negligence is a matter of major concern today not only in India but all over the world. Medical errors are associated with inexperienced physicians; new procedures; extremes of age; complex care and urgent care; poor communication whether in ones own language or in another language for medical tourists; improper documentation, illegible handwriting, inadequate nurse-to-patient ratios, etc., which contribute to the problem. Thus, the standards in the medical profession are deteriorating. Pursuits of money rather than the pursuit of excellence appear to be the most important motive force in patient care.

PROLOGUE

Health is a state of complete physical, mental and social well-being and not merely the absence of disease or infirmity (www.who.int), and *healthcare* is the prevention, treatment, and management of illness, and the preservation of mental and physical well-being through the services offered by the medical and allied health professions.

There is considerable lack of agreement about the precise meaning of the term *patient*. It is diversely defined by different experts with different perspectives. To illustrate, Patient is a person who requires medical care; an individual who is receiving needed professional services that are directed by a licensed practitioner of the healing arts toward maintenance, improvement or protection of health or lessening of illness, disability or pain.

Medical negligence is defined as a failure to exercise reasonable skill and care in diagnosis and treatment as per the prevalent standards as that particular point of time. An aggrieved patient who believes that he is a victim of medical negligence can now approach the Consumer Courts for fair compensation, and expect results in a relatively shorter period of two to three years. The procedure is comparatively simple and inexpensive.

Negligence is the omission to do something which a reasonable man, guided upon those considerations which regulate the conduct of human affairs would do, or doing something which a prudent and reasonable man would not do.

Negligence and rashness on the part of a medical practitioner, whilst treating a patient, is considered by the Courts as deficiency in services. Medical negligence arises from an act or omission by a medical practitioner, which no reasonably competent and careful practitioner would have committed. What is expected of a medical practitioner is reasonably skilful behaviour adopting the ordinary skills and practices of the profession with ordinary care.

Traditionally, patients in India have unquestioning trust in their doctors. Most doctors deserve it. But in some cases, medical negligence has resulted in severe harm physical, mental and financial. In addition, unqualified practitioners have brought suffering to gullible patients. Doctors have been liable to prosecution in civil court, but few malpractice victims sue for compensation, fearing years (even decades) of costly litigation. Fortunately, in 1995 the Supreme Court decreed the medical profession to be a "service" under the Consumer Protection Act, 1986. It set aside a writ Petition challenging the same by the Indian medical Association.

CONSUMER PROTECTION ACT AND MEDICAL NEGLIGENCE

The important question is that what was the necessity for applying the Consumer Protection Act, to the Medical Profession. This Act was made applicable to the doctors because there are no provisions in the Indian Medical Council Act, 1956 to entertain any complaint from the patient; to take action against the Medical Practitioner in case any negligence, and to award any compensation, etc. in case the negligence is proved. This necessity aroused because the laws which provide for action in cases of medical negligence were under the under the umbrella of Law of Tort and Indian Penal Code, which have some well documented problems such as delay in medical negligence cases tends to be greater; the cost of bringing an action, which is notoriously high in relation to the sums recovered in damages; limited access to the courts. Further, the success depends on proof of both negligence and causation which can be particularly difficult in cases of medical negligence.

The Consumer Protection Act, 1986 (CPA) is a unique legislation which provides for speedy and economical redressal in a simple manner. It has been held in a number of cases under CPA that instances of medical negligence are covered by CPA. Those unfortunate enough to experience gross malpractice may approach, in writing or in person, the District Consumer Disputes Redressal Forum when the compensation claims amount to less than Rs.5 lakhs. Claims between Rs.5 lakhs and Rs.20 lakhs may be taken to the State Consumer Dispute Commission. Claims above Rs.20 lakhs may be placed before the National Consumer Disputes Redressal Commission. The addresses of the above bodies may be obtained from your local consumer organisation. All complaints must be endorsed by the written opinion of two expert specialists in the medical field.

REVIEW OF LITERATURE ON PATIENTS' PROTECTION

An attempt has been made to offer a comprehensive review of literature on patients' protection as follows.

Stavroula A. Papadodima (2008) discussed the situation and legislation in Greece in terms of codes of ethics and law to protect patients' interest. He was of the opinion that medical care and the patients' trust depend on the ability of the doctors to maintain confidentiality. Without a guarantee of confidentiality, many patients would want to avoid seeking medical assistance. The principle of confidentiality, however, is not absolute and may be overridden by public interests. On some occasions such as birth, death, infectious disease, there is a legal obligation on the part of the doctor to disclose but only to the appropriate authorities.

Permissible disclosure can be granted by the patients' consent, for example, for the purpose of insurance they may wish to take out. Moreover, there are some ambivalent situations such as criminal acts, or notification of sexual partner in case of a patient with AIDS, for which Greek law does not include relevant provisions, and the Codes of Medical Ethics do not offer clear guidelines. Therefore, the Greek doctor is called to estimate the situation and assume full responsibility for his decision (Stavroula A. Papadodima 2008).

David Orentlicher (2010) considers the legislative efforts by United States to address a long-standing, but increasingly refined practice that pharmaceutical companies use to enhance their drug-detailing efforts which is against interest of patients. Given the high costs of their detailing efforts, drug companies are eager to employ the most efficient ways to identify physicians who might be persuaded to prescribe their drugs.

It was argued that drug detailing results in sub-optimal prescribing decisions by physicians, compromising patient health. Health care information organizations employ computer technology to collect and analyze data from prescriptions as they are filled at pharmacies. The organizations sell their analyses, which can include general prescribing trends as well as physician-specific data, to pharmaceutical companies so the companies' sales representatives can better target their marketing activities. This "data mining" has provoked concern because it can not only exacerbate the effects of drug detailing but also compromise other interests of patients (David Orentlicher, 2010).

Scott E. Harrington (2010) highlighted in his article which provides an overview of the Patient Protection and Affordable Care Act, which was approved by the U.S. Congress and signed by President Barack Obama in March 2010, with an emphasis on provisions related to the expansion of health insurance. It highlighted key provisions concerning coverage expansion, insurance market reforms, and the projected costs and financing of the legislation.

It also discussed that this law will transform private health insurance markets through its creation of state-level exchanges and federal government prescription of individual and small-group health insurance benefits, coverage, and allowable underwriting/rating criteria. It also raised issue that cost of health care and insurance will likely remain problematic in the United States for the foreseeable future (Scott E. Harrington, 2010).

John D. Goodson (2010) discussed about the Patient Protection and Affordable Care Act (PPACA) of 2010 of USA which brings both promise and peril for primary care. This Act has the potential to reestablish primary care as the foundation of U.S. health care delivery. The legislation authorizes specific programs to stabilize and expand the primary care physician workforce, provides an immediate 10 per cent increase in primary care physician payment, creates an opportunity to correct the skewed resource-based relative value scale, and supports innovation in primary care practice. Nevertheless, the threat is that the PPACA initiatives may not alter the current trend toward an increasingly specialized physician workforce. To realize the potential for the PPACA to achieve a more equitable balance between generalist and specialist physicians, all primary care advocates must actively engage in the long rebuilding process (John D. Goodson, 2010).

Bob Brown (2010) advocated that the administrative simplification provisions of the Health Insurance Portability and Accountability Act of USA (HIPAA) were intended to lead to the standardization of electronic transactions between providers and health plans resulting in significant improvements in efficiency and cost savings. But, actually the savings and efficiencies that have been achieved have been disappointing. He focused on understanding the strategic focus areas such as patient care, employee engagement, and financial health.

Such an effective compliance programs enhance an organization's reputation capital, promote an ethical workplace, and contribute to the delivery of high-quality health care and protect the interest of patients (Bob Brown, 2010).

William H. Dow (2006) conducted a study in USA to know the impact of differential effectiveness of different patient protection laws on length of stay of patients in different states. Data are drawn from the Agency for Healthcare Research and Quality's Nationwide Inpatient Sample from 1993 to 1998, which includes data from approximately 20 percent of all hospital discharges nationwide. Study analyzed only private payer patients only, because all laws were targeted at private insurance.

In the mid-1990s, many states as well as the federal Government began to regulate early postpartum hospital discharge. Length-of-stay patterns changed markedly in response, but effects were much greater in some states than others. In particular, laws directly empowering patients appeared more effective than laws requiring providers to follow practice guidelines. A primary finding of this study is the significant heterogeneity in the effect of early discharge laws in different states which suggests that law details and the state environment can greatly influence the effectiveness of regulation. Findings from this study could provide lessons for patient protection initiatives (William H. Dow 2006).

ILLUSTRATIONS OF MEDICO NEGLIGENCE

An attempt has been made by the researchers to offer few illustrations of healthcare errors to highlight the fact that patients have suffered largely due to negligence of healthcare service providers.

A Diabetic Patient suffered from myocardial infarction was admitted in hospital (05/11/1993) for chest pain, retrosternal discomfort. Patient started vomiting, pain radiating to are, profuse sweating and ECG showed complete heart block and was admitted in Bombay hospital under care of cardiologist, no senior doctor attended the patient during patient's stay of about 15 hours in I.C.U. of hospital except a brief visit by cardiologist. No insulin was administered between which increased further complications and patient died. State Commission held hospital negligent and compensation of Rs. 4.5 lacs with 12 per cent interest awarded. Appeal was dismissed by national Consumer disputes redressal commission. [Decision of national consumer disputes redressal Commission, dated 22/09/2003 in case of Bombay hospital and Medical Research Centre vs. Kishnabehari M. Agrawal, 2004 CTJ 468 (CP) (NCDRC)]. (S.S. Purnapatre, 2004).

A young man met with an accident and developed fracture left leg. The Bokaro general Hospital doctor plastered the fractured leg and refereed to orthopedic surgeon and he was further referred to the other hospitals and Medical research centre, Calcutta. It is because of deficiency on the part of successive doctors right from the Bokaro General Hospital to other hospital, entire leg had suffered from Gangrene. If the treatment of such fracture was not possible at Bokaro General Hospital the patient should have been referred to some specialized centre. Compensation of Rs. 10 lacs was offered to be paid jointly and severally by Bokaro general hospital. [Decision of Jharkhand State Consumer Disputes Redressed Commission, Ranchi, dated in case of devendra Singh Vs. Bokaro general Hospital and Others, 2005 (3) CPR 385]. (S.S. Purnapatre, 2007).

A Carpenter operated (03/01/1996) for Fractured Right Leg was given four bottles of blood. Subsequent tests revealed that patient has become HIV Positive; blood of one of the four donors was HIV Positive. Hospital did not carry out HIV test of donor's blood. Hospital management found guilty of negligence and compensation of Rs. 2 lacs awarded. [Decision of Karnataka State Consumer Disputes Redressal Commission, Bangalore, dated 05/11/2004 in case of Shri S. Murlidhar and other Vs. Administrator and others, 2004 (3) CPR 581]. (S.S. Purnapatre, 2007).

A couple having a son suffering from Thalassaemia Major, at the time of next pregnancy approached All India Institute of Medical sciences (AIIMS) for consultation regarding prenatal diagnosis of Thalassaemia (19/12/1989) and whether the baby in womb would suffer from the same or not.

The blood sample was collected at AIIMS and sent to UK for report. The UK Institute reports the C.V.S. DNA SAMPLE AS Beta Thalassaemia trait. However, after delivery child (25/06/1990) was found to be suffering from Thalassaemia Major. Compensation of 1, 95, 00,000/- was claimed. It was held that error in carrying out test cannot be termed as negligence. However, AIIMS was directed to provide free treatment to the child for all his life. [Decision of State Consumer Disputes redressal Commission, New Delhi, dated 20/05/2004 in the case of Sailesh Munjal and another vs. AIIMS and others, 2004 CTJ 940 (CP) (NCDRC), 2004 (3) CPR 2 (NC)]. (S.S. Purnapatre, 2005).

Coper-T broke when doctor was trying (18/12/1996) to take it out. Doctor inserted her hand leading to Uterine and Ileac Perforation with Hamoperitoneum and peritonitis. Doctor held negligent and compensation of Rs. 35,000 was awarded for pain and suffering.

[Decision of Meghalaya State Consumer Disputes Redressal Commission, Shillong, dated 10/01/2004, in case of Smt. J. S. Paul Vs. Dr. Mrs. Barkataki and others, 2004 (3) CPR 333]. (S.S. Purnapatre, 2005).

A minor was suffering from typhoid brought to the hospital and was examined by the senior consultant and the doctor. The nurse of the hospital wrote out a prescription and gave to the minor's father to bring the injection 'chloroquine' instead of 'chloramphenecol'. After the nurse injected it intravenously the child immediately collapsed and went into cardiac arrest. The child on account of the negligence and deficiency on part of the hospital authorities suffered irreparable damages and could survive only as a mere vegetative body. A complaint was filed before the national commission by the parents on behalf of the minor patients. It was thus held that the patient suffered on account of negligence, error, and omission on the part of the nurse as well as the resident doctor. Thus, paid compensation of Rs. 12.5 lacks to the minor patient and Rs 5 lacks to the parents for the mental agony they suffered (Supriya Srivastava, Retrieved on 08/02/2009).

ILLUSTRATIONS OF FOOD INFECTION/POISONING

The 30 girls students of the SC welfare hostel at Tirumalayapalem were hospitalized on 02/02/2002 because of food poisoning. A team of doctors were deputed from the District Headquarters Hospital for attending on the students who were recovering at the Primary Health Centre. The Minister for Roads and Buildings, Tummala Nageswara Rao, and the district Collector, Shri Giridhar, visited the students.

They also took stock of the conditions in the hostel premises. An enquiry into the incident was made and the hostel cook was placed under suspension (K. Samu, 2002, Hindu 2.2.2002).

Three persons were died after eating bad meat in South Delhi and two others were seriously taken ill after consuming "Contaminated pork" in the Ambedkar Nagar area on 02/02/2002. All the five persons who consumed pork were taken ill in the Dakshinpuri area. Two people died at their residence and one person at AIIMS hospital, Delhi. One person was treated at the AIIMS, while other person was admitted to the Safdarjung hospital, Delhi (K. Samu, 2002, Asian Age 2.2.2002).

The 23 villagers were fall ill and hospitalized after they consumed wild, mushrooms in Orissa's Bolangir area on 19/08/2002. The Government acted promptly and all the affected villagers in the Bongamunda block were hospitalized. The task force was constituted by the State Government which has a led of senior doctor to tour Bangamunda and nearby blocks of Bolangir and administer necessary treatment to those suffering from food poisoning and also to those suspected to be starving. They were discharged after necessary treatment. (K. Samu, 2002, Hindustan Times 19.8.2002).

About 1,200 students of Government and aided schools in Pondicherry were hospitalized as they developed food poisoning symptoms after consuming milk and bread served under a free breakfast scheme today. The children were rushed to hospital when they complained of nausea and began vomiting. The Chief Minister, N. Rangasamy, had immediately ordered suspension of the scheme, and the Collector had held an inquiry into food poisoning. Samples of the milk and bread have been sent for laboratory examination (K. Samu, 2002, Hindu 6.9.2002).

Five members of a family in Butudi village in the backward district of Kandhamal, Orissa, were dead on 18/09/2002 due to consumption of mango kernel powder. The post-mortem report had indicated that all of them had consumed gruel prepared from mango kernel powder and the deaths had been caused due to food poisoning. (K. Samu, 2002, Indian Express 18.9.2002).

Over 50 inmates of the Don Bosco Navajeevan Rehabilitation Centre at Ramanthapur, Andhra Pradesh, fell sick after having tamarind rice for breakfast on 08/10/2002 and were admitted to the Fever Hospital in Nallakunta for treatment.

The children, who are picked up from streets and taken care of by the centre, complained of vomiting sensation and diarrhea after having their breakfast. They later went to play cricket and started vomiting. They were immediately shifted to the Fever Hospital where doctors put them on drips. (K. Samu, 2002, Hindu 8.10.2002).

The 4 children died after eating ice-cream at a fair of the Bhil community at a village in Udaipur district on 09/10/2002, and four more died later. More than 80 children who also ate the ice-cream were in hospital with food poisoning. The district administration had treated the incident in Barodia village as it would treat an epidemic and it has dispatched medical relief to 53 villages where the problem may spread. (K. Samu, 2002, Hindustan Times 9.10.2002).

Suspected food poisoning led to the death of 12 members of the nomadic Moghya community in Bundi district, Rajasthan, Nainwa sub division on 03/12/2002. The victims belonged to two families who share the meal of chicken were given treatment in the Bundi Government hospital. (K. Samu, 2002, Hindu 3.12.2002).

About 30 tribal girl students of the AP Residential Girls Junior College at Paderu who were taken ill on 12/02/2002 after their breakfast at the hostel have been hospitalized with complaints of fever, vomiting and motions. Doctors at Paderu Government community hospital worked hard to improve the health condition of all the students. (K. Samu, 2002, Hindu 12.2.2002).

An Outbreak of Food Poisoning in a Military Establishment was observed on 23 September 2000. A total of 391 persons had consumed meals in the mess and detailed food history was taken from available persons and the attack rates of each specific food items were calculated with the relative risks. Chicken served was brought from a civil contractor, weighed on a dirty scale and then kept overnight in the mess freezer. The time gap between receipt of chicken from the civil source to the time it was kept in the freezer was more than 3 hours, permitting adequate time for thawing and bacterial multiplication. Laboratory investigations were carried out at the local military hospital. Attempt was made to collect food histories and signs and symptoms from all those dining in the mess whether affected or unaffected. Of the 391 persons who had consumed meals at the mess, 123 were affected giving an overall attack rate of 31.5 per cent. Majority of the cases had loose motions, fever, pain abdomen and vomiting. The maximum attack rate, 65.1 per cent, was for those who had eaten chicken preparation.

The chicken dish was the epidemiologically incriminating food item responsible for the outbreak. Clinical and epidemiological features were suggestive of salmonella food poisoning (Lt Col SL Jadhav, 2007).

An outbreak of food poisoning involving 121 persons of a military establishment was registered on 2nd February, 2007. These 94 persons reported to the hospital soon after having lunch, with complaints of nausea, vomiting, abdominal pain and loose motions.

The index case reported within 30 minutes after having lunch. All persons had taken lunch that had been prepared from a single cookhouse. The lunch consisted of chapati, dal, rice, vegetable consisting of potato and brinjal, raita and kheer. Of those affected, 37 were seriously ill and had to be admitted. The 'raita' as the food item responsible for the outbreak, with a risk ratio of 21.35. On investigation, a total of 94 persons became ill, with an attack rate of 77.7 per cent. The symptoms included nausea, vomiting, abdominal pain, diarrhoea, weakness and fever. There were no deaths and all affected persons recovered within 24 hours. The aggravating factor was the storage of raita at room temperature before its consumption, which provided ideal conditions for enterotoxin formation.

With use of locally grown plants in the food preparation without knowledge of local flora, resulting in accidental food poisoning. Such outbreak of food poisoning was due to use of a locally grown plant as vegetable, amongst soldiers of a unit in high altitude. Of the 39 people who consumed the meal, 29 fell ill with an attack rate of 74.35 per cent. All the cases presented with classical features of atropine poisoning and were managed with supportive care. Twenty one had symptoms severe enough to warrant hospitalization. All the cases made complete recovery. An outbreak of non-bacterial food poisoning in soldiers at high altitude, caused by accidental ingestion of a dish made out of Atropa acuminata plant leaves containing atropine related alkaloids (Lt Col AS Kushwaha, 2008).

PATIENTS' RIGHTS, OBLIGATIONS AND PRECAUTIONS TO PROTECT THEIR INTEREST

An attempt has been made to give a brief idea about patients' rights, obligations, and precautions which help them to protect their interest and safeguard them from malpractices of healthcare service providers, are given as follows.

The consumer protection act preserves several rights of consumer viz., right to be protected from hazardous goods and services; right to be informed about the quality and performance of goods and services; rights to free choice of goods and services; right to be heard in decision making process concerning consumer interests; right to redressed if consumer rights are infringed, and right to consumer education.

Patients' Rights

In the interest of a healthy doctor patient relationship, a patient should know his rights as a consumer which includes right to get all the facts about his/her illness; to have your medical records explained; and to be made aware of risks and side effects, if any, of the treatment prescribed for patient; do not hesitate to question your doctor about any of these aspects; right to be handled with consideration and due regard for their modesty in case of physical examination; right to know their doctor's qualifications and in case his inability to evaluate they can ask someone.

Further it includes the right to complete confidentiality regarding their illness; right to get a second opinion from any specialist if patient are doubtful about the treatment prescribed and especially an operation suggested; patients or their nearest relatives have right to be informed in advance what an operation is for and the possible risks involved; if patient are to be discharged or moved to another hospital, patient have a right to be informed in advance and to make his/her own choice of hospital of nursing home, in consultation with the doctor; and right to get your case papers upon request.

Precautionary Measures and or obligations for a Patients' Planning for Undergoing Medical Treatment

Patients' should make sure they have disclosed all relevant facts to the doctor before deciding any treatment. Except emergency, the final decision about the treatment should be taken after proper deliberation and/or second opinion. Take clarification for all the doubts regarding diagnosis/ treatment/investigation.

Patients' should discuss with their doctor the cost of the treatment which includes possible complications. During the treatment, patients should seek clarification from the doctor if they are not satisfied with any aspect and/or have doubts. They should keep all receipts/prescriptions/reports/discharge cards safely and keep extra photo copies. After treatment clarify all doubts regarding bills/payments etc., before discharge.

Patients should involve family physician in the discussion with the specialist doctor. In case of a death during the treatment, if any one related person of patient not satisfied with the cause of death, demand a post mortem examination and get copies of the entire indoor Case Record. It is necessary and correct on the part of patient to discuss with the concerned doctor all the doubts before resorting to any legal action. Many of the complications/delays/mishaps in any medical treatment can be genuine.

In case patient requires expert medical advice regarding the legitimacy of their complaint about medical malpractice or deficiency in service they may approach the Association for Consumer Action on Safety and Health (ACASH) or any similar organisation.

DOCTORS' RIGHTS, OBLIGATIONS AND PRECAUTIONS TO PROTECT THEIR INTEREST

An attempt has been made to give a brief idea about doctors' rights, obligations, and precautions which help them to protect their interest and safeguard the interest of their patients, are given as follows.

A duly qualified medical professional, i.e. a doctors' have a right to seek to medical practice by registering himself with the Medical Council of the State of which he is a resident, by following the procedure as prescribed under the Medical Act of the State.

The State Medical Council has the power to warn, refuse to register/remove from register or re enter the name of the doctor who has been sentenced by any court for any non-bailable offence or found to be guilty of infamous conduct in any professional respect. The appropriate Medical Councils are empowered to award such punishment as deemed necessary or direct the removal of the name of the delinquent registered practitioner from the register either permanently or for a specified period, if he has been found guilty of serious professional misconduct. No action against a medical practitioner can be taken unless an opportunity has been given to him to be heard in person or through an advocate.

Duties and Obligations of Doctors

The duties and obligations of doctors are enlisted in ordinary laws of the land and various Codes of Medical Ethics and Declarations in Indian and International context, which includes Code of Medical Ethics of Medical Council of India; Hippocratic Oath; Declaration of Geneva; Declaration of Helsinki; International Code of Medical Ethics; Government of India Guidelines or Sterilization. On the basis of these various Codes of Ethics and Declarations, the duties of the doctors can be summarized as under.

Doctors' Duties to Patients

It includes providing Standard Care which an average person takes while doing similar job in a similar situation. It includes use of standard, suitable, equipment in good repair; standard assistants, junior doctor or paramedical staff, sufficiently competent and experienced to do the job, and fulfills the prescribed qualifications; standard procedure; Standard premises, e.g. nursing home, hospital; standard proper reference to appropriate specialist; Standard proper record keeping for treatment given and no experiment on patients.

Another duty is to provide information to the Patient /Attendant regarding necessity of treatment; Alternative modalities of treatment; duration of treatment; regarding expenses and break-up thereof; consent for treatment, and emergency care; risks of pursuing the treatment, including inherent complications of drugs, investigations, procedure, surgery etc.

Doctors' Duties to the Public

Doctors' duty to public includes providing health education; medical help when natural calamities like drought, flood, earth-quakes, train accidents, etc. occur; to help victims of house collapse, road accidents, fire, etc. education for compulsory notification of births, deaths, infectious diseases, food poisoning etc.

Doctors' Duty towards Law Enforcers, Police, Courts, any Legal Authorities and Others

It is Doctors' duty to inform the police all cases of poisoning, burns, injury, illegal abortion, suicide, homicide, manslaughter, grievous hurt and its natural complications like tetanus, gas-gangrene, etc.; to call a Magistrate for recording dying declaration etc.

Doctors' Duty not to Violate Professional Ethics

Few important professional ethics for Doctors' includes not to associate with unregistered medical practitioner who is not qualified; not to indulge in self-advertisement except authorized by the Code of Medical Ethics; not to issue false certificates and bills; not to run a medical store/open shop for sale of medical and surgical instruments; not to refuse professional service on grounds of religion, nationality, race, party politics or social status; not to attend patient when under the effect of alcohol; no fee sharing (Dichotomy); not to talk loose about colleagues; keep information given by patient /attendant to be kept as secret; not to recover any money (in cash or kind) in connection with services rendered to a patient other than a proper professional fee, even with the knowledge of the patient.

Doctors' should not Indulge in any Illegal or Hide Illegal Acts

Doctors' should not indulge in illegal acts such as performing illegal abortions/ sterilization's; issue death certificates where cause of death is not know; not informing police a case of accident, burns, poisoning, suicide, grievous hurt, gas gangrene; not calling Magistrate for recording dying declaration; unauthorized, unnecessary, uninformed treatment and surgery or procedure; sex determination in certain States.

Doctors' should not to undertake any Procedure Beyond his Skill

This depends upon his qualifications, special training and experience. The doctor must always ensure that he is reasonably skilled before undertaking any special procedure/treating a complicated case. To quote an example, a doctor who is not sufficiently trained or qualified should not administer anesthesia.

Doctors' Duty to Avoid Professional, Medical, and Criminal Negligence

Professional negligence is the breach of a duty caused by the omission to do something which a reasonable man guided by those considerations which ordinarily regulate the conduct of human affairs would do or doing something which a prudent and reasonable man would not do. Medical negligence or malpractice is related with lack of reasonable care and skill or willful negligence on the part of a doctor in the treatment of a patient whereby the health or life of a patient is endangered. Criminal negligence is so great that it goes beyond matter of mere compensation. Not only has the doctor made a wrong diagnosis and treatment, but also that he has shown such gross ignorance, gross carelessness or gross neglect for the life and safety of the patient that a criminal charge is brought against him.

CONCERNS FOR HEALTHCARE SECTOR OF INDIA

Critical Aspects of Health

India has made rapid strides in the health sector since Independence: life expectancy has gone up markedly, the infant mortality rate has been halved, and 42 per cent of children receive the essential immunizations. We have a huge private healthcare infrastructure. And yet, critical health issues remain, infectious diseases continue to claim a large number of lives, babies continue to die needless deaths from diarrhoea and respiratory infections, and millions still do not have access to the most basic healthcare.

Difficulty in filing Complaint against Medico Negligence

The Consumer Protection Act now permits the people to claim compensation for deficient services in consumer courts. But, in many cases patients who have filed cases of negligence in consumer courts have complained that hospitals do not make available copies of medical records of the patients.

In some states consumer courts do not accept medical cases unless they are accompanied by the written testimony of at least one independent doctor supporting the allegations of medical negligence made by the consumers. Many cases are dismissed not because they are baseless or frivolous but because patients can often not prove their charges.

Availability of Basic Healthcare Infrastructure to Protect Interest of Healthcare Service Users

There are four key challenges that would need to be addressed viz., how much more medical infrastructure is required to adequately take care of India's healthcare needs? How to reduce the inequity in distribution of healthcare facilities? What are the measures that need to be implemented to enable the majority of the Indian population to avail healthcare facilities?

What are the initiatives required to assure consumers about the quality of medical care provided?

Medical Confidentiality a Part of Protection of Human Dignity and Freedom

Medical care and the patients' trust depend on the ability of the doctors to maintain confidentiality. Without a guarantee of confidentiality, many patients would want to avoid seeking medical assistance. Everyone has the right to respect for his private and family life.

The physician must maintain complete secrecy about anything he saw, heard, learned or understood during the practice of his profession, which is confidential and can be disclosed only to the patient or his family. Medical confidentiality is an important feature of the doctor-patient relationship. Doctors owe a duty not to disclose information against the patient's wishes (Stavroula A. Papadodima, *et al.,* 2008).

PROPOSITIONS FOR PROTECTING PATIENTS' INTEREST

Compliance to Medical Ethics

There is nowadays a growing trend for medical ethics to be considered as a part of the international human rights in many important aspects of professional regulation and normative theory, including development, communication, interpretation, implementation, and credibility of medical ethics (Stavroula A. Papadodima, *et al.,* 2008).

Maintain Confidentiality

The obligation of the medical, paramedical and nursing staff to maintain confidentiality needs to be established as a binding by making provisions in law whose violation makes the offenders liable to penal, civil and disciplinary sanctions (Stavroula A. Papadodima, *et al.,* 2008).

Common Situations Requiring Extra Caution

Doctors should avoid common causes for medical negligence. They should keep in mind certain high risk situations which are actions, and require extra caution. Some illustration of such situation are discussed below which needs extra caution on the part of healthcare/medical service provider.

Failure to attend the patient and are particularly frequent where children are concerned, especially in relation to acute abdominal emergencies, meningitis and chest infections.

Retention of objects in operations sites such as Swabs, packs, instruments or towels may be left behind in the field of operation. The responsibility remains with the surgeon. *Accident and Emergency Departments* which is the most hazardous part of the hospital and senior staff must be readily available to supervise the work.

Subtraction of the wrong limb, digit or operation of wrong eye/tooth which is a common mishap.

Carelessness in hospital notes, errors in pre-operative skin marking and failure to check notes against the patient in the operating theater are the common reasons for the misadventure.

A high risk specialty needs special attention such as emergency, orthopedics, obstetrics, surgery, plastic-surgery, and gynecology. Missed fractures tight plaster casts and poor results from spinal procedures are common complaints in orthopedics. In obstetrics, damage to the newborn from anoxia or forceps procedures major damage claims. Failed sterilization/Vasectomy are again a common cause for litigation. *Anesthesia* that is Anesthetists along with surgeons, present a common target for litigation ; the actual administration of the anesthetic is not usually the cause of complaint, but the many ancillary responsibilities such as transfusions, injections, etc.

Therapeutic hazards can be avoided by administering the right drug, the right dose, via the right route; by informing patients /attendants of the potential risks of treatment by taking all possible steps to avoid undesirable consequences.

Failure of Communication by doctor about the patient's medical condition in comprehensible language. In case of reference to another doctor, it is his responsibility to communicate directly with the second doctor and not rely on the patient to carry any informal message.

Non-profit Patient-Centered Outcomes Research

Focus should be on development and support to comparative effectiveness research by establishing a Research Institute for research on non-profit Patient-Centered Outcomes to identify research priorities and conduct research that compares the clinical effectiveness of medical treatments.

Focus on Health Prevention and Promotion

Emphasis should be on establishing the National Prevention, Health Promotion and Public Health Council to coordinate federal prevention, wellness, and public health activities. Develop a national strategy to improve, monitor, and amend the nation's health.

Generation of Funds for Prevention and Healthcare Programmes

Focus should be on to establish a Prevention and Public Health Fund for prevention, wellness, and public health activities including prevention research and health screenings, the Education and Outreach Campaign for preventive benefits, and immunization programmes.

Disclosure of Financial Relationships between Health Entities

Need to establish disclosure of financial relationships between health entities, including physicians, hospitals, pharmacists, other providers, and manufacturers and distributors of covered drugs, devices, biological, and medical supplies.

Offer Rewards to Healthcare Employees

Employers related to providing healthcare services should offer rewards to their employees in the form of premium discounts, waivers of cost-sharing requirements, or benefits that would otherwise not be provided for participating in a wellness program and meeting certain health-related standards.

CONCLUSION REMARKS

Healthcare systems are complex and diverse in both structure (e.g. nursing units, pharmacies, emergency departments, operating rooms) and professional mix (e.g. nurses, physicians, pharmacists, administrators, therapists) and made up of multiple interconnected elements with adaptive tendencies in that they have the capacity to change and learn from experience. The health care error is a preventable adverse effect of care, whether or not it is evident or harmful to the patient.

Food poisoning outbreaks are common in institutions and restaurants schools, colleges armed forces etc. Outbreaks of food poisoning are recognized or reported frequently by a large number of persons affected at the same time, similarity of signs and symptoms, and history of ingestion of common meal. In case of food infection an investigation of food borne outbreaks is important to identify and rapidly control the source and to prevent similar outbreaks from happening again.

It can be inferred by saying that medical negligence arises from an act or omission by a medical practitioner, which no reasonably competent and careful practitioner would have committed. When the concept of negligence is extended to professional people such as a doctor the test is that the medical practitioner must bring to his task a reasonable degree of skill and knowledge and must exercise a reasonable degree of care. Neither the very highest nor a very low degree of care and competence judged in the light of the particular circumstances of each case is what the law requires. But where you get a situation, which involves the use of some special skill or competence, then the test as to whether there has been negligence or not is the standard of the ordinary skill, a man exercising and professing to have that special skill.

In medical malpractice litigation, juries have the responsibility to decide whether a medical practitioners conduct in a particular instance fell below an acceptable professional standard of care, and if so, was that conduct a proximate cause of injury to the plaintiff.

One can conclude that if enough care is taken to avoid the common mistakes committed by healthcare service providers such healthcare errors can be minimised, and the more important aspect is that the patients and doctors should understand their rights, duties, obligations and precautionary measures, implement them in reality.

Through this doctors will get success in achieving the goal of preventing such healthcare errors. The focus should be on establishing the standard procedures for critical aspects of healthcare services where the probabilities of common errors are high, and continuous monitoring of the same with the help of checklist of the activities will help in reducing and preventing the healthcare errors. Doctors practicing ethically and honestly should not have any reason for fear. Law whether civil, criminally or consumer law, can only set the outer limits of acceptable conduct i.e. minimum standards of professional care and skill, leaving the question of ideal to the profession itself.

PATIENTS' SAFETY: EMERGING ISSUES AND CHALLENGES

Introduction

Health is a state of complete physical, mental and social well-being and not merely the absence of disease or infirmity, and healthcare is the prevention, treatment, and management of illness, and the preservation of mental and physical well-being through the services offered by the medical and allied health professions. Patient satisfaction is the degree to which the patient regards the health care service or product or the manner in which it is delivered by the medical service provider as useful, effective, or beneficial to patient. It has been observed that the modern healthcare facilities continues to achieve excellent results in improving health conditions of people worldwide, but, one can still come across the events that show that the patients are put at risk either through errors of healthcare service providers through failure to assess patients' needs properly, or manage their care and recognize deterioration in the patients' health conditions. Health Care Error is a preventable adverse effect of care, whether or not it is evident or harmful to the patient that occurs due to complex and diverse Health Care System in form of Structure that is Nursing Units, Pharmacies, Emergency Departments, Operating Rooms, and Professional Mix that is Nurses, Physicians, Pharmacists, Administrators, Therapists made up of multiple interconnected elements with adaptive tendencies having the capacity to change and learn from experience. Such healthcare errors are responsible for the emerging issues related with Patient Safety.

The Patient Safety is a new healthcare concerning prevention of medical error that often leads to adverse healthcare events. It was not familiar until the 1990s, till various countries begun to report on staggering numbers of patients who were either harmed and or killed due to medical errors. The World Health Organization [WHO] has therefore described Patient Safety an endemic concern recognizing its impact of 1 in every 10 patients around the world. One of the global issues that have affected both developed and developing countries in the recent past is the Patient Safety. The need to consider and manage the safety of patients within healthcare has been widely recognized. The 'science' of Patient Safety has grown, and is constantly seeking to identify how and why things go wrong in patient care and what one can learn from other industries and from other disciplines such as psychology to make healthcare safer. The emphasis has moved away from blame towards looking at how modern healthcare is delivered in complex, busy hospitals and clinics, and recognizing that sometimes the systems themselves create problems. Each year the treatment and care of hundreds of millions of patients worldwide is complicated by infections acquired during healthcare. The impact of healthcare-associated infection may imply prolonged stays in hospital, long-term disability, massive additional financial burden, and deaths.

Patient Safety is the mechanism that prevents or mitigates patients' harm stemming from complex and diverse healthcare processes that are compromised due to medical errors viz., an improper and wrong medication; improper medical treatment; incorrect and delayed test results; and avoidance of healthcare-related infections. It is a global issue affecting developed and developing countries and the healthcare errors are more prevalent in countries having weak healthcare systems. The major causes of insufficient Patient Safety are lack of training of healthcare workers; time constraints on healthcare workers; and insufficient reporting and learning systems to prevent errors in the future. Due to the growth of the research evidence in the field of patient safety, an increasing number of countries have placed systematic action on Patient Safety on their political agenda as a policy priority.

To illustrate, the World Health Organization globally launched the World Alliance for Patient Safety to tackle healthcare-associated infections regardless of the level of development of healthcare systems and the availability of resources as well as to co-ordinate and accelerate improvements in Patient Safety in October 2004. Implementation strategies include the integration amongst different healthcare settings of multiple interventions in the areas of Blood Safety, Injection Safety, and Clinical Procedure Safety, as well as Water, Sanitation, and Waste Management with the promotion of hand hygiene in healthcare as the cornerstone.

Healthcare Errors and Patients' Safety: A Critique

An attempt has been made by the researchers to outline the areas of healthcare errors due to which patient has to suffer as follows.

There are many areas which can be attributed to healthcare errors such as receiving the wrong drug or wrong surgery, or complications of surgery and other treatments, or failure to diagnose correctly or to spot the patient whose condition is deteriorating and to do something about it. The outcomes of healthcare error are different for patients, his/her families, and for healthcare service provider. It can be in terms of patients' health improvement; permanent disability or even death. The earlier research supports evidence that a significant number of healthcare errors are preventable.

According to estimate of the European Commission in Europe, 1 out of 10 patients are affected by healthcare-related infections. 3 Million Deaths are caused by healthcare-related infections. 50,000 people die each year because of healthcare-related infections which can be attributed to health care errors (http://www.healthfirsteurope.org). It is estimated that in European Union (EU) Member States around 8 to 12 per cent of patients admitted to hospitals suffer from healthcare errors much of which is preventable.

A conservative average of the Institute of Medicine and Health Grades Reports, USA had indicated that there were about 400,000 to 1.2 million healthcare error-induced deaths attributed to human factors, medical complexity, system failures, infrastructure failure during the year 1996 to 2006.

Human factors that causes healthcare errors consists of variations in healthcare provider training and experience, fatigue, depression and burnout; diverse patients', unfamiliar settings, time pressures, and failure to acknowledge the prevalence and seriousness of medical errors. Medical complexity resultant in to healthcare error is caused due to complicated technologies; powerful drugs; Intensive care and prolonged stay in hospital. A system failure that leads to healthcare errors included poor communication, unclear lines of authority of physicians, nurses, and other healthcare providers. It is also caused by complications increase as patient to nurse staffing ratio increases. Disconnected reporting systems within a hospital, fragmented systems in which numerous hand-offs of patients results in lack of coordination and errors, and drug names that look alike or sound alike also result into healthcare errors.

Other reasons for the healthcare error may be due to an impression that action is being taken by other groups within the institution; reliance on automated systems to prevent error; inadequate systems to share information about medical errors hampering analysis of contributory causes, and improvement strategies. The healthcare error is many times result of cost-cutting measures put in by hospitals in response to reimbursement cutbacks; environment and design factors. The American Institute of Architects has identified concerns for the safe design and construction of health care facilities. According to the WHO, 50 per cent of medical equipment in developing countries is only partly usable due to lack of skilled operators or parts. As a result, diagnostic procedures or treatments cannot be performed, leading to substandard medical treatment. Other leading causes of healthcare errors include inadequate assessment of the patient's condition, and poor leadership or training.

An attempt has been made by the researchers to offer few illustrations of healthcare errors to highlight the fact that patients have suffered largely due to negligence of healthcare service providers.

*On 23/06/1997, MS. Sheetali Bhargawa, aged 17 years, were given blood transfusion, the 5 units of blood platelet concentrate prepared in blood bank from five different donors was transfused. On 25/06/1997, patient's blood was tested and found that patient was suffering from Hepatitis C. Patient had to spend huge amounts for her treatment of hepatitis infection. It was the negligence of hospital and compensation of 18 lakhs was ordered by National Consumer Disputes Redressal Commission, New Delhi to Indraprastha Apollo Hospital. (MS. S.S. Purnapatre, 2005).

*A lady was admitted in Civil Hospital, Aurangabad, on 10/07/1963, for delivery of child and subsequent sterilization operation. The hospital is associated with Medical College. After operation patient developed high fever and acute pain in abdomen.

The patient was examined by surgeon attached to the hospital and advised that patient should be reopened and on reopening it was found that a mop (Towel) was left in the abdomen of patient during sterilization operation.

Condition of patient did not improved and patient died because of negligence of Gynecologists and Medical Officer. Trial Court held Medical Officer guilty of negligence and ordered compensation of Rs. 36,000 to be paid by Medical Officer, Gynecologist and Government of Maharashtra. High Court reverses the decision but Supreme Court set aside High Court decision and upheld Trial Court decision. [Decision of Supreme Court in Civil Appeal No. 3318/1979 dated 20/02/1996. published in AIR 1996 Supreme Court 2377] [Ibid].

*A Patient was operated for Hernia by Surgeon, on 08/01/1995, under general anesthesia and after operation Anesthetist and Surgeon left Operation Theatre immediately after operation without checking whether patient is out of Anesthesia. Patient's breathing stopped and Surgeon rushed to hospital but patient remained unconscious and died.

District Forum held Anesthetist and Surgeon negligent and compensation of Rs. 4 lakh was awarded. Appeal of doctors was not considered and State Commission too upheld decision of District Forum due to Anesthetist and Surgeon found guilty [Ibid].

World Health Organization's Initiatives and Patients' Safety

The World Health Organization launched the World Alliance for Patient Safety in response to World Health Assembly Resolution In the month of October, 2004 that urged WHO and Member States to pay the closest possible attention to the problem of patients' safety. It is aimed at raising awareness and political commitment to improve Patients' Safety, and Medical Care and also for developing Patients' Safety Policy and Practices. Each year the core element is the formulation of Global Patient Safety Challenges. Every two years a Challenge is formulated to stimulate global commitment and action on a patients' safety issue addresses a significant area of risk for all WHO Member States. The first Challenge concerning patients' safety has focused on health care-associated aspect of infection, while safe surgery was chosen as the topic for the second challenge of the global patient safety. It is fact that surgical care is an essential component of health care worldwide for over a century. As the incidences of traumatic injuries, cancers and cardiovascular disease continued to increase the impact of surgical intervention on public health systems will grow. An estimated 234 Million major operations are performed around the world each year, corresponding to one operation for every 25 people alive. Yet, surgical services are unevenly distributed with 30 per cent of the world's population receiving 75 per cent of major operations. Lack of access to high quality surgical care remains a significant problem in much of the world despite the fact that surgical interventions can be cost effective in terms of lives saved and disability averted. Surgery is often the only therapy that can alleviate disabilities and reduce the risk of death from common conditions.

Each year an estimated 63 million people undergo surgical treatment due to traumatic injuries, another 10 million operations are performed for pregnancy-related complications, and 31 million more are undertaken to treat malignancies.

WHO's World Alliance Action Areas for Patient Safety

The World Alliance for Patient Safety has identified six action areas viz., Patient Taxonomy, Research; Solutions for Patient Safety; Reporting; Learning, and a biennial Global Patient Safety Challenge. The first Challenge covered in the year 2005 to 2006 launched in the month of October, 2005 under the banner of Clean Care is Safer Care addressed health care-associated infection, a major, Patient Safety problem affecting hundreds of millions of people worldwide. Three core principles underlie the choice of these action areas viz, First, a commitment to placing patients at the centre of efforts to improve Patient Safety worldwide. Second, a focus on improving the ways to detect and learn from information about Patient Safety problems within and across countries, with a particular emphasis on methods and tools for detecting Patient Safety problems in developing countries.

Third, a need to build up the knowledge base of interventions which have been shown to help solve Patient Safety problems, together with a more rapid and systematic dissemination of information worldwide on successful strategies (Didier Pittet, Liam Donaldson, 2006). Patients for Patient Safety (PFPS) emphasize the central role patients and consumers can play in efforts to improve the quality and safety of healthcare around the world. It works with a global network of patients, consumers, caregivers, and consumer organizations to support patient involvement in Patient Safety programmes, both within countries and in the global programmes of the world alliance for patient safety. Its ultimate purpose was to improve health care safety in all health care settings throughout the world by involving consumers and patients as partners. Taxonomy for Patient Safety is working to develop an internationally acceptable framework for defining and classifying adverse events and near misses. Prevention and mitigation of adverse events require improved information sharing about the prevalence, types, causes, severity, and consequences of near misses and adverse events at both national and international levels. The lack of a standardized nomenclature and taxonomy of near misses and adverse events hinders this effort. Research for Patient Safety is an attempt to develop an agreed International Research Agenda for Patient Safety that was set up by the WHO to foster research on Patient Safety research agendas aimed at to facilitate the spread and use of research findings to inform safer health care in all WHO Member States. The goal of Solutions for Patient Safety is to increase International Collaborations for the promotion of existing Patient Safety interventions and better co-ordination of efforts to develop future solutions. It is defined as any system design or intervention that has demonstrated the ability to prevent or mitigate patient harm stemming from the processes of health care.

The International Steering Committee approved 09 solutions available for use by WHO Member States from the month of May, 2007 viz, look-alike, sound-alike medication names; patient identification; Communication during patient hand-over; Performance of correct procedure at correct body site; Control of concentrated electrolyte solutions; Assuring medication accuracy at transitions in care; Avoiding catheter and tubing Mis-connections; Single use of injection devices, and Improved hand hygiene to prevent health care-associated infections. Reporting and Learning Systems have emerged as a major tool to help identify Patient Safety problems, and provide data for organizational and system learning. The most important knowledge in the field of Patient Safety is how to prevent harm to patients during treatment and care. Its fundamental role is to enhance Patient Safety by learning from failures of the health care system. Health-care errors are often provoked by weak systems and often have common root causes which can be generalized and corrected. Although, each event is unique, there are likely to be similarities and patterns in sources of risk which may otherwise go unnoticed if incidents are not reported and analyzed (http://www.who.int/patientsafety/research/en).

The Alliance is to identify specific topics for action which address significant risk to Patient Safety relevant to all countries each 2 years. The first theme called as 'Clean Care is Safer Care' for the year 2005-2006, whereas the second challenge is 'Safe Surgery Saves Lives', and third one is 'Tackling Antimicrobial Resistance' (Didier Pittet, Liam Donaldson, 2006).

WHO Guidelines on Health Care

WHO has developed new Guidelines described as 'Hand Hygiene in Health Care (Advanced Draft)' with a thorough review, and specific recommendations to improve practices and reduce transmission of pathogenic microorganisms to patients and HCWs to provide Health Care Workers [HCWs], Hospital Administrators, and Health Authorities with the best scientific evidence and recommendations to improve practices intended to be implemented in any situation for delivery of the healthcare to a patient or a specific group of population (World Alliance for Patient Safety, 2006).

Principles and Quality of the Health Care

The basic principles for Patient Safety are the principles for Quality of Health Care which includes to do the Right Thing for the Right Patient Using The Right Method and at the Right Time, and To Communicate Well with the Patient and the Rest of the Clinical Team to facilitate recording of the findings; planning of prompt and clear actions to ensure that instructions are understood and carried out, and report concerns to a senior colleague when necessary. (Sarah Williamson, www.asianhhm.com)

Enhance Effectiveness by Doing the Right Thing

It means to ensure the conduct of the correct test in line with the patient's symptoms based on choosing of correct drug that is given in the correct doze, and that surgery is performed on the correct side of the body supported with recording of correct observations on a sick patient at the correct frequency. The procedures and training to guide all the staff implies improving safety and quality of care in form of unambiguous and clear prescription of drugs, proper and safe administration of drugs, marking and preparing patients for surgery, knowledge of appropriate timing of tests and different methods of interpretation of results that are provided. The right thing might also convey having up-to-date knowledge and skills to allow clinicians to give their patients the best care. All healthcare organizations need to consider how much they can rely on individual clinicians' judgment and to what extent they can intervene with directives or by taking action to force compliance with changes.

By Offering Medical Treatment to the Right Patient

Although, it sounds painfully obvious, but many health care errors occur because patients have similar names. Errors could occur when the wrong patient is taken to

X-ray, or a doctor picks up the wrong set of notes, or specimens are mislabeled, or even because in a busy ward there is a new patient on the bed. It should be routine for staff to check at each stage of care that they are dealing with the correct patient, and if they have heard the patient's name correctly when they are asked to carry out an instruction.

By Providing Medical Treatment Using the Right Method

It implies ensuring of diagnostic tests that are correctly performed and interpreted. Similarly, many errors occur where drugs are given by the wrong route or in the wrong concentration. It is also very important that untrained staff know that, and abstain from that they should not perform certain tasks that carry significant risks. It also suggests keeping medical equipment clean and in good working order.

To Provide Medical Treatment at the Right Time

It includes giving of drugs as prescribed time as well as checking the patient and recording observations to avoid the patient's deteriorating condition. Some of the hospitals in UK and USA uses early warning systems designed to alert staff about a deteriorating patient, and to guide and empower them for seeking required assistance.

To Ensure Effective Communication

In most cases, faulty treatments can be attributed to improper communication of critical data. It helps not only patients in understanding their condition but also healthcare providers in providing proper care to patients. Listening to patients and respecting their wishes shall form the basis of offering effective healthcare in the 21st century. Many industries have learnt that it is important for Patients' Safety to have a culture where no one is above criticism because any human being can make a mistake, and where junior staff can put forward suggestions or concerns, and have these treated with respect.

To Maintain Proper Medical Records of Patients

Multiple medical teams are involved for record keeping and providing health care facilities to the patients consisting of Doctors, Nurses, Therapists, Technicians, and Pharmacists whose relationship with each other requires sharing of information and acting on instructions.

It is highly desirable that in each of their shift s/he must record changes in the patient's condition, results of tests, new plans for care, and anything else that everyone caring for the patient needs to know.

To Develop A Culture and Systems of Patient Safety

There exists a need to set up policies, procedures and for providing training to multiple medical teams involved for record keeping and providing health care facilities to the patients for ensuring patient safety. These teams should clearly understand instructions; ensure proper use of the equipment to avoid infection and improve hygiene by following safety norms and use of incident reporting system (Sarah Williamson).

Conclusion Remarks

India's healthcare sector is on a high-growth trajectory propelled by domestic economic optimism, increasing public health awareness, and growing global interest in India's low-cost service delivery systems. But, the major issue is the growth of private players' that has leaded to rise in real estate costs. To attract investments amounting of $ 70 billion that is Rs 2, 86,930 Crores in the healthcare sector of India by the year 2012, the Government's increased emphasis on primary healthcare, an explosion in patient base, and a boom in medical tourism call for a strategic emphasis on cost reduction and quality of the healthcare in India.

To ensure better implementation of the WHO's World Alliance for Patient Safety aimed at handling the global challenge of Patient Safety and for ensuring a high level of hygiene, it is essential that health care facilities focuses on viz., clean hands; clean equipment; clean products; clean practices; and above all clean environment. One also finds presence of a large number of innovative technologies aimed at enhancing and strengthening patient safety. Despite the introduction of Blood Screening and Testing Measures, patients remain at risk of Infection and Transfusion-Associated Reactions because Micro-Organisms such as Viruses, Bacteria and Parasites likely to be present in Blood and Blood Products that remains invisible. New medical technologies such as Pathogen Inactivation Technologies have been developed for improving Blood Products. The single use medical devices such as Syringes, Surgical Drapes and Surgical Gowns to more complex technologies such as Biopsy Forceps and Balloon Catheters have been developed to increase standards of health care worldwide. In general, the use of safety features including Alarms, Programs, and Automatic Identification Technology in Medical Equipment have increased patients' safety (Sarah Williamson).

There is a significant transdisciplinary body of theoretical and research literature available on the science of patient safety. It has emerged as a distinct healthcare discipline supported by an immature yet developing scientific framework.

It calls for ssystem-wide action on a broad range of fronts to identify and manage actual and potential risks concerning Patient Safety that calls for actions in areas viz., Performance Improvement, Environmental Safety, and Risk Management, including Infection Control, Safe use of Medicines, Equipment Safety, Safe Clinical Practice, and Safe Environment of health care. It embraces that the challenges faced by the world populations for Patient Safety are enormous, but the rewards too are important if appropriate actions are planned and implemented in near future.

USING INFORMATION TECHNOLOGY [IT] FOR IMPROVING QUALITY OF HEALTHCARE SERVICES

Prologue

Globally, the quality of healthcare services and measurement of the performance of medical care providers has become an important facet of the health care system. Worldwide people seek to improve quality of their life. But, majority of them who live in overcrowded houses with inadequate sanitation and unsafe water supply becomes victims of infectious disease and children too are commonly found suffering due to malnutrition resultant into high death rate and low life expectancy. There exists a need to improve provision, availability and accessibility, and above all the quality of healthcare services, and also its physical and human infrastructure and ensuring offering of health insurance. One of the most commonly sought approaches therefore adopted by large number of economies is to induce participation of the private sector in the healthcare sector through greater emphasis laid upon Public Private Partnerships [PPPs].

Health for all is meant for everybody over ages, demography, sex and society. The new paradigm of development in health care has shifted the curative and rehabilitation principles into prevention and promotion of health care; it is also meant to empower people for self care to have healthy life style. Health has always been a matter of universal concern, but at no other time in history has it assumed the legal and political implications that it has today, not only in India, but also worldwide. It is said that the Internet should be used for the benefit of mankind. Internet experts have always felt that development and delivery of medicine will be one area where this medium is likely to have immense benefit to mankind. The evolution of the role and use of the Information Technology [IT] in the healthcare industry is a topic of much interest to those who are involved in the delivery of healthcare services.

A NEED FOR IMPROVING QUALITY OF HEALTHCARE SERVICES

Gradually, one finds a shift in the healthcare market from conditions of the sellers' market to a buyers' market. Therefore, it has become crucial to design, communicate and timely deliver patients' satisfaction by effective and efficient adoption of the service oriented approach considering the fact that now hospitals are compelled to reach out to its patients to better survive and grow in prevalent competitive business environment. It is crucial to accept the fact that this can be achieved by hospitals only by building a bridge of trust between hospitals in general and its customers in particular a, and also the community that is surrounded and covered by hospital so that the community can cross over it. One also need to understand the fact that patients do not visit a particular hospital just because its services are low-cost , but largely because of its name and perceived positive image build up because of consistent and often delivery of healthcare services of good quality to its patients from time to time. Further, one should also note that the customer of the hospital, unlike other service experiences gets a close look at all the steps of the hospital. S/he gets a chance to interact practically with medical, para-medical, administrative and other supporting staff and gets first-hand experience on the workings of the hospital that largely not only determines his/her satisfaction but also perceived positive image of the hospital that is directly affected by the quality of the health care services offered by the hospitals to its patients (Rashmi and Vijay Kumar B., 2010).

A model of service quality was originally developed through an exploratory research by Parasuraman, Zeithaml, and Berry (1985), in four services categories viz., retail banking; credit card; securities brokerage, and product repair and maintenance that was conducted with the help of total 12 focus group interviews.

It revealed that the criteria used by consumers in assessing service quality fit in potentially overlapping dimensions called as viz., dimensions were reliability, responsiveness, competence, access, courtesy, communication, credibility, security, understanding/knowing the customer, and tangibles Further, the same group of authors also focused on conceptualization and operationalisation of the service quality construct that described the development of 22 items instrument popularly now called as SERVQUAL used for assessing customers' perceptions of service quality in service and retailing organizations that finally provided five distinct dimensions viz., Tangibles; Reliability; Responsiveness; Assurance, and Empathy. Thereafter, Parasuraman Zeithaml and Berry (1991) also carried out a follow up study to redefine the SERVQUAL and concluded favourably about usefulness of the SERVQUAL (A. Parasuraman, Valarie A.Zeithaml, and Leonard L. Berry, 1985, 1988 and1991).

One finds some of the efforts put in by the researchers also in the area of the healthcare sector that has been outlined in brief as follows.

C. Jeanne Hill, *et al.,* (1989) examined the importance of nineteen selected criteria consumer might use in their choice of a professional service provider. Factor analysis reduced the variables to five factors which included knowledge; comfort; time, social reputation, and accessibility. Its results presented strong implications for competitiveness of professional service providers with knowledge and comfort items representing as the most important to individuals (C. Jeanne Hill, *et al.,* 1989).

Pauy Cheng Lim and Nelson K.H. Tang (2000) conducted study based on 252 patients at Singapore to determine the expectations and perceptions of patients which revealed an overall service quality gap between patients' expectations and perceptions suggesting need for improvements. It inferred that assurance and responsiveness were the critical dimensions of service quality (Pauy Cheng Lim and Nelson K.H. Tang, 2000).

De Dennis McBride *et al.,* (2002/2003) conducted survey of consumers and visitors at Western State Hospital (WSH), Washington to gain their perspective on the quality of care, services, and hospital environment suggested that, consumers and visitors at WSH were generally satisfied with their hospital experience. (De Dennis McBride, Jonathan Lindsay and Morgan Wear, 2002/2003).

Yves Eggli, Patricia Halfon (2003) viewed that most of the conceptual frameworks used for hospital quality management exhibit shortcomings, terminology barriers or too much complexity, and proposed a simple model specific to hospitals based on four entities viz., Patients; activities; resources, and effects, and six levels viz., representations; priorities; measures; standards; evaluation, and accountability, which can be plotted against the four entities in order to measure the development of quality (Yves Eggli, Patricia Halfon, 2003).

Mik Wisniewski and hazel Wisniewski (2005) undertook study at the Scottish Colposcopy Clinic between October 2000 and 2001 aimed to measure service quality using both the gap concept and service quality dimensions using SERVQUAL instrument which revealed that largest service quality gap was observed for the reliability of services and the need for improved premises (Mik Wisniewski and hazel Wisniewski, 2005).

There are six basic aims identified for improvement in healthcare viz., (*i*) Safe: Avoiding injuries to patients from care that is intended to help them. (*ii*) Effective: Providing services based on scientific knowledge to all who could benefit, and refraining from providing services to those unlikely to benefit, avoiding underuse and overuse. (*iii*) Patient-centered: Providing care that is respectful of and responsive to individual patient preferences, needs, and values and ensuring that patient values guide clinical decisions. (*iv*) Timely: Reducing waits and sometimes harmful delays for both those who receive and give care. (*v*) Efficient: avoiding waste, such as waste of equipment, supplies, ideas, and energy, and (*vi*) Equitable: providing care that does not differ in quality because of personal characteristics such as gender, ethnicity, geographic location, and socioeconomic status (Sarah F. Schillie, 2007).

Many in healthcare today are interested in improvement of Quality of Healthcare services by the efforts of everyone involved in providing healthcare service (Fig. 4.4).

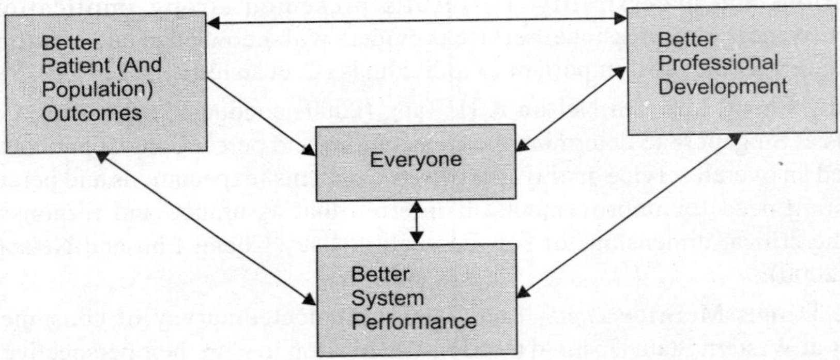

Fig. 4.4: Linked Aims of Improvement of Quality in Healthcare Services

Source: Paul B Batalden and Frank Davidoff (2007).

The idea of linked aims of improvement of quality in healthcare services defined as the combined and continuous efforts of everyone that is healthcare professionals, patients and their families, researchers, payers, planners and educators, to make the changes that will lead to better patient outcomes (health), better system performance (care) and better professional development (learning). This definition arises from the conviction that healthcare will not realize its full potential unless change making becomes an intrinsic part of everyone's job, every day, in all parts of the healthcare system (Paul B Batalden and Frank Davidoff, 2007).

For improvement in quality of healthcare services three important aspects are focused by the researchers which are given in Fig. 6.5.

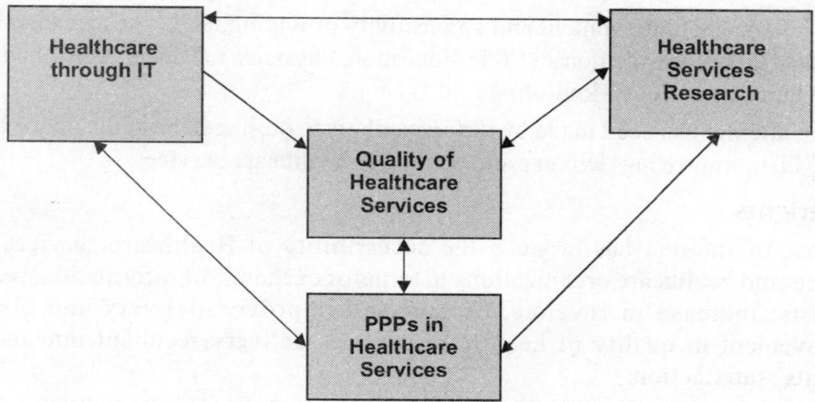

Fig. 4.5: Important Aspects of Quality of Healthcare

KEY PERSPECTIVES OF INFORMATION TECHONOLOGY IN HEALTH CARE SERVICES

With the ushering in of new technologies and the convergence of Information Technology [IT] into the domain of healthcare, the healthcare sector has received a new set of opportunities in form of e-healthcare for the masses. The use and applications of IT has not only improved the delivery system of healthcare services but has also facilitated the sharing of knowledge among the medico-professionals (Debashree Mukherjee, 2009). e-Health tools facilitate the interaction among the patients, medico and clinical professionals which mainly consists of tools such as viz., (*i*) Electronic Health Records (e-HR), (*ii*) Patients Information Systems (PIS), (*iii*) Hospital Information Systems (HIS), (*iv*) General Practitioner Information System (GPIS), (*v*) National Electronic Registries, (*vi*) National Drug Registries, (*vii*) Directories of Healthcare Professional and Institutions, and (*viii*) Decision Support Systems (DSS) (Suchitra Mohanty, 2009).

Various e-health tools that have been identified and put to use has yielded a positive and mutually beneficial outcome in terms of strengthening of the physician-patient relationships resultant into bolstering of patients confidence and trust on the medical professionals (Debashree Mukherjee, 2009). The use and application of e-healthcare results into improvement of connectivity as sharing and moving of information is the vital idea of e-healthcare functionality. E-healthcare provides all healthcare related information to anyone, at any time, any place in a timely and an efficient way (Suchitra Mohanty, 2009).

Further, it leads to improvement relationships between patient and physician which is crucial and integral aspect for the successful implementation of e-healthcare services that is based on five pillars of e-healthcare services called as viz., (*i*) Content: Medical Information Databases, Healthcare Provider Directories; (*ii*) Commerce: Online Pharmacies and Shopping Portals, Transfer of Healthcare Billing Data.

It has also further included (*iii*) Connectivity: Interconnection of Involved Parties i.e. Physicians, Laboratory, Pharmacy, Hospital, Insurance; (*iv*) Computer Application:

Applications enabling content and connectivity providing, and (*v*) Care: Physician to Physician- Tele-Consultation and Tele-Education, Physician to Patient- Tele-Diagnostics, Tele-Therapy and Tele-Monitoring.

An attempt has been made by the researchers to outline in brief the major benefits of use IT in improving delivery and quality of healthcare services.

To Patients

The use of Internet has broaden the accessibility of Healthcare services for its patients and healthcare organizations in terms of exchange of information; reduction in costs, increase in revenue, prompt and improved delivery and above all improvement in quality of healthcare services delivery resultant into increased patients' satisfaction.

To Administrators/Organizations

The hospital and clinic administrators can now largely choose to become proactive for delivery of timely, cost-effective and prompt healthcare services of a good quality to its patients by using Information and Communication Technologies [ICTs] within their organizations. Although, challenges and unexpected costs have also arise due to ever-changing nature and advancements in ICTS.

To Community

The Internet, as a public network has opened an open flow of global communication and information sharing. The major Internet applications for healthcare organizations are unlimited such as viz., website development and business strategies, education and research, disease management programs, electronic medical records, and e-mail.

To Medico and Clinical Professionals

The Internet is also being put to use by healthcare organizations to guide the medico and clinical professionals' on evolving best medical and clinical practices for efficient and effective clinical diagnosis, treatment and delivery of healthcare services to its patients. Internet-based applications are crucial and critically useful in improving quality assurance and clinical benchmarks that might act as an integral role in improving healthcare services to its patients (Madison, James, 2002).

HEALTHCARE THROUGH IT: PROS AND CONS

In current globalised scenario, e-Health or electronically enabled healthcare can provide the much-needed silver lining and bridge the gaps in healthcare access that is prevalent in the Indian society.

In fact, India and many other developing countries need e-Health more than the developed world, because conventional healthcare has failed to reach the large sections of underserved population.

For example, a team of medical experts sitting in London or the USA can impart their diagnostic skills or prescribe appropriate medication to a critically ill patient in rural Bihar, through the help of effective information technology networks.

Telemedicine can also help in training of medical personnel across the country, and thereby India can improve its human resource in health sector, by making them abreast of the current developments in the field of medicine. However, before all things, the government and the private players have to collectively ensure that the cost to incur the benefits of e-Health are within the reach of the majority of India; otherwise the entire exercise will be a futile one from a development perspective, though reflecting mercenary dividends (Fig. 4.6).

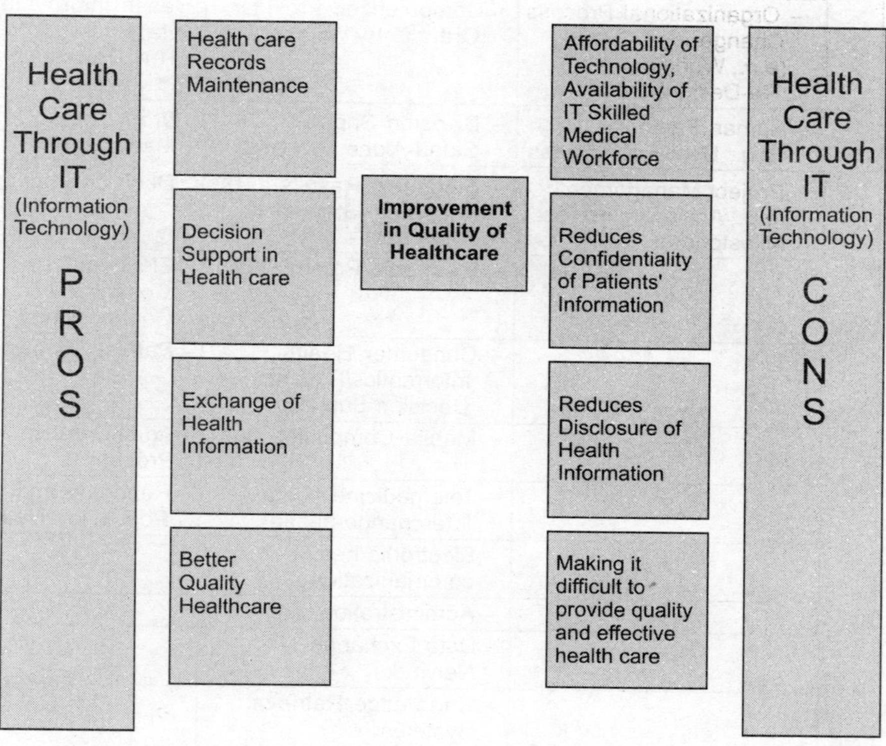

Fig. 4.6: HEALTHCARE THROUGH IT: PROS and CONS

Healthcare through Information Technology reflect the potential of information technology (IT) in reducing medical errors, lower costs, and improve patient care. It also recommends a technological framework for transitioning from manual, paper-based health records to a modern, computerized electronic records infrastructure. It facilitates the electronic health records maintenance, computer-assisted decision support, and exchange of health information. Due care must be taken for maintaining confidentiality of patients' information (Rakesh Agarwal *et al.* 2007).

HEALTH INFORMATION TECHNOLOGY (HIT) FRAMEWORKS

An attempt has been made by researcher to give brief idea about health information technology framework and its elements as follows (Table 4.1).

Table 4.1: Health Information Technology (HIT) Frameworks and its Elements

Elements		
Components of an HIT Implementation	Types of HIT Systems	Functional Capabilities of an HIT System
– Technological (*e.g.*, System Applica-tions)	– Electronic Health Records	– Clinical Documentation
– Organizational Process Change (*e.g.*, Workflow Re-Design)	– Computerized Provider Order Entry	(Health Information/ Data) – Results Management
– Human Factors (*e.g.*, User-Friendliness)	– Decision Support Stand-Alone Systems)	– Order Entry Management
Project Management (*e.g.*, Achieving Project Milestones)	– Electronic Results Reporting (Standalone Systems)	Decision Support
	– Electronic Prescribing	– Electronic Communication and Connectivity
	– Consumer Health Informatics/Patient Decision Support	– Patient Support
	– Mobile Computing	– Administrative Processes
	– Telemedicine (Data Interchange-based)	– Reporting and Population Health
	– Electronic health communication	
	– Administration	
	– Data Exchange Networks	
	– Knowledge Retrieval Systems –HIT in general –Others	

Source: Basit Chaudhry, www.annals.org

The framework (Components, Types and Functional capabilities) of HIT provide an idea about the benefits it generate for healthcare services, provided proper care is taken to make the use of Information Technology in healthcare services (Basit Chaudhry,).

BARRIERS CONFRONTING USE AND APPLICATIONS OF INFORMATION TECHNOLOGY IN DELIVERY OF HEALTH CARE SERVICES

The challenge is related with using IT that supports the sharing of medical e-records while maintaining patient privacy. Using information technology in healthcare services posing patients' health information assurance and security challenge and make it difficult to provide quality and effective health care by service providers. Disclosures of sensitive information by people such as emotional problems, sexually transmitted diseases, substance abuse, and genetic predispositions to diseases, could cause embarrassment and affect insurability.

Most consumers were uncomfortable with their health plan, sharing health information with a hospital, a specialist or their primary care doctor as they were concerned with who saw their information and were worried that the information could be made available online.

Clearly, patients or consumers feel that it is critical that their medical information is held in confidence. If patients do not feel that their personal medical information will be kept confidential, they may withhold important medical information from health care providers and making it difficult to provide quality and effective health care. Presenting a significant information assurance and security is challenge to the health care industry as reflected by the consumers' concerns related to building trust with health care community. If the health care industry falls behind in assuring the public that it can indeed safeguard patient information, then the initiative to create a more efficient and cost effective health care system by using Information Technology will be in serious jeopardy (Sherrie Drye Cannoy and A. F. Salam, 2010).

Despite the Internet's growing popularity and use, several barriers prevent full implementation of IT in delivery of healthcare services that has been outlined as follows.

For Patients

From the point of view of patients', lack of universal access to the Internet, especially among low-income families; computer illiteracy; and comparatively high cost of computers are a few barriers that are adversely affecting use of IT in availing of healthcare services.

Besides, a widening gap between those who have and those who do not have access to use of Internet too poses a big a challenge to healthcare service providers that too adversely influences use of IT in case of healthcare services.

Many times, consumers are also reluctant to make use of Internet because of difficulty in discerning the quality of healthcare websites and medical information posted on Internet (Madison, James, 2002).

For Physicians

Many physicians are cautious of new computer applications as they believe that they are unskilled in electronic communication and data searching; they will become even more time constrained as patients who have gathered large amounts of online medical information increasingly bombard them with questions; physicians fear a greater possibility of malpractice suits as well as inadequate reimbursement because they devote more time to replying to patients' e-mails (ibid).

For Administrators/Organizations

Administrators might be reluctant to adopt ever-changing IT as they are not ready to invest substantial finances in a system that is not fully mature. They are often cautious in adopting ICTs because of their desire to ensure patients' safety. Some of them are unwilling to have Web-based Information shared among the many diverse groups affiliated with their organizations. Many Web-based services that could potentially be utilized by an organization require major systemic investment and organizational change. Lack of System compatibility across healthcare organizations and between patients and Web-based organizations too act as a significant barrier use of IT in availing of healthcare services (ibid).

Generalizability: A Key Limitation in Use of IT

One of the key limitations of using IT is its Generalizability as health care experts; policymakers; payers, and patients' consider health ICTs, such as electronic health records and computerized provider order entry as critical to transforming the health care industry. (Basit Chaudhry, www.annals.org.)

Issues Concerning Privacy and Confidentiality

Privacy and confidentiality issues too are a primary concern underscoring the reluctance of administrators, physicians, and patients to completely embrace Internet technologies. (Madison, James, 2002).

IT AND HEALTHCARE SERVICES IN NEAR FUTURE: A CRITIQUE

It would be true to state that the health care services have lagged far behind compared to many other industries in using and harnessing the capabilities and competencies of IT in enhancing and improving delivery of healthcare services.

Given the complexity of modern medicine, it has become evident that IT can certainly play a very crucial role in delivering and improving quality of health care services in India and worldwide through re-design and re-engineering of the entire health care delivery system. It also necessitates corresponding favourable changes in various other macro-environmental forces such as technological, socio-cultural, educational, financial, and ecological factors that require in-depth research in near future. One need to critically evaluate the role of IT in improving clinical decision making, information management, communication, costs, and access to care.

We need to overcome barrier of access so that large number of patients and health care service providers can improve safety and quality of healthcare services that are delivered worldwide. It also calls for generating of generic indigenous solutions to minimize the digital divide. It also necessitates reduction in the Costs of documentation and other resources that is associated with use and adoption of IT in delivery of healthcare services.

One shall also critically evaluate transferability of IT solutions in various other health care settings (Eduardo Ortiz and Carolyn M. Clancy, 2003). Although, various IT tools that are being thought in to operation to make healthcare easily accessible to the masses, it is still less understood because of the lack of imparting of the basic e-education. Further, National Information Systems on healthcare are necessary to be maintained by the Governmental at all levels so that the messes have the opportunity to have easier and continuous access of the basic e-health practices. Further, norms and guidelines on the delivery of e-healthcare services need to be provided by the economies worldwide so that delivery of e-healthcare services by each country can take place on a through use of a standardized framework that can also be evaluated from time to time (Debashree Mukherjee, 2009).

But, the important question related with use of IT in delivering of healthcare services is that weather a regulation can help us in bringing about such radical change? The regulatory system can help in implementation of use of IT in delivering of healthcare services to a certain extent, but crucial aspect concerning it shall be that of an its enforcement. In a country like India and other economies, enforcement shall play an important role. This kind of regulation shall encourage application of IT in delivering of healthcare services. Considering the increasing number of medical tourists visiting India, Electronic Health Records (EHR) seems to be necessity for the Indian Healthcare industry. We need to adopt an efficient Electronic Information System to stay connected to the patients post-treatment in order to have an easier access of the patients' medical history in India. The advantage of providing quality care and lowering the costs associated with the induction of IT cannot be ignored. The healthcare services industry therefore must make some conscious efforts to implement this exigent task but gains are also higher. All that is needed now is the willpower and resources to deliver the solution nationwide. The impact of a successful implementation of a globally interoperable EHR will be definitely beneficial.

Doctors as well as patients would be saved from the pain of preserving the paper records and access would become much quicker. Information Technology should synergize the stakeholders towards a common goal 'Quality healthcare for all at affordable price (N. Janardhan Rao and Feroz Zaheer, 2009).

CONCLUDING REMARKS

Good health is universally acknowledged to be of intrinsic value and therefore constitutes an integral element of development. One can be rich but sick enough to not enjoy any opportunities that wealth opens up, and poor health may translate into worsening economic opportunities as well. In fact, one can also be healthy but too poor to pursue valued objectives. Quality is an increasingly important issue to the health care sector. Health care professionals around the world apply all sorts of methods to improve the quality of care delivery. The tools range from the very sophisticated to simpler ones. Nonetheless, the aims of all of these efforts are to increase the benefits to patients. Although, most of these kinds of efforts stem from health care providers' own initiatives, those from Governments and third-party payers certainly play a pivotal role in promoting improvements in quality of care. For better healthcare quality service the use of Information Technology in healthcare, healthcare service research and public private partnership play important role.

IT in healthcare is the better solution as by application of e-Health, knowledge or information pertaining to a quality and sophisticated healthcare system can be made accessible to remote corners of India, where only basic health infrastructure is available. However, before all things, the Government and the private players have to collectively ensure that the costs to incur the benefits of e-Health are within the reach of the majority of India.

Besides, ensuring a more equitable access to healthcare delivery, e-Health in India, among myriad other welfare-oriented aspects, can also ensure knowledge management in healthcare industry and facilitate a more optimal utilization of limited medical facilities.

e-Health's usage must be very prudent, and care should be taken to see that the benefits of ICT revolution helps to transmit the benefits of medical knowledge effectively to the underserved sections of the population of India, without compromising on their privacy, which may be revealed through insensitive dissemination of sensitive electronic health records among other things.

Health service research is on the threshold of relevance to a burning social need. Health services research would really help. It must come from the healthcare leadership to begin to organize their goals into patterns and to interpret for others; researchers have to begin to assemble some tools and clarify utilities of decision science used; the social and psycho-logic sciences can draw out from people the goals they cannot express.

Inequalities in Indian healthcare give rise to paradoxical situation in which we have on one side, super specialty medical centers which cater to the needs of patients requiring specialized and speedy treatment and on the other hand, a very large number of our population remains deprived of basic medical facilities and healthcare. Professionals and stakeholders have to minimize these distressing inequalities in healthcare and make it accessible to one and all.

There is a need to promote health as a human right by launching a primary healthcare movement and using Information Technology, Healthcare service research and Public Private Partnership in Healthcare services.

The science of economics can calculate the costs and benefits of healthcare policies; the clinical sciences can reach back to their traditions to reconsider what patients really want after all, and to speak for the voiceless, the poor, and the future. There exist need for "Value-Driven Health Care Initiative" which called for measuring and publishing information about quality and using this information to improve quality and promote the efficiency of medical care.

The rapidly growing worldwide use of Internet and its role in enhancing quality of healthcare are especially relevant to administrators, physicians, and above all patients. Although, one finds increased use and wider applications of Internet it is not free from the barriers of cost, culture, availability, and accessibility that are likely to stay on even in near future. Healthcare administrators should be encouraged to consider the value of the Internet and related technologies. Clearly, all decisions on Internet use to support quality care must be specific to each healthcare organization. Given the fragmented nature of health care, the large volume of transactions in the system, there exist need to integrate new scientific evidence into practice, and other complex information management activities, the limitations of paper-based information management are intuitively apparent.

While the benefits of health Information Technology are clear in theory, adapting new information systems to health care has proven difficult and rates of use have been limited as most information technology applications have centered on administrative and financial transactions rather than on delivering clinical care services.

Administrators should have the goal to safeguard each patient's privacy and confidential information. The healthcare industry even today, since computers started influencing our society, is standing at the threshold of a world of possibilities thrown up by technologies such as Virtual Reality; Cyber surgery; Micro-robotic Surgery etc.

Then only, 'Health for all' can still be achieved by the year 2020 by making befitting use of Information Technology Revolution that has already begun to happen in delivery of healthcare services in India (Dr. Sunil Shroff, http://www.medindia.net/articles/article1.asp).

It is time we change the existing systems and bring about a refreshing change in the healthcare industry to better the lives of people through better IT solutions (N. Janardhan Rao and Feroz Zaheer, 2009).

REFERENCES

Agarwal, Rakesh, Tyrone Garndison, Christopher Johnson and Jerry Kiernan (2007); "Enabling The 21st Century Health Care Information Technology Revolution"; Communications of the ACM (Association for Computing Machinery); Vol. 50, No. 2; February 2007, pp. 35-42.

Batalden, Paul B and Frank Davidoff (2007); "What is "quality improvement" and how can it transform healthcare?" Qual Safe Health Care (QSHC); 2007, Vol. 16, pp. 2-3.

Biology-Online.org, http://www.biology-online.org/dictionary/Patient_satisfaction.

Brown, Bob (2010); "The New HIPAA Provisions of the Patient Protection and Affordable Care Act"; Journal of Health Care Compliance; July-August 2010; pp. 36-63.

Cannoy, Sherrie Drye and A. F. Salam (2010); "A Framework for Health Care Information Assurance Policy and Compliance"; Communications of the ACM (Association for Computing Machinery); Vol. 53, No. 3, March 2010, pp. 126-131.

Chaudhry, Basit; Jerome Wang; Shinyi Wu; Margaret Maglione; Walter Mojica; Elizabeth Roth; Sally C. Morton; and Paul G. Shekelle; "Systematic Review: Impact of Health Information Technology on Quality, Efficiency, and Costs of Medical Care"; Annals of Internal Medicine; http://www.annals.org/content/ 144/10/742.full, Retrieved on 14/11/2010.

Dow, William H., Dean M. Harris, Zhimei Liu (2006); "Differential Effectiveness in Patient Protection Laws: What Are the Causes? An Example from the Drive-Through Delivery Laws"; Journal of Health Politics, Policy and Law, December, 2006, by Duke University Press Vol. 31, No. 6, pp. 1107-1127.

Eggli, Yves, Patricia Halfon (2003); "A Conceptual Framework for Hospital Quality"; International Journal of Health Care Quality Assurance, MCB UP Limited; Vol., 16/1, 2003, pp. 29-36.

Emerging Market Report: Health in India 2007; Price Waterhouse Coopers (PWC).

Goodson, John D. (2010); "Patient Protection and Affordable Care Act: Promise and Peril for Primary Care"; Perspective, Annals of Internal Medicine; June 2010; Vol. 152, No. 11; pp. 742-744.

Guadagnino, Christopher (2003); "Role of Patient Satisfaction"; Physician's News Digest, Press Ganey Associates' Robert Wolosin, December 2003; http://www.physiciansnews.com/cover /1203.html, Retrieved on 26/12/2009.

Harrington, Scott E. (2010); "U.S. Health-Care Reform: The Patient Protection and Affordable Care Act"; The Journal of Risk and Insurance, 2010, Vol. 77, No. 3, pp. 703-708.

Hellings, Johan *et. al.* (2007); "Challenging Patient Safety culture: survey results"; International Journal of Health Care Quality Assurance; Emerald Group Publishing Limited; Vol. 20 No. 7, 2007, pp. 620-632.

Hill, C. Jeanne, S.J. Garner, and Michael E. Hanna (1989); "Selection Criteria For Professional Service Providers"; The Journal Of Services Marketing; Vol. 3 No. 4 fall, 1989, pp. 61-69.

http://ec.europa.eu/health/ph_systems/patient_safety_en.htm Retrieved on 03/02/2009.

http://en.wikipedia.org/wiki/Healthcare_error, Retrieved on 13/09/2009.

http://infochangeindia.org/200210045930/Health/Backgrounder/Health-Background-Perspective.html, Retrieved on 23/01/2010.

http://linkinghub.elsevier.com/retrieve/pii/S1201971206001251, Retrieved on 03/02/2009.

http://mdrf-eprints.in/264/1/Why_hospital_should_go_in_for_ISO_9002_ certification.pdf, Retrieved on 26/12/2009.

http://medind.nic.in/jac/t00/i3/jact00i3p210.pdf.

http://www.bmj.com/content/316/7144/1558.2.full.

http://www.cgsiindia.org/knowyourrights.html, Retrieved on 30/08/2010.

http://www.ehealthonline.org/articles/article-etails.asp?Title=Healthcare%20in%20India: Problems%20and%20ProspectsandArticalID=1364andType=PERSPECTIVE

http://www.healthfirsteurope.org/index. php? pid=82, Retrieved on 03 02 2009.

http://www.indialaws.info/display.aspx?4273, Retrieved on 08/02/2009.

http://www.ispub.com/journal/the_internet_journal_of_world_health_and_societal_politics/volume_7_number_1_33/article/public-private-partnerships-for-healthcare-delivery-in-india.html.

http://www.ncbi.nlm.nih.gov/pmc/articles/PMC1390481/pdf/annsurg00531-0112.pdf.

http://www.vegsource.com/news/2010/04/the-patient-protection-and-affordable-care-act-a-big-step-forward.html (The Patient Protection and Affordable Care Act: A Big Step Forward).

http://www.who.int/patientsafety/research/en/ Retrieved on 03/02/2009.

Human development in South Asia, 2004 (2005); Published for the Mahbubul Haq Human Development Center; Oxford University press, 2005.

Kathleen L. McFadden, Gregory N. Stock, Charles R. Gowen (2006); "Implementation of Patient Safety Initiatives in US Hospitals"; International Journal of Operations and Production Management, Emerald Group Publishing Limited, Vol. No. 26, No. 3, 2006, pp. 326-347.

Kravitz, Richard (1998); "Patient Satisfaction with Health Care Critical Outcome or Trivial Pursuit?"; Center of Health Services Research in Primary Care, University of California, Davis; J Gen Intern Med. 1998 April; 13(4): pp. 280-282; (http://www.ncbi.nlm.nih.gov/pmc/articles/PMC1496942, Retrieved on 26/12/2009).

Kushwaha, Lt Col AS, Brig SK Aggarwal, Brig LR Sharma,, Maj Gen M Singh, Maj R Nimonkar (2008); "Accidental Outbreak of Non-Bacterial Food Poisoning"; Medical journal Armed Forces India (MJAFI) 2008; Vol. No. 64, pp. 346-349 (http://medind.nic.in /maa/t08/i4/maat08i4p346.pdf).

Lim, Pauy Cheng and Nelson K.H. Tang (2000); "A study of Patients' Expectations and Satisfaction in Singapore Hospitals"; International Journal of Health care Quality Assurance, MCB University Press, Vol. 13/7, pp. 290-299.

Lt Col SL Jadhav, Surg Lt Cdr AK Sinha, Col A Banerjee, Lt Col PS Chawla (2007) "An Outbreak of Food Poisoning in a Military Establishment"; Medical journal Armed Forces India (MJAFI) 2007; Vol. 63, pp. 130-133 (http://medind.nic.in/maa/t07/i2/maat07i2p130.pdf).

Madison, James (2002); "The Role of the Internet in Improving Healthcare Quality" Journal of Healthcare Management; July 2002; http://www.allbusiness.com/management/3604751-1.html.

Maj MS Mustafa, Lt Col S Jain, Col VK Agrawal (2009); "Food Poisoning Outbreak in a Military Establishment"; Medical journal Armed Forces India (MJAFI) 2009; Vol. 65, pp. 240-243 (http://medind.nic.in/maa/t09/i3/maat09i3p240.pdf).

McBride, De Dennis, Jonathan Lindsay and Morgan Wear (2002/2003); "Western state Hospital Consumer and Visitor Satisfaction Survey"; University of Washington School of Medicine Division of Psychiatry and Behavioral Sciences, Survey of The year 2002/2003.

McKinley, Robert K, Terjinder Manku-Scott, Adrian M Hastings, David P French, Richard Baker (1997); "Reliability and validity of a new measure of patient satisfaction with out of hours primary medical care in the united kingdom: development of a patient questionnaire"; http://www.bmj.com/cgi/content /full/314/7075/193?ijkey=9a90838dbd4d711cde5d2215365d 1864 bf76045e.

Medicinenet.com; www.medterms.com /script/main/art.asp?articlekey=39154-36k.

Mohanty, Suchitra (2009); "E-Healthcare Introducing a New Horizon in Health System"; E-Healthcare Modernizing Healthcare; Edited by Debashree Mukherjee, Icfai Books.

Mukherjee, Debashree (2009); "Latest Developments in IT Healthcare"; E-Healthcare Modernizing Healthcare; Edited by Debashree Mukherjee, Icfai Books, The Icfai University Press, Hyderabad, First Edition, 2009, pp. 18.

Orentlicher, David (2008); "Prescription Data Mining and the Protection of Patients' Interests"; journal of law, medicine and ethics; The Effects of Health Information Technology on the Physician-Patient Relationship, Spring 2010; pp. No. 74-84.

Ortiz, Eduardo and Carolyn M. Clancy (2003); "Use of Information Technology to Improve the Quality of Health Care in the United States"; Health Services Research; Vol 38, No. 2, April 2003, pp. xi-xxii.

Papadodima, Stavroula A., Chara A. Spiliopoulou and Emmanouil I. Sakelliadis (2008); "Medical Confidentiality: Legal and Ethical Aspects In Greece"; Bioethics, The

Authors. Journal compilation; 2008; Blackwell Publishing Ltd.; Volume 22 Number 7 2008, pp. 397-405.

Parasuraman, Valarie A. Zeithaml, and Leonard L. Berry (1985); "A Conceptual Model of Service Quality and its Implications for Future Research"; Journal of Marketing, Vol. 49 (Fall 1985). pp. 41-50.

Parasuraman, Valarie A. Zeithaml, and Leonard L. Berry (1988); "SERVQUAL: A Multiple-Item Scale for Measuring Consumer Perceptions of Service Quality"; Journal of Retailing, Vol, 64, No. 1, spring 1988, pp. 12-40.

Parasuraman, Valarie A. Zeithaml, and Leonard L. Berry (1991); "Refinement and Reassessment of the SERVQUAL Scale"; Journal of Retailing, Vol, 67, Spring No. 4, winter 1991, pp. 420-450.

Purnapatre, S.S., *et.al.,* Editors (2004); Journal of Doctors in the Court; Actual CPA cases from Indian Courts; Quarterly Issue III, 2004 Edition, pp. 11-13.

Purnapatre, S.S., *et.al.,* Editors (2004); Journal of Doctors in the Court; Actual CPA cases from Indian Courts; Quarterly Issue IV, 2004 Edition, pp. 18-20.

Purnapatre, S.S., *et.al.,* Editors (2004); Journal of Doctors in the Court; Actual CPA cases from Indian Courts; Quarterly Issue IV, 2004 Edition, pp. 21-22.

Purnapatre, S.S., *et.al.,* Editors (2005); Journal of Doctors in the Court; Actual CPA cases from Indian Courts; Quarterly Issue VIII, 2005 Edition, pp. 22-24.

Purnapatre, S.S., *et.al.,* Editors (2005); Journal of Doctors in the Court; Actual CPA cases from Indian Courts; Quarterly Issue VIII, 2005 Edition, pp. 25-26.

Purnapatre, S.S., *et.al.,* Editors (2007); Journal of Doctors in the Court; Actual CPA cases from Indian Courts; Quarterly Issue XII, 2007 Edition, pp. 21-23.

Purnapatre, S.S., *et.al.,* Editors (2007); Journal of Doctors in the Court; Actual CPA cases from Indian Courts; Quarterly Issue XII, 2007 Edition, pp. 26-28.

Rao, N. Janardhan and Feroz Zaheer (2009); "IT in Healthcare Time for a Change"; E-Healthcare Modernizing Healthcare; Edited by Debashree Mukherjee, Icfai Books, The Icfai University Press, Hyderabad, First Edition, 2009, pp. 15-17.

Rashmi and Vijay kumar B. (2010); "Client Satisfaction in Rural India for Primary Health Care-A Tool for Quality Assessment"; Al Ame en J Med S c i (Al Ameen Charitable Fund Trust, Bangalore; Vol. 3 No.2; (2 010; pp. 1 0 9 -1 1 4.

Samu, K. (2002); "Health /Medical Negligence- 2002"; Compiled Documents, Human Rights Documentation, Indian Social Institute, Lodi Road, New Delhi, India (http://www.isidelhi.org.in/hrnews/HR_THEMATIC_ISSUES/Health/Health-2002.pdf).

Schillie, Sarah F. (2007); "Quality Improvement in Healthcare"; Medscape CME Public Health and Prevention, Perspectives in Prevention from the American College of Preventive Medicine, 09/12/2007; http://cme.medscape.com/viewarticle/561651.

Shroff, Sunil, "Information Technology Revolution in Healthcare"; http://www.medindia.net/articles/article1.asp, Retrieved on 14/11/2010.

Srivastava, Supriya (Retrieved on 08/02/2009); Medical Negligence and the Professional Standard of Care; http://www.indialaws.info/display.aspx?4273, Retrieved on 08/02/2009.

The Free Dictionary; www.thefreedictionary.com /health+care-32k.

Williamson, Sarah (Freelance Consultant Patient Safety and Risk Management SalSafe, UK) (Retrieved on 03/02/2009);" Patient Safety and Risk Management";

Asian Hospital and Healthcare Management; http://www.asianhhm.com/facilities_operations/patient_safety_ risk management .htm, Retrieved on 03/02/2009.

Wisniewski, Mik and hazel Wisniewski (2005); "Measuring Service Quality in a Hospital Colposcopy Clinic"; International Journal of Health care Quality Assurance, Emerald Group Publishing Ltd., Vol. 18 No. 3, 2005, pp. 217-228.

World Alliance for Patient Safety (2006); "WHO Guidelines on Hand Hygiene in Health Care (Advanced Draft): Global Patient Safety Challenge 2005-2006, Clean Care is Safer Care" World Health Organization, April, 2006: http://www.who.int/patientsafety /events /05/HH_en.pdf, Retrieved on 03/02/2009.

www.ficci-heal2008.com/Executive_Summary.ppt.

www.iapindia.org/iapfiles/ASPP/Patient_Satisfaction.ppt, Retrieved on 26/12/2009.

www.who.int (harold-jr.tripod.com/sitebuildercontent/sitebuilderfiles/definitions_of_health. pdf).

www.who.int (harold-jr.tripod.com/sitebuildercontent/sitebuilderfiles/definitions_of_health. pdf).

5 Research Methodology

The author have attempted to outline various areas of the research methodology which includes key terms, scope and coverage, rationale of the research study as well as its, research design, objectives and hypothesis of the research study, sources of information, and sampling decisions.

KEY WORDS OF THE RESEARCH STUDY

Health, Satisfaction, Patient, Hospital, Hospital Services, Health Care, Patient satisfaction.

The key terms are defined as follows:

Health

World Health Organization's has defined health as a state of complete physical, mental and social well-being and not merely the absence of disease or infirmity (www.who.int,).

Satisfaction

Satisfaction is a person's feelings of pleasure or disappointment resulting from comparing a product's perceived performance or outcome in relation to his or her expectations (Philip Kotler and Kevin Lane Keller, 2006).

Patient

There is considerable lack of agreement about the precise meaning of the term patient. It is diversely defined by different experts with different perspectives. To illustrate, Patient is a person who requires medical care; A person receiving medical or dental care or treatment; A person under a physician's care for a particular disease or condition; A person who is waiting for or undergoing medical treatment and care; An individual who is receiving needed professional services that are directed by a licensed practitioner of the healing arts toward maintenance, improvement or protection of health or lessening of illness, disability or pain.

Hospital

As per the Directory of Hospitals in India, 1988, a hospital is described as an institution which is operated for the medical, surgical and/or obstetrical care of in-patient and it is treated as a hospital by the Central/State Government/Local body/Private and licensed by the appropriate authority (R.C. Goyal, 2005).

Hospital Services

Hospital service is a term that has been referred with reference to medical and surgical services and the supporting laboratories, equipment and personnel that make up the medical and surgical mission of a hospital or hospital system.

Health Care

Healthcare has been defined as the prevention, treatment, and management of illness and the preservation of mental and physical well-being through the services offered by the medical and allied health professions.

Patient Satisfaction

The degree to which the individual regards the health care service or product or the manner in which it is delivered by the provider as useful, effective, or beneficial.

SCOPE AND COVERAGE OF THE RESEARCH STUDY

The scope of research study was restricted to selected hospital services as provided to patients by doctors, paramedical staff, and also administrative staff amongst selected hospitals such as Government hospitals (GHs); Trust hospitals (THs); as well as Private hospitals (PHs); located in the Baroda City of the State of Gujarat, India.

RATIONALE OF THE RESEARCH STUDY

An attempt in this research study has been made to put forward findings and results of the research study aimed at measurement of selected patients' overall satisfaction/ dissatisfaction on selected criteria, who were conveniently drawn from selected hospitals of the Government Hospital (GHs), Trust Hospital (THs), and private Hospital (PHs).

RESEARCH DESIGN

The research design followed has been essentially descriptive one in nature considering objectives identified and hypothesis tested in this research study.

OBJECTIVES OF THE RESEARCH STUDY

The research study was undertaken mainly keeping in mind following major objectives.

(*i*) To measure patients' overall satisfaction /dissatisfaction as experienced and reported by selected patients on selected hospital services;

(*ii*) To collect selected patients' opinion on selected criteria on hospital services, and

(*iii*) To evaluate the actual experience of selected patients' on selected hospital services.

HYPOTHESES OF THE RESEARCH STUDY

A list of hypotheses tested has been given as follows:

- The average opinion of selected patients' in the selected type of hospitals (GHs; THs; and PHs), on selected criteria used to measure selected patients' responses for the selection of a given type of hospital (GHs; THs; and PHs), is equal.
- The average opinion of selected patients' in the selected type of hospitals (GHs; THs; and PHs), on selected criteria used to measure selected patients' responses, for the various medical; paramedical; and administrative services provided to him/her as well as the environment (physical facilities), and tangible facilities, of the given type of hospital (GHs; THs; and PHs), is equal.
- The average opinion of selected patients' in the selected type of hospitals (GHs; THs; and PHs), on selected criteria used to measure selected patients' responses for the reliability of services; responsiveness of service providers; assurance from hospital services; empathy experienced by from hospital services; dignity maintained by service providers, and accessibility and affordability of hospital services, of a given type of hospital (GHs; THs; and PHs), is equal.
- The overall response of the patients in the selected type of hospitals, with respect to their overall satisfaction with regard to medical treatment, nursing staff services, administrative staff, and environment facilities, on selected criteria, is equal.
- Selected patients' overall experience in the selected type of hospital, on the selected criteria, is equal.
- The average opinion of selected patients, in the selected type of hospitals, on selected criteria, with respect to their post purchase behaviour, is equal.
- Mean of patients' view about selected type of hospitals is equal in terms of decision regarding selection of hospital; medical, paramedical, and administrative services; as well as environment (physical facilities) of hospitals; and tangible facilities of hospitals.
- Mean of patients' response about selected category of hospitals is equal in terms of reliability criteria; responsiveness criteria; assurance criteria; empathy criteria; dignity criteria, and accessibility and affordability of hospital services.

SOURCES OF INFORMATION and DATA

The researcher has made possible efforts in order to collect available information from various secondary sources that have been outlined in brief as follows:

Secondary Data

The researcher has collected Secondary data mainly from various sources, such as, Business Newspapers viz., The Economic Times, *The Times of India*, and *Express Healthcare* etc. The authors have referred various magazines viz., *Economic Political Weekly, Gujarat Health line*. Research Journals that were reviewed by the researcher viz., *Vikalpa the Journal for Decision Makers*; *Psychiatric Services*; International Jour*nal of Healthcare Quality Assurance*; *Journal of the Academy of Hospital Administration*; *Journal of Child and Family Studies*; *Managing Service Quality*; *Journal of Healthcare Marketing*; *Australian and New Zealand Journal of Psychiatry; Psycho-Oncology*;

Journal of Nursing Care Quality; International Journal for Quality in Healthcare; Journal of Clinical Psychology; Journal of Retailing; Journal of Marketing; Health Manpower Management; Journal of Management Development; Journal of Management in Medicine; Journal of Economic and Social Research; Journal of Ecotourism; Journal of Managerial Issue. The researchers research has studied few Reports viz., Human Development in South Asia by Mahbubul Haq Human Development Center; Gujarat *Human Development Report*; *Human Development Report*; *World Health Statistics; The World Health Report*; Government Publications such as: *National Health Policy*; *Report of the National Commission on Macroeconomics and Health*; *The Economic Survey*; *Annual Report of Health* and *Family Welfare*, etc. The researchers have also used Internet and few of the search engines to collect data and information on this study.

Primary data

The primary data were collected by the authors, during September to December 2007, from the total number of 519 patients who were hospitalized and had availed hospital services from amongst selected government hospitals, trust hospitals and Private Hospitals located in the city of Baroda in the State of Gujarat. Out of total number of 519 responses 500 responses were finally considered for data analysis and interpretation. The Structured Non-Disguised Questionnaire was also thereafter translated in Gujarati language to help patients to better understand and to respond to it.

It consisted of total number of fifteen questions, apart from questions related to profile of respondents viz., personal aspects on patients' selected background variables viz., types of hospitals from where selected patients had availed hospital services; duration of hospitalisation; type of medical treatment availed by selected patients; availability of supporting medical facilities nearby hospitals; issues related to selection of hospitals by the patients; overall opinion on selected statements on selected criteria of hospitals pertaining to actual experience as reported by selected patients; and suggestions to improve hospital services.

SCALE DEVELOPMENT FOR MEASUREMENT OF PATIENTS' SATISFACTION

A brief outline of literature on methodological issues and scale development with regard to patients' satisfaction survey has been given as follows:

Clara Martinez Fuentes (1999) had developed a methodological analysis for the use of the SERVQUAL measure scale in the Spanish public health sector to focus on the analysis of the quality of the service given by public hospitals, on one hand, and on the dimensions of this service, which were appreciated by customers, on the other hand. The conceptual basis of this study centered on the quality of service in public hospitals and measured satisfaction by focusing on structure, process and result. In the literature on service quality, two models have emerged and the first model was posited by Gronroos (1982) known as the Image Model which advocated that perceived total quality will depend basically on two variables that is, what the customer already expects of the service; and the manner in which this service has been performed in its technical and functional aspects. The second model, known as the Gap Model was developed by Parasuraman *et al.* (1985), also from the idea that the quality of a service depends on experience and perception and it presented five kinds of gaps. By synthesizing these two models, quality in a service, in a positive sense, will exist when perceived quality exceeds the expected quality. Cronin and Taylor (1992, 1994) made most criticisms of the SERVQUAL gap model that measurement of quality exclusively by means of perceptions of the result is more valid than by the difference between expectations and perceptions of the result. This scale, which they call SERVPERF, is equivalent to SERVQUAL but excluding the statements about expectations, and the weightings. To carry out the research a questionnaire defined based on the SERVQUAL was administered on 170 patients in the city of Valencia, and findings were presented in to three important measures aimed at measuring service quality which included, tangibles, reliability or technical quality and process of performance of the service or functional quality of the process (Clara Martinez Fuentes, 1999).

Reva Berman Brown, Louise Bell (1998) described the research process and the development of the instrument employed in auditing patients' perceptions of quality and it also described the adaptation processes used in order to place the Parasuraman SERVQUAL instrument into the health setting in the UK. The researcher examined the issue of auditing from a new perspective that focused solely on the views of the service user. It was guided by two already-validated research instruments that is, the first model Parasuraman SERVQUAL instrument (Parasuraman *et al.,* 1988), and second model developed by the Heywood- Farmer instrument (Heywood-Farmer and Stuart, 1990), which looked at professional service quality, and was originally used to audit the quality of service provided by General Practitioner (GPs) (Reva Berman Brown, Louise Bell, 1998).

Emilie Roberts *et al.,* (1994) developed a method of assessing the quality of health care to highlight the areas of greatest concern to patients designed to examine patients' experience with care starting with the concerns expressed by patients and using it as a basis for evaluating and ranking different aspects of the service which needed improvement. The paired comparison technique was successfully used and validated in a variety of commercial and business environments. The aim of this case study was to assess the feasibility of the paired comparison technique in rating patients' satisfaction with aspects of their care in a hospital. The results of the study indicated that the paired comparison technique, at least in its present form, cannot be recommended as a tool to aid understanding of patients' satisfaction. The findings from this case study also indicated that there were drawbacks in using the paired comparison technique to assess service quality in a highly specialized hospital setting dealing with an acute and potentially life threatening condition (Emilie Roberts *et al.,* 1994).

Thomas Meehan *et al.* (2002) conducted a research study to report on the development, testing and psychometric properties of a brief consumer satisfaction measure for use with psychiatric inpatients. Focus group discussions with inpatients were used to develop a pool of items related to satisfaction with hospital stay. Instrument development employed three separate but related phases. In Phase I, focus group discussions with 66 inpatients at three acute care units with the aim to generate a pool of items related to patients' satisfaction with hospital stay was conducted. In Phase II, a second sample of 72 patients from the same three acute units was asked to rate the 51 items in terms of importance in contributing to their satisfaction. During Phase III, the draft questionnaire was administered to 494 consecutive inpatients who were approaching discharge in acute and rehabilitation facilities, and 356 completed surveys were returned. Factor analysis yielded three factors comprising a staff-patients alliance; doctor/treatment issue, and an environmental component. The Inpatients' Evaluation of Service Questionnaire addresses many of the shortcomings of existing satisfaction measures. It was developed through extensive consumer involvement, it is simply worded, easy to score and appears to perform well with acute and rehabilitation inpatients (Thomas Meehan *et al.,* 2002).

Reva Berman Brown, Louise Bell, (2005) conducted study aimed to describe the research process, and the development of the instrument now employed in auditing patients' perceptions of quality improvement in a community health care trust in a coastal town in Essex, England. The questionnaire was administered in two ways that is, by means of face-to-face meetings in the respondents' homes, and through the mail and 123 patients out of the sample of 210 participated in the research. The instrument had measured health outcomes in terms of quality improvement from the users' perspective, and had also highlighted gaps between what the service offers in terms of quality and users' perceptions of what is delivered. Factor analysis was carried out and three factors or areas of importance emerged which includes, physical surroundings; treatment by staff; and understanding of treatment. It offered that patient-centered quality improvement audit should be undertaken regularly so that both non-clinical managers and health care professionals can establish whether or not they are providing services that are patient-friendly and effective from the user's viewpoint or not (Reva Berman Brown, Louise Bell, 2005).

Zack Z. Cernovsky *et al.,* (1997) made efforts to explore the relationship of treatment satisfaction to another personality questionnaire, the Zuckerman's Sensation Seeking Scales. Satisfaction of 119 addicts with an addiction treatment program was measured by an 11 item satisfaction scale. The Sensation Seeking scales included 40 items. In the questionnaire, the patients' were asked to rate their satisfaction with psychotherapeutic interventions, psychological tests, medical laboratory tests, with hospital rules, and hospital meals and snack foods. Results indicated overall high level of satisfaction with the programme (Zack Z. Cernovsky *et al.,* 1997).

Ingemar Eckerlund *et al.,* (1997) presented a pilot study at three departments of ophthalmology in Sweden and the data were collected via questionnaire involving a new method which met reasonable demands for validity and reliability, and was explicitly change-oriented. A method called quality, satisfaction, and performance (QSP) was used to measure quality and to focus on quality improvement and consisted of three integrated components. One component measured the degree of patients' satisfaction, and different aspects thereof, among different patients groups. Second component measured patients'-perceived quality levels of various quality dimensions. Finally, the model also contained a component on goals, with questions directed at what patients' satisfaction should ultimately lead to, viz., increased trust, increased likelihood for positive recommendations, etc. The questionnaire addressed eight different quality dimensions viz., accessibility; hospitality; service commitment; environment; information advice,; staff knowledge; participation influence, and continuity freedom of choice. What distinguishes this model from most others used in healthcare is that it not only it measured the degree of satisfaction but also the impact that various quality dimensions/ factors had on patients' satisfaction. Another advantage with the QSP method is the linkage to the goal side, which secured validity in the model. This aspect of the model required the user to specify organizational goals. A department obviously cannot aim only towards satisfying patients. Other longer-term goals are also important to an organization's future (Ingemar Eckerlund *et al.,* 1997).

Ulf Goran Ahlfors *et al.,* (2001) focused on development and clinical evaluation of a brief consumer satisfaction rating scale (UKU-ConSat). UKU (Udvalg for Kliniske Undersøgelser that is Committee for Clinical Trials), a working group within the Scandinavian Society for Psychopharmacology (SSP), had designed a brief consumer satisfaction rating scale, the UKU-ConSat. A field trial of UKU-ConSat took place at three clinical study sites (Sites A, B, and C) during 1994-1996 in Finland and Sweden. The UKU-ConSat rating scale consisted of eight items in two groups viz., structure and process and outcome, and these items included, availability of care covering access to treatment as well as waiting list issues; environment of the clinic; availability and access to various treatment modalities and specialists; information regarding state of health, drug treatment, attitude to psychosocial measures, patients' assessment of the outcome, patients' opinion of his her general well-being after the treatment. Its results showed that it could be applied to several relevant patient categories viz., psychotic; affective; neurotic, organic and alcohol and substance abuse disorders. According to both patients and staff the rating scale promises to become useful both for research and for improvement of routine psychiatric services. The construction of the scale permitted both an overall assessment of patients' satisfaction and a more detailed assessment of specific ingredients of the structure and process of care and the outcome (Ulf Goran Ahlfors *et al.,* 2001).

Ugur Yavas, Natalia Romanova (2005) made efforts partially to address various decidedly critical questions, related to hospitals and conducted study aimed at introduction of a measure to assess the perceived effectiveness of Multi-Hospital organizations (MOs). The data were collected by mailing survey questionnaire were to top managers of non-profit hospitals based on list compiled by American Hospital Association and usable responses were obtained from 189 hospitals (Ugur Yavas, Natalia Romanova, 2005).

Susan Michie, Che Rosebert (1994) described the stages involved in developing a satisfaction survey for out-patients attending a London teaching hospital, using existing expertise within the organization. The Service Development manager approached the Health Psychologist for scientific and technical advice and a psychology student provided the practical work of carrying out the pilot study. Of the 377 patients approached, 330 agreed to complete the questionnaire. Its results showed that overall, greatest dissatisfaction was expressed about the length of time spent waiting to see a doctor, one of the clinical support services and the facilities such as car parking and refreshments. Greatest satisfaction was expressed for the personal consideration shown by doctors, nurses and other clinic staff, the manner of being received at the hospital clinic and reception, and the contact with the hospital when booking the appointment (Susan Michie, Che Rosebert, 1994).

Jessie L. Tucker, Sheila R. Adams (2001) investigated the apparent methodological shortcomings of the literature that considered patients' evaluations of their care. The multidimensional aspects of satisfaction suggested by previous studies to predict satisfaction were access, communication, and outcomes. As suggested by other previous studies, the independent variables used to predict quality were caring, empathy, reliability, and responsiveness. Its results suggested that just two distinct dimensions of the care experience were found to capture 74 per cent of the variance in satisfaction-quality, with patients' socio-demographic differences accounting for only one per cent. These two distinct dimensions include provider performance aspects and access (Jessie L. Tucker, Sheila R. Adams, 2001).

Binshan Lin, Eileen Kelly (1995) focused on how to reassert the importance of studying patients satisfaction surveys and to clarify and illuminate some of the methodological problems. Attention was focused on four aspects of the problems which were of general interest to those conducting surveys, namely the sampling frames, quality of survey data and instrument, non-response problems, and reporting of results and the interpretation. This article provided several implications for researchers (Binshan Lin, Eileen Kelly, 1995).

Steven A, Taylor and J, Joseph Cronin Jr., (1994) attempted to clarify and extend the conceptualization and measurement of consumer satisfaction and service quality in health services. Although, the two constructs SERVQUAL and SERVPERF served as cornerstones in the design and implementation of health care marketing strategies, a literature review suggested that satisfaction and service quality are difficult to distinguish, both conceptually and operationally, in health care settings. The findings from two studies conducted by the authors to distinguish the nature of these two important constructs within a health care marketing context revealed that a non-recursive relationship between service quality and patients' satisfaction. Health services marketers should be careful about trying to apply broad theories and scales-such as SERVQUAL and SERVPERF-used in other service settings because they may translate poorly to health care. (Steven A, Taylor and J, Joseph Cronin Jr., 1994).

Eileen Evason, Dorothy Whittington, (1997) presented some of the results of a focus group exercise conducted in July 1993 with ten groups of people who had been in-patients, or who had children who had been in-patients, at a complex of hospital facilities in Northern Ireland. It was found that the focus group methodology was successful in amplifying feedback previously gleaned from surveys. It also highlighted patients' tolerance of shortcomings and their appreciation of staff providing high quality care while under pressure. It was concluded that patients regarded the National Health Service as deteriorating generally (Eileen Evason, Dorothy Whittington, 1997).

A. Gigantesco, P Morosini, A. Bazzoni, (2003) conducted study with an objective to validate a brief self-completed questionnaire for routinely assessing patients' opinions on the quality of care in inpatients' psychiatric wards (Rome Opinion Questionnaire for Psychiatric Wards). It concluded that the questionnaire seemed to be adequate for evaluating patients' opinions on care in inpatient psychiatric wards. Because of its user-friendliness, it may be particularly suitable for routine use (A. Gigantesco, P Morosini, A. Bazzoni, 2003).

Hana Kasalova (1995) demonstrated that the apparent generosity error that is, subjectivity in rating service quality may be compensated for by a mathematical process that is, rectification, which is derived from the assessment of every respondent's general scale. A questionnaire was designed after many preliminary interviews, tested in a preliminary survey (101 respondents out of 150 addresses) and eventually sent to 1,110 ex-patients of a Prague hospital University Hospital Královské Vinohrady, out of which 545 patients have responded. In all cases (545 persons) the patients' satisfaction was found to be very high in spite of the fact that the originally used five-point scale was changed to a nine-point one in order to give respondents the chance to measure more accurately the quality of individual services. However, the generosity error intervened again: even with detailed instructions that five points would mean "good, fair quality", most questions again elicited an "excellent" (nine points) as answers. (Hana Kasalova, 1995).

While designing the study questionnaire various dimensions, variables and sub variables (statements or questions), as per details provided in Table 5.1 and 5.2, were selected from which Structured Non-Disguised questionnaire developed with the help of some of the earlier research studies with necessary alterations.

Table 5.1: List of References of Selected Criteria Used in Design of Structured Questionnaire for Measurement of Patients' Actual Experience, Overall Satisfaction/Dissatisfaction on Selected Hospital Services

Name of Author	Time Period and Place of Research Study Conducted	No. of Criteria used in the questio-nnaire	Total No. of Criteria
Demographic Criteria			
Prof.(Dr.) Parimal H. Vyas and Shri P.D.Thakkar (2005).	2002-20003 (Baroda)	03	* **07**
De Dennis McBride, Jonathan Lindsay, Morgan Wear, Genevieve Smith, and Terri Villanueva (2002/2003).	2002-2003 (Washington)	02	
Prof. R.D. Sharma and Hardeep Chahal (1999).	April 1996 to March 1997 (Jammu City)	01	
General information about Hospital, Reasons for selection of Hospital, Type of Medical treatment undergone and Availability of Medical Facilities within and Nearby Hospital (Q-1 to Q-7).			
Prof.(Dr.) Parimal H. Vyas and Shri P.D. Thakkar (2005).	2002-20003 (Baroda)	17	**27**
De Dennis McBride, Jonathan Lindsay, Morgan Wear, Genevieve Smith, and Terri Villanueva (2002/2003)..	2002-2003 (Washington)	01	
Prof. R.D. Sharma and Hardeep Chahal (1999).	April 1996 to March 1997 (Jammu City)	07	
Puay Cheng Lim and Nelson K.H. Tang (2000).	October 1998 (Singapore)	01	
Rob Baltussen and Yazoume Ye (2005).	{Burkina Faso (Rural Area), Nouna District situated at the Border of the Sahel Region in West Africa}	01	
Criteria for Measuring Patients' Actual Experience with Hospital service (Q-8 01 to 64)			
Naceur Jabnoun and Mohammed Chaker (2003).	(2002) Abu Dhabi, Sharjah and Dubai in UAE.	07	* **64**
Mik Wisniewski and Hazel Wisniewski (2005).	October 2000 to August 2001. (Scotland)	07	
Anne E. Tomes and Stephen Chee Peng Ng (2000).	(1993) NHS Trust Hospital, U.K.	09	

...(Contd.)

...(Contd.)

Prof.(Dr.) Parimal H. Vyas and Shri P.D. Thakkar (2005).	2002-2003 (Baroda)	01	
Prof. R.D. Sharma and Hardeep Chahal (1999).	April 1996 to March 1997 (Jammu City)	24	
Rob Baltussen and Yazoume Ye (2005).	Burkina Faso (Rural Area) situated at the Border of the Sahel Region in West Africa, Nouna District.	09	
De Dennis McBride, Jonathan Lindsay, Morgan Wear, Genevieve Smith, and Terri Villanueva (2002/2003).	2002-03 (Washington)	03	
Four criteria added based on suggestion during pilot study	Result of Pilot Study	04	
Overall Satisfaction Experienced by Patients from Overall Hospital Services (Q-9 to Q-14)			
Prof. R.D. Sharma and Hardeep Chahal (1999).	April 1996 to March 1997 (Jammu City)	04	* **17**
Prof.(Dr.) Parimal H. Vyas and Shri P.D. Thakkar (2005).	2002-2003 (Baroda)	01	
De Dennis McBride, Jonathan Lindsay, Morgan Wear, Genevieve Smith, and Terri Villanueva (20022003).	2002-03 (Washington)	11	
One question (No. 14) added on the basis of suggestions received during (Pilot Study) based on discussion about Research Instrument that is, questionnaire, with doctors.		01	

Prof.(Dr.) Parimal H. Vyas and Shri P.D. Thakkar (2005); "Market Performance Analysis and Measurement of Patients' Satisfaction in Healthcare Services"; "The Indian Journal of Commerce", Vol.58, No.1, January-March, 2005, PP.150-161. Quarterly Publication of the Indian Commerce Association, School of Management Studies, IGNOU, New Delhi.

De Dennis McBride, Jonathan Lindsay, Morgan Wear, Genevieve Smith, and Terri Villanueva (2002/2003); "Western state hospital Consumer and Visitor Satisfaction Survey 2002/2003"; Survey report Published by The Washington Institute-For Mental Illness Research and Training-western Branch, 2003 (www.wimirt.washington.edu).

Prof. R.D. Sharma and Hardeep Chahal (1999); "A Study of Patients' Satisfaction of Private Health Care facilities"; "Vikalpa The Journal for Decision Makers", Vol, 24 No. 4, October- December 1999, PP. 69-76. Indian Institute of Management, Ahmedabad, India.

Puay Cheng Lim and Nelson K.H. Tang (2000); "A Study of Patients' Expectations and Satisfaction in Singapore Hospitals"; "International Journal of Health Care Quality Assurance", Vol. 13, No. 7, 2000, PP. 290-299. MCB University Press.

...(Contd.).

...(Contd.).

Rob Baltussen and Yazoume Ye (2005); "Quality of Care of Modern Health Services as perceived by Users and Non-users in Burkina Faso"; "International Journal for Quality in Health care, Vol. 18, No. 01, 2005, pp. 30-34. Advance Access Publication. (Published by Oxford University Press on Behalf of International society for Quality Health Care).

Naceur Jabnoun and Mohammed Chaker (2003); "Comparing the Quality of Private and Public Hospitals"; "Managing Service Quality", Vol. 13 No. 4, 2003, pp. 209-299. MCB University Press .

Mik Wisniewski and Hazel Wisniewski (2005); "Measuring Service Quality in a Hospital Colposcopy Clinic"; "International Journal of Health Care Quality Assurance", Vol. 18, No.3, 2005, pp. 217-228. Emerald Group Publishing Limited.

Anne E. Tomes and Stephen Chee Peng Ng (2000); "Service Quality in Hospital care: the Development of an in-patient Questionnaire"; "International Journal of Health Care Quality Assurance", Vol. 8, No. 3, 2000, pp. 25-33. MCB University Press.

* Adapted as per Objectives of the Study

Table 5.2: Summary of Factors and Major Criteria Used in Study (Please Refer Question Number 08)

Factors Used in study	Major Criteria Used in The Study				
	Medical Services	Paramedical Services	Administrative Services	Environment (Physical Facilities)	Total
	Number of Criteria used in Study				
Tangibility	01	–	–	14	15
Reliability	03	02	–	–	05
Responsiveness	02	04	07	01	14
Assurance	03	04	–	–	07
Empathy	06	01	03	–	10
Accessibility and Affordability	01	–	–	04	05
Dignity	01	04	03	–	08
Total	17	15	13	19	64

Source: Parsuraman *et al.,* 1988 ; Puay Cheng Lim et al. 2000; and Anne E. Tornes *et al.,* 1995

In all, total seven number of statements were used for collection of data on Demographic information about selected patients (Prof. (Dr.) Parimal H. Vyas and P.D. Thakkar 2005; De Dennis McBride *et al.,* 2002/2003, and Prof. R.D. Sharma and Hardeep Chahal 1999).

Total numbers of 27 statements were used for collection of general information such as, hospital in which treatment was given to patients; reasons for selection of the hospital; type of medical treatment received and availability of medical treatment within and nearby hospital. (Prof. (Dr.) Parimal Vyas *et al.,* 2005; De Dennis McBride *et al.,*

2002/2003; Prof. R.D. Sharma *et al.,* 999; Puay cheng Lim and H.K.G. Tang 2000; and Rob Baltussen *et al.,* 2005).

Sixty four statements were selected for measuring patients' actual experience with regard to hospital services. (Naceur Jabnoun 2003; Prof. (Dr.) Parimal Vyas and Thakkar 2005; and Prof. R.D. Sharma and Hardeep Chahal 1999).

All the above mentioned 64 statements were grouped in to four major variables such as, behaviour of doctors; behaviour of medical assistant; quality of administrative service and physical environment (Parsuraman *et al.,* 1988; Puay Cheng Lim *et al.,* 2000; 27 and Anne E. Tornes *et al.,* 1995).

Total number of 17 statements were put to use for measuring overall satisfaction/dissatisfaction as experienced by selected patients from overall hospital services (Prof. (Dr.) Parimal Vyas *et al.,* 2005; Prof. R.D. Sharma *et al.,* 1999; and Dennis McBride *et al.,* 2003).

A five point Likert scale was used defined as 01 = Least Important; and 5 = Most Important (Question number 07); 01 = Strongly Disagree; and 5 = Strongly Agree (Question number 08, 12, 13 and 14) and 1 represents Highly Dissatisfied and 5 represents Highly Satisfied (Question number 10).

RELIABILITY AND VALIDITY OF RESEARCH INSTRUMENT USED FOR MEASUREMENT OF PATIENTS' SATISFACTION/DISSATISFACTION

RELIABILITY

Reliability refers to the extent to which a scale produces consistent results if repeated measurements are made on the characteristics. One of the popular approach for assessing reliability includes the Internal Consistency Reliability method which is used to assess the reliability of a summated scale where several items are summed to form a total score. The simplest measure of internal consistency is split-half-reliability. A popular approach of overcoming this problem is to use the Coefficient Alpha or Cronbach's Alpha, which is the average of all possible split-half coefficients resulting from different ways of splitting the scale items. This coefficient varies from 0 to 1, and average of 0.6 or less generally indicates unsatisfactory internal consistency reliability.

In our study, reliability tests were run to determine how strongly the attitudes were related to each other and to the composite score. All dimensions of the questionnaire related with measuring patient satisfaction were tested and the Cronbach's alpha ranged from 0.671 to 0.894 which really shows Internal reliability of the scale. The reliability of a scale as measured by coefficient alpha reflects the degree of cohesiveness among the scale items (Naresh K. Malhotra, 2007; Jum C. Nunnally, 1981, and Puay Cheng Lim and Nelson K. H. Tang, 2000).

The summary of Cronbach's Alpha score for all 14 groups of criteria is given in Table 4.3.

Table 5.3: Summary of Indicators and Reliability Alpha Score

Sl. No.	Grouped Indicator Items	Cronbach Reliability Alpha Coefficient
01	Patients' Perceptions for Doctors' Performance	**0.864**
02	Patients' Perceptions for Paramedical Staff Performance	**0. 883**
03	Patients' Perceptions for Administrative Staff Performance	**0. 894**
04	Patients' Perceptions for Environment (Physical Facilities) of Hospital Staff Performance	**0. 695**
05	Patients' Perceptions of hospital service against Tangible Criteria	**0. 836**
06	Patients' Perceptions of hospital service against Reliability Criteria	**0. 714**
07	Patients' Perceptions of hospital service against Responsiveness Criteria	**0. 839**
08	Patients' Perceptions of hospital service against Assurance Criteria	**0. 720**
09	Patients' Perceptions of hospital service against Empathy Criteria	**0. 779**
10	Patients' Perceptions of hospital service against Dignity Criteria	**0. 795**
11	Patients' Perceptions of hospital service against Accessibility/Affordability Criteria	**0. 716**
12	Patients' Perceptions of hospital service against Overall Responses against Selected Criteria	**0. 671**
13	Patients' Perceptions of hospital service against Best Thing of the Hospital against Selected criteria	**0. 770**
14	Patients' Perceptions of hospital service against Worst Thing of the Hospital against Selected criteria	**0. 725**

VALIDITY

In our empirical research study while undertaking the pilot study the structured questionnaire was given to people, who were related with medical discipline, for their valuable feedback and opinion on design of questionnaire to be used for collection of primary data on measurement of patients' satisfaction. It had total number of 14 questions (Total 110 criteria), which consists of Demographic variables (06 criteria); General variables of hospital information relating to patients' medical treatment (27 criteria grouped under Q. No. 01 to Q. No. 07); variables related to measurement of patient satisfaction (60 criteria under Q. No. 08), and overall satisfaction (17 criteria under Q.No. 09 to Q. No. 14) (Naresh K. Malhotra, 2007; R.D. Sharma and Hardeep Chahal, 1999; Parasuraman *et. al.,* 1991).

Table 5.4: Comparison of Mean Scores of Extent of Patients' Satisfaction/Dissatisfaction

Patients' Satisfaction with respect to		Patients' Satisfaction with respect to		Patients' Satisfaction with respect to		Patients' Satisfaction with respect to	
Rating Scale 1 (Strongly Agree) to 5 (Strongly Disagree)							
(Q-8 -1 to 64)	Mean Score (Rank)	(Q-9 -1 to 4)	Mean Score (Rank)	(Q-12 -1 to 4)	Mean Score (Rank)	(Q-13 -1 to 4)	Mean Score (Rank)
Medical Services	4.31 (1)	Overall Satisfaction with Medical treatment	4.63 (1)	Best Service is Medical Treatment in Hospital	4.62 (1)	Worst Service is Medical Treatment in Hospital	1.38 (1)
Paramedical Services	4.03 (3)	Overall Satisfaction with Nursing	4.23 (3)	Best Service is Nursing Staff Services	4.19 (3)	Worst Service is Nursing Staff Services	1.78 (3)
		Staff		in Hospital		in Hospital	
		services					
Administrative Services	3.86 (4)	Overall Satisfaction with Administrative Staff	4.02 (4)	Best Service is Administrative Staff Services in Hospital	4.00 (4)	Worst Service is Administrative Staff Services in Hospital	1.94 (4)
Environment (Physical Facilities) of Hospital	4.21 (2)	Overall Satisfaction with Environment	4.37	Best Service is Environment in Hospital	4.33 (2)	Worst Service is Environment in Hospital	1.69 (2)
Overall Average	**4.10**		**4.31**		**4.29**		**1.70**

The authors have measured convergent validity by comparing mean scores of scale with other measures of the same construct. It becomes clear from above given table number 4.4, that the means of same construct were measured and less variation was observed in the given question categories and average satisfaction score was found to be as similar. Majority of the respondents were found placed between Strongly Agree to Agree.

If we give rank to average score of the patients' satisfaction, it reveals the uniform preference in case of all the four categories of questions group, that is, medical services; environment (physical facilities); paramedical services; administrative services. It supports the strength of linkage between the three statements thus fulfils the condition of convergent validity.

A BRIEF ABOUT SAMPLING DECISIONS

In view of available time and other constraints being faced by the researcher, it was decided to conduct a sample survey, to measure selected patients' overall satisfaction/

dissatisfaction based on evaluation of his/her own actual experience, using structured non-disguised questionnaire which was put to use based on a pilot study conducted in the city of Baroda.

A representative sampling unit was defined as a patient who was actually hospitalized, amongst any of the Government Hospital, Trust Hospital and Private Hospital, and had availed hospital services located in the Baroda. The non-probability sampling approach was put to use based on convenience sampling method supported with Personal interviews for drawing of sampling units.

The hospitals were selected based on sources such as, Directory of Medical College of Baroda as well as available information from Baroda Municipal Corporation and also through various other sources such as Yellow Pages of the Telephone Directory, and a Guide to Medical Services in Baroda City.

DESIGNING OF STRUCTURED NON-DISGUISED QUESTIONNAIRE

The pilot study questionnaire consisted of total 14 number of questions (Total 110 criteria), subdivided in to Demographic Variables (06 criteria); General Variables of Hospital Information in which patient had availed medical treatment (27 criteria grouped under Q.-1 to Q.-7); It also included variables related to measurement of patients' satisfaction/dissatisfaction (60 criteria under Q.-8), and variables related to measurement of patients' overall satisfaction/dissatisfaction (17 criteria under Q.-9 to Q.-14). The pilot study questionnaires were provided to 19 persons, who were related with medical discipline, for their valuable feedback suggestions and opinion to facilitate on capability of questionnaire instrument to collection of the data and information for measuring patients' satisfaction/dissatisfaction.

The composition of such 19 persons include 02 Doctors (MBBS), 03 Doctors (MD-Medicine), 01 Doctor (MD-Anesthesia), 01 Doctor (MD-Pathology), 02 Doctors (MS-General Surgeon), 01 Doctor (MS-Orthopedic), 01 Doctor (MS-ENT), 01 Doctor (BDS), 01 Doctor (DHMS), 01 Doctor (Gynecologists), 01 Doctor (Physiotherapists), 01 Nurse (Matron), 02 Administrator of Hospital and 01 Patient}.

Based on feedback/opinion on received from the doctors and other persons, the questionnaire is rephrased few questions and an additional 04 criteria (No. 17, 28, 33, 60 under Q.-08) and 01 question (Q.-14) were added. So the questionnaire after pilot study (Opinion of Doctors) has 15 questions consists of total 116 criteria.

EXPLANATORY NOTES

The researcher has used five scale questions (Question Nos. 07 to 08, 09, 12 and 13) to know the patients' reasons for selection of hospital as well as to measure patients' responses on their overall experiences with regard to doctors, paramedical staff, administrative staff behaviour and environment (physical facilities). The five scale response categories defined as: Least Important to Most Important which were clubbed together, as important and unimportant, to evaluate rated importance (Q. No. 07) as first three response categories: Least Important, Unimportant and somewhat important provided negative importance whereas remaining two response categories: Important and Most Important revealed positive importance of the Internet users.

It was followed consistently to measure patients' overall experiences on selected criteria by using five scales defined as: Strongly Agree to Strongly Disagree which were clubbed together, as agree and disagree, to evaluate rated importance (Q. No. 08, 12, and 13) wherein first three response categories provided Negative, and remaining two revealed response categories provided Positive responses.

Further, another five scale response category is used defined as: Highly Dissatisfied to Highly Satisfied which were clubbed together, as Satisfied and Dissatisfied, to evaluate rated importance (Q. No. 09) wherein first three response categories provided Negative, and remaining two revealed response categories provided Positive responses. Similarly the responses were combined as Important-Unimportant (Q. No. 7) or Agree-Disagree (Q. No. 08, 12 and 13) or Satisfied-Dissatisfied (Q. No. 09). The Chi-square at 5 Per cent level of Significance has been applied to test hypotheses relating to measurement of patients' overall experience with regard to services provided to medical, paramedical, and administrative staff environment (physical facilities).

LIMITATIONS OF THE RESEARCH STUDY

- The present study is limited to the study of measuring patients' satisfaction on the hospital services in case of selected type of the located hospitals in Baroda city only.
- The present study is restricted to patients selected as the sample for the purpose of collecting required information.
- Willingness of the hospitals to allow the researcher to meet the patients for data collection and willingness of patients for providing information has influenced the results.
- Due to constraints of time, the study could not be broad based and was confined to only Baroda city.
- The limitation of threat of the secondary data sources employed to the research project does prevail.
- The patients' responses are subject to their own personal biases, as patients have a complex set of important beliefs that cannot be captured through questionnaire or research instrument used.
- In present study, though data were collected from selected three types of hospitals (GHs, THs and PHs), the researcher has made an overall analysis based on all collected data, rather than analyzing each type of hospitals separately.
- Though, results of the study obtained from selected samples are fairly meaningful, due care should be exercised in extending its conclusions to other healthcare service providers.
- The quantitative method used is valuable in establishing relationships between variables, but is considered weak in identifying the reasons for those relationships when an attempt is made to do so.

- The generalizability of the study findings are limited by the small sample size.
- Errors due to question misinterpretation or misunderstanding or patients' inattention might or might not have affected results systematically.

REFERENCES

Ahlfors, Ulf Goran, Tommy Lewander, Eva Lindstrom, Ulrik Fredrik Malt, Henrik Lublin, Ulf Malm (2001); "Assessment of Patients' Satisfaction With Psychiatric Care"; Nord J Psychiatry, Taylor and Francis, Vol 55, Suppl 44, 2001, pp. 71-90.

Baltussen, Rob and Yazoume Ye (2005); "Quality of Care of Modern Health Services as perceived by Users and Non-users in Burkina Faso"; "International Journal for Quality in Health care, Vol. 18, No. 01, 2005, pp. 30-30. Advance Access Publication. (Published by Oxford University Press on Behalf of International society for Quality Health Care).

Biology-Online.org, http://www.biology-online.org/dictionary/Patient_satisfaction.

Brown, Reva Berman, Louise Bell (1998); "Patient-Centered Audit: A Users' Quality Model"; Managing Service Quality, MCB University Press, Vol. No. 8, No. 2, 1998, pp. 88 -96.

Brown, Reva Berman, Louise Bell (2005); "Patient-Centered Quality Improvement Audit"; International Journal of Health Care Quality Assurance, Emerald Group Publishing Limited, Vol. 18 No. 2, 2005.

Cernovsky, Zack Z., Richard L. O'Reilly, Maureen Pennington (1997); "Sensation Seeking Scales and Consumer Satisfaction with a Substance Abuse Treatment Program"; Journal of Clinical Psychology, John Wiley and Sons. Inc., Vol. No. 53 (8), 1997, pp. 779-784.

Eckerlund, Ingemar, Bengt Jönsson, Magnus Tambour, Anders H. Westlund (1997); "Change-Oriented Patient Questionnaires-Testing A New Method at Three Departments of Ophthalmology"; International Journal of Health Care Quality Assurance, MCB University Press, Vol. No.10/7, 1997, pp. 254-259.

Evason, Eileen, Dorothy Whittington (1997); "Patients' Perceptions of Quality In A Northern Ireland Hospital Trust: A Focus Group Study"; International Journal of Health Care Quality Assurance, MCB University Press, Vol. No. 10/1, 1997, pp. 7-19.

Fuentes, Clara Martinez (1999); "Measuring Hospital Service Quality: A Methodological Study"; Managing Service Quality, MCB University Press, Vol. No. 9, No. 4, 1999, pp. 230-239.

Goyal, R.C. (2005); "Hospital Administration and Human Resource management"; Prentice Hall of India Private limited, New Delhi, 4th edition, 2005, p. 03.

Jabnoun, Naceur and Mohammed Chaker (2003); "Comparing the Quality of Private and Public Hospitals"; "Managing Service Quality", Vol. 13 No. 4, 2003, pp. 209-299. MCB University Press .

Kasalova, Hana (1995); "Rectification of the Primary Data Obtained by a Patients' Satisfaction Survey"; International Journal of Health care Quality Assurance; MCB University Press Limited; Vol. No. 8, No. 1, pp. 15-17.

Kotler, Philip and Kevin Lane Keller (2005); "Marketing Management"; Prentice Hall of India Private limited, New Delhi, 12th edition, 2005, p. 144.

Lim, Puay Cheng and Nelson K.H. Tang (2000); "A Study of Patients' Expectations and Satisfaction in Singapore Hospitals"; "International Journal of Health Care Quality Assurance", Vol. 13, No. 7, 2000, pp. 290-299. MCB University Press.

Lin, Binshan, Eileen Kelly (1995); "Methodological Issues in Patients' Satisfaction Surveys"; International Journal of Health Care Quality Assurance, MCB University Press Limited, Vol. No. 8 No. 6, 1995, pp. 32-37.

Malhotra, Naresh K. (2007); "Marketing Research An Applied Orientation"; Peearson Prentice Hall;Fiofth Edition, 2007, p. 315.

McBride, De Dennis, Jonathan Lindsay, Morgan Wear, Genevieve Smith, and Terri Villanueva (2002/2003); "Western state hospital Consumer and Visitor Satisfaction Survey 2002/2003"; Survey report Published by The Washington Institute-For Mental Illness Research and Training-western Branch, 2003 (www.wimirt.washington.edu).

Medicinenet.com; www.medterms.com /script/main/art.asp?articlekey=39154-36k.

Meehan, Thomas, Helen Bergen, Terry Stedman (2002); "Monitoring Consumer Satisfaction with Inpatients' Service Delivery: the Inpatients' Evaluation of Service Questionnaire"; Australian and New Zealand Journal of Psychiatry; Vol. No.36, 2002, pp., 807-811.

Michie, Susan, Che Rosebert (1994); "Developing an Out-patients' Satisfaction Survey"; Journal of Managerial Psychology, MCB University Press, Vol. No. 9 No. 1,1994, pp. 26-31.

Morosini, Gigantesco, P, A. Bazzoni (2003); "Quality Of Psychiatric Care: Validation of an Instrument for Measuring Inpatient Opinion"; International Journal for Quality in Health Care, Published by Oxford University Press, 2003, Vol. No. 15, No. 1, pp. 73-78.

Nunnally, Jum C. (1981); "Psychometric Theory"; Tata Mcgraw-Hill Publishing Ltd. New Delhi, 1981.

Parasuraman, Valarie A.Zeithaml, and Leonard L. Berry (1988); "SERVQUAL: A Multiple-Item Scale for Measuring Consumer Perceptions of Service Quality"; Journal of Retailing, Vol, 64, No. 1, Spring 1988, pp. 12-40.

Parasuraman, Valarie A.Zeithaml, and Leonard L. Berry (1991); "Refinement and Reassessment of the SERVQUAL Scale"; Journal of Retailing, Vol, 67, Spring No. 4, Winter 1991, pp. 420-450.

Roberts, Emilie, Ralph Leavey, David Allen, Graham Gibbs (1994); "Feedback on Quality: Patients' Experience of Surgical Care" International Journal of Health Care Quality Assurance, MCB University Press Limited, Vol. No.7, No. 3, 1994, pp. 27-32.

Sharma, Prof. R.D. and Hardeep Chahal (1999); "A Study of patients' Satisfaction of private Health Care facilities"; "Vikalpa The Journal for Decision Makers", Vol, 24 No. 4, October- December 1999, pp. 69-76. Indian Institute of Management, Ahmedabad, India.

Steven, A, Taylor and J, Joseph Cronin Jr. (1994); "Modeling Patients' Satisfaction and Service Quality"; Journal of Health Care Marketing, Vol. 14, No. 1, Spring 1994, pp. 34-44.

The Free Dictionary; www.thefreedictionary.com /health+care-32k .

Tomes, Anne E. and Stephen Chee Peng Ng (2000); "Service Quality in Hospital care: the Development of an in-patient Questionnaire"; "International Journal of Health Care Quality Assurance", Vol. 8, No. 3, 2000, pp. 25-33. MCB University Press.

Tucker, Jessie L., Sheila R. Adams (2001); "Incorporating Patients' Assessments of Satisfaction And Quality: An Integrative Model of Patients' Evaluations of Their Care"; Managing Service Quality; MCB University Press, Vol. No. 11,No. 4, 2001, pp. 272-286.

Vyas, Prof.(Dr.) Parimal H. and Shri P.D. Thakkar (2005); "Market Performance Analysis and Measurement of Patients' Satisfaction in Healthcare Services"; "The Indian Journal of Commerce", Vol.58, No.1, January-March, 2005, pp. 150-161. Quarterly Publication of the Indian Commerce Association, School of Management Studies, IGNOU, New Delhi.

Wisniewski, Mik and Hazel Wisniewski (2005); "Measuring Service Quality in a Hospital Colposcopy Clinic"; "International Journal of Health Care Quality Assurance", Vol. 18, No.3, 2005, pp. 217-228. Emerald Group Publishing Limited.

www.surgeryencyclopedia.com/ Fi-La/Hospital-Services.html-26k.

www.who.int (harold-jr.tripod.com/sitebuildercontent/sitebuilderfiles/definitions _of_health.pdf.

Yavas, Ugur, Natalia Romanova (2005); "Assessing Performance of Multi-Hospital Organizations: A Measurement Approach"; International Journal of Health Care Quality Assurance, Emerald Group Publishing Limited, Vol. No. 18 No. 3, 2005, pp. 193-203.

WELCOME TO THIS QUESTIONNAIRE

I am a faculty member of the Faculty of Commerce, M.S. University of Baroda, pursuing a research study on measuring Patients' Satisfaction. I will be grateful to you if you spare your valuable time and provide me your valuable views on the subject of the research study. I assure you that it is purely an academic exercise and the information supplied by you would be kept strictly confidential.

Thank you.

ABOUT YOU

Name : ______________________________

Gender : Male ☐ Female ☐

Your-

Personal Status : Single ☐ Married ☐

Education : Below 10th std. ☐ Under Graduate ☐

Graduate ☐ Post Graduate ☐

Age : Below 30 Years ☐ 30-45 years ☐

45-60 years ☐ Above 60 Years ☐

Occupation : Business ☐ Service ☐ Dependents ☐

Monthly Income : Below Rs. 8,000 ☐ Rs.8,001 to Rs.14,000 ☐

Rs. 14,001 to Rs. 20,000 ☐

Rs.20,001 to Rs. 30000 ☐

More than Rs.30,000 ☐

Date:___________

(Please put a tick (✓) as applicable to you)

[Q.1] Please state the Name of the hospital in which you underwent your last major treatment ______________________________

[Q.2] Hospital belongs to which category?

(1) Government Hospital ☐

(2) Hospital of Trust ☐

(3) Private Hospital ☐

(4) Any Other, (Please specify)______________________________.

[Q.3] Period of Hospitalization: From (Date) _____ to (Date) _____ = _____ days.

(1) Week or Less ☐

(2) 1 Month or Less ☐

(3) 3 Months or less ☐

(4) More than 3 Months ☐

[Q.4] What do you think of the charges of the hospital?

(1) Very High ☐

(2) High ☐

(3) Reasonable ☐

(4) Low ☐

(5) Very Low ☐

[Q.5] Type of medical treatment that you had undergone at this hospital

Sr.No.	Type of Medical treatment	Please put a tick (✓)
(1)	Cardiac (Heart)	
(2)	Renal (Kidney)	
(3)	Eyes, Nose, Throat	
(4)	Cancer	
(5)	Orthopedic Surgery	
(6)	Any Other (Please specify)	

[Q.6] Availability of Supporting Medical facilities: [Please put a tick (✓)]

Sr. No.	Medical facilities	With in the Hospital	Nearby the Hospital
(1)	Medical Store		
(2)	Pathological Laboratory		
(3)	Blood Bank		
(4)	Radiologist/X-ray testing laboratory		
(5)	Sonography		
(6)	Other Doctors' services e.g. anesthetist, child specialist		

[Q.7] Please encircle ANY ONE of the following numbers given against each of the statements being the likely reasons that may have influenced your decision regarding selection of this hospital. **(1= Least Important; 2=Unimportant; 3 = Somewhat Imp.; 4 = Important; 5 = Most Important)**.

Sr. No.	Reasons	Your Score				
(1)	It was my own decision.	1	2	3	4	5
(2)	Our relatives suggested it.	1	2	3	4	5
(3)	Our friend suggested it.	1	2	3	4	5
(4)	It was suggested by our family doctor.	1	2	3	4	5
(5)	Based on Past Performance of Hospital/Past Efficient Doctors' Performance	1	2	3	4	5
(6)	It was the only the hospital where this kind of medical treatment facility is available.	1	2	3	4	5
(7)	Overall reputation of hospital.	1	2	3	4	5
(8)	Hospital Located Nearby.	1	2	3	4	5
(9)	Hospital Service is Economical.	1	2	3	4	5
(10)	Accessibility of Supply of medicine and other Medical test facilities	1	2	3	4	5
(11)	Sanitation in the Hospital	1	2	3	4	5

[Q.8] Please encircle ANY ONE of the following numbers given against each of the statements relating to your actual Experiences that represent your feelings about the features of your health care service organization. (*Actual Experience* = Degree of Excellence with which service is provided. 1= Strongly Disagree. 2= Disagree. 3= Somewhat Agree. 4= Agree. 5= Strongly Agree).

Sr. No.	Health Care Service Major Variables and its Features	*Actual Experience*				
During my Hospital Stay						
(1)	On the basis of explanation given by Doctor about my treatment I felt Doctor has good Knowledge and Efficiency.	1	2	3	4	5
(2)	I felt Doctors were better in extending Cooperation to me/patients.	1	2	3	4	5
(3)	I experienced that doctors were polite in dealing with me/patients.	1	2	3	4	5
(4)	I experienced Impartial Attitude of Doctors.	1	2	3	4	5
(5)	I felt comfortable during doctors' Examination.	1	2	3	4	5
(6)	On the basis of the way he treated me/patients I found doctor was well Experienced in curing Patient.	1	2	3	4	5
(7)	I experienced thorough checkup by Doctor.	1	2	3	4	5
(8)	I experienced that doctors work according to Patient Expectation	1	2	3	4	5
(9)	I felt Doctors give Individual consideration and maintain confidentiality.	1	2	3	4	5
(10)	I felt Doctors show respect and support patients.	1	2	3	4	5

Contd.

Contd.

(11)	On the basis of my recovery from illness I felt Doctor makes a good diagnosis.	1	2	3	4	5
(12)	I felt Doctors prescribe good drugs.	1	2	3	4	5
(13)	For performing any test on me Doctors ask for my permission.	1	2	3	4	5
(14)	I felt Comfortable asking question to Doctors about my Treatment and Medications.	1	2	3	4	5
(15)	I felt Doctor is honest in dealing and treating me.	1	2	3	4	5
(16)	I felt sufficient good doctors remain present for providing treatment.	1	2	3	4	5
(17)	I felt doctor were easily available or remain present for providing treatment in case of emergency.	1	2	3	4	5
During my Hospital Stay						
(18)	On the basis of explanation given by Nurse about my treatment I felt Nurse had good Knowledge and Efficiency.	1	2	3	4	5
(19)	I felt Nurses were better in extending cooperation to me/ Patients.	1	2	3	4	5
(20)	I experienced that nurses show politeness in dealing with me/patients.	1	2	3	4	5
(21)	I Experienced Impartial Attitude of Nurses and ward boys.	1	2	3	4	5
(22)	On the basis of feedback provided about my health I felt Nurse maintains proper records of patients' treatment.	1	2	3	4	5
(23)	On the basis of regular response I felt that Nurses handled patient quarries properly.	1	2	3	4	5
(24)	On the basis of the way she treats me/patients I found Nurse is well Experienced in curing me/Patient.	1	2	3	4	5
(25)	I had good experience about approach of those who perform the test on me/patient.	1	2	3	4	5
(26)	I experienced that Nurses give personal attention to patients.	1	2	3	4	5
(27)	I experienced that Nurses provide prompt service.	1	2	3	4	5
(28)	I felt the Nurses and other staff responded well and remains present for providing treatment in case of emergency.	1	2	3	4	5
(29)	I experienced that Nurses explain procedure and take permission before applying any test on me.	1	2	3	4	5
(30)	I experienced that Nurses explain the rules, regulation in ward.	1	2	3	4	5
(31)	I experienced that Nurses are kind, gentle and sympathetic all the time.	1	2	3	4	5

Contd.

Contd.

(32)	I was given Information about how to manage my side effects of my medication.	1	2	3	4	5
(33)	I felt good for prompt services provided by sanitation staff like 'Ayas', 'Mahetarani' or Mehtar'.	1	2	3	4	5
During my Hospital Stay						
(34)	I felt less Waiting Time for Consultation and treatment.	1	2	3	4	5
(35)	I felt less Waiting Time for Tests.	1	2	3	4	5
(36)	I felt Hospital has Simple Checking Procedure.	1	2	3	4	5
(37)	I experienced Speed and ease of Admission and Discharge from hospital.	1	2	3	4	5
(38)	I found Convenient Office hours in the hospital.	1	2	3	4	5
(39)	I felt Staff gives Prompt services	1	2	3	4	5
(40)	I experienced No Overcrowding in hospital.	1	2	3	4	5
(41)	I appreciate good Grievances Handling System in hospital.	1	2	3	4	5
(42)	I felt Administrative staff welcome and implement patients' suggestion.	1	2	3	4	5
(43)	I felt Staff gives patients Personal attention.	1	2	3	4	5
(44)	I am treated with dignity and given adequate privacy during stay in hospital.	1	2	3	4	5
(45)	I felt that staff shows good concern for my Family and Visitor.	1	2	3	4	5
(46)	I experienced Simple Billing Procedure in hospital.	1	2	3	4	5
During my Hospital Stay						
(47)	I found hospital Well-equipped units.	1	2	3	4	5
(48)	I found Proper Sitting and Bedding Arrangements in hospital.	1	2	3	4	5
(49)	I felt Physical Comfort in Examination and waiting room.	1	2	3	4	5
(50)	I found sufficient Natural light or Illumination in hospital.	1	2	3	4	5
(51)	I observed sufficient number of Dust Bins and Spittoons are provided.	1	2	3	4	5
(52)	I experienced No Flies/ Mosquitoes in hospital.	1	2	3	4	5
(53)	I found adequate Parking Arrangements made by hospital.	1	2	3	4	5
(54)	I felt surroundings of Hospital were Clean.	1	2	3	4	5
(55)	I felt Pleasing and appealing room of he Hospital.	1	2	3	4	5
(56)	I felt Good food served by Hospital.	1	2	3	4	5
(57)	I found Staff neat in appearance.	1	2	3	4	5
(58)	I experienced the noise occurring inside and outside ward was kept at minimum.	1	2	3	4	5
(59)	I found the hospital ward well decorated and ventilated.	1	2	3	4	5

Contd.

Contd.

(60)	I felt better for music facilities provided in the morning hours for the betterment and liveliness of indoor patients or I feel such music facilities should be provided	1	2	3	4	5
(61)	I found Quick Payment arrangements made by hospital.	1	2	3	4	5
(62)	I found Costs were adequate or affordable.	1	2	3	4	5
(63)	I experienced that Drugs would be obtained easily in the hospital.	1	2	3	4	5
(64)	I found that Distance to the health centre is adequate.	1	2	3	4	5

[Q.9] Overall how satisfied you are with your hospital on following aspects? Please state your score against each of these aspects.
1=Highly Dissatisfied; 2=Disatisfied; 3=Somewhat Satisfied/Can't Say/ Undecided; 4=Satisfied; 5= Highly Satisfied

Sr. No.	Reasons	Your Score				
(1)	On Medical Treatment that was provided to you.	1	2	3	4	5
(2)	On Supporting Medicare services provided to you by the nursing staff.	1	2	3	4	5
(3)	On Supporting services provided to you by the administrative staff.	1	2	3	4	5
(4)	On Physical Environment or Atmospherics	1	2	3	4	5

(Please put a tick (✓) as the case may be)

[Q.10] Overall Satisfaction Experienced by you from Overall Hospital Services.

(1) Highly Dissatisfied ☐ (2) Dissatisfied ☐
(3) Somewhat Satisfied ☐ (4) Satisfied ☐
(5) Highly Satisfied ☐

[Q.11] Would you prefer to recommend this hospital to others in future?

(1) Definitely yes ☐ (2) Probably Yes ☐
(3) Undecided ☐ (4) Probably No ☐
(5) Definitely No ☐

[Q.12] I felt the best service of the hospital is: (Give your Score-1= Strongly Disagree. 2 = Disagree. 3 = Somewhat Agree. 4 = Agree. 5 = Strongly Agree).

Sr. No.	Reasons	Your Score				
(1)	Treatment provided to cure my illness.	1	2	3	4	5
(2)	Supporting Medicare services provided to me by the nursing staff.	1	2	3	4	5
(3)	Supporting services provided to me by the administrative staff.	1	2	3	4	5
(4)	Environment and/or facilities.	1	2	3	4	5
(5)	Any other please specify____________________	1	2	3	4	5

[Q.13] I felt the worst service of the hospital is: (Give your Score-**1= Strongly Disagree. 2= Disagree. 3= Somewhat Agree. 4= Agree. 5= Strongly Agree).**

Sr. No.	Reasons	Your Score				
(1)	Treatment provided to cure my illness.	1	2	3	4	5
(2)	Supporting Medicare services provided to me by the nursing staff.	1	2	3	4	5
(3)	Supporting services provided to me by the administrative staff.	1	2	3	4	5
(4)	Environment and/or facilities.	1	2	3	4	5
(5)	Any other please specify____________________	1	2	3	4	5

[Q.14] On the basis of my experience I prefer that all kinds of Medical facilities should be available in the same hospital.

(1) Strongly Disagree ☐ (2) Disagree ☐

(3) Somewhat Agree ☐ (4) Agree ☐

(5) Strongly Agree ☐

[Q.15] Please give your valuable suggestions to improve the services of this hospital.

____

____

____

____

6

Data Analysis and Interpretation

The authors after the collection of primary data had made an attempt to analyse, interpret, and report its results, by using SPSS 12.0 for windows, and derived from the data analysis and following results. In this chapter, abbreviations used are, GHs = Government Hospitals; THs = Trust Hospitals; PHs = Private Hospitals; IM = Important; UI = Unimportant; AG = Agree, DA = Disagree; SD = Standard Deviations; MI = Most important; SWA = Some What Important; LI = Least Important; SA = Strongly Agree; SDA = Strongly Disagree ST = Satisfied; DS = Dissatisfied; HS = Highly Satisfied, SWS = Some What Satisfied, HDS = Highly Dissatisfied.

PROFILE OF SELECTED PATIENTS

The researchers have provided profile of the respondents that is, patients on the basis of gender, marital status, education, age, occupation, and monthly income as follows.

Profile of the Patients is given below in Table 6.1 to Table 6.6.

Table 6.1: Patients' Gender and Type of Hospitals

Sl. No.	Gender	Type of Hospitals (Number and Percentages of Patients)				Total Number and Percentages of Patients
		GHs	THs	PHs	Total	
01	Male	112 (39.0)	120 (41.8)	55 (19.2)	287 (100)	287 (57.4)
02	Female	88 (41.3)	80 (37.6)	45 (21.1)	213 (100)	213 (42.6)
	Total	200 (40.0)	200 (40.0)	100 (20.0)	500 (100)	500 (100)

In case of gender, it was found that overall 57 per cent of patients were males and 43 per cent of females who had availed hospital services. According to type of hospitals, it was found that 41 per cent patients were females in GHs followed by 38 per cent in THs, and 21 per cent in PHs, whereas 42 per cent were males in THs followed by 39 per cent in GHs and 19 per cent in PHs respectively.

Graph 6.1: Patients' Gender and Type of Hospitals

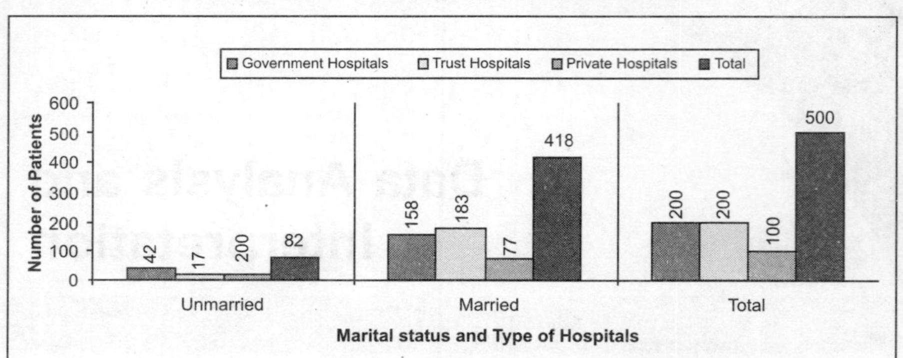

Table 6.2: Patients' Marital Status and Type of Hospitals

Sr. No.	Marital Status	Type of Hospitals (Number and Percentages of Patients)				Total Number and Percentages of Patients
		GHs	THs	PHs	Total	
01	Single	42 (51.2)	17 (20.7)	23 (28.0)	82 (100)	82 (16.4)
02	Married	158 (37.8)	183 (43.8)	77 (18.4)	418 (100)	418 (83.6)
	Total	200 (40.0)	200 (40.0)	100 (20.0)	500 (100)	500 (100)

Graph 6.2: Patients' Marital Status and Type of Hospitals

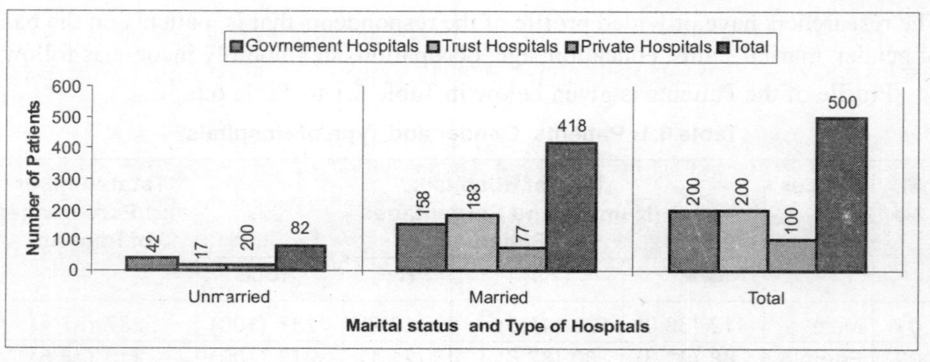

In case of marital status, it was found that overall 84 per cent of patients were married and 16 per cent were unmarried. According to the type of hospitals, it was found that 44 per cent of patients were married in case of THs followed by 38 per cent from GHs and 18 per cent from PHs, where as, 51 per cent of patients were unmarried in case of GHs followed by 28 per cent from PHs and 21 per cent from THs respectively.

Table 6.3: Patients' Educational Qualifications and Type of Hospitals

Sl. No.	Educational Qualification	Type of Hospitals (Number and Percentages of Patients)				Total Number and Percentages of Patients
		GHs	THs	PHs	Total	
01	Below 10th Std.	152(50.3)	116(38.4)	34(11.3)	302(100)	302(60.4)
02	Under Graduate	36(28.1)	60(46.9)	32(25.0)	128(100)	128(25.6)
03	Graduate	11(19.0)	21(36.2)	26(44.8)	58(100)	58(11.6)
04	Post Graduate	1(8.3)	3(25.0)	8(66.7)	12(100)	12(2.4)
	Total	200 (40.0)	200 (40.0)	100 (20.0)	500 (100)	500 (100)

Graph 6.3: Patients' Educational Qualifications and Type of Hospitals

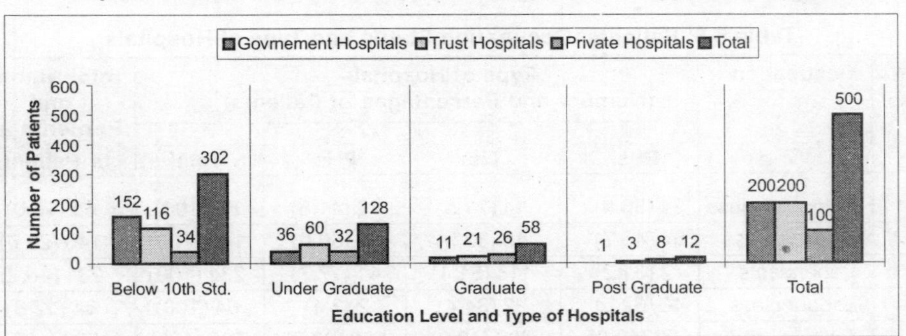

In case of educational qualifications of selected patients', it was observed that with the increase in educational qualification of patients, the preference for hospitals shifted from GHs to THs to PHs. In case of graduates and more than graduates, 56 per cent patients' were from PHs followed by 31 per cent from THs and 13 per cent were from GHs respectively. In case of patients' below 10th standard the reverse trend noticed.

Table 6.4: Patients' Age Groups and Type of Hospitals

Sl. No.	Age Group	Type of Hospitals (Number and Percentages of Patients)				Total Number and Percentages of Patients
		GHs	THs	PHs	Total	
01	Below 30 Years	83 (53.2)	37 (23.7)	36 (23.1)	156 (100)	156 (31.2)
02	30-45 Years	46 (38.7)	51 (42.9)	22 (18.5)	119 (100)	119 (23.8)
03	45-60 Years	48 (35.8)	61 (45.5)	25 (18.7)	134 (100)	134 (26.8)
04	Above 60 Years	23 (25.3)	51 (56.0)	17 (18.7)	91 (100)	91 (18.2)
	Total	200 (40.0)	200 (40.0)	100 (20.0)	500 (100)	500 (100)

Graph 6.4: Patients' Age Groups and Type of Hospitals

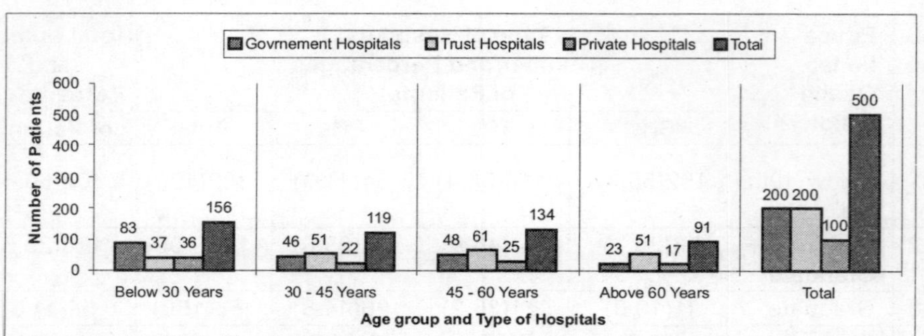

In case of age groups, it was revealed that more than 40 per cent of the patients of the THs were from the age group of more than 30 years, followed by GHs, and PHs. Average percentages, for the age group of more than 30 years, were 48 per cent in THs, 33 per cent in GHs and 19 per cent in case of PHs respectively.

Table 6.5: Patients' Occupation Status and Type of Hospitals

Sl. No.	Occupation	Type of Hospitals (Number and Percentages of Patients)				Total Number and Percentages of Patients
		GHs	THs	PHs	Total	
01	Business class	24 (36.9)	14 (21.5)	27 (41.5)	65 (100)	65 (13.0)
02	Service class	64 (45.7)	46 (32.9)	30 (30.0)	140 (100)	140 (28.0)
03	Dependents	72 (31.2)	118 (51.1)	41 (17.7)	231 (100)	231 (46.2)
04	Labour class	40 (62.5)	22 (34.4)	2 (3.1)	64 (100)	64 (12.8)
	Total	200 (40.0)	200 (40.0)	100 (20.0)	500 (100)	500 (100)

Graph 6.5: Patients' Occupation Status and Type of Hospitals

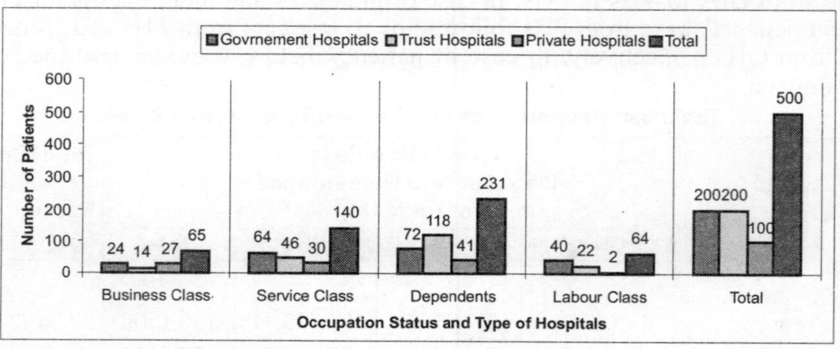

In case of occupation status, overall 60 per cent of patients were from dependents and labour class followed by 40 per cent were from service and business class. According to the type of hospitals, it was found that majority (63 per cent) of the patients were labour class from GHs, followed by 34 per cent from THs, and 3 per cent were from PHs. In case of dependents, 51 per cent of patients were from THs followed by 31 per cent from GHs, and 18 per cent from PHs. In case of business class, 41 per cent of patients were from PHs followed by 37 per cent from GHs, and 22 per cent were from THs. In short, the GHs were preferred by labour class, the THs were preferred by dependents and PHs was preferred by business class people. The preference of service class people was found as favourable for GHs followed by THs, and PHs.

Table 6.6: Patients' Monthly Income and Type of Hospitals

Sl. No.	Monthly Income	Type of Hospitals (Number and Percentages of Patients)				Total Number and Percentages of Patients
		GHs	THs	PHs	Total	
01	Below Rs. 8,000	171 (41.5)	173 (42.0)	68 (16.5)	412 (100)	412 (82.4)
02	Rs.8,001 to Rs. 14,000	23 (35.9)	22 (34.4)	19 (29.7)	64 (100)	64 (12.8)
03	Rs.14,001 to Rs.20,000	6 (40.0)	4 (26.7)	5 (33.3)	15 (100)	15 (3.0)
04	Rs.20,001 to Rs. 30,000	0 (0.0)	1 (16.7)	5 (83.3)	6 (100)	6 (1.2)
05	More than Rs. 30,000	0 (0.0)	0 (0.0)	3 (100)	3 (100)	3 (0.6)
	Total	200 (40.0)	200 (40.0)	100 (20.0)	500 (100)	500 (100)

Graph 6.6: Patients' Monthly Income and Type of Hospitals

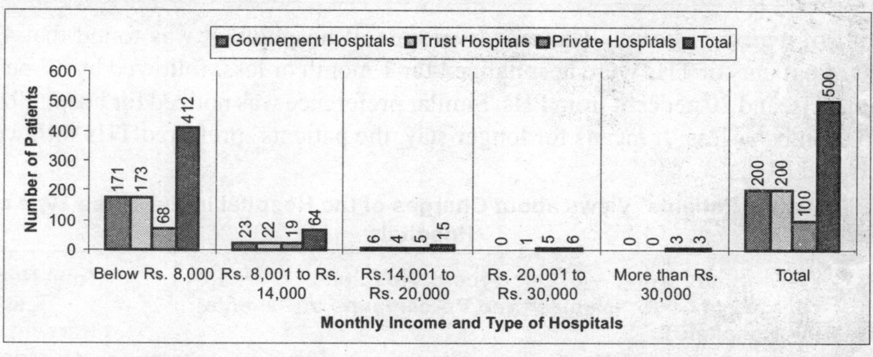

If one compares monthly income versus type of hospitals, it was found that 39 per cent of patients of GHs were from below Rs. 14000 income group, followed by 38 per cent from THs, and 23 per cent were from PHs. In case of income groups, more than Rs. 14,001, the 72 per cent of patients were from PHs followed by 15 per cent from THs, and 13 per cent from GHs. It means lower income group patients preferred Government hospital followed by THs whereas higher income group preferred PHs followed by THs.

DATA ANALYSIS (ACCORDING TO TYPE OF HOSPITALS)

Table 6.7: Patients' Period of Hospitalization in the Three Type of Hospitals

Sl. No.	Period of Hospitalization	Type of Hospitals (Number and Percentages of Patients)				Total Number and Percentages of Patients
		GHs	THs	PHs	Total	
01	1 Week or Less	166 (42.8)	144 (37.1)	78 (20.0)	388 (100)	388 (77.6)
02	1 Month or Less	30 (30.9)	48 (49.5)	19 (19.6)	97 (100)	97 (19.4)
03	3 Months or Less	4 (28.6)	8 (57.1)	2 (14.3)	14 (100)	14 (2.8)
04	More than Three Months	0 (0.0)	0 (0.0)	1 (100)	1 (100)	1 (0.2)
	Total	200 (40.0)	200 (40.0)	100 (20.0)	500 (100)	500 (100)

Graph 5.7: Patients' Period of Hospitalization in the Three Type of Hospitals

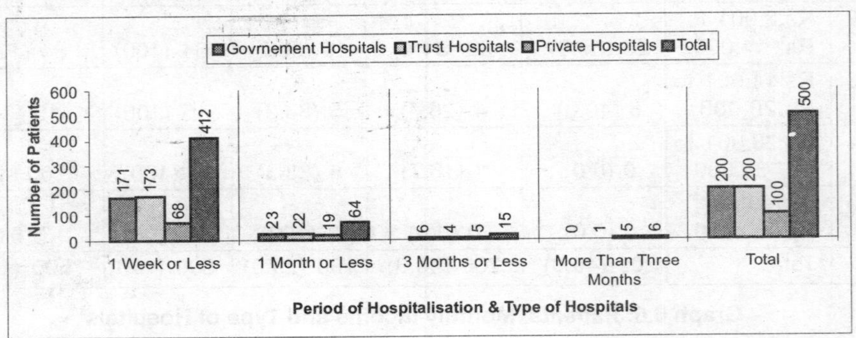

If of period of hospitalization versus type of hospitals, it was found that 43 per cent of patients of THs were hospitalized for 1 month or less, followed by 37 per cent from GHs, and 20 per cent from PHs. Similar preference was noticed for hospitalization of 3 months or less. It means for longer stay, the patients' preferred THs followed by GHs and PHs.

Table 6.8: Patients' Views about Charges of the Hospital in the Three Type of Hospitals

Sl. No.	View about charges of the Hospitals	Type of Hospitals (Number and Percentages of Patients)				Total Number and Percentages of Patients
		GHs	THs	PHs	Total	
01	Very High	0 (0.0)	0 (0.0)	10 (100)	10 (100)	10 (2.0)
02	High	1 (2.9)	9 (25.7)	25 (71.4)	35 (100)	35 (7.0)
03	Reasonable	14 (7.6)	111 (60.3)	59 (32.1)	184 (100)	184 (36.8)
04	Lower	17 (22.7)	52 (69.3)	6 (8.0)	75 (100)	75 (15.0)
05	Very Low	168 (85.7)	28 (14.3)	0 (0.0)	196 (100)	196 (39.2)
	Total	200 (40.0)	200 (40.0)	100 (20.0)	500 (100)	500 (100)

Graph 6.8: Patients' Views about Charges of the Hospital in the three type of Hospitals

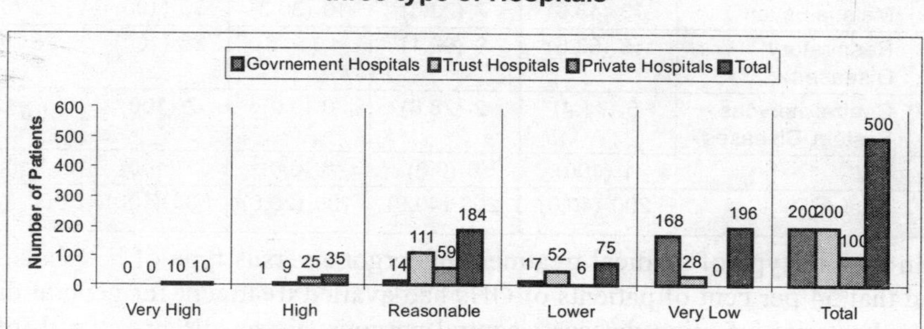

In case of patients' views about charges of hospitals, overall half of the (54 per cent) patients viewed charges of hospitals were lower; 37 per cent viewed it charges as reasonable, and 9 per cent viewed it as higher. If one analyze according to type of hospitals, patients viewed GHs were charging lower followed by THs and PHs, whereas THs were viewed by patients as charging reasonable followed by PHs. The PHs viewed by patients as charging higher followed by THs and GHs. An interpretation about charges of hospitals can be made that PHs were viewed by patients as expensive, THs were reasonable and GHs viewed as charging lower.

Table 6.9: Type of Medical Treatment Undergone by Patients in All the Three Type of Hospitals

Sl. No.	Type of Medical Treatment	Type of Hospitals (Number and Percentages of Patients)				Total Number and Percentages of Patients
		GHs	THs	PHs	Total	
01	Cardiac (Heart)	14 (34.1)	19 (46.3)	8 (19.5)	41 (100)	41 (8.2)
02	Renal (Kidney)	10 (26.3)	17 (44.7)	11 (28.9)	38 (100)	38 (7.6)
03	Eyes, Nose, Throat	5 (35.7)	8 (57.1)	1 (7.1)	14 (100)	14 (2.8)
04	Cancer	3 (6.5)	42 (91.3)	1 (2.2)	46 (100)	46 (9.2)
05	Orthopedic Surgery	11(17.7)	33 (53.2)	18 (29.0)	62 (100)	62 (12.4)
06	Obstratics and Gynechological Diseases	22 (56.4)	7 (17.9)	10 (25.6)	39 (100)	39 (7.8)
07	Abdomen Diseases	37 (63.8)	11 (19.0)	10(17.2)	58 (100)	58 (11.6)
08	Metabolic Diseases	6 (33.3)	4 (22.2)	8 (44.4)	18 (100)	18 (3.6)
09	Viral Infection Diseases	33 (68.8)	11 (22.9)	4 (8.3)	48 (100)	48 (9.6)
10	Bacterial Infection Diseases	10 (71.4)	2 (14.3)	2 (14.3)	14 (100)	14 (2.8)
11	Surgical Operation	5 (13.2)	22 (57.9)	11(28.9)	38 (100)	38 (7.6)
12	Skin Diseases	1 (50.0)	1 (50.0)	0 (0.0)	2 (100)	2 (0.4)
13	Blood Disorders	9 (56.3)	5 (31.3)	2 (12.5)	16 (100)	16 (3.2)

...(Contd.).

...(Contd.)

14	Malaria Fever	13 (43.3)	7 (23.3)	10 (33.3)	30 (100)	30 (6.0)
15	Respiratory Diseases	15 (53.6)	9 (32.1)	4 (14.3)	28 (100)	28 (5.6)
16	Central nervous System Diseases	5 (71.4)	2 (28.6)	0 (0.0)	7 (100)	7 (1.4)
17	HIV	1 (100)	0 (0.0)	0 (0.0)	1 (100)	1 (0.2)
	Total	200 (40.0)	200 (40.0)	100 (20.0)	500 (100)	500 (100)

In case of type of medical treatment undergone versus type of hospitals, it was found that 54 per cent of patients of GHs had availed treatment for general diseases that is, bacterial infection diseases; central nervous system diseases; viral infection diseases; abdomen diseases, and obstratics and gynechological diseases; 70 per cent patients of THs has availed treatment for specific kind of diseases that is, cancer; surgical operation; eyes, nose, throat; orthopedic surgery; cardiac (heart), and renal (kidney). In case of PHs, 78 per cent of patients had availed treatment for mixed kind of diseases such as, metabolic diseases; orthopedic surgery; renal (kidney); malaria fever; obstratics and gynechological diseases, and abdomen diseases.

Table 6.10: Availability of Supporting Medical Facilities within the Hospitals in All the Three Type of Hospitals

Sl. No.	Supporting Medical Facilities		Type of Hospitals (Number and Percentages of Patients)				Total Number and Percentages of Patients
			GHs	THs	PHs	Total	
01	Medical Store Available	Within Hospitals	199 (45.9)	199 (45.9)	36 (8.3)	434 (100)	434 (86.8)
		Nearby Hospitals	1 (1.6)	1 (1.6)	62 (96.9)	64 (100)	64 (12.8)
02	Pathological Laboratory Available	Within Hospitals	200 (44.4)	197 (43.8)	53 (11.8)	450 (100)	450 (90.0)
		Nearby Hospitals	0 (0.0	2 (4.8)	40 (95.2)	42 (100)	42 (8.4)
03	Blood Bank/ Blood storage Facilities Available	Within Hospitals	5 (2.5)	179 (90.9)	13 (6.6)	197 (100)	197 (39.4)
		Nearby Hospitals	4 (11.1)	1 (2.8)	31 (86.1)	36 (100)	36 (7.2)
04	Radiologists/ X-ray testing Laboratory Available	Within Hospitals	200 (47.3)	198 (46.8)	25 (5.9)	423 (100)	423 (84.6)
		Nearby Hospitals	0 (0.0)	2 (3.1)	63 (96.9)	65 (100)	65 (13.0)
05	Sonography Available	Within Hospitals	192 (48.4)	179 (45.1)	26 (6.5)	397 (100)	397 (79.4)
		Nearby Hospitals	0 (0.0)	1 (1.6)	62 (98.4)	63 (100)	63 (12.6)
06	Other Doctors' services Available	Within Hospitals	177 (47.2)	178 (47.5)	20 (5.3)	375 (100)	375 (75.0)
		Nearby Hospitals	0 (0.0)	2 (4.7)	41 (95.3)	43 (100)	43 (8.6)

In case of availability of medical facilities versus type of hospitals, 90 per cent of patients reported that the blood bank facilities were available in THs, whereas in case of both GHs and THs, on an average near 45 per cent of patients reported about kind of facilities were available within the hospitals, which included, medical store; pathological laboratory; radiologists/x-ray testing laboratory; sonography, and other doctors' services. In case of PHs on an average only around 7 per cent of patients reported that all kinds of above mentioned facilities were available within the hospitals, whereas most of the (around 90 per cent) PHs patients' reported that all kinds of above mentioned facilities were available nearby hospitals.

It means Government and THs provide some basic supporting medical facilities within the hospitals whereas such facilities were not generally made available within the PHs but, such facilities were available in nearby areas of PHs.

NOTE

In the Table 5.11 (Q. No. 07) the responses are combined for analysis purpose in two categories as Important (Most Important + Important) and Unimportant (Somewhat Important + Unimportant + Least Important) which should be noted.

In the Tables 5.12 to 5.23 and Tables 5.26 to 5.27 (Q. NOs. 08, 09, 12, 13) also the responses are combined for analysis purpose in two categories as Agree (Strongly Agree + Agree), and Disagree (Somewhat Agree + Disagree + Strongly Disagree) that should be noted.

Table 6.11: Patients' Reasons for Selection of All the Three Type of Hospitals (Q. No. 07)

Sl. No.	Selected Criteria	Type of Hospitals (Number and Percentages of Patients)							
		GHs		THs		PHs		Total	
		IM	UI	IM	UI	IM	UI	IM	UI
01	Own Decision	179 (89.5)	21 (10.5)	117 (58.5)	83 (41.5)	63 (63.0)	37 (37.0)	359 (71.8)	141 (28.2)
02	Relatives Suggested	103 (51.5)	97 (48.5)	123 (61.5)	77 (38.5)	31 (31.0)	69 (69.0)	257 (51.4)	243 (48.6)
03	Friends Suggested	94 (47.0)	106 (53.0)	112 (56.0)	88 (44.0)	23 (23.0)	77 (77.00	229 (45.8)	271 (54.2)
04	Suggested by Family Doctor	39 (19.5)	161 (80.5)	81 (40.5)	119 (59.5)	36 (36.0)	64 (64.0)	156 (31.2)	344 (68.8)
05	Performance of Hospitals/ Doctor	181 (90.50)	19 (09.5)	168 (84.0)	32 (16.0)	88 (88.0)	12 (12.0)	437 (87.4)	63 (12.6)
06	Only in this Hospitals such kind of facility is available	82 (41.0)	118 (59.0)	150 (75.0)	50 (25.0)	45 (45.0)	55 (55.0)	277 (55.4)	223 (44.6)
07	Overall Reputation of Hospitals	190 (95.0)	10 (5.0)	182 (91.0)	18 (9.0)	89 (89.0)	11 (11.0)	461 (92.2)	39 (7.8)

...(Contd.)

...(Contd.)

08	Hospitals Located Nearby	169 (84.5)	31 (15.5)	99 (49.5)	101 (50.5)	38 (38.0)	62 (62.0)	306 (61.2)	194 (38.8)
09	Hospitals is economical	196 (98.0)	4 (2.0)	102 (51.0)	98 (49.0)	19 (19.0)	81 (81.0)	317 (63.4)	183 (36.6)
10	Accessibility of Medicine and Test Facilities	181 (90.5)	19 (9.5)	186 (93.0)	14 (7.0)	81 (81.0)	19 (19.0)	448 (89.6)	52 (10.4)
11	Sanitation in the Hospitals	190 (95.0)	10 (5.0)	191 (95.5)	9 (4.5)	94 (94.0)	6 (6.0)	475 (95.0)	25 (5.0)

In case of reasons for selection of hospitals, the important reasons considered by above 60 per cent of all the patients together, were sanitation in the hospitals followed by overall reputation of hospitals; accessibility of medicine and test facilities; performance of hospitals/doctor; own decision and hospitals was economical, whereas, reasons considered unimportant by above 40 per cent of patients for selection of the hospitals were suggested by family doctor followed by friends suggested; relatives suggested and only in this hospitals such kind of facility is available.

In case of reasons which were common and equally important for each category of hospital, on an average above 85 per cent of patients considered sanitation in the hospitals followed by overall reputation of hospitals; accessibility of medicine and test facilities, and performance of hospitals/doctors.

Over and above the common reasons for selection of hospitals, the other reasons which were important for selection of GHs by the patients that hospitals were economical and hospitals located nearby, whereas, the reason namely, patients' own decision was important to PHs patients and other reasons such as only in this hospitals such kind of facility is available followed by relatives suggested; friends suggested; hospitals was economical, and suggested by family doctor were important to THs.

In case of unimportant reasons for selection of hospitals, it was found that around and above 50 per cent of GHs patients' considered reasons such as, suggested by family doctor followed by only in this hospitals such kind of facility is available; friends suggested and relatives suggested; whereas in case of THs around 40 per cent and above patients considered reasons such as, hospitals located nearby and own decision; and above 60 per cent of patients of PHs considered reasons such as, hospitals is economical followed by friends suggested, relatives suggested, suggested by family doctor, and hospitals located nearby.

MEDICAL SERVICES, PARAMEDICAL SERVICES, ADMINISTRATIVE SERVICES, AND ENVIRONMENT (PHYSICAL FACILITIES) OF ALL THE THREE TYPE OF HOSPITALS

Table 6.12: Patients' Responses for Medical Services for All the Three Type of Hospitals

Sl. No.	Selected Criteria	Type of Hospitals (Number and Percentages of Patients)							
		GHs		THs		PHs		Total	
		AG	DA	AG	DA	AG	DA	AG	DA
01	Doctors' Knowledge and Efficiency	192 (96.0)	8 (4.0)	189 (94.5)	11 (5.5)	94 (94.0)	6 (6.0)	475 (95.0)	25 (5.0)
02	Doctors' Cooperation to patients	182 (91.0)	18 (9.0)	191 (95.5)	9 (4.5)	95 (95.0)	5 (5.0)	468 (93.6)	32 (6.4)
03	Doctors' were polite with patients	182 (91.0)	18 (9.0)	193 (96.5)	7 (3.5)	95 (95.0)	5 (5.0)	470 (94.0)	30 (6.0)
04	Impartial Attitude of Doctors	185 (92.5)	15 (7.5)	192 (96.0)	8 (4.0)	88 (88.0)	12 (12.0)	465 (93.0)	35 (7.0)
05	Patients' Felt Comfortable During Doctors Examination	179 (89.5)	21 (10.5)	184 (92.0)	16 (8.0)	94 (94.0)	6 (6.0)	457 (91.4)	43 (8.6)
06	Doctors' Experience in Curing Patients	188 (94.0)	12 (6.0)	184 (92.0)	16 (8.0)	96 (96.0)	4 (4.0)	468 (93.6)	32 (6.4)
07	Thorough Checkup by Doctors	187 (93.5)	13 (6.5)	184 (92.0)	16 (8.0)	95 (95.0)	5 (5.0)	466 (93.2)	34 (6.8)
08	Doctors' Work according to Patients Expectations	62 (31.0)	138 (69.0)	122 (61.0)	78 (39.0)	53 (53.0)	47 (47.0)	237 (47.4)	263 (52.6)
09	Doctors' Gave Individual Consideration and Confidentiality	128 (64.0)	72 (36.0)	172 (86.0)	28 (14.0)	80 (80.0)	20 (20.0)	380 (76.0)	120 (24.0)
10	Doctors' Showed Respect and Support patients	172 (86.0)	28 (14.0)	188 (94.0)	12 (6.0)	93 (93.0)	7 (7.0)	453 (90.6)	47 (9.4)
11	Doctors' Makes Good Diagnosis	192 (96.0)	8 (4.0)	192 (96.0)	8 (4.0)	91 (91.0)	9 (9.0)	475 (95.0)	25 (5.0)
12	Doctors' Prescribed Good Drugs	186 (93.0)	14 (7.0)	189 94.5)	11 (5.5)	93 (93.0)	7 (7.0)	468 (93.6)	32 (6.4)
13	Doctor' ask for patients Permission for performing Test	73 (36.5)	127 (63.5)	135 (67.5)	65 (32.5)	61 (61.0)	39 (39.0)	269 (53.8)	231 (46.2)
14	Patients' Felt Comfortable asking Questions to Doctors	183 (91.5)	17 (8.5)	189 (94.5)	11 (5.5)	89 (89.0)	11 (11.0)	461 (92.2)	39 (7.8)
15	Doctors' Honesty in Dealing with patients	195 (97.5)	5 (2.5)	190 (95.0)	10 (5.0)	89 (89.0)	11 (11.0)	474 (94.8)	26 (5.2)
16	Sufficient number of Doctors Remained Present	179 (89.5)	21 (10.5)	181 (90.5)	19 (9.5)	87 (87.0)	13 (13.0)	447 (89.4)	53 (10.6)
17	Doctors' Availability in Emergency	175 (87.5)	25 (12.5)	178 (89.0)	22 (11.0)	90 (90.0)	10 (10.0)	443 (88.6)	57 (11.4)

In case of medical services versus type of hospitals, on an average 87 per cent of all patients together showed agreement with most of the above criteria, whereas above 25 per cent of all patients showed disagreement to criteria viz., doctors' work according to patients' expectations followed by doctors' gave individual consideration and confidentiality, and doctors' ask for patients' permission for performing test. Type of hospitals wise also, these criteria remained common for each type of hospitals.

Over and above these criteria, if one considers responses according to type of hospitals' responses, 10 per cent and above patients showed disagreement to one criteria namely, sufficient number of doctors' remained present in case of GHs; whereas, in case of PHs the patients' considered certain criteria viz., sufficient number of doctors remained present followed by impartial attitude of doctors; felt comfortable asking questions to doctors, and doctors' honesty in dealing with patients.

In case of type of hospitals, for the medical services, on an average 90 per cent of patients from THs; 87 per cent from PHs, and 84 per cent from GHs showed agreement with the above mentioned criteria. So in case of medical services, the patients showed first preference to THs followed by private and GHs.

Table 6.13: Patients' Responses for Paramedical Services for All the Three Type of Hospitals

Sl. No.	Selected Criteria	Type of Hospitals (Number and Percentages of Patients)							
		GHs		THs		PHs		Total	
		AG	DA	AG	DA	AG	DA	AG	DA
01	Nurses' Knowledge and Efficiency	172 (86.0)	28 (14.0)	180 (90.0)	20 (10.0)	90 (90.0)	10 (10.0)	442 (88.4)	58 (11.6)
02	Nurses' Cooperation to Patients	146 (73.0)	54 (27.0)	183 (91.5)	17 (8.5)	95 (95.0)	5 (5.0)	424 (84.8)	76 (15.2)
03	Nurses' Showed Politeness with Patients	160 (80.0)	40 (20.0)	179 (89.5)	21 (10.5)	91 (91.0)	9 (9.0)	430 (86.0)	70 (14.0)
04	Impartial Attitude of Nurses	170 (85.0)	30 (15.0)	186 (93.0)	14 (7.0)	85 (85.0)	15 (15.0)	44 (88.2)	59 (11.8)
05	Nurses' Maintain Proper records of	174 (87.0)	26 (13.0)	181 (90.5)	19 (9.5)	91 (91.0)	9 (9.0)	446 (89.2)	54 (10.8)
06	Nurses' Handled Patients Query	123 (61.5)	77 (38.5)	162 (81.0)	38 (19.0)	88 (88.0)	12 (12.0)	373 (74.6)	127 (25.4)
07	Nurses' Experience in Curing Patients	149 (74.5)	51 (25.5)	164 (82.0)	36 (18.0)	86 (86.0)	14 (14.0)	399 (79.8)	101 (20.2)
08	Good Experience of Those who Perform	179 (89.5)	21 (10.5)	177 (88.5)	23 (11.5)	86 (86.0)	14 (14.0)	442 (88.4)	58 (11.6)
09	Nurses' Gave Personal Attention to Patients	95 (47.5)	105 (52.5)	153 (76.5)	47 (23.5)	79 (79.0)	21 (21.0)	327 65.4)	173 (34.6)
10	Nurses' Provided Prompt Service	54 (27.0)	146 (73.0)	114 (57.0)	86 (43.0)	72 (72.0)	28 (28.0)	240 (48.0)	260 (52.0)
11	Nurses' and Staff Remained Present in Emergency	119 (59.5)	81 (40.5)	167 (83.5)	33 (16.5)	86 (86.0)	14 (14.0)	372 (74.4)	128 (25.6)

...(Contd.)

Sl. No.	Selected Criteria	Type of Hospitals (Number and Percentages of Patients)							
		GHs		THs		PHs		Total	
		AG	DA	AG	DA	AG	DA	AG	DA
12	Nurses' Explain Procedures and take Patient Permission before Test	120 (60.0)	80 (40.0)	170 (85.0)	30 (15.0)	71 (71.0)	29 (29.0)	361 (72.2)	139 (27.8)
13	Nurses' Explain Rules Regulation in ward	179 (89.5)	21 (10.5)	180 (90.0)	20 (10.0)	82 (82.0)	18 (18.0)	441 (88.2)	59 (11.8)
14	Nurses' are Kind, Gentle and Sympathetic	184 (92.0)	16 (8.0)	178 (89.0)	22 (11.0)	90 (90.0)	10 (10.0)	452 (90.4)	48 (9.6)
15	Information Provided to patients for Managing Side Effects	76 (38.0)	124 (62.0)	148 (74.0)	52 (26.0)	51 (51.0)	49 (49.0)	275 (55.0)	225 (45.0)
16	Prompt Service Provided by Sanitation Staff	155 (77.5)	45 (22.5)	184 (92.0)	16 (8.0)	91 (91.0)	9 (9.0)	430 (86.0)	70 (14.0)

In case of paramedical services versus type of hospitals, on an average 79 per cent of all patients together showed agreement with most of the above mentioned selected criteria, whereas above 25 per cent of patients showed disagreement with some criteria viz., nurses' provided prompt service followed by information provided to patients for managing side effects; nurses gave personal attention to patients; nurses' explain procedures and take patient permission before test; nurses' and staff remained present in emergency, and nurses' handled patients query properly. From these, three criteria viz, nurses' provide prompt service; information provided to patients for managing side effects, and nurses' gave personal attention to patients showed common disagreement for all the three type of selected hospitals.

Over and above, if one considers responses as per the type of hospitals, 20 per cent and above patients of GHs showed disagreement with some criteria viz., nurses' and staff remains present in emergency followed by nurses' explain procedures and take patient permission before test; nurses' handled patients query properly, nurses' cooperation to patients; nurses' experience in curing patients; nurses' showed politeness with patients, and prompt service provided by sanitation staff; whereas, in case of PHs patients showed disagreement to criteria namely, nurses' and staff remained present in emergency in case of THs; and nurses' explain procedures and take patient permission before test.

In case of paramedical services of selected type of hospitals, on an average 85 per cent of patients from THs; 83 per cent from PHs and 70 per cent from GHs showed agreement with the above mentioned criteria. So, in case of paramedical services, the patients showed first preference to THs, followed by private and GHs.

Table 6.14: Patients' Responses for Administrative Services for All the Three Type of Hospitals

Sl. No.	Selected Criteria	Type of Hospitals (Number and Percentages of Patients)							
		GHs		THs		PHs		Total	
		AG	DA	AG	DA	AG	DA	AG	DA
01	Less Waiting Time For Consultation and Treatment	116 (58.0)	84 (42.0)	174 (87.0)	26 (13.0)	80 (80.0)	20 (20.0)	370 (74.0)	130 (26.0)
02	Less Waiting Time for Test	145 (72.5)	55 (27.5)	161 (80.5)	39 (19.5)	85 (85.0)	15 (15.0)	391 (78.2)	109 (21.8)
03	Simple Checking Procedure	151 (75.5)	49 (24.5)	180 (90.0)	20 (10.0)	88 (88.0)	12 (12.0)	419 (83.8)	81 (16.2)
04	Speed, Ease of Admission and Discharge form Hospitals	162 (81.0)	38 (19.5)	174 (87.0)	26 (13.0)	85 (85.0)	15 (15.0)	421 (84.2)	79 (15.8)
05	Convenient Office Hours	184 (92.0)	16 (8.0)	177 (88.5)	23 (11.5)	86 (86.0)	14 (14.0)	447 (89.4)	53 (10.6)
06	Staff Gave Prompt Services	56 (28.0)	144 (72.0)	153 (76.5)	47 (23.5)	74 (74.0)	26 (26.0)	283 (56.6)	217 (43.4)
07	No Overcrowding in Hospitals	117 (58.5)	83 (41.5)	177 (88.5)	23 (11.5)	82 (82.0)	18 (18.0)	376 (75.2)	124 (24.8)
08	Good Grievance handling System	35 (17.5)	165 (82.5)	152 (76.0)	48 (24.0)	66 (66.0)	34 (34.0)	253 (50.6)	247 (49.4)
09	Adm. Staff Welcome and Implement Suggestion	44 (22.0)	156 (78.0)	138 (69.0)	62 (31.0)	48 (48.0)	52 (52.0)	230 (46.0)	270 (54.0)
10	Adm. Gives Personal Attention To Patient	45 (22.5)	155 (77.5)	149 (74.5)	51 (25.5)	66 (66.0)	34 (34.0)	260 (52.0)	240 (48.0)
11	Patients' were Treated With Dignity and Privacy	157 (78.5)	43 (21.5)	178 (89.0)	22 (11.0)	89 (89.0)	11 (11.0)	424 (84.8)	76 (15.2)
12	Good Concern for Patients' Family and Visitor	164 (82.0)	36 (18.0)	182 (91.0)	18 (9.0)	88 (88.0)	12 (12.0)	434 (86.8)	66 (13.2)
13	Simple Billing Procedures	184 (92.0)	16 (8.0)	180 (90.0)	20 (10.0)	86 (86.0)	14 (14.0)	450 (90.0)	50 (10.0)

In case of administrative services versus type of hospitals, on an average 73 per cent of all patients together showed agreement with most of the above mentioned criteria whereas, above 25 per cent of all respondent showed disagreement with administrative services in some of the criteria viz., administrative staff welcome and implement suggestion followed by good grievance handling system; administrative gives personal attention to patient; staff gave prompt services; less waiting time for consultation and treatment, and no overcrowding in hospitals. From these criteria patients' showed common disagreement for all selected hospitals for the four criteria namely, administrative staff welcome and implement suggestion; good grievance handling system; administrative gives personal attention to patient, and staff gives prompt services.

Over and above this common criteria, if one considers responses as per the type of hospitals, 20 per cent and above patients of GHs showed disagreement to some criteria viz., less waiting time for consultation and treatment followed by no overcrowding in hospitals; less waiting time for test; simple checking procedure, and patients' were treated with dignity and privacy ; whereas, patients' showed disagreement for criteria namely, less waiting time for test in case of THs and in case of PHs less waiting time for consultation and treatment.

In case of patients' responses for administrative services as per the type of hospitals, on an average 84 per cent of patients from THs; 79 per cent from PHs and 60 per cent from GHs showed agreement with the above mentioned criteria. Thus, in case of administrative services, the patients showed first preference to THs followed by PHs and GHs.

Table 6.15: Patients' Responses for Environment (Physical Facilities) of All the Three Type of Hospitals

Sl. No.	Selected Criteria	Type of Hospitals (Number and Percentages of Patients)							
		GHs		THs		PHs		Total	
		AG	DA	AG	DA	AG	DA	AG	DA
01	Well Equipped Units	181 (90.5)	19 (9.5)	187 (93.5)	13 (6.5)	88 (88.0)	12 (12.0)	456 (91.2)	44 (8.8)
02	Proper Sitting and Bedding Arrangements	186 (93.0)	14 (7.0)	186 (93.0)	14 (7.0)	90 (90.0)	10 (10.0)	462 (92.4)	38 (7.6)
03	Comfort in Examination and waiting Room	185 (92.5)	15 (7.5)	187 (93.5)	13 (6.5)	85 (85.0)	15 (15.0)	457 (91.4)	43 (8.6)
04	Natural Light or Illumination in Hospitals	194 (97.0)	6 (3.0)	196 (98.0)	4 (2.0)	88 (88.0)	12 (12.0)	478 (95.6)	22 (4.4)
05	Sufficient Number of Dust Bins and Spittoons	187 (93.5)	13 (6.5)	190 (95.0)	10 (5.0)	88 (88.0)	12 (12.0)	465 (93.0)	35 (7.0)
06	No Flies and Mos-quitoes in Hospitals	159 (79.5)	41 (20.5)	167 (83.5)	33 (16.5)	93 (93.0)	7 (7.0)	419 (83.8)	81 (16.2)
07	Adequate parking Arrangements	197 (98.5)	3 (1.5)	178 (89.0)	22 (11.0)	69 (69.0)	31 (31.0)	44 (88.8)	56 (11.2)
08	Clean Surroundings of Hospitals	195 (97.5)	5 (2.5)	182 (91.0)	18 (9.0)	90 (90.0)	10 (10.0)	467 (93.4)	33 (6.6)
09	Pleasing and Appealing Room of Hospitals	184 (92.0)	16 (8.0)	189 (94.5)	11 (5.5)	85 (85.0)	15 (15.0)	458 (91.6)	42 (8.4)
10	Good Food Served by Hospitals *	146 (73.0)	54 (27.0)	107 (93.0)	8 (7.0)	46 (79.3)	12 (20.7)	299 (80.2)	74 (19.8)
11	Staff Neat in Appearance	193 (96.5)	7 (3.5)	119 (91.5)	11 (8.5)	90 (90.0)	10 (10.0)	402 (93.5)	28 (6.5)
12	Inside and Out side Noise kept Minimum	172 (86.0)	28 (14.0)	180 (90.0)	20 (10.0)	89 (89.0)	11 (11.0)	441 (88.2)	59 (11.8)
13	Wards Well Decorated and Ventilated	190 (95.0)	10 (5.0)	194 (97.0)	6 (3.0)	81 (81.0)	19 (19.0)	465 (93.0)	35 (7.0)
14	Music Facilities should be provided	181 (90.5)	19 (9.5)	180 (90.0)	20 (10.0)	81 (81.0)	19 (19.0)	465 (88.4)	35 (11.6)

...(Contd.).

...(Contd.)

15	Quick Payment Arrangements	176 (88.0)	24 (12.0)	198 (99.0)	2 (1.0)	87 (87.0)	13 (13.0)	461 (92.2)	39 (7.8)
16	Costs were Adequate or Affordable	198 (99.0)	2 (1.0)	113 (56.5)	87 (43.5)	13 (13.0)	87 (87.0)	324 (64.8)	176 (35.2)
17	Drugs Easily Obtained in Hospitals	183 (91.5)	17 (8.5)	192 (96.0)	8 (4.0)	83 (83.0)	17 (17.0)	458 (91.6)	42 (8.4)
18	Distance to Healthcare is Adequate	175 (87.5)	25 (12.5)	114 (57.0)	86 (43.0)	43 (43.0)	57 (57.0)	332 (66.4)	168 (33.6)

* Total Patients were 373 as 127 Patients have not replied for question "Good Food Served by Hospitals" as food services were not provided by hospital.

In case of environment (physical facilities) versus type of hospitals, on an average 88 per cent of all patients together showed agreement with most of the above mentioned criteria whereas, above 20 per cent of all patients showed disagreement with some of the criteria namely, costs were adequate or affordable followed by distance to healthcare was adequate; and good food served by hospitals.

As per the patients' responses considering type of hospitals, 20 per cent and above patients of GHs showed disagreement with two criteria namely, good food served by hospitals and no flies and mosquitoes in hospitals; whereas in case of THs patients' showed disagreement with some criteria viz., costs were adequate or affordable, and distance to healthcare was adequate. In case of PHs, patients' showed disagreement with some criteria viz., costs were adequate or affordable followed by distance to healthcare was adequate; adequate parking arrangements; good food served by hospitals; music facilities should be provided, and wards well decorated and ventilated.

In case of environment (physical facilities) of selected type of hospitals, on an average 89 per cent of patients from THs; 91 per cent from GHs and 78 per cent from PHs showed agreement with the above mentioned selected criteria. Thus, in case of responses for environment (physical facilities), the patients showed first preference to GHs followed by THs and PHs.

DATA ANALYSIS OF INTANGIBLE SERVICE CHARACTERISTICS

Table 6.16: Patients' Responses on Tangible Criteria for All the Three Types of Hospitals

Sl. No.	Selected Criteria	Type of Hospitals (Number and Percentages of Patients)							
		GHs		THs		PHs		Total	
		AG	DA	AG	DA	AG	DA	AG	DA
01	Sufficient number of Doctors' Remained Present	179 (89.5)	21 (10.5)	181 (90.5)	19 (9.5)	87 (87.0)	13 (13.0)	447 (89.4)	53 (10.6)
02	Well Equipped Units	181 (90.5)	19 (9.5)	187 (93.5)	13 (6.5)	88 (88.0)	12 (12.0)	456 (91.2)	44 (8.8)
03	Proper Sitting and Bedding Arrangements	186 (93.0)	14 (7.0)	186 (93.0)	14 (7.0)	90 (90.0)	10 (10.0)	462 (92.4)	38 (7.6)

...(Contd.)

...*(Contd.)*

04	Comfort in Examination and waiting Room	185 (92.5)	15 (7.5)	187 (93.5)	13 (6.5)	85 (85.0)	15 (15.0)	457 (91.4)	43 (8.6)
05	Natural Light or Illumination in Hospitals	194 (97.0)	6 (3.0)	196 (98.0)	4 (2.0)	88 (88.0)	12 (12.0)	478 (95.6)	22 (4.4)
06	Sufficient Number of Dust Bins and Spittoons	187 (93.5)	13 (6.5)	190 (95.0)	10 (5.0)	88 (88.0)	12 (12.0)	465 (93.0)	35 (7.0)
07	No Flies and Mos-quitoes in Hospitals	159 (79.5)	41 (20.5)	167 (83.5)	33 (16.5)	93 (93.0)	7 (7.0)	419 (83.8)	81 (16.2)
08	Adequate parking Arrangements	197 (98.5)	3 (1.5)	178 (89.0)	22 (11.0)	69 (69.0)	31 (31.0)	444 (88.8)	56 (11.2)
09	Clean Surroundings of Hospitalss	195 (97.5)	5 (2.5)	182 (91.0)	18 (9.0)	90 (90.0)	10 (10.0)	467 (93.4)	33 (6.6)
10	Pleasing and Appealing Room of Hospitals	184 (92.0)	16 (8.0)	189 (94.5)	11 (5.5)	85 (85.0)	15 (15.0)	458 (91.6)	42 (8.4)
11	Good Food Served by Hospitals*	146 (73.0)	54 (27.0)	107 (93.0)	8 (7.0)	46 (79.3)	12 (20.7)	299 (80.2)	74 (19.8)
12	Staff Neat in Appearance	193 (96.5)	7 (3.5)	119 (91.5)	11 (8.5)	90 (90.0)	10 (10.0)	402 (93.5)	28 (6.5)
13	Inside and Out side Noise kept Minimum	172 (86.0)	28 (14.0)	180 (90.0)	20 (10.0)	89 (89.0)	11 (11.0)	441 (88.2)	59 (11.8)
14	Wards Well Decorated and Ventilated	190 (95.0)	10 (5.0)	194 (97.0)	6 (3.0)	81 (81.0)	19 (19.0)	465 (93.0)	35 (7.0)
15	Music Facilities should be provided	181 (90.5)	19 (9.5)	180 (90.0)	20 (10.0)	81 (81.0)	19 (19.0)	442 (88.4)	58 (11.6)

* Total Patients were 373 as 127 Patients have not replied for question "Good Food Served by Hospitals" as food services were not provided by hospital.

In case of tangible facilities versus type of hospitals, on an average 90 per cent of all patients' showed agreement with most of the above mentioned criteria whereas, above 15 per cent of all patients' showed disagreement with two criteria namely, good food served by hospitals and no flies and mosquitoes in hospitals.

As per the patients' responses considering type of hospitals, 15 per cent and above patients' of GHs showed disagreement with some criteria viz., good food served by hospitals followed by no flies and mosquitoes in hospitals; and inside and out side noise kept minimum; whereas, in case of THs the patients' showed disagreement with criteria namely, no flies and mosquitoes in hospitals; and in case of PHs the patients' showed disagreement with criteria viz., adequate parking arrangements followed by good food served by hospitals; music facilities should be provided; wards well decorated and ventilated; pleasing and appealing room of hospitals, and comfort in examination and waiting room.

In case of tangible facilities of selected type of hospitals, on an average 92 per cent of patients' from THs; 91 per cent from GHs and 86 per cent from PHs showed agreement with the above mentioned criteria. Thus, in case of responses for environment (physical facilities), the patients showed first preference to THs followed by GHs and PHs.

Table 6.17: Patients' Responses on Reliability Criteria for All the Three Type of Hospitals

Sl. No.	Selected Criteria	Type of Hospitals (Number and Percentages of Patients)							
		GHs		THs		PHs		Total	
		AG	DA	AG	DA	AG	DA	AG	DA
01	Impartial Attitude of Doctors	185 (92.5)	15 (7.5)	192 (96.0)	8 (4.0)	88 (88.0)	12 (12.0)	465 (93.0)	35 (7.0)
02	Doctors' Makes Good Diagnosis	192 (96.0)	8 (4.0)	192 (96.0)	8 (4.0)	91 (91.0)	9 (9.0)	475 (95.0)	25 (5.0)
03	Doctors' Prescribeed Good Drugs	186 (93.0)	14 (7.0)	189 (94.5)	11 (5.5)	93 (93.0)	7 (7.0)	468 (93.6)	32 (6.4)
04	Impartial Attitude of Nurses	170 (85.0)	30 (15.0)	186 (93.5)	14 (7.0)	85 (85.0)	15 (15.0)	441 (88.2)	59 (11.8)
05	Nurses' Maintain Proper records of	174 (87.0)	26 (13.0)	181 (90.5)	19 (9.5)	91 (91.0)	9 (9.0)	445 (89.2)	54 (10.8)

In case of reliability criteria that was measured for the of hospital services versus type of hospitals, on an average 92 per cent of all patients together showed agreement with most of the above mentioned criteria whereas, above 10 per cent of all patients' showed disagreement with two criteria namely, impartial attitude of nurses and nurses' maintain proper records of patients. From the point of view of responses for the type of hospitals, 10 per cent and above patients showed disagreement with some criteria namely, impartial attitude of nurses and nurses' maintain proper records of patients in case of GHs; whereas nurses' maintain proper records of patients in case of THs; and impartial attitude of nurses and impartial attitude of doctors in case of PHs.

Patients' responses on reliability criteria as per the type of hospitals, on an average 94 per cent of patients from THs; 91 per cent from GHs and 90 per cent from PHs showed agreement with the selected criteria. Thus, in case of responses for reliability of hospital services, the patients showed first preference to THs followed by Government and PHs.

Table 6.18: Patients' Responses on Responsiveness Criteria for All the Type of Hospitals

Sl. No.	Selected Criteria	Type of Hospitals (Number and Percentages of Patients)							
		GHs		THs		PHs		Total	
		AG	DA	AG	DA	AG	DA	AG	DA
01	Doctors' Cooperation to patients	182 (91.0)	18 (9.0)	191 (95.5)	9 (4.5)	95 (95.0)	5 (5.0)	468 (93.6)	32 (6.4)
02	Patients' Felt Comfortable asking Questions to Doctors	183 (91.5)	17 (8.5)	189 (94.5)	11 (5.5)	89 (89.0)	11 (11.0)	461 (92.2)	39 (7.8)
03	Nurses' Cooperation to Patients	146 (73.0)	54 (27.0)	183 (91.5)	17 (8.5)	95 (95.0)	5 (5.0)	424 (84.8)	76 (15.2)
04	Nurses' Provided Prompt Service	54 (27.0)	146 (73.0)	114 (57.0)	86 (43.0)	72 (72.0)	28 (28.0)	240 (48.0)	260 (52.0)

...(Contd.)

...(Contd.)

05	Nurses' and Staff Remained Present in Emergency	119 (59.5)	81 (40.5)	167 (83.5)	33 (16.5)	86 (86.0)	14 (14.0)	372 (74.4)	128 (25.6)
06	Information Provided to patients for Managing Side Effects	76 (38.0)	124 (62.0)	148 (74.0)	52 (26.0)	51 (51.0)	49 (49.0)	275 (55.0)	225 (45.0)
07	Prompt Service Provided by Sanitation Staff	155 (77.5)	45 (22.5)	184 (92.0)	16 (8.0)	91 (91.0)	9 (9.0)	430 (86.0)	70 (14.0)
08	Less Waiting Time For Consultation and Treatment	116 (58.5)	84 (42.0)	174 (87.0)	26 (13.0)	80 (80.0)	20 (20.0)	370 (74.0)	130 (26.0)
09	Less Waiting Time for Test	145 (72.5)	55 (27.5)	161 (80.5)	39 (19.5)	85 (85.0)	15 (15.0)	391 (78.2)	109 (21.8)
10	Speed, Ease of Admission and Discharge form Hospitals	162 (81.0)	38 (19.0)	174 (87.0)	26 (13.0)	85 (85.0)	15 (15.0)	421 (84.2)	79 (15.8)
11	Convenient Office Hours	184 (92.0)	16 (8.0)	177 (88.5)	23 (11.5)	86 (86.0)	14 (14.0)	447 (89.4)	53 (10.6)
12	Adm. Staff Gives Prompt Services	56 (28.0)	144 (72.0)	153 (76.5)	47 (23.5)	74 (74.0)	26 (26.0)	283 (56.6)	217 (43.4)
13	No Overcrowding in Hospitals	117 (58.5)	83 (41.5)	177 (88.5)	23 (11.5)	82 (82.0)	18 (18.0)	376 (75.2)	124 (24.8)
14	Good Grievance handling System	35 (17.5)	165 (82.5)	152 (76.0)	48 (24.0)	66 (66.0)	34 (34.0)	253 (50.6)	247 (49.4)

Patients' responses in case of responsiveness of hospital staff members as per type of hospitals, on an average 74 per cent of all patients together showed agreement with most of the above mentioned criteria whereas, above 25 per cent of all respondent showed disagreement with some criteria viz., nurses' provided prompt service followed by good grievance handling system; information provided to patients for managing side effects; administrative staff gave prompt services; less waiting time for consultation and treatment; nurses' and staff remained present in emergency, and no overcrowding in hospitals.

From these seven criteria, four criteria namely, nurses' provide prompt service; good grievance handling system; information provided to patients for managing side effects, and administrative staff gave prompt services showed common disagreement for all selected type of hospitals.

The patients' responses as per the type of hospitals, nearly 25 per cent and above patients showed disagreement with some criteria viz., less waiting time for consultation and treatment followed by no overcrowding in hospitals; nurses' and staff remained present in emergency; nurses' cooperation to patients, and prompt service provided by sanitation staff in case of GHs.

Patients' responses on selected criteria of responsiveness of the staff of the selected type of hospitals, on an average 84 per cent of patients from THs; 81per cent from PHs and 62 per cent from GHs showed agreement with selected criteria. In case of responsiveness of the hospital staff, the patients' showed first preference to THs followed by PHs and GHs.

Table 6.19: Patients' Responses on Assurance Criteria for All the Three Type of Hospitals

Sl. No.	Selected Criteria	Type of Hospitals (Number and Percentages of Patients)							
		GHs		THs		PHs		Total	
		AG	DA	AG	DA	AG	DA	AG	DA
1	Doctors' Knowledge and Efficiency	192 (96.0)	8 (4.0)	189 (94.5)	11 (5.5)	94 (94.0)	6 (6.0)	475 (95.0)	25 (5.0)
2	Doctors' Experience in Curing Patients	188 (94.0)	12 (6.0)	184 (92.0)	16 (8.0)	96 (96.0)	4 (4.0)	468 (93.6)	32 (6.4)
3	Thorough Checkup by Doctors	187 (93.5)	13 (6.5)	184 (92.0)	16 (8.0)	95 (95.0)	5 (5.0)	466 (93.2)	34 (6.8)
4	Nurses' Knowledge and Efficiency	172 (86.0)	28 (14.0)	180 (90.0)	20 (10.0)	90 (90.0)	10 (10.0)	442 (88.4)	58 (11.6)
5	Nurses' Handled Patients Query Properly	123 (61.5)	77 (38.5)	162 (81.0)	38 (19.0)	88 (88.0)	12 (12.0)	373 (74.6)	127 (25.4)
6	Nurses' Experience in Curing Patients	149 (74.5)	51 (25.5)	164 (82.0)	36 (18.0)	86 (86.0)	14 (14.0)	399 (79.8)	101 (20.2)
7	Good Experience of Those who Perform Test on Patients	179 (89.5)	21 (10.5)	177 (88.5)	23 (11.5)	86 (86.0)	14 (14.0)	442 (88.4)	58 (11.6)

In case of patients' responses on criteria of assurance for hospital services as provided to them by the various type of hospitals, on an average 88 per cent of all patients together showed agreement with most of the above mentioned selected criteria whereas, above 10 per cent of all patients showed disagreement with some of the selected criteria viz., nurses' handled patients query properly followed by nurses' experience in curing patients; nurses' knowledge and efficiency, and good experience of those who perform test on patients.

In case of selected patients' hospital-wise responses on criteria of assurance disagreement was commonly observed for the same criteria with little criteria wise difference in preference. On an average 91 per cent of patients from PHs; 89 per cent from THs and 85 per cent from GHs showed agreement on the selected criteria. Thus, in case of assurance, the patients showed first preference to PHs followed by THs and GHs.

Table 6.20: Patients' Responses on Empathy Criteria for All the Three Types of Hospitals

Sl. No.	Selected Criteria	Type of Hospitals (Number and Percentages of Patients)							
		GHs		THs		PHs		Total	
		AG	DA	AG	DA	AG	DA	AG	DA
01	Doctors' were polite with patients	182 (91.0)	18 (9.0)	193 (96.5)	7 (3.5)	95 (95.0)	5 (5.0)	470 (94.0)	30 (6.0)
02	Patients' Felt Comfortable During Doctors Examination	179 (89.5)	21 (10.5)	184 (92.0)	16 (8.0)	94 (94.0)	6 (6.0)	457 (91.4)	43 (8.6)

...(Contd.)

...(Contd.)

03	Doctors' Work According to Patients Expectations	62 (31.0)	138 (69.0)	122 (61.0)	78 (39.0)	53 (53.0)	47 (47.0)	237 (47.4)	263 (52.6)
04	Doctors' Gave Individual Consideration and Confidentiality	128 (64.0)	72 (36.0)	172 (86.0)	28 (14.0)	80 (80.0)	20 (20.0)	380 (76.0)	120 (24.0)
05	Doctors' Showed Respect and Support patients	172 (86.0)	28 (14.0)	188 (94.0)	12 (6.0)	93 (93.0)	7 (7.0)	453 (9.6)	27 (5.4)
06	Doctors' Honesty in Dealing with patients	195 (97.5)	5 (2.5)	190 (95.0)	10 (5.0)	89 (89.0)	11 (11.0)	474 (94.8)	26 (5.2)
07	Nurses' Showed Politeness with Patients	160 (80.0)	40 (20.0)	179 (89.5)	21 (10.5)	91 (91.0)	9 (9.0)	430 (86.0)	70 (14.0)
08	Simple Checking Procedure	151 (75.5)	49 (24.5)	180 (90.0)	20 (10.0)	88 (88.0)	12 (12.0)	419 (83.8)	81 (16.2)
09	Good Concern for Patient's Family and Visitor	164 (82.0)	36 (18.0)	182 (91.0)	18 (9.0)	88 (88.0)	12 (12.0)	434 (86.8)	66 (13.2)
10	Simple Billing Procedures	184 (92.0)	16 (8.0)	180 (90.0)	20 (10.0)	86 (86.0)	14 (14.0)	450 (90.0)	50 (10.0)

In case of empathy experienced by patients from hospital services from the various type of hospitals, on an average 84 per cent of all patients together showed agreement with most of the selected criteria whereas, nearly 15 per cent and above of all patients' showed disagreement with some criteria viz., doctors' work according to patients expectations followed by doctors' gave individual consideration and confidentiality; simple checking procedure; nurses' showed politeness with patients, and good concern for patient's family and visitor.

From these five selected criteria, in the two of the criteria viz., doctors' work according to patients' expectations and doctors' gave individual consideration and confidentiality showed common disagreement for all the selected type of hospitals that is GHs, PHs, and THs..

Over and above, if one considers patients' responses as per the type of hospitals, nearly 15 per cent and above patients showed disagreement with some selected criteria viz., simple checking procedure followed by nurses' showed politeness with patients; good concern for patient's family and visitors; and doctors' showed respect and support to patients in case of GHs.

In case of patients' responses on criterion of empathy vis-à-vis type of hospitals, 89 per cent of patients from THs; 86 per cent from PHs and 79 per cent from GHs showed agreement with the selected criteria. Thus, in case of empathy as experienced by selected patients from hospitals' services, the patients showed first preference to THs followed by PHs and GHs.

Table 6.21: Patients' Responses on Dignity Criteria for All the Three Type of Hospitals

Sl. No.	Selected Criteria	Type of Hospitals (Number and Percentages of Patients)							
		GHs		THs		PHs		Total	
		AG	DA	AG	DA	AG	DA	AG	DA
01	Doctors' ask for patients Permission for performing Test	73 (36.5)	127 (63.5)	135 (67.5)	65 (32.5)	61 (61.0)	39 (39.0)	269 (53.8)	231 (46.2)
02	Nurses' Gave Personal Attention to Patients	95 (47.5)	105 (52.5)	153 (76.5)	47 (23.5)	79 (79.0)	21 (21.0)	327 (65.4)	173 (34.6)
03	Nurses' Explain Procedures and take Patient Permission before Test	120 (60.0)	80 (40.0)	170 (85.0)	30 (15.0)	71 (71.0)	29 (29.0)	361 (72.2)	139 (27.8)
04	Nurses' Explain Rules Regulation in ward	179 (89.5)	21 (10.5)	180 (90.0)	20 (10.0)	82 (82.0)	18 (18.0)	441 (88.2)	59 (11.8)
05	Nurses' were Kind, Gentle and Sympathetic	184 (92.0)	16 (8.0)	178 (89.0)	22 (11.0)	90 (90.0)	10 (10.0)	452 (90.4)	48 (9.6)
06	Adm. Staff Welcome and Implement Suggestion	44 (22.0)	156 (78.0)	138 69.0)	62 (31.0)	48 (48.0)	52 (52.0)	230 (46.0)	270 (54.0)
07	Adm. Gives Personal Attention To Patient	45 (22.5)	155 (77.5)	149 (74.5)	51 (25.5)	66 (66.0)	34 (34.0)	260 (52.0)	240 (48.0)
08	Patients' were Treated With Dignity and Privacy	157 (78.5)	43 (21.5)	178 (89.0)	22 (11.0)	89 (89.0)	11 (11.0)	424 (84.8)	76 (15.2)

In case of dignity as maintained by selected hospital service providers vis-à-vis type of hospitals, on an average 69 per cent of all patients together showed agreement with most of the selected criteria whereas, above 25 per cent of patients showed disagreement with some of the selected criteria viz., administrative staff welcome and implement suggestion followed by administrative staff gave personal attention to patient; doctors' ask for patients permission for performing test; nurses' gave personal attention to patients and nurses' explain procedures, and take patients' permission before test.

From the above mentioned five criteria, the three criteria namely, administrative staff welcome and implement suggestion; administrative gives personal attention to patient, and nurses explain procedures and take patient permission before test revealed a disagreement by patients for all selected type of hospitals.

Over and above, if one considers patients' responses from the point of view of type of hospitals, above 25 per cent patients showed disagreement with some selected criteria viz., nurses' gave personal attention to patients, and nurses' explain procedures and take patient permission before test in case of GHs; nurses' gave personal attention to patients in case of THs and nurses' explain procedures and take patient permission before test in case of PHs.

As per the type of hospitals wise responses of selected patients for the criteria of dignity towards patients as maintained by hospital service providers, on an average 80 per cent of patients from THs; 73 per cent from PHs and 56 per cent from GHs showed agreement with the selected criteria. Thus, in case of dignity towards patients as maintained by hospital service providers, the patients' showed first preference to THs followed by PHs and GHs.

Table 6.22: Patients' Responses on Accessibility/Affordability Criteria for All the Three Type of Hospitals

Sl. No.	Selected Criteria	Type of Hospitals (Number and Percentages of Patients)							
		GHs		THs		PHs		Total	
		AG	DA	AG	DA	AG	DA	AG	DA
1	Doctors' Easily Available in Emergency	175 (87.5)	25 (12.5)	178 (89.0)	22 (11.0)	90 (90.0)	10 (10.0)	443 (88.6)	57 (11.4)
2	Quick Payment Arrangements	176 (88.0)	24 (12.0)	198 (99.0)	2 (1.0)	87 (87.0)	13 (13.0)	461 (92.2)	39 (7.8)
3	Costs were Adequate or Affordable	198 (99.0)	2 (1.0)	113 (56.5)	87 (43.5)	13 (13.0)	87 (87.0)	324 (64.8)	176 (35.2)
4	Drugs Easily Obtained in Hospitals	183 (91.5)	17 (8.5)	192 (96.0)	8 (4.0)	83 (83.0)	17 (17.0)	458 (91.6)	42 (8.4)
5	Distance to Healthcare is Adequate	175 (87.5)	25 (12.5)	114 (57.0)	86 (43.0)	43 (43.0)	57 (57.0)	332 (66.4)	168 (33.6)

In case of accessibility and affordability of hospital services *vis-à-vis* type of hospitals, 81 per cent of patients together showed agreement with most of the identified criteria whereas, above 30 per cent of them showed disagreement with two criteria viz., costs were adequate or affordable, and distance to healthcare was adequate.

If one considers patients' responses as per the type of hospitals, the patients' showed disagreement for the same above mentioned criteria. That is, above 50 per cent of patients from PHs and above 40 per cent of patients from THs showed disagreement. Accessibility and affordability of hospital services as per type of hospitals, on an average 91 per cent of patients from GHs; 80 per cent from THs and 63 per cent from PHs showed agreement with the above mentioned criteria. In brief, on the criteria of accessibility and affordability of hospital services, the patients' showed first preference to GHs followed by THs and PHs.

Table 6.23: Patients' Overall Responses on Selected Criteria for All the Three Type of Hospitals

Sl. No.	Selected Criteria	Type of Hospitals (Number and Percentages of Patients)							
		GHs		THs		PHs		Total	
		AG	DA	AG	DA	AG	DA	AG	DA
01	Overall Satisfaction with Medical Services	195 (97.5)	5 (2.5)	186 (93.0)	14 (7.0)	97 (97.0)	3 (3.0)	478 (95.6)	22 (4.4)
02	Overall Satisfaction with Nursing Services	177 (88.5)	23 (11.5)	184 (92.0)	16 (8.0)	92 (92.0)	8 (8.0)	453 (90.6)	47 (9.4)
03	Overall Satisfaction with Administrative Services	140 (70.0)	60 (30.0)	186 (93.0)	14 (7.0)	85 (85.0)	15 (15.0)	411 (82.2)	89 (17.8)
04	Overall Satisfaction with Environment (Physical Facilities)	193 (96.5)	7 (3.5)	191 (95.5)	9 (4.5)	88 (88.0)	12 (12.0)	472 (94.4)	28 (5.6)

The overall responses, against selected criteria, of all the patients showed the favourable preferences for overall satisfaction with medical services; environment; paramedical services, and the administrative services, whereas reverse preference was observed for disagreement for the same criteria.

In case of GHs, the patients showed same preferences as showed by responses of all patients together. In case of THs, the patients showed the favourable preference for overall satisfaction with environment (physical facilities) followed with medical services; administrative services, and paramedical services, whereas in case of PHs, the patients showed preference for overall satisfaction with medical services, followed by paramedical services; environment (physical facilities), and administrative services.

Table 6.24: Overall Satisfaction Experienced by Selected Patients from Overall Hospital Services (Q. No. 10)

Sl. No.	Selected Criteria	Type of Hospitals (Number and Percentages of Patients)			
		GHs	THs	PHs	Total
01	Highly Satisfied	22(28.2)	29(37.2)	27(34.6)	78(100)
02	Satisfied	147(41.5)	143(40.4)	64(18.1)	354(100)
03	Somewhat satisfied/ Undecided	26(44.1)	24(40.7)	9(15.3)	59(100)
04	Dissatisfied	5(62.5)	3(37.5)	0(0.0)	8(100)
05	Highly Dissatisfied	0(0.0)	1(100)	0(0.0)	1(100)
	Total	200(40.0)	200(40.0)	100 20.0)	500(100)

In case of overall satisfaction, as experienced by selected patients' from overall hospital services, 86 per cent of patients' showed satisfactions, whereas 14 per cent of them were dissatisfied.

If one considers patients' responses as per the type of hospitals, 91 per cent of the satisfied patients were from PHs followed by 86 per cent from THs and 85 per cent of GHs, whereas reverse results were found in case of dissatisfied patients.

Table 6.25: Post-Purchase Behaviour of Selected Patients (Q. No. 11)

Sl. No.	Selected Criteria	Type of Hospitals (Number and Percentages of Patients)			
		GHs	THs	PHs	Total
1	Definitely Yes	165(40.8)	155(38.4)	84(20.8)	404(100)
2	Probably Yes	27(34.2)	39(49.4)	13(16.5)	79(100)
3	Undecided	7(46.7)	5(33.3)	3(20.0)	15(100)
4	Probably No	1(100)	0(0.0)	0(0.0)	1(100)
5	Definitely No	0(0.0)	1(100)	0(0.0)	1(100)
	Total	200(40.0)	200(40.0)	100(20.0)	500(100)

In case of selected patients' recommendation of the hospitals to others, it was found that most of them (97 per cent) were positive about recommending hospitals to others in future, and if one considers type of hospitals, uniform pattern was found for each type of hospitals.

Table 6.26: Patients' Views About Best Service of the Hospital for the Three Type of Hospitals (Q. No. 12)

Sl. No.	Selected Criteria	Type of Hospitals (Number and Percentages of Patients)							
		GHs		THs		PHs		Total	
		AG	DA	AG	DA	AG	DA	AG	DA
01	Best Service is Medical Treatment in Hospitals	196 (98.0)	4 (2.0)	181 (90.5)	19 (9.5)	99 (99.0)	1 (1.0)	476 (95.2)	24 (4.8)
02	Best Service is Nursing Staff Services in Hospitals	176 (88.0)	24 (12.0)	178 (89.0)	22 (11.0)	92 (92.0)	8 (8.0)	446 (89.2)	54 (10.8)
03	Best Service is Administrative Staff Services in Hospitals	138 (69.0)	62 (31.0)	180 (90.0)	20 (10.0)	89 (89.0)	11 (11.0)	407 (81.4)	93 (18.6)
04	Best Service is Environment in Hospitals	192 (96.0)	8 (4.0)	185 (92.5)	15 (7.5)	87 (87.0)	13 (13.0)	464 (92.8)	36 (7.2)

In case of overall responses of patients about best services of hospital on the selected criteria, all the patients showed favourable preferences for best services viz., medical treatment in hospitals followed by environment in hospitals; nursing staff services in hospitals, and administrative staff services in hospitals, whereas reverse preference was noticed for disagreement on the same criteria.

In case of GHs, the patients showed similar preference alike all patients together whereas In case of THs, the patients' showed the favourable preference for best service was environment (physical facilities) in hospitals followed by medical services; administrative services, and paramedical services. But, in case of PHs, the patients showed preference for best services was medical services; followed by paramedical services; administrative services, and environment (physical facilities) in the hospitals.

Table 6.27: Patients' Views about Worst Service of the Hospitals for All the Three Type of Hospitals (Q. No. 13)

Sl. No.	Selected Criteria	Type of Hospitals (Number and Percentages of Patients)							
		GHs		THs		PHs		Total	
		AG	DA	AG	DA	AG	DA	AG	DA
01	Worst Service is Medical Services in Hospitals	4 (2.0)	196 (98.0)	2 (1.0)	198 (99.0)	1 (1.0)	99 (99.0)	7 (1.4)	493 (98.6)
02	Worst Service is Paramedical Services in Hospitals	3 (1.5)	197 (98.5)	1 (0.5)	199 (99.5)	4 (4.0)	96 (96.0)	8 (1.6)	492 (98.4)
03	Worst Service is Administrative Services in Hospitals	3 (1.5)	197 (98.5)	5 (2.5)	195 (97.5)	3 (3.0)	97 (97.0)	11 (2.2)	489 (97.8)
04	Worst Service is related with Environment (physical facilities) in the Hospitals	4 (2.0)	196 (98.0)	5 (2.5)	195 (97.5)	4 (4.0)	96 (96.0)	13 (2.6)	487 (97.4)

In case of overall responses of patients about worst service of hospital, against selected criteria, all the patients showed their preference for worst services was environment (physical facilities) in hospitals followed by administrative services; paramedical services, and medical services in the hospitals.

In case of GHs, the patients showed their agreement about worst services of hospitals for environment physical facilities) in the hospital followed by medical services; paramedical services and administrative services.

In case of THs, the patients showed their agreement about worst service of hospital for environment (physical facilities) in the hospital followed by administrative services followed by medical services and paramedical services, whereas in case of PHs, the patients showed their agreement about worst service of hospital for environment (physical facilities) and paramedical services followed by administrative and medical services.

Table 6.28: Patients' Preferences About Availability of Medical Facilities (Q. No. 14)

Sl. No.	Selected Criteria	Type of Hospitals (Number and Percentages of Patients)			
		GHs	THs	PHs	Total
01	Strongly Agree	59 (38.8)	42 (27.6)	51 (33.6)	152 (100)
02	Agree	131 (41.2)	145 (45.6)	42 (13.2)	318 (100)
03	Somewhat Agree	9 (36.0)	11 (44.0)	5 (20.0)	25 (100)
04	Disagree	1 (20.0)	2 (40.0)	2 (40.0)	5 (100)
	Total	200 (40.0)	200 (40.0)	100 (20.0)	500 (100)

In case of patients' preference about whether, all kinds of medical facilities should be made available in the same hospital or not, it was found that most of the patients (94 per cent) agreed and showed positive preference for all kinds of medical facilities that should be made available in the same hospital.

DATA ANALYSIS (Overall-All Hospitals Together)

Table 6.29: Patients' Views About Charges of the Hospitals (Q. No. 04)

Sl. No.	Selected Criteria	No of Patients (Percentages)	Mean	SD
01	Very High	10 (2.0)		
02	High	35 (7.0)		
03	Reasonable	184 (36.8)	3.82	1.092
04	Low	75 (15.0)		
05	Very Low	196 (39.2)		
	Total	500 (100)		

The overall responses of all the patients about charges of hospitals revealed that above half of the (54 per cent) patients reported charges as low, 37 per cent reported charges as reasonable and 9 per cent reported charges as high.

Table 6.30: Patients' Reasons for the Selection of the Hospitals (Q. No. 07)

Sl. No.	Selected Criteria	MI	IM	SWA	UI	LI	Total	Mean	SD
		(Number and Percentages of Patients)							
01	Own Decision	287 (57.4)	72 (14.4)	49 (9.8)	61 (12.2)	31 (6.2)	500	4.05	1.311
02	Relatives Suggested	113 (22.6)	144 (28.8)	82 (16.4)	104 (20.8)	57 (11.4)	500	3.30	1.329
03	Friends Suggested	101 (20.2)	128 (25.6)	92 (18.4)	114 (22.8)	65 (13.0)	500	3.17	1.336
04	Suggested by Family Doctor	77 (15.4)	79 (15.8)	85 (17.0)	155 (31.0)	104 (20.8)	500	2.74	1.361
05	Past performance of Hospitals/Doctor	185 (37.0)	252 (50.4)	38 (7.6)	13 (2.6)	12 (2.4)	500	4.17	0.859
06	Only in this Hospitals such kind of facility is available	65 (13.0)	212 (42.4)	135 (27.0)	59 (11.8)	29 (5.8)	500	3.45	1.046
07	Overall Reputation of Hospitals	187 (37.4)	274 (54.8)	26 (5.2)	05 (1.0)	08 (1.6)	500	4.25	0.739
08	Hospitals Located Nearby	123 (24.6)	183 (36.6)	65 (13.0)	33 (6.6)	96 (19.2)	500	3.41	1.422
09	Hospitals is economical	195 (39.0)	122 (24.4)	150 (30.0)	19 (3.8)	14 (2.8)	500	3.93	1.045
10	Accessibility of Medicine and Test Facilities	154 (30.8)	294 (58.8)	42 (8.4)	07 (1.4)	03 (0.6)	500	4.18	0.686
11	Sanitation in the Hospitals	225 (45.0)	250 (50.0)	12 (2.4)	08 (1.6)	05 (1.0)	500	4.36	0.705
	Average	155 (31.0)	183 (36.6)	70 (14.0)	53 (10.6)	39 (7.8)	500	3.73	1.22

The overall responses of all the patients about reasons for selection of hospital revealed that 67 per cent of patients agreed with above given reasons for selection of hospitals whereas, 33 per cent of patients showed their disagreement which mainly comprises of reasons such as suggestions of family doctors followed by suggestion of friends; suggestion of relatives; location of hospital, and availability of specific facility in hospital.

Thus, on the basis of an average score which felt in the range from highest mean score of 4.36 to lowest mean score 2.74, first preference of patients as a reason for selection of hospital was sanitation of the hospitals followed by overall reputation of hospitals; accessibility of medical and test facilities; past performance of hospital/doctor, and patient patients' own decision.

MEDICAL SERVICES, PARAMEDICAL SERVICES, ADMINISTRATIVE SERVICES, AND ENVIRONMENT (PHYSICAL FACILITIES) OF HOSPITALS.

Table 6.31: Patients' Responses for Medical Services of the Selected Hospitals (Q. No. 08-1 to 17)

Sl. No.	Selected Criteria	SA	AG	SWA	DA	SDA	Total	Mean	SD
		(Number and Percentages of Patients)							
01	Doctors' Knowledge and Efficiency	306 (61.2)	169 (33.8)	23 (4.6)	1 (0.2)	1 (0.2)	500	4.56	0.613
02	Doctors' Cooperation to patients	305 (61.0)	163 (32.6)	28 (5.6)	3 (0.6)	1 (0.2)	500	4.54	0.649
03	Doctors' were polite with patients	324 (64.8)	146 (29.2)	26 (5.2)	3 (0.6)	1 (0.2)	500	4.58	0.639
04	Impartial Attitude of Doctors	301 (60.2)	164 (32.8)	22 (4.4)	8 (1.6)	5 (1.0)	500	4.50	0.745
05	Patients' Felt Comfortable During Doctors' Examination	219 (43.8)	238 (47.6)	40 (8.0)	3 (0.6)	0 (0.0)	500	4.35	0.65
06	Doctors' Experience in Curing Patients	268 (53.6)	200 (40.0)	27 (5.4)	5 (1.0)	0 (0.0)	500	4.46	0.646
07	Thorough Checkup by Doctors	252 (50.4)	214 (42.8)	29 (5.8)	4 (0.8)	1 (0.2)	500	4.42	0.658
08	Doctors' Work according to Patients Expectations	101 (20.2)	136 (27.2)	190 (38.0)	54 (10.8)	19 (3.8)	500	3.49	1.049
09	Doctors' Gave Individual Consideration and Confidentiality	164 (32.8)	216 (43.2)	90 (18.0)	25 (5.0)	5 (1.0)	500	4.02	0.894
10	Doctors' Showed Respect and Support patients	211 (42.2)	242 (48.4)	38 (7.6)	07 (1.4)	02 (0.4)	500	4.31	0.705
11	Doctors' Makes Good Diagnosis	296 (59.2)	179 (35.8)	20 (4.0)	4 (0.8)	1 (0.2)	500	4.53	0.634
12	Doctors' Prescribed Good Drugs	305 (61.0)	163 (32.6)	26 (5.2)	3 (0.6)	3 (0.6)	500	4.53	0.68
13	Doctor' ask for patients Permission for performing Test	138 (27.6)	131 (26.2)	145 (29.0)	63 (12.6)	23 (4.6)	500	3.60	1.15
14	Patients' Felt Comfortable asking Questions to Doctors	177 (35.4)	284 (56.8)	36 (7.2)	3 (0.6)	0 (0.0)	500	4.26	0.641
15	Doctors' Honesty in Dealing with patients	320 (64.0)	154 (30.8)	20 (4.0)	6 (1.2)	0 (0.0)	500	4.58	0.63
16	Sufficient number of Doctors Remained Present	198 (39.6)	249 (49.8)	46 (9.2)	4 (0.8)	3 (0.6)	500	4.27	0.709
17	Doctors' Availability in Emergency	191 (38.2)	252 (50.4)	49 (9.8)	7 (1.4)	1 (0.2)	500	4.25	0.702
	Average	240 (48.0)	194 (38.8)	50 (10.0)	12 (2.4)	4 (0.8)	500	4.31	0.81

The overall response of all the patients, about medical services in the hospitals revealed that most of the (86 per cent) patients showed agreement with all selected criteria, whereas 14 per cent of patients showed disagreement with some criteria namely, doctors' work according to patients expectations; doctors' ask for patients permission for performing test; and doctors' gave individual consideration and confidentiality.

On the basis of an average score, which felt in the range from highest mean score 4.58 to lowest mean score 3.49, first preference of patients for medical services was for some criteria namely, doctors' were polite with patients, followed by doctors' honesty in dealing with patients; doctors' knowledge and efficiency; doctors' cooperation to patients; doctors' made good diagnosis; doctors' prescribed good drugs; impartial attitude of doctors; doctors' experience in curing patients; thorough checkup by doctors; patients' felt comfortable during doctors' examination; doctors' showed respect and support to patients; sufficient number of doctors remained present, patients' felt comfortable asking questions to doctors, and doctors' availability in emergency.

Table 6.32: Patients' Responses for Paramedical Services of the Selected Hospitals (Q. No. 08-18 to 33)

Sl. No.	Selected Criteria	SA	AG	SWA	DA	SDA	Total	Mean	SD
		(Number and Percentages of Patients)							
01	Nurses' Knowledge and Efficiency	137 (27.4)	305 (61.0)	48 (9.6)	06 (1.2)	04 (0.8)	500	4.13	0.689
02	Nurses' Cooperation to Patients	171 (34.2)	253 (50.6)	67 (13.4)	07 (1.4)	02 (0.4)	500	4.17	0.735
03	Nurses' Showed Politeness with Patients	248 (49.6)	182 (36.4)	61 (12.2)	07 (1.4)	02 (0.4)	500	4.33	0.774
04	Impartial Attitude of Nurses	235 (47.0)	206 (41.2)	48 (9.6)	07 (1.4)	04 (0.8)	500	4.32	0.769
05	Nurses' Maintain Proper records of Patients	173 (34.6)	273 (54.6)	50 (10.0)	03 (0.6)	01 (0.2)	500	4.23	0.661
06	Nurses' Handled Patients Quarry Properly	136 (27.2)	237 (47.4)	117 (23.4)	08 (1.6)	02 (0.4)	500	3.99	0.779
07	Nurses' Experience in Curing Patients	133 (26.6)	266 (53.2)	91 (18.2)	07 (1.4)	03 (0.6)	500	4.04	0.747
08	Good Experience of Those who Perform Test on Patients	159 (31.8)	283 (56.6)	54 (10.8)	04 (0.8)	00 (0.0)	500	4.19	0.649
09	Nurses' Gave Personal Attention to Patients	108 (21.6)	219 (43.8)	137 (27.4)	33 (6.6)	03 (0.6)	500	3.79	0.875
10	Nurses' Provide Prompt Service	62 (12.4)	178 (35.6)	229 (45.8)	21 (4.2)	10 (2.0)	500	3.52	0.838
11	Nurses' and Staff Remains Present in	58 (11.6)	314 (62.8)	121 (24.2)	07 (1.4)	00 (0.0)	500	3.85	0.625
12	Nurses' Explain Procedures and take Patient Permission before Test	98 (19.6)	263 (52.6)	102 (20.4)	28 (5.6)	09 (1.8)	500	3.83	0.870

...(Contd.).

...(*Contd.*)

13	Nurses' Explain Rules Regulation in ward	132 (26.4)	309 (61.8)	45 (9.0)	10 (2.0)	04 (0.8)	500	4.11	0.703
14	Nurses' were Kind, Gentle and Sympathetic	256 (51.2)	196 (39.2)	39 (7.8)	07 (1.4)	02 (0.4)	500	3.83	0.870
15	Information Provided to patients for Managing Side Effects	103 (20.6)	172 (34.4)	128 (25.6)	66 (13.2)	31 (6.2)	500	3.50	1.140
16	Prompt Service Provided by Sanitation Staff	131 (26.2)	299 (59.8)	60 (12.0)	07 (1.4)	03 (0.6)	500	4.10	0.696
	Average	146 (29.2)	248 (49.6)	87 (17.4)	14 (2.8)	05 (1.0)	500	4.03	0.82

The overall response of all the patients about paramedical services in the hospital revealed that 79 per cent of the patients showed agreement with selected criteria, whereas 21 per cent of patients showed disagreement with some criteria viz., information provided to patients for managing side effects; nurses' provided prompt service; nurses' gave personal attention to patients; nurses' explain procedures and take patient permission before test, and nurses' and staff remained present in emergency.

Thus, on the basis of an average score, which felt in the range from highest mean score 4.39 to lowest mean score 3.5, the order of the preference, for the paramedical services, showed by the patients was nurses' were kind, gentle and sympathetic; nurses' showed politeness with patients; impartial attitude of nurses; nurses' maintain proper records of patients; good experience of those who perform test on patients; nurses' cooperation to patients;, nurses' knowledge and efficiency; nurses' explain rules regulation in ward; prompt service provided by sanitation staff;, nurses' experience in curing patients, and nurses' handled patients quarry properly.

Table 6.33: Patients' Responses for Administrative Services of the Selected Hospitals (Q. No. 0 8-34 to 46)

Sl. No.	Selected Criteria	SA	AG	SWA	DA	SDA	Total	Mean	SD
		(Number and Percentages of Patients)							
01	Less Waiting Time For Consultation and Treatment	75 (15.0)	295 (59.0)	114 (22.8)	10 (2.0)	06 (1.2)	500	3.85	0.737
02	Less Waiting Time for Test	71 (14.2)	320 (64.0)	96 (19.2)	12 (2.4)	01 (0.2)	500	3.90	0.662
03	Simple Checking Procedure	145 (29.0)	274 (54.8)	69 (13.8)	08 (1.6)	04 (0.8)	500	4.10	0.746
04	Speed, Ease of Admission and Dis-charge form Hospitals	128 (25.6)	293 (58.6)	65 (13.0)	11 (2.2)	03 (0.6)	500	4.06	0.725
05	Convenient Office Hours	142 (28.4)	305 (61.0)	38 (7.6)	09 (1.8)	06 (1.2)	500	4.14	0.723
06	Adm. Staff Gives Prompt Services	90 (18.0)	193 (38.6)	169 (33.6)	38 (7.6)	11 (2.2)	500	3.63	0.938

...(*Contd.*).

...(Contd.)

07	No Overcrowding in Hospitals	151 (30.2)	225 (45.0)	91 (18.2)	20 (4.0)	13 (2.6)	500	3.96	0.937
08	Good Grievance handling System	88 (17.6)	165 (33.0)	148 (29.6)	63 (12.6)	36 (7.2)	500	3.41	1.132
09	Adm. Staff Welcome and Implement Suggestion	95 (19.0)	135 (27.0)	125 (25.0)	108 (21.6)	37 (7.4)	500	3.29	1.210
10	Adm. Gives Personal Attention To Patient	77 (15.4)	183 (36.6)	121 (24.2)	95 (19.0)	24 (4.8)	500	3.39	1.103
11	Patients' were Treated With Dignity and Privacy	166 (33.2)	258 (51.6)	63 (12.6)	12 (2.4)	01 (0.2)	500	4.15	0.742
12	Good Concern for Patients' Family and Visitor	130 (26.0)	304 (60.8)	55 (11.0)	09 (1.8)	02 (0.4)	500	4.10	0.684
13	Simple Billing Procedures	149 (29.8)	301 (60.2)	35 (7.0)	09 (1.8)	06 (1.2)	500	4.16	0.724
	Average	116 (23.2)	250 (50.0)	91 (18.2)	31 (6.2)	12 (2.4)	500	3.86	0.92

The overall response of all the patients about administrative services in the hospital revealed that 73 per cent of the patients showed agreement with selected criteria, whereas 27 per cent of patients showed disagreement with some criteria viz., administrative staff welcome and implement suggestion; administrative staff gave personal attention to patient; good grievance handling system; administrative staff gave prompt services; less waiting time for consultation and treatment, and less waiting time for test.

Thus, on the basis of an average score, which felt in the range from highest mean score 4.16 to lowest mean score 3.29, first preference of patients for administrative services was for simple billing procedures; followed by patients' were treated with dignity and privacy; convenient office hours; simple checking procedure; good concern for patient family and visitor; speed, ease of admission and discharge form hospitals, and no overcrowding in hospitals.

Table 6.34: Patients' Responses for Environment (Physical Facilities) of the Selected Hospitals (Q. No. 08-47 to 64)

Sl. No.	Selected Criteria	SA	AG	SWA	DA	SDA	Not Applicable	Total	Mean	SD
		(Number and Percentages of Patients)								
01	Well Equipped Units	232 (46.4)	224 (44.8)	38 (7.6)	05 (1.0)	01 (0.2)	–	500	4.36	0.684
02	Proper Sitting and Bedding Arrangements	253 (50.6)	209 (41.8)	35 (7.0)	02 (0.4)	01 (0.2)	–	500	4.42	0.658
03	Comfort in Examination and waiting Room	226 (45.2)	231 (46.2)	39 (7.8)	03 (0.6)	01 (0.2)	–	500	4.36	0.668

...(Contd.).

...*(Contd.)*

04	Natural Light or Illumination in Hospitals	230 (46.0)	248 (49.6)	16 (3.2)	05 (1.0)	01 (0.2)	–	500	4.40	0.624
05	Sufficient Number of Dust Bins and	228 (45.6)	237 (47.4)	25 (5.0)	08 (1.6)	02 (0.4)	–	500	4.36	0.690
06	No Flies and Mosquitoes in Hospitals	155 (31.0)	264 (52.8)	64 (12.8)	16 (3.2)	01 (0.2)	–	500	4.11	0.757
07	Adequate parking Arrangements	319 (63.8)	125 (25.0)	30 (6.0)	22 (4.4)	04 (0.8)	–	500	4.47	0.855
08	Clean Surroundings of Hospitals	206 (41.2)	261 (52.2)	21 (4.2)	09 (1.8)	03 (0.6)	–	500	4.32	0.694
09	Pleasing and Appealing Room of Hospitals	212 (42.4)	246 (49.2)	36 (7.2)	06 (1.2)	00 (0.0)	–	500	4.33	0.661
10	Good Food Served by Hospital*	149 (29.8)	150 (30.0)	40 (8.0)	25 (5.0)	09 (1.8)	127 (25.4)*	500	3.05	0.994
11	Staff Neat in Appearance	184 (36.8)	288 (57.6)	26 (5.2)	02 (0.4)	00 (0.0)	–	500	4.31	0.585
12	Inside and Out side Noise kept Minimum	157 (31.4)	284 (56.8)	36 (7.2)	18 (3.6)	05 (1.0)	–	500	4.14	0.776
13	Wards Well Decorated and Ventilated	182 (36.4)	283 (56.6)	28 (5.6)	05 (1.0)	02 (0.4)	–	500	4.28	0.649
14	Music Facilities should be provided	203 (40.6)	239 (47.8)	29 (5.8)	19 (3.8)	10 (2.0)	–	500	4.21	0.868
15	Quick Payment Arrangements	265 (53.0)	196 (39.2)	32 (6.4)	06 (1.2)	01 (0.2)	–	500	4.44	0.686
16	Costs were Adequate or Affordable	282 (56.4)	42 (8.4)	141 (28.2)	25 (5.0)	10 (2.0)	–	500	4.12	1.102
17	Drugs Easily Obtained in Hospitals	246 (49.2)	212 (42.4)	35 (7.0)	04 (0.8)	03 (0.6)	–	500	4.39	0.706
18	Distance to Healthcare is Adequate	197 (39.4)	135 (27.0)	55 (11.0)	25 (5.0)	88 (17.6)	–	500	3.66	1.474
	Average	218 (43.6)	215 (43.0)	40 (8.0)	12 (2.4)	08 (1.6)	07 (1.4)	500	4.21	0.83

* Total Patients were 373 as 127 Patients have not replied for question "Good Food Served by Hospitals" as food services were not provided by hospital.

The overall response of all the patients about environment (physical facilities) in the hospitals revealed that 87 per cent of the patients showed agreement with selected criteria, whereas 13 per cent of them showed disagreement with two criteria namely, good food served by hospitals and distance to healthcare was adequate.

Thus, on the basis of an average score, which felt in the range from highest mean score 4.47 to lowest mean score 3.05, first preference of patients for environment (physical facilities) was for adequate parking arrangements; quick payment arrangements; proper sitting and bedding arrangements; natural light or illumination in hospitals; drugs easily obtained in hospitals; well equipped units; comfort in examination and waiting room; sufficient number of dust bins and spittoons; pleasing and appealing room of hospitals; clean surroundings of hospitals; staff neat in appearance, wards well decorated and ventilated; music facilities should be provided; inside and out side noise kept minimum; costs were adequate or affordable, and no flies and mosquitoes in hospitals.

DATA ANALYSIS OF VARIABLES: INTANGIBLE SERVICES CHARACTERISTICS

Table 6.35: Patients' Responses on Tangible Criteria of the Selected Hospitals (Q. No. 08-16, 47 to 58)

Sl. No.	Selected Criteria	SA	AG	SWA	DA	SDA	Not Applicable	Total	Mean	SD
		(Number and Percentages of Patients)								
01	Sufficient Doctors Remain Present	198 (39.6)	249 (49.8)	46 (9.2)	04 (0.8)	03 (0.6)	–	500	4.27	0.709
02	Well Equipped Units	232 (36.4)	224 (44.8)	38 (7.6)	5 (1.0)	01 (0.2)	–	500	4.36	0.684
03	Proper Sitting and	253 (50.6)	209 (41.8)	35 (7.0)	02 (0.4)	01 (0.2)	–	500	4.42	0.658
04	Comfort in Examination and waiting Room	226 (45.2)	231 (46.2)	39 (7.8)	3 (0.6)	01 (0.2)	–	500	4.36	0.668
05	Natural Light or Illumination in Hospitals	230 (46.0)	248 (49.6)	16 (3.2)	05 (1.0)	01 (0.2)	–	500	4.40	0.624
06	Sufficient Number of Dust Bins and Spittoons	228 (45.6)	237 (47.4)	25 (5.0)	08 (1.6)	02 (0.4)	–	500	4.36	0.690
07	No Flies and Mosquitoes in Hospitals	155 (31.0)	264 (52.8)	64 (12.8)	16 (3.2)	01 (0.2)	–	500	4.11	0.757
08	Adequate parking Arrangements	319 (63.8)	125 (25.0)	30 (6.0)	22 (4.4)	04 (0.8)	–	500	4.47	0.855
09	Clean Surroundings of Hospitals	206 (41.2)	261 (52.2)	21 (4.2)	09 (1.8)	03 (0.6)	–	500	4.32	0.694
10	Pleasing and Appealing Room of Hospitals	212 (42.4)	246 (49.2)	36 (7.2)	06 (1.2)	00 (0.0)	–	500	4.33	0.661
11	Good Food Served by Hospital*	149 (29.8)	150 (30.0)	40 (8.0)	25 (5.0)	09 (1.8)	127*	500	3.05	0.994
12	Staff Neat in Appearance	184 (36.8)	288 (57.6)	26 (5.2)	02 (0.4)	00 (0.0)	–	500	4.31	0.585
13	Inside and Out side Noise kept Minimum	157 (31.4)	284 (56.8)	36 (7.2)	18 (3.6)	05 (1.0)	–	500	4.14	0.776
14	Wards Well Decorated and Ventilated	182 (39.4)	283 (56.6)	28 (5.6)	05 (1.0)	02 (0.4)	–	500	4.28	0.649
15	Music Facilities should be provided	203 (40.6)	239 (47.8)	29 (5.8)	19 (3.8)	10 (2.0)	–	500	4.21	0.868
	Average	209 (41.8)	239 (47.2)	34 (6.8)	10 (2.0)	03 (0.6)	08 (1.6)	500	4.23	0.73

* Total Patients were 373 as 127 Patients have not replied for question "Good Food Served by Hospitals" as food services were not provided by hospital.

The overall response of all the patients about tangible facilities of the hospital revealed that 89 per cent of the patients showed agreement with selected criteria, whereas 11 per cent of them showed disagreement on two criteria viz., good food served by hospitals, no flies and mosquitoes in hospitals and adequate parking arrangements.

Thus, on the basis of an average score, which felt in the range from highest mean score 4.47 to lowest mean score 3.05, first preference of patients for tangible criteria was for adequate parking arrangements, followed by proper sitting and bedding arrangements; natural light or illumination in hospitals; well equipped units; comfort in examination and waiting room, sufficient number of dust bins and spittoons;, pleasing and appealing room of hospitals; clean surroundings of hospitals; staff neat in appearance; wards well decorated and ventilated; sufficient doctors remain present; music facilities should be provided, and inside and out side noise kept minimum.

Table 6.36: Patients' Responses on Reliability Criteria of the Selected Hospitals (Q. No. 08-04, 11, 12, 21, 22)

Sl. No.	Selected Criteria	SA	AG	SWA	DA	SDA	Total	Mean	SD
		(Number and Percentages of Patients)							
01	Impartial Attitude of Doctors	301 (60.2)	164 (32.8)	22 (4.4)	08 (1.6)	05 (1.0)	500	4.50	0.745
02	Doctors' Made Good Diagnosis	296 (59.2)	179 (35.8)	20 (4.0)	04 (0.8)	01 (0.2)	500	4.53	0.634
03	Doctors' Prescribed Good Drugs	305 (61.0)	163 (32.6)	26 (5.2)	03 (0.6)	03 (0.6)	500	4.53	0.680
04	Impartial Attitude of Nurses	235 (47.0)	206 (41.2)	48 (9.6)	07 (1.4)	04 (0.8)	500	4.32	0.769
05	Nurses' Maintain Proper records of Patients	173 (34.6)	273 (54.6)	50 (10.0)	03 (0.6)	01 (0.2)	500	4.23	0.661
	Average	262 (52.4)	197 (39.4)	33 6.6)	05 (1.0)	03 (0.6)	500	4.42	0.71

The overall response of all the patients about reliability of the hospital services revealed that 92 per cent patients showed agreement with selected criteria, whereas only 8 per cent of them showed disagreement with this criteria which spread among all the criteria.

Thus, on the basis of an average score, which felt in the range from highest mean score 4.53 to lowest mean score 4.23, first preference of patients against reliability criteria was for doctors' makes good diagnosis; doctors' prescribed good drugs; impartial attitude of doctors; impartial attitude of nurses, and nurses' maintain proper records of patients.

Table 6.37: Patients' Responses on Responsiveness Criteria of the Selected Hospitals (Q. No. 08-02, 14, 19, 27, 28, 32, 33, 34, 35, 37 to 41)

Sl. No.	Selected Criteria	SA	AG	SWA	DA	SDA	Total	Mean	SD
		(Number and Percentages of Patients)							
01	Doctors' Cooperation to patients	305 (61.0)	163 (32.6)	28 (5.6)	03 (0.6)	01 (0.2)	500	4.54	0.649
02	Patients' Felt Comfortable asking Questions to Doctors	177 (35.4)	284 (56.8)	36 (7.2)	03 (0.6)	00 (0.0)	500	4.26	0.641
03	Nurses' Cooperation to Patients	171 (34.2)	253 (50.6)	67 (13.4)	07 (1.4)	02 (0.4)	500	4.17	0.735

...(Contd.)

...(Contd.)

04	Nurses' Provided Prompt Service	62 (12.4)	178 (35.6)	229 (45.8)	21 (4.2)	10 (2.0)	500	3.52	0.838
05	Nurses' and Staff Remains Present in Emergency	58 (11.6)	314 (62.8)	121 (24.2)	07 (1.4)	00 (0.0)	500	3.85	0.625
06	Information Provided to patients for Managing Side Effects	103 (20.6)	172 (34.4)	128 (25.6)	66 (13.2)	31 (6.2)	500	3.50	1.140
07	Prompt Service Provided by Sanitation Staff	131 (26.2)	299 (59.8)	60 (12.0)	07 (1.4)	03 (0.6)	500	4.10	0.696
08	Less Waiting Time For Consultation and Treatment	75 (15.0)	295 (59.0)	114 (22.8)	10 (2.0)	06 (1.2)	500	3.85	0.737
09	Less Waiting Time for Test	71 (14.2)	320 (64.0)	96 (19.2)	12 (2.4)	01 (0.2)	500	3.90	0.662
10	Speed, Ease of Admi-ssion and Discharge form Hospitals	128 (25.6)	293 (58.6)	65 (13.0)	11 (2.2)	03 (0.6)	500	4.06	0.725
11	Convenient Office Hours	142 (28.4)	305 (61.0)	38 (7.6)	09 (1.8)	06 (1.2)	500	4.14	0.723
12	Adm. Staff Gives Prompt Services	90 (18.0)	193 (38.6)	168 (33.6)	38 (7.6)	11 (2.2)	500	3.63	0.938
13	No Overcrowding in Hospitals	151 (30.2)	225 (45.0)	91 (18.2)	20 (4.0)	13 (2.6)	500	3.96	0.937
14	Good Grievance handling System	88 (17.6)	165 (33.0)	148 (29.6)	63 (12.6)	36 (7.2)	500	3.41	1.132
	Average	125 (25.0)	247 (49.4)	99 (19.8)	20 (4.0)	9 (1.8)	500	3.92	0.87

The overall response of all the patients about responsiveness of the hospital staff services revealed that 75 per cent of the patients showed agreement with selected criteria, whereas 25 per cent of them showed disagreement with these criteria viz., good grievance handling system; followed by information provided to patients for managing side effects; nurses provide prompt service; administrative staff gives prompt services; nurses and staff remains present in emergency; less waiting time for consultation and treatment, and less waiting time for test.

Thus, on the basis of an average score, which felt in the range from highest mean score 4.54 to lowest mean score 3.41, first preference of patients against responsiveness criteria was for doctors' cooperation to patients; patients' felt comfortable asking questions to doctors; nurses' cooperation to patients; convenient office hours; prompt service provided by sanitation staff; speed, ease of admission and discharge form hospitals, and no overcrowding in hospitals.

Table 6.38: Patients' Responses on Assurance Criteria of the Selected Hospitals (Q. No. 08-01, 06, 07, 18, 23, 24, 25)

Sl. No.	Selected Criteria	SA	AG	SWA	DA	SDA	Total	Mean	SD
		(Number and Percentages of Patients)							
01	Doctors' Knowledge and Efficiency	306 (61.2)	169 (33.8)	23 (4.6)	01 (0.2)	01 (0.2)	500	4.56	0.613
02	Doctors' Experience in Curing Patients	268 (53.6)	200 (40.0)	27 (5.4)	05 (1.0)	00 (0.0)	500	4.46	0.646
03	Thorough Checkup by Doctors	252 (50.4)	214 (42.8)	29 (5.8)	04 (0.8)	01 (0.2)	500	4.42	0.658
04	Nurses' Knowledge and Efficiency	137 (27.4)	305 (61.0)	48 (9.6)	06 (1.2)	04 (0.8)	500	4.13	0.689
05	Nurses' Handled Patients Quarry Properly	136 (27.2)	237 (47.4)	117 (23.4)	08 (1.6)	02 (0.4)	500	3.99	0.779
06	Nurses' Experience in Curing Patients	133 (26.6)	266 (53.2)	91 (18.2)	07 (1.4)	03 (0.6)	500	4.04	0.747
07	Good Experience of Those who Perform Test on Patients	159 (31.8)	283 (56.6)	54 (10.8)	04 (0.8)	00 (0.0)	500	4.19	0.649
	Average	199 (39.7)	238 (47.8)	56 (11.1)	05 (1.0)	02 (0.4)	500	4.26	0.72

The overall response of all the patients about assurance from hospital services revealed that 75 per cent of the patients showed agreement with selected criteria, whereas, 25 per cent of them showed disagreement with two criteria namely, nurses' handled patients quarry properly and nurses' experience in curing patients.

Thus, on the basis of an average score, which felt in the range from highest mean score 4.56 to lowest mean score 3.99, first preference of patients against assurance criteria was for doctors' knowledge and efficiency; followed by doctors' experience in curing patients; thorough checkup by doctors; good experience of those who perform test on patients, and nurses' knowledge and efficiency.

Table 6.39: Patients' Responses on Empathy Criteria of the Selected Hospitals (Q. No. 08-03, 05, 08, 09, 10, 15, 20, 36, 45, 46)

Sl. No.	Selected Criteria	SA	AG	SWA	DA	SDA	Total	Mean	SD
		(Number and Percentages of Patients)							
01	Doctors' were polite with patients	324 (64.8)	146 (29.2)	26 (5.2)	03 (0.4)	01 (0.2)	500	4.58	0.639
02	Patients' Felt Comfortable During Doctors Examination	219 (43.8)	238 (47.6)	40 (8.0)	03 (0.6)	00 (0.0)	500	4.35	0.650
03	Doctors' Work According to Patients Expectations	101 (20.2)	136 (27.2)	190 (38.0)	54 (10.8)	19 (3.8)	500	3.49	1.049
04	Doctor's Gave Individual Consideration and Confidentiality	164 (32.8)	216 (43.2)	90 (18.0)	25 (5.0)	05 (1.0)	500	4.02	0.894

...(Contd.)

...(Contd.)

05	Doctors' Showed Respect and Support patients	211 (42.2)	242 (48.4)	38 (7.6)	07 (1.4)	02 (0.4)	500	4.31	0.705
06	Doctors' Honesty in Dealing with patients	320 (64.0)	154 (30.8)	20 (4.0)	06 (1.2)	00 (0.0)	500	4.58	0.630
07	Nurses' Showed Politeness with Patients	248 (49.6)	182 (36.4)	61 (12.2)	07 (1.4)	02 (0.4)	500	4.33	0.774
08	Simple Checking Procedure	145 (29.0)	274 (54.8)	69 (13.8)	08 (1.6)	04 (0.8)	500	4.10	0.746
09	Good Concern for Patients' Family and Visitor	130 (26.0)	304 (60.8)	55 (11.0)	09 (1.8)	02 (0.4)	500	4.10	0.684
10	Simple Billing Procedures	149 (29.4)	301 (60.2)	35 (7.0)	09 (1.8)	06 (1.2)	500	4.16	0.724
	Average	201 (40.2)	219 (43.8)	63 (12.6)	13 (2.6)	04 (0.8)	500	4.20	0.82

The overall response of all the patients about empathy experienced by patients from hospital services revealed that 84 per cent of the patients showed agreement with selected criteria, whereas 16 per cent of them showed disagreement with two criteria namely, doctors' work according to patients' expectations and doctors' gave individual consideration and confidentiality.

Thus, on the basis of an average score, which felt in the range from highest mean score 4.58 to lowest mean score 3.49, first preference of patients against empathy criteria was for doctors' were polite with patients followed by doctors' honesty in dealing with patients; patients' felt comfortable during doctors' examination; nurses' showed politeness with patients; doctors' showed respect and support patients; simple billing procedures; simple checking procedure, and good concern for patient family and visitor.

Table 6.40: Patients' Responses on Dignity Criteria of the Selected Hospitals (Q. No. 08-13, 26, 29, 30, 31, 42, 43, 44)

Sl. No.	Selected Criteria	SA	AG	SWA	DA	SDA	Total	Mean	SD
		(Number and Percentages of Patients)							
01	Doctors' ask for patients Permission for performing Test	138 (27.6)	131 (26.2)	145 (29.0)	63 (12.6)	23 (4.6)	500	3.60	1.150
02	Nurses' Gave Personal Attention to Patients	108 (21.6)	219 (43.8)	137 (27.4)	33 (6.6)	03 (0.6)	500	3.79	0.875
03	Nurses' Explain Procedures and take Patient Permission before Test	98 (19.6)	263 (52.6)	102 (20.4)	28 (5.6)	09 (1.8)	500	3.83	0.870
04	Nurses' Explain Rules Regulation in ward	132 (26.4)	309 (61.8)	45 (9.0)	10 (2.0)	04 (0.8)	500	4.11	0.703

...(Contd.)

...(*Contd.*)

05	Nurses' are Kind, Gentle and Sympathetic	256 (51.2)	196 (39.2)	39 (7.8)	07 (1.4)	02 (0.4)	500	4.39	0.727
06	Adm. Staff Welcome and Implement Suggestion	95 (19.0)	135 (27.0)	125 (25.0)	108 (21.6)	37 (7.4)	500	3.29	1.210
07	Adm. Gives Personal Attention To Patient	77 (15.4)	183 (36.6)	121 (24.2)	95 (19.0)	24 (4.8)	500	3.39	1.103
08	Patients' were Treated With Dignity and Privacy	166 (33.2)	258 (51.6)	63 (12.6)	12 (2.4)	01 (0.2)	500	4.15	0.742
	Average	134 (26.8)	212 (42.4)	97 (19.4)	44 (8.8)	13 (2.6)	500	3.82	1.01

The overall response of all the patients about dignity as maintained with patients by hospital staff revealed that majority of the patients (69 per cent) showed agreement with selected criteria, whereas 31 per cent of them showed disagreement with some criteria viz., administration staff welcome and implement suggestion followed by administration gives personal attention to patient; doctors' ask for patients permission for performing test; nurses' gave personal attention to patients, and nurses' explain procedures, and take patient permission before test.

Thus, on the basis of an average score, which felt in the range from highest mean score 4.39 to lowest mean score 3.29, first preference of patients against dignity criteria was for nurses' were kind, gentle and sympathetic; patients' were treated with dignity and privacy, and nurses' explain rules regulation in ward.

Table 6.41: Patients' Responses on Accessibility/Affordability Criteria of the Selected Hospitals (Q. No. 08-17, 61 to 64)

Sl. No.	Selected Criteria	SA	AG	SWA	DA	SDA	Total	Mean	SD
		(Number and Percentages of Patients)							
01	Doctors' Availability in Emergency	191 (38.2)	252 (50.4)	49 (9.8)	07 (1.4)	01 (0.2)	500	4.25	0.702
02	Quick Payment Arrangements	265 (53.0)	196 (39.2)	32 (6.4)	06 (1.2)	01 (0.2)	500	4.44	0.686
03	Costs were Adequate or Affordable	282 (56.4)	42 (8.4)	141 (28.2)	25 (5.0)	10 (2.0)	500	4.12	1.102
04	Drugs Easily Obtained in Hospitals	246 (49.2)	212 (42.4)	35 (7.0)	04 (0.8)	03 (0.6)	500	4.39	0.706
05	Distance to Healthcare is Adequate	197 (39.4)	135 (27.0)	55 (11.0)	25 (5.0)	88 (17.6)	500	3.66	1.474
	Average	236 (47.2)	167 (33.4)	63 (12.6)	13 (2.6)	21 (4.2)	500	4.17	1.02

The overall response of all the patients about accessibility and affordability of hospital services revealed that 81 per cent of the patients showed agreement with selected criteria, whereas 19 per cent of them showed disagreement with one criterion namely, distance to healthcare was adequate.

Thus, on the basis of an average score, which felt in the range from highest mean score 4.44 to lowest mean score 3.66, first preference of patients against accessibility/

affordability criteria was for quick payment arrangements; followed by drugs easily obtained in hospitals; doctors' availability in emergency, and costs were adequate or affordable.

Table 6.42: Patients' Overall Satisfaction on Selected Criteria of the Selected Hospitals (Q. No. 09)

Sl. No.	Selected Criteria	HS	ST	SWA	DS	HDS	Total	Mean	SD
		(Number and Percentages of Patients)							
01	Overall Satisfaction with Medical Services	338 (67.6)	140 (28.0)	19 (3.8)	03 (0.6)	00 (0.0)	500	4.63	0.589
02	Overall Satisfaction with Paramedical Services	163 (32.6)	290 (58.0)	45 (9.0)	01 (0.2)	01 (0.2)	500	4.23	0.626
03	Overall Satisfaction with Administrative Services	108 (21.6)	303 (60.6)	82 (16.4)	05 (1.0)	02 (0.4)	500	4.02	0.676
04	Overall Satisfaction with Environment (Physical Facilities)	219 (43.8)	253 (50.6)	22 (4.4)	06 (1.2)	00 (0.0)	500	4.37	0.628
	Average	207 (41.4)	246 (49.2)	42 (8.4)	04 (0.8)	01 (0.2)	500	4.31	0.67

The overall response of all the patients about their overall satisfaction against selected criteria revealed that 91 per cent of the patients showed agreement with selected criteria, whereas 9 per cent of them showed disagreement with this criteria and it mainly comprises one criterion namely, overall satisfaction with administrative services.

Thus, on the basis of an average score which felt in the range from highest mean score 4.63 to lowest mean score 4.02, first overall preference of patients against selected criteria was overall satisfaction with medical treatment, followed by overall satisfaction with environment, and overall satisfaction with paramedical staff.

Table 6.43: Patients' Overall Satisfaction As Experienced on Hospital Services (Q. No. 10)

Sl. No.	Selected Criteria	Number and Percentages of Patients' Responses	Mean	SD
01	Highly Satisfied	78 (15.6)	4.00	0.597
02	Satisfied	354 (70.8)		
03	Somewhat satisfied	59 (11.8)		
04	Dissatisfied	08 (1.6)		
05	Highly dissatisfied	01 (0.2)		
	Total	500 (100)		

Overall satisfaction as experienced by patients from overall services against all selected criteria revealed that, 86 per cent of them expressed satisfaction with hospital services and 14 per cent of patients' were dissatisfied.

Table 6.44: Patients' Post-Purchase Behaviour (Q. No. 11)

Sl. No.	Selected Criteria	Number and Percentages of Patients' Responses	Mean	SD
01	Definitely yes	404 (80.8)	4.77	0.524
02	Probably Yes	79 (15.8)		
03	Undecided	15 (3.0)		
04	Probably No	01 (0.2)		
05	Definitely No	01 (0.2)		
	Total	500 (100)		

Patients' responses towards their intention to recommend the selected hospitals to others in near future revealed that 97 per cent of the patients agreed to it, whereas 3 per cent of patients showed their disagreement to it.

Table 6.45: Patient's Views About Best Service of the Selected Hospitals (Q. No. 12)

Sl. No.	Selected Criteria	SA	AG	SWA	DA	SDA	Total	Mean	SD
		(Number and Percentages of Patients)							
01	Best Service is Medical Treatment	345 (69.0)	131 (26.2)	18 (3.6)	01 (0.2)	05 (1.0)	500 500	4.62 4.62	0.664 0.664
02	Best Service is Nursing Staff Services in Hospitals	163 (32.6)	283 (56.6)	45 (9.0)	07 (1.4)	02 (0.4)	500	4.19	0.693
03	Best Service is Administrative Staff Services in Hospitals	108 (21.6)	299 (59.8)	82 (16.4)	07 (1.4)	04 (0.8)	500	4.00	0.715
04	Best Service is Environment in Hospitals	212 (42.4)	252 (50.4)	27 (5.4)	04 (0.8)	05 (1.0)	500	4.33	0.702
	Average	207 (41.4)	241 (48.2)	43 (8.6)	5 (1.0)	4 (0.8)	500	4.29	0.727

The overall response of all the patients about best service of hospital services revealed that 90 per cent of the patients showed agreement with all selected criteria, whereas 10 per cent of patients showed disagreement with this criteria and it mainly comprises one criteria viz., services provided by administrative staff.

Thus, on the basis of an average score which felt in the range from highest mean score 4.62 to lowest mean score 4.00, first overall preference of patients about best services of the hospital was medical treatment in hospitals, followed by environment in hospitals, and nursing staff services in hospitals.

Table 6.46: Patient's Views About Worst Service of the Selected Hospitals (Q. No. 13)

Sl. No.	Selected Criteria	SA	AG	SWA	DA	SDA	Total	Mean	SD
		(Number and Percentages of Patients)							
01	Worst Service is Medical Services in Hospitals	04 (0.8)	03 (0.6)	21 (4.2)	122 (24.4)	350 (70.0)	500	1.38	0.672
02	Worst Service is Paramedical Services in Hospitals	01 (0.2)	07 (1.4)	40 (8.0)	286 (57.2)	166 (33.2)	500	1.78	0.663
03	Worst Service is Administrative Services in Hospitals	01 (0.2)	10 (2.0)	70 (14.0)	296 (59.2)	123 (24.6)	500	1.94	0.694
04	Worst Service is related with Environment (Physical Facilities) in Hospitals	01 (0.2)	12 (2.4)	28 (5.6)	250 (50.0)	209 (41.8)	500	1.69	0.703
	Average	2 (0.4)	7 (1.4)	40 (8.0)	239 (47.8)	212 (42.4)	500	1.70	0.71

The overall response of all the patients about worst service of hospitals revealed that 98 per cent of the patients showed disagreement with all selected criteria, whereas 2 per cent of them showed agreement with one criteria namely, services provided by administrative staff.

Thus, on the basis of an average score, which felt in the range from highest mean score 1.94 to lowest mean score 1.38, overall preference of patients about worst services of the hospital was administrative services in hospitals; followed by paramedical services in hospitals; environment (physical facilities) in hospitals, and last preference was medical services in hospitals.

Table 6.47: Patients' Preferences About Availability of Medical Facilities (Q. No. 14)

Sl. No.	Selected Criteria	Number (Percentages) of Patients' Responses	Mean	SD
01	Strongly Agree	152 (30.4)	4.23	0.583
02	Agree	318 (63.6)		
03	Somewhat Agree	25 (5.0)		
04	Disagree	05 (1.0)		
05	Strongly Disagree	00 (0.0)		
	Total	500 (100)		

The patients views were also collected on their preferences for different kinds of medical facilities that should be made available in the same hospitals or not, and findings showed that 94 per cent of the patients agreed to it and only 6 per cent of patients disagreed to it.

7 Findings of the Research Study

FINDINGS OF THE RESEARCH STUDY

The researcher has applied Chi-square test, ANOVA and factor analysis to test various hypothesis formulated based on the primary data which were collected from the selected patients' of the Government Hospitals (GHs), Trust Hospitals (THs), and Private hospitals (PHs) from the city of Baroda of the Gujarat State.

CHI SQUARE

The results of the testing hypothesis are put forward as follows.

In order to apply the Chi- Square the responses given by patients, on five rating scales, were combined into two groups as Important-Unimportant (Q No. 07); Agree-Disagree (Q No. 08, Q No.12 and Q No.13); and Satisfied-Dissatisfied (Q No. 09).

The results of Chi square test is put forward as follows:

(Abbreviations used in following tables are GHs = Government Hospitals; THs = Trust Hospitals; PHs = Private Hospitals; S = Significant; NS = Not Significant)

Hypothesis: 1

The average opinion of selected patients' in the selected type of hospitals (GHs; THs; and PHs), on selected criteria used to measure selected patients' responses for the selection of a given type of hospital (GHs; THs; and PHs), is equal. (Q. No.07)

The average opinion of selected patients' on various reasons for selection of type of hospitals was found to be uniform in some of the selected criteria viz., past performance of hospital/doctor; overall reputation of hospital; sanitation in the hospital, wherein average opinion of selected patients was different with regard to other selected items.

Hypothesis: 2

The average opinion of selected patients' in the selected type of hospitals (GHs; THs; and PHs), on selected criteria used to measure selected patients' responses for the various medical services provided to him/her by doctors' of the given type of hospital (GHs; THs; and PH)s, is equal. (Q. No. 08-01 to 08-17).

Table 7.1: Selected Patients' Reasons for Selection of Hospitals

Sl. No.	Selected Criteria	Computed Value of χ^2
01	Own Decision	S (52.24)
02	Relatives Suggested	S (24.83)
03	Friends Suggested	S (29.44)
04	Suggested by Family Doctor	S (21.89)
05	Past performance of Hospital/Doctor	NS (3.88)
06	Only in this Hospital such kind of facility is available	S (52.26)
07	Overall Reputation of Hospital	NS (4.00)
08	Hospital Located Nearby	S (79.92)
09	Hospital is economical	S (201.39)
10	Accessibility of Medicine and Test Facilities	S (10.59)
11	Sanitation in the Hospital	NS (0.32)

TV= 0.05=5.99 (DF=2)

Table 7.2: Selected Patients' Responses for Medical Services Provided in the Hospitals

Sl. No.	Selected Criteria	Computed Value of χ^2
01	Doctors' Knowledge and Efficiency	NS (0.74)
02	Doctors' Cooperation to patients	NS (3.79)
03	Doctors' were polite with patients	NS (5.59)
04	Impartial Attitude of Doctors	S (6.68)
05	Patients' Felt Comfortable During Doctors Examination	NS (1.87)
06	Doctors' Experience in Curing Patients	NS (1.87)
07	Thorough Checkup by Doctors	NS (0.99)
08	Doctors' Work according to Patients Expectations	S (37.67)
09	Doctors' Gave Individual Consideration and Confidentiality	S (27.63)
10	Doctors' Showed Respect and Support patients	S (192.75)
11	Doctors' Makes Good Diagnosis	NS (4.21)
12	Doctors' Prescribed Good Drugs	NS (0.45)
13	Doctor' ask for patients Permission for performing Test	S (41.27)
14	Patients' Felt Comfortable asking Questions to Doctors	NS (3.03)
15	Doctors' Honesty in Dealing with patients	S (9.80)
16	Sufficient number of Doctors Remained Present	NS (0.87)
17	Doctors' Availability in Emergency	NS (0.47)

TV= 0.05=5.99 (DF=2)

The average opinion of selected patients on various medical services being provided by doctors to them, was found to be different in some of the selected criteria viz., impartial attitude of doctors; doctors' work according to patient expectations; doctors' gave individual considerations and maintain confidentiality; doctors' showed respect and support to patients; doctor's ask for patients' permission for performing tests and doctors' honesty in dealing with patients, wherein average opinion of selected patients' was uniform with regard to other selected items.

Hypothesis: 3

The average opinion of selected patients' in the selected type of hospitals (GHs; THs; and PHs), on selected criteria used to measure selected patients' responses for the various services provided to him/her by paramedical staff of the given type of hospital (GHs; THs; and PHs), is equal. (Q. No.08-18 to 08-33)

Table 7.3: Selected Patients' Responses for Services of Paramedical Staff

Sl. No.	Selected Criteria	Computed Value of χ^2
01	Nurses' Knowledge and Efficiency	NS (1.87)
02	Nurses' Cooperation to Patients	S (36.64)
03	Nurses' Showed Politeness with Patients	S (10.09)
04	Impartial Attitude of Nurses	S (7.38)
05	Nurses' Maintain Proper records of Patients	NS (1.69)
06	Nurses' Handled Patients Query Properly	S (31.91)
07	Nurses' Experience in Curing Patients	S (6.47)
08	Good Experience of Those who Perform Test on Patients	NS (0.80)
09	Nurses' Gave Personal Attention to Patients	S (47.38)
10	Nurses' Provided Prompt Service	S (64.90)
11	Nurses' and Staff Remained Present in Emergency	S (39.07)
12	Nurses' Explain Procedures and take Patient Permission before Test	S (31.23)
13	Nurses' Explain Rules Regulation in ward	NS (4.64)
14	Nurses' are Kind, Gentle and Sympathetic	NS (1.06)
15	Information Provided to patients for Managing Side Effects	S (53.17)
16	Prompt Service Provided by Sanitation Staff	S (20.06)

TV= 0.05=5.99 (DF=2)

The average opinion of selected patients' on various services being provided to them by paramedical staff, was found to be different in some of the selected criteria viz., nurses' knowledge and efficiency; nurses' maintain proper records of patients; good experience of those who perform test on patients; nurses' explain rules regulation in ward; nurses' were kind, gentle and sympathetic; wherein, average opinion of selected patients' was uniform with regard to other selected items.

Hypothesis: 4

The average opinion of selected patients' in the selected type of hospitals (GHs; THs; and PHs), on selected criteria used to measure selected patients' responses for the various services provided to him/her by administrative staff of the given type of hospital (GHs; THs; and PHs), is equal. *(Q. No.08-34 to 08-46)*

Table 7.4: Selected Patients' Responses for Services of Administrative Staff

Sl. No.	Selected Criteria	Computed Value of χ^2
01	Less Waiting Time For Consultation and Treatment	S (46.05)
02	Less Waiting Time for Test	S (97.14)
03	Simple Checking Procedure	S (17.11)
04	Speed, Ease of Admission and Discharge form Hospital	NS (2.77)
05	Convenient Office Hours	NS (2.82)
06	Staff Gives Prompt Services	S (111.16)
07	No Overcrowding in Hospital	S (51.36)
08	Good Grievance handling System	S (148.77)
09	Adm. Staff Welcome and Implement Suggestion	S (89.13)
10	Adm. Gives Personal Attention To Patient	S (109.94)
11	Patients' Were Treated With Dignity and Privacy	S (10.26)
12	Good Concern for Patients' Family and Visitor	S (7.23)
13	Simple Billing Procedures	NS (2.67)

TV= 0.05=5.99 (DF=2)

The average opinion of selected patients' on various services being provided to them by administrative staff was found to be uniform in some of the selected criteria viz., speed, ease of admission and discharge form hospital; convenient office hours; simple billing procedures, wherein, average opinion of selected patients' was different with regard to other selected items.

Hypothesis: 5

The average opinion of selected patients' in the selected type of hospitals (GHs; THs; and PHs), on selected criteria used to measure selected patients' responses for the environment (physical facilities) of the given type of hospital (GHs; THs; and PHs), is equal. *(Q. No.08-47 to 08-64)*

The average opinion of selected patients' on environment (physical facilities) of the hospitals was found to be similar in some of the selected criteria viz., well equipped units; proper sitting and bedding arrangements; sufficient number of dust bins and spittoons; staff neat in appearance; inside and out side noise kept minimum; wherein, average opinion of selected patients' was different with regard to other selected items.

Table 7.5: Selected Patients' Responses to Environment (Physical Facilities) of Hospitals

Sl. No.	Selected Criteria	Computed Value of χ^2
01	Well Equipped Units	NS (2.72)
02	Proper Sitting and Bedding Arrangements	NS (1.03)
03	Comfort in Examination and waiting Room	S (6.64)
04	Natural Light or Illumination in Hospital	S (17.40)
05	Sufficient Number of Dust Bins and Spittoons	NS (5.15)
06	No Flies and Mosquitoes in Hospital	S (8.97)
07	Adequate parking Arrangements	S (58.35)
08	Clean Surroundings of Hospitals	S (9.20)
09	Pleasing and Appealing Room of Hospital	S (7.89)
10	Good Food Served by Hospital*	S (18.48)
11	Staff Neat in Appearance	NS (5.79)
12	Inside and Out side Noise kept Minimum	NS (1.61)
13	Wards Well Decorated and Ventilated	S (28.26)
14	Music Facilities should be provided	S (6.70)
15	Quick Payment Arrangements	S (21.53)
16	Costs were Adequate or Affordable	S (226.23)
17	Drugs Easily Obtained in Hospital	S (14.65)
18	Distance to Healthcare is Adequate	S (72.37)

TV= 0.05=5.99 (DF=2)

Hypothesis: 6

The average opinion of selected patients' in the selected type of hospitals (GHs; THs; and PHs), on selected criteria used to measure selected patients' responses for the tangible facilities of the given type of hospital (GHs; THs; and PHs), is equal. *(Q. No. 08 -16, 47, 48, 49, 50, 51, 52, 53, 54, 55, 56, 57, 58, 59, and 60)*

Table 7.6: Selected Patients' Responses on Tangibles Criterion of the Hospital Services

Sl. No.	Selected Criteria	Computed Value of χ^2
01	Sufficient Doctor's Remained Present	NS (0.87)
02	Well Equipped Units	NS (2.72)
03	Proper Sitting and Bedding Arrangements	NS (1.03)
04	Comfort in Examination and waiting Room	S (6.64)
05	Natural Light or Illumination in Hospital	S (17.40)
06	Sufficient Number of Dust Bins and Spittoons	NS (5.15)

...(Contd.)

...(Contd.)

Sl. No.	Selected Criteria	Computed Value of χ^2
07	No Flies and Mosquitoes in Hospital	S (8.97)
08	Adequate parking Arrangements	S (58.35)
09	Clean Surroundings of Hospitals	S (9.20)
10	Pleasing and Appealing Room of Hospital	S (7.89)
11	Good Food Served by Hospital	S (18.48)
12	Staff Neat in Appearance	NS (5.79)
13	Inside and Out side Noise kept Minimum	NS (1.61)
14	Wards Well Decorated and Ventilated	S (28.26)
15	Music Facilities should be provided	S (6.70)

TV= 0.05=5.99 (DF=2)

The average opinion of selected patients' on tangible facilities of the hospitals was found to be identical. In some of the selected criteria viz., sufficient doctors' remained present; well equipped units; proper sitting and bedding arrangements; sufficient number of dust bins and spittoons; staff neat in appearance; inside and out side noise kept minimum; wherein, average opinion of selected patients' was different with regard to other selected items.

Hypothesis: 7

The average opinion of selected patients' on the selected type of hospitals (GHs; THs; and PHs), on selected criteria used to measure selected patients' responses for the reliability of service provided in the given type hospital (GHs; THs; and PHs), is equal. *(Q. No. 08 -04, 11, 12, 21, and 22,*

Table 7.7: Selected Patients' Responses on Reliability Criterion of the Hospital Services

Sl. No.	Selected Criteria	Computed Value of χ^2
01	Impartial Attitude of Doctors	S (6.68)
02	Doctors' Makes Good Diagnosis	NS (4.21)
03	Doctors' Prescribed Good Drugs	NS (0.45)
04	Impartial Attitude of Nurses	S (7.38)
05	Nurses' Maintain Proper records of Patients	NS (1.69)

TV= 0.05=5.99 (DF=2)

The average opinion of selected patients' on the reliability of the services of the hospitals provided to them was found to be different in some of the selected criteria viz., impartial attitude of doctors and impartial attitude of nurses wherein, average opinion of selected patients' was uniform with regard to other selected items.

Hypothesis: 8

The average opinion of selected patients' in the selected type of hospitals (GHs; THs; and PHs), on selected criteria used to measure selected patients' responses for the responsiveness of services providers of the given type of hospital (GHs; THs; and PHs), is equal. *(Q. No. 08 -02, 14, 19, 27, 28, 32, 33, 34, 35, 37, 38, 39, 40, and 41)*

Table 7.8: Selected Patients' Responses on Responsiveness Criterion of the Hospital Services

Sl. No.	Selected Criteria	Computed Value of χ^2
01	Doctor's Cooperation to patients	NS (3.79)
02	Patients' Felt Comfortable asking Questions to Doctors	NS (3.03)
03	Nurses' Cooperation to Patients	S (36.64)
04	Nurses' Provided Prompt Service	S (64.90)
05	Nurses' and Staff Remained Present in Emergency	S (39.07)
06	Information Provided to patients for Managing Side Effects	S (53.17)
07	Prompt Service Provided by Sanitation Staff	S (20.06)
08	Less Waiting Time For Consultation and Treatment	S (46.05)
09	Less Waiting Time for Test	S (7.14)
10	Speed, Ease of Admission and Discharge form Hospital	NS (2.77)
11	Convenient Office Hours	NS (2.82)
12	Adm. Staff Gives Prompt Services	S (111.16)
13	No Overcrowding in Hospital	S (51.36)
14	Good Grievance handling System	S (148.77)

TV= 0.05=5.99 (DF=2)

The average opinion of selected patients' on various criteria related with responsiveness of the hospitals, was found to be uniform in some of the selected criteria viz., doctors' cooperation to patients; patients' felt comfortable asking questions to doctors; speed, ease of admission and discharge form hospital; convenient office hours; wherein, average opinion of selected patients' was different with regard to other selected items.

Hypothesis: 9

The average opinion of selected patients' in the selected type of hospitals (GHs; THs; and PHs), on selected criteria used to measure selected patients' responses for the assurance from the hospital services of the given type of hospital (GHs; THs; and PHs), is equal. *(Q. No.08 -01, 06, 07, 18, 23, 24, and 25)*

Table 7.9: Selected Patients' Responses on Assurance Criterion of the Hospital Services

Sl. No.	Selected Criteria	Computed Value of χ^2
01	Doctors' Knowledge and Efficiency	NS (0.74)
02	Doctors' Experience in Curing Patients	NS (1.87)
03	Thorough Checkup by Doctors	NS (0.99)

...(Contd.)

...(Contd.)

Sl. No.	Selected Criteria	Computed Value of χ^2
04	Nurses' Knowledge and Efficiency	NS (1.87)
05	Nurses' Handled Patients Query Properly	S (31.91)
06	Nurses' Experience in Curing Patients	S (6.47)
07	Good Experience of Those who Perform Test on Patients	NS (0.80)

TV= 0.05=5.99 (DF=2)

The average opinion of selected patients' on various criteria related with assurance from the hospital services, was found to be different in terms of two criteria viz., nurses' handled patients' query and nurses' experience in curing patients; wherein, average opinion of selected patients' was uniform with regard to other selected items.

Hypothesis: 10

The average opinion of selected patients' in the selected type of hospitals (GHs; THs; and PHs), on selected criteria used to measure selected patients' responses for the empathy experienced from the hospital services of the given type of hospital (GHs; THs; and PHs), is equal. *(Q. No. 08 -03, 05, 08, 09, 10, 15, 20, 36, 45, and 46)*

Table 7.10: Selected Patients' Responses on Empathy Criterion of the Hospital Services

Sl. No.	Selected Criteria	Computed Value of χ^2
01	Doctors' were polite with patients	NS (5.59)
02	Patients' Felt Comfortable During Doctors Examination	NS (1.87)
03	Doctors' Work According to Patients Expectations	S (37.67)
04	Doctors' Gave Individual Consideration and Confidentiality	S (27.63)
05	Doctors' Showed Respect and Support patients	S (192.75)
06	Doctors' Honesty in Dealing with patients	S (9.80)
07	Nurses' Showed Politeness with Patients	S (10.09)
08	Simple Checking Procedure	S (17.11)
09	Good Concern for Patients' Family and Visitor	S (7.23)
10	Simple Billing Procedures	NS (2.67)

TV= 0.05=5.99 (DF=2)

The average opinion of selected patients' on various criteria related with empathy experienced by patients from the hospital services, was found to be uniform in some of the criteria viz., doctors' were polite with patients; patients' felt comfortable during doctors' examination; simple billing procedures; wherein, average opinion of selected patients' was different with regard to other selected items.

Hypothesis: 11

The average opinion of selected patients' in the selected type of hospitals (GHs; THs; and PHs), on selected criteria used to measure selected patients' responses for the dignity maintained by the services providers of the given type of hospital (GHs; THs; and PHs), is equal. *(Q. No. 08 -13, 26, 29. 30, .11, 42, 43, and 44)*

Table 7.11: Selected Patients' Responses on Dignity Criterion of the Hospital Services

Sl. No.	Selected Criteria	Computed Value of χ^2
01	Doctors' ask for patients Permission for performing Test	S (41.27)
02	Nurses' Gave Personal Attention to Patients	S (47.38)
03	Nurses' Explain Procedures and take Patient Permission before Test	S (31.23)
04	Nurses' Explain Rules Regulation in ward	NS (4.64)
05	Nurses' were Kind, Gentle and Sympathetic	NS (1.06)
06	Adm. Staff Welcome and Implement suggestion	S (89.13)
07	Adm. Gives Personal Attention To Patient	S (109.94)
08	Patients' Were Treated With Dignity and Privacy	S (10.26)

TV= 0.05=5.99 (DF=2)

The average opinion of selected patients' on various criteria related with dignity maintained by the hospital service provides was found to be uniform in some of the criteria viz., nurses' explain rules regulation in ward; nurses' were kind, gentle and sympathetic; wherein, average opinion of selected patients' was different with regard to other selected items.

Hypothesis: 12

The average opinion of selected patients' in the selected type of hospitals (GHs; THs; and PHs), on selected criteria used to measure selected patients' responses for the accessibility/affordability of the hospital services of the given type of hospital (GHs; THs; and PHs), is equal. *(Q. No. 08 -17, Q, 62. 63, and 64)*

Table 7.12: Selected Patients' Response against Accessibility/Affordability Criterion of the Hospital Services

Sl. No.	Selected Criteria	Computed Value of χ^2
01	Doctors' Availability in Emergency	NS (0.47)
02	Quick Payment Arrangements	S (21.53)
03	Costs were Adequate or Affordable	S (226.23)
04	Drugs Easily Obtained in Hospital	S (14.65)
05	Distance to Healthcare is Adequate	S (72.37)

TV= 0.05=5.99 (DF=2)

The average opinion of selected patients on various criteria related with accessibility and affordability of the hospital services was found to be uniform in some of the criteria viz., 'doctors' availability in emergency'; wherein, average opinion of selected patients' was different with regard to other selected items.

Hypothesis: 13

The average opinion of selected patients' in the selected type of hospitals (GHs; THs; and PHs), on selected criteria used to measure selected patients' responses for the overall satisfaction with selected criteria of the given type of hospital (GHs; THs; and PHs), is equal. *(Q. No. 09)*

Table 7.13: Selected Patients' Overall Satisfaction on the Hospital services

Sl. No.	Selected Criteria	Computed Value of χ^2
01	Overall Satisfaction with Medical treatment	NS (5.40)
02	Overall Satisfaction with Nursing Staff services	NS (1.73)
03	Overall Satisfaction with Administrative Staff	S (36.82)
04	Overall Satisfaction with Environment	S (9.87)

TV= 0.05=5.99 (DF=2)

The average opinion of selected patients' on various criteria with regard to overall response against selected criteria was found as different in terms of two criteria viz., overall satisfaction with administrative staff and with environment of the hospital; wherein, average opinion of selected patients' was uniform with regard to other selected items.

Hypothesis: 14

The average opinion of selected patients' in the selected type of hospitals (GHs; THs; and PHs), on selected criteria used to measure selected patients' responses for the overall satisfaction with the given type of hospital (GHs; THs; and PHs), is equal. *(Q. No. 10)*

Table 7.14: Selected Patients' Overall Satisfaction on Hospital Services

Sl. No.	Selected Criteria	Computed Value of χ^2
01	Highly Satisfied	Significant (17.11)
02	Satisfied	
03	Somewhat satisfied /Undecided	
04	Dissatisfied	
05	Highly Dissatisfied	

TV= 0.05=15.5 (DF=8)

The average opinion of selected patients' on overall satisfaction experienced from hospital services was found to be different, which implies significant results.

Hypothesis: 15

The average opinion of selected patients' in the selected type of hospitals (GHs; THs; and PHs), on selected criteria used to measure selected patients' post-purchase behaviour vis-a vis the given type of hospital (GHs; THs; and PHs), is equal. *(Q. No.-11)*

Table 7.15: Selected Patients' Post-Purchase Behaviour

Sl. No.	Selected Criteria	Computed Value of χ^2
01	Definitely Yes	Not Significant (6.70)
02	Probably Yes	
03	Undecided	
04	Probably No	
05	Definitely No	
	Total	

TV= 0.05=15.5 (DF=8)

The average opinion of selected patients' was found to be equal with regard to post-purchase behaviour for hospitals.

Hypothesis: 16

The average opinion of selected patients' in the selected type of hospitals (GHs; THs; and PHs), on selected criteria used to measure selected patients' responses medical services (best services) of the given type of hospital (GHs; THs; and PHs), is equal. *(Q. No.-12)*

Table 7.16: Selected Patients' Positive Experiences on Best Medical Services

Sl. No.	Selected Criteria	Computed Value of χ^2
01	Best Service is Medical Treatment in Hospital	S (16.26)
02	Best Service is Nursing Staff Services in Hospital	NS (1.12)
03	Best Service is Administrative Staff Services in Hospital	S (33.90)
04	Best Service is Environment in Hospital	S (8.13)

TV= 0.05=5.99 (DF=2)

The average opinion of selected patients' on various criteria about best service of the hospital was found to be equal in one criterion namely; best service is nursing staff service in the hospital; wherein average opinion of selected patients' was different with regard to other selected items.

Hypothesis: 17

The average opinion of selected patients' in the selected type of hospitals (GHs; THs; and PHs), on selected criteria used to measure selected patients' responses for medical service (worst services) of the given type of hospital (GHs; THs; and PHs), is equal. *(Q. No. 13)*

Table 7.17: Selected Patients' Experiences on Worst Medical Services

Sl. No.	Selected Criteria	Computed Value of χ^2
01	Worst Service is Medical Treatment in Hospital	NS (0.87)
02	Worst Service is Nursing Staff Services in Hospital	NS (5.21)
03	Worst Service is Administrative Staff Services in Hospital	NS (0.84)
04	Worst Service is Environment in Hospital	NS (1.07)

TV= 0.05=5.99 (DF=2)

The average opinion of selected patients' on various criteria about medical services (worst) of the hospital was found to be uniform on selected criteria.

IMPLICATIONS OF THE RESEARCH STUDY BASED ON THE CHI-SQUARE (χ^2)

- The research study provided an understanding, based on confirmatory evidence, to the hospitals that past performance of the hospitals and doctors; overall reputation of hospitals, and sanitation in the hospitals were the major reasons for choosing particular hospital, so due consideration to these criteria will help the hospitals in attracting the patients to hospitals. It has an important implication in determining future potential of hospital business. Past performance of hospitals and doctors have an impact on quality of service and will be an important criteria for potential research for searching innovative ways of delivering services. The overall reputation has economic implications on business which includes survival; profit; growth, and future plan.
- In terms of medical services of the hospitals, the research study provided confirmatory evidence which provided an understanding to the hospitals in determining implications of medical services on business. Impartial attitude of doctors will have an impact on reputation or goodwill of business through maintaining transparency by doctors while dealing with patients. If doctors' work according to patients' expectations it will have an adverse impact on quality of services provided to patients or on health of a patient, so the doctors should consider the expectations of patients but not at the cost of quality of treatment or services. Giving individual considerations and maintaining confidentiality, and showing respect and support to patients by doctors will have an impact on psychological satisfaction of patients and it creates an environment of ethical behaviour in the hospitals. Further, doctors' can develop a rapport with the patients and improve their patients' satisfaction.

  If the doctors' does not ask for patients' permission for performing test on them and if doctors' does not show honesty in dealing with patients, doctors' may invite legal complications for hospitals and will also have an impact on reputation of the hospitals.
- In terms of paramedical services of the hospitals, the research study provided confirmatory evidence, which provides an understanding to the hospitals in

determining implications of paramedical services on business. Knowledge and efficiency of nursing staff, and the habit of maintaining good records of patients by nurses and other paramedical staff will help the hospitals in improving patients' satisfaction and reputation of hospitals. If nurses of the hospitals take due care in explaining rules, regulations in the wards and remained kind, gentle and sympathetic with the patients, the patients' will carry the good impression of hospital in society and will have a positive word of mouth for the hospital.

- In terms of administrative services of the hospital, the research study provided confirmatory evidence, which provides an understanding to the hospitals in determining implications of administrative services on business. The speed, ease of admission and discharge from hospital; convenient office hours, and simple billing procedures will provide the comfort to the patients during their hospitalization. So, due recognition to these administrative procedures will help the hospital in creating a comfortable environment for patients and in providing mental peace to patients.
- In terms of environment (physical facilities) and tangible criteria of the hospitals, the research study provided confirmatory evidence, which provides an understanding to the hospitals in determining implications of environment and tangible facilities on business. The criteria, viz., well equipped units; proper sitting and bedding arrangement; sufficient number of dust bins and spittoons; staff neat in appearance, and inside out side noise in the hospital kept minimum, will add to the comfort of patients and affect positively the patients' intention to visit the hospital in future.
- In terms of reliability of the hospitals, the research study provided confirmatory evidence, which provides an understanding to the hospitals in determining implications of important reliability criteria on business. As per the findings of the research study the reliability of hospital services depends on impartial attitudes of doctors and nurses and will have an impact on the patients' loyalty towards hospital, so due recognition to it will definitely affect the future profit and growth of the business.
- In terms of responsiveness of the service providers of the hospitals, the research study provided confirmatory evidence, which provides an understanding to the hospitals in determining implications of important responsiveness criteria on business. The responsiveness of doctors' in terms of extending cooperation to patients and making patient feel comfortable in asking questions to doctors, will have an impact on satisfaction of patients.

  The responsiveness of administrative staff in terms of sped, ease of admission and discharge from hospital, and convenient office hours will have an impact on mental peace of patients, which ultimately leads to patient satisfaction.
- In terms of assurance from the hospital services, the research study provided confirmatory evidence, which provides an understanding to the hospitals in

determining implications of important assurance criteria on business. The proper handling of patients quarry by nurses and nurses' experience in curing patients, will help the hospitals in creating a trust and confidence in patients about hospital services, which have an impact on patients intention to visit hospital again in future and also affect survival of the hospital.

- In terms of empathy experienced by patients' from hospital services, the research study provided confirmatory evidence, which provides an understanding to the hospitals in determining implications of empathy criteria on business. The politeness of doctors with patients and making patients felt comfortable during doctors' examination will help the hospitals in improving the patient satisfaction and in influencing patients to have positive word of mouth in favour of hospitals.
- In terms of dignity maintained by the service providers of the hospitals, the research study provided confirmatory evidence, which provides an understanding to the hospitals in determining implications of dignity criteria on business. If the nursing staff explain the rules and regulation in the wards and are kind, gentle and sympathetic with the patients, it will provide psychological satisfaction to patients and create an environment in which people follow the ethical behaviour.
- In terms of accessibility and affordability of the hospital services, the research study provided confirmatory evidence, which provides an understanding to the hospitals in determining implications of accessibility and affordability criteria on business. The accessibility of services in terms of availability of doctors in emergency will have an impact not only on satisfaction of patients but, also affect intention of patients to visit hospital in future illness. The due recognition by the hospital in making doctors' availability in emergency will help the hospital in attracting the patients in case of his/her illness in future.
- In case of overall response of all the patients, against selected criteria, the due recognition of the hospitals in terms of satisfactory services of administrative staff and the environment of hospital will have an impact in creating better satisfaction of patients from the hospital services and the positive post purchase behaviour from patients.
- All type of hospitals understand that developing different medical practices and strategies will have an impact on satisfaction of patients from overall services of hospital as the patients' covered under research study responded differently for expressing their overall satisfaction with all kinds of hospitals services.
- The research study has provided confirmatory evidence that all patients have reported uniformly for expressing their intention to recommend the hospital to others in future, and therefore, it becomes clear that satisfying patients is imperative as the patients will recommend the hospital to others only when they are satisfied with hospital services.

- In case of patients' views about best service of the hospital, the research study provided confirmatory evidence that all patients have reported uniformly for one criterion that is, best service is provided by the nursing staff of the hospital. In implies that nursing staff services will have an impact on level of patients' satisfaction and due recognition to it will help the hospitals in providing better satisfaction to their patients.
- In case of patients' views about worst service of the hospital, the research study provided confirmatory evidence that all patients have reported uniformly for all criteria, and therefore, it implies that due recognition to all kinds of hospitals services will help the hospitals in avoiding the dissatisfaction of patients.

ONE WAY ANNOVA AND FACTOR ANALYSIS FOR SELECTED PATIENTS' REASONS FOR SELECTION OF TYPE OF THE HOSPITALS

ONE WAY ANNOVA FOR PATIENTS' REASONS FOR SELECTION OF HOSPITAL

(Abbreviations used in following tables are, GHs = Government Hospitals; THs = Trust Hospitals; PHs = Private Hospitals; SD = Standard Deviation; SE = Standard Error)

Hypothesis: 18

Mean of patients' view about selected type of hospital is equal in terms of decision regarding selection of hospital and an alternative hypothesis is at least one mean is different from other.

Table 7.18: Descriptive Statistics of Patients' Reasons in Selection of the Type of Hospitals

Type of Hospitals	N	Mean	SD	SE
GHs	200	42.85	3.698091	0.261495
THs	200	40.81	5.309885	0.375466
PHs	100	37.76	5.142652	0.514265
Total	500	41.016	5.043274	0.225542

Table 7.18 indicates the descriptive statistics of type of hospitals. The Government hospital has highest mean value of 42.85. The second highest mean value is 40.81 of trust hospital, and private hospital having lower mean value of 37.76.

Table 7.19: Test of Homogeneity of Variances for Patients' Reasons on Selection of the Type of Hospitals

Levene's Statistic	df1	df2	Sig.
12.47583	2	497	0.00

Table 7.19 indicates the Levene's test of homogeneity of variance through which verification can be done about the equality of variance of all group of hospital. Results of Levene's test showed that the significant value (0.00) which is less then 0.05. It

means that our null hypothesis has been rejected as significant value does not exceed 0.05. It means variance of all groups is not equal.

Analysis of Variance

Table 7.20: ANOVA Table for Patients' Reasons for Selection of the Type of Hospitals

Particulars	Sum of Squares	df	Mean Square	F	Sig.
Between Groups	1741.352	2	870.676	39.51648	0.00
Within Groups	10950.52	497	22.03324		
Total	12691.87	499			

The variation between the groups of all hospitals is 1741 and within group the variation is 10950. The variation within groups was higher then variation between groups of type of hospitals.

According to null hypothesis variance of all groups was equal and our alternative hypotheses states that at least one variance is different from other. As null hypotheses is rejected because of significance value (0.00) is < 0.05 that means at least one type of hospitals is different from the other type of hospitals.

Post-Hoc Test (Tamhane)

Table 7.21: Multiple Comparisons of Patients' Reasons for Selection of the Type of Hospital Through Tamhane Test

Type of Hospitals		Mean Difference	SE	Sig.
GHs	GHs			
	THs	2.04	0.457552	0.00
	PHs	5.09	0.57693	0.00
THs	GHs	–2.04	0.457552	0.00
	THs			
	PHs	3.05	0.636744	0.00
PHs	GHs	–5.09	0.57693	0.00
	THs	–3.05	0.636744	0.00
	PHs			

Based on test of homogeneity of variance, it becomes clear that variance of three type of hospitals is not equal. It means that at least one variance is different from other. ANOVA table also indicated that mean of three type of hospitals is not equal, therefore, the Post-Hog test is applied by assuming unequal variance. Government Hospitals are different from Trust Hospital and Private Hospital. Trust hospitals are different from Government and Private Hospitals. Private hospitals are also different from Government and Trust Hospitals because of significant value, of all type of hospital, is < 0.05 with their other type of hospitals.

Post-Hoc Test (Tukey HSD)

Table 7.22: Multiple Comparisons of Patients' Reasons for Selection of the Type of Hospitals Through Tukey HSD Test

Type of Hospitals	N	Subset for alpha = .05		
		1	2	3
Private Hospital	100	37.76		
Trust Hospital	200		40.81	
Government Hospital	200			42.85
Sig.		1	1	1

From the Table 7.22 it becomes clear that all three type of hospitals were different. Private hospital was different then trust and Government hospitals, trust hospitals were different then private and Government hospitals and Government hospitals were also different then private and trust hospitals.

Graph 7.1 also shows through Means Plot how three types of hospitals are different.

Graph 7.1: Means Plots of Type of Hospitals for Decision Regarding Selection of Hospital for All the Three Type of Hospitals

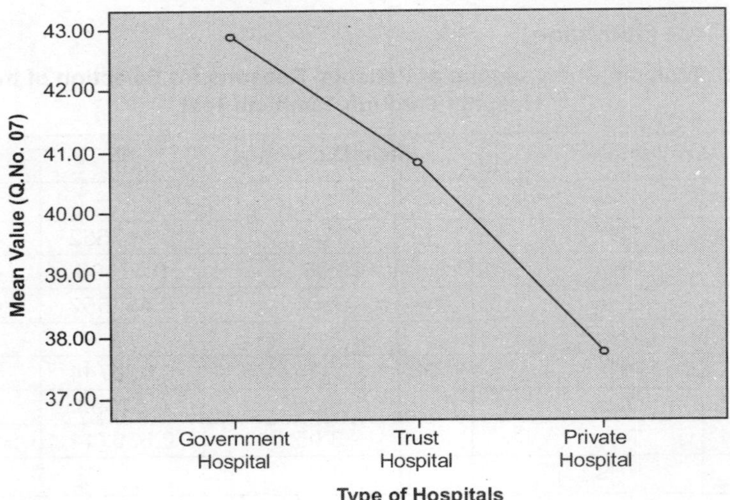

Graph 7.1 indicates different Type of Hospitals with their mean value. The Government hospital had large mean value of 42.85. Trust hospital had second highest mean value of 40.80 and private hospital had lowest mean value of 37.76. So based on Means plot it becomes clear that all three type of hospitals are different.

Note: *To measure the suitability of the data for factor analysis the adequacy of the data is evaluated on the basis of the results of Kaiser-Meyaer-Oklin (KMO) measures of sampling adequacy and Bartiet's test of spehericity (homogeneity of variance). This exercise is done for all the group of data in which factor analysis is applied.*

FACTOR ANALYSIS OF PATIENTS' REASONS FOR SELECTION OF THE TYPE OF HOSPITALS

Factor Analysis: Decision Regarding Selection of the Type of Hospitals

Table 7.23: Patients' Reasons for Selection of the Type of Hospitals Through KMO and Bartlett's Test

Kaiser-Meyer-Olkin Measure of Sampling Adequacy		0.606223
Bartlett's Test of Sphericity	Approx. Chi-Square	1005.048
	df	55
	Sig.	0.00

In case of reasons for the selection of type of hospitals the results showed that the KMO measure of sampling adequacy was 0.60, which indicated that the present data were suitable for Factor Analysis. Similarly, Bartlett's Test of sphericity (0.00) was significant ($p<.005$), indicating sufficient correlation exist between the criteria to proceed with the Factor Analysis.

Table 7.24: Total Variance on Patients' Responses for Selection of the Type of Hospitals

Com-ponent	Initial Eigen values			Extraction Sums of Squared Loadings			Rotation Sums of Squared Loadings		
	Total	Percent-ages of Varia-nce	Cumul-ative per cent	Total	Percent-ages of Vari-ance	Cumu-lative per cent	Total	% age of Vari-ance	Cumu-lative per cent
01	2.2499	20.45	20.453	2.2499	20.4534	20.453	2.091	19.01	19.01
02	1.8166	16.51	36.968	1.8166	16.5148	36.968	1.723	15.66	34.675
03	1.6177	14.71	51.674	1.6177	14.706	51.674	1.721	15.64	50.319
04	1.1998	10.91	62.581	1.1998	10.9073	62.581	1.349	12.26	62.581

The first four components (factors) in the initial solution have an Eigen values over 1 and it accounted for about 62 per cent of the observed variations in the decision regarding selection of hospital in Baroda city. According to Kaiser Criterion, only the first four factors should be used because subsequent Eigenvalues are all less then 1. Graph 7.2 is also useful tool to decide about the number factors. If one has draw parallel line to horizontal (dotted line) at Eigenvalues to 1 in Scree plot, it will tell us how many factors are going to be extracted. In our analysis Scree plot showed that four factors are going to be extracted.

The above scree plot shows the graphical presentation of four components which can be extracted for further analysis. (*Refer to Table 7.25*)

All the extracted communalities are acceptable and all criteria are fit for the factor solution as their extraction values are large enough.

Factor loadings were used to measure correlation between criteria and the factors. A factor loading close to 1 indicates a strong correlation between a criteria and factor, while a loading closer to zero indicated weak correlation. The factors are rotated with

Graph 7.2: Component-wise Scree Plot of Eigenvalues for Decision Regarding Selection of Hospitals for All The Three Type of Hospitals

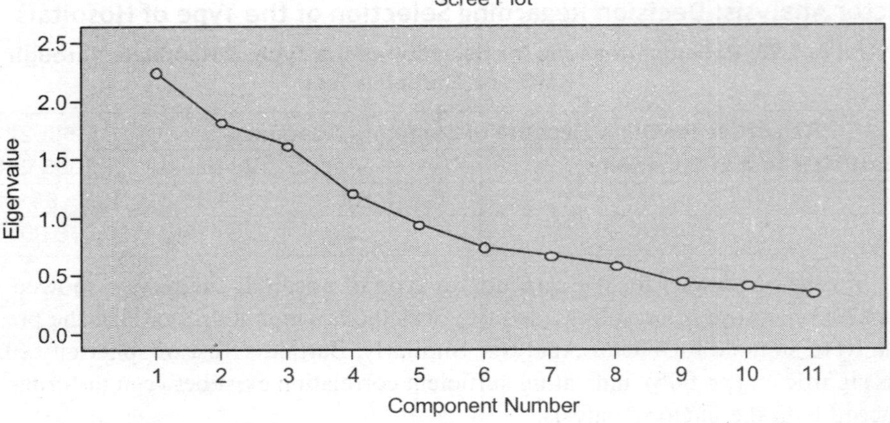

Table 7.25: Communalities and Rotated Component Matrix of Patients' Reasons for Selection of the Type of Hospitals

Sl. No.	Selected Criteria	Communalities Extraction	Rotated Component			
			1	2	3	4
01	Own Decision	0.464487	0.620307	0.214553	–0.14497	–0.11251
02	Relatives Suggested	0.771968	0.020699	–0.06035	0.876146	–0.01631
03	Friends Suggested	0.763095	0.095356	0.034191	0.864116	0.078336
04	Suggested by Family Doctor	0.360135	–0.18015	–0.19825	0.221452	0.489222
05	Past performance of Hospital/Doctor	0.734961	0.055234	0.851889	–0.0132	–0.0776
06	Only in this Hospital such kind of facility is available	0.553727	–0.32065	0.367515	0.279908	0.487333
07	Overall Reputation of Hospital	0.772639	0.13817	0.865542	–0.03085	0.058585
08	Hospital Located Nearby	0.672733	0.815313	–0.06517	0.061193	–0.00245
09	Hospital is economical	0.672765	0.797741	0.063362	0.179528	–0.01135
10	Accessibility of Medicine and Test Facilities	0.540125	0.48697	0.121505	0.035889	0.535662
11	Sanitation in the Hospital	0.577329	0.033209	0.001832	–0.14076	0.745929

the used of Varimax with Kaiser Normalization rotation method. Principle Component Analysis (PCA) method is used for factor extraction and consider only those factors for interpretation purpose whose values are greater then 0.5.

From the above table it becomes clear that how much different criteria were correlated with four components. The criterion 1 (Own decision), criterion 8 (Hospital located nearby) and criterion 9 (Hospital is economically) were more correlated with component 1. Criterion 5 (Past performance of Hospital/Doctor) and criterion 7 (Overall

Reputation of Hospital) was more correlated with component 2. Criterion 2 (Relatives Suggested) and criterion 3 (Friends Suggested) was more correlated with component 3. And criterion 11 (Sanitation in the Hospital) was more correlated with component 4.

Table 7.26: Component-wise Mean Value for Patients' Reasons for Selection of the Type of Hospitals

Component	Mean Value	Selected Criteria	Selected Factors
01	11.38	Own Decision	Affordable
		Hospital Located Nearby	
		Hospital is economical	
02	8.42	Past performance of Hospital/ Doctor	Performance
		Overall Reputation of Hospital	
03	6.48	Relatives Suggested	Reference/ Suggestion
		Friends Suggested	
04	4.36	Sanitation in the Hospital	Sanitation

Table 7.26 indicates component wise mean value. The component 1 have higher mean value of 11.38 and which found to be more correlated with three criteria (Own decision, hospital is located nearby and hospital is economical).

The component 1 make one group as affordability and it explained 19 per cent variation from data that means these three criteria were important for different type of hospitals.

Component 2 have second highest mean value of 8.42 and it makes one group as performance because it is more correlated with (past performance of hospital/doctor and overall reputation of hospital) and it also explains 16 per cent variation from data. Component 3 having 6.48 mean values and it make one group related with suggestion because of it is more correlated with (relative suggestion and friends' suggestion) and it explain 16 per cent variation from data. And component 4 have lowest mean value of 4.36 and have only one criteria namely, sanitation of hospital and make one group as (sanitation). It explains 12 per cent variation from data.

Importance of Components for Selected Type of Hospitals

The importance of each component to different type of hospitals can be understood with the help of below given box plots. The following box plot explain the total score of component 1 (Affordability) for three type of Hospitals *(Refer Graph 7.3).*

From the above box plot interpretation can be made that Government hospitals have higher median value and has many of the extreme point and outliers but it have less variation then trust and private hospitals.

Trust hospital has second highest median value but it has more variation then Government and private hospitals, and a private hospital has lower median value and second highest variation.

Graph 7.3: Hospitals-wise Box Plot for Component 1 for Patients' Reasons for Selection of the Type of Hospitals

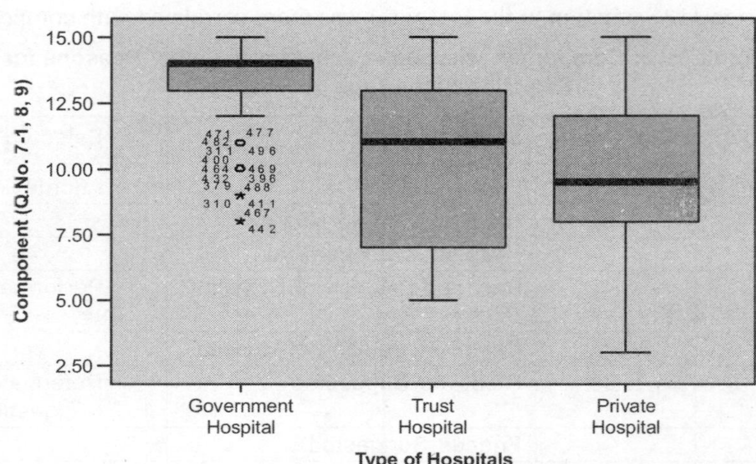

So finally it can be concluded that component 1 (Affordability) was important for Government hospitals. That means three criteria, i.e. patients' own decision, hospital located nearby and hospital is economical are important for patients to make a choice of Government hospitals.

Following Box plot explain type of hospitals and total score of component 2 (Performance) as a criteria (Graph 7.4).

Graph 7.4: Hospitals-wise Box Plot for Component 2 for Selected Patients' Reasons for Selection of the Type of Hospitals

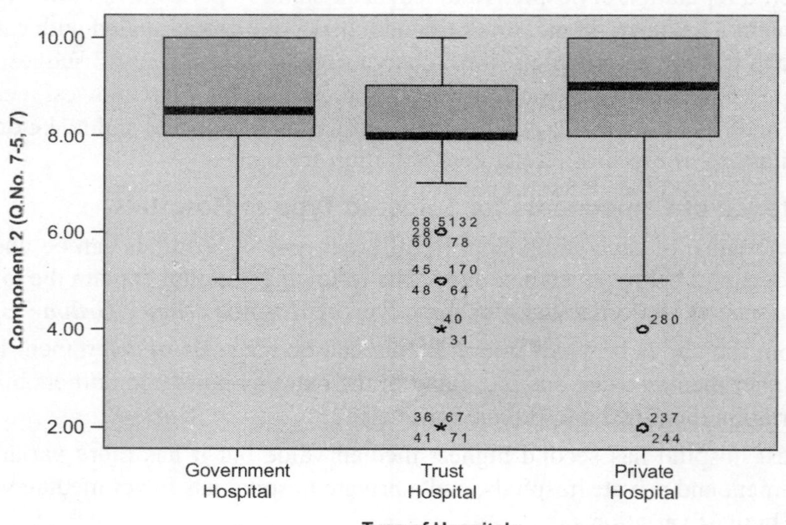

From the above box plot (Graph 7.4) one can be observed that private hospitals have higher median value and have few outliers and less variation then Government hospitals. The Government hospitals have second highest median value but it has large variation. And trust hospitals have lower median value and it also have many of the outliers and extreme points.

So finally it can be concluded that component 2 (Performance) was important for private hospital. That means two criteria i.e., past performance of hospital/doctor and overall reputation of hospital were important for private hospital.

Graph 7.5 explain type of hospitals total score of component 3 (Suggestion) as a factor.

Graph 7.5: Hospitals-wise Box Plot for Component 3 for Selected Patients' Reasons for Selection of the Type of Hospitals

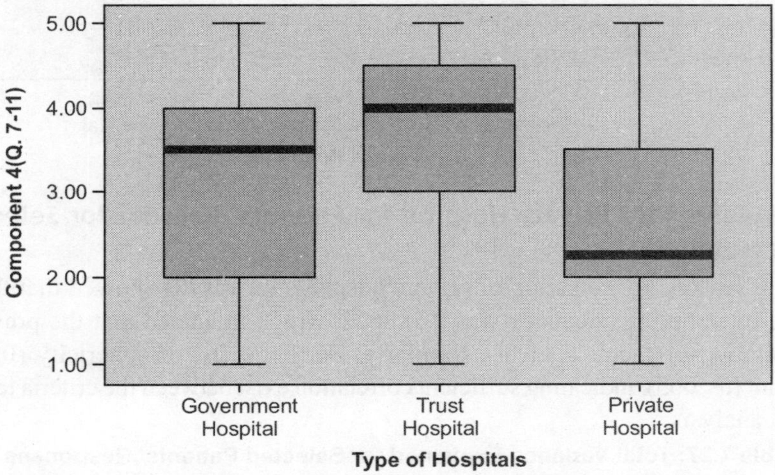

From the above box plot Graph 7.5 it becomes clear that component 3 (Suggestion) was important for Trust hospitals as it has large median value and lower variation then Government and private hospitals. So patients' prefer trust hospitals on the basis of recommendation made by their relatives and friends.

Following Box plot explain Type of Hospitals and total score of component 4 (Sanitation) as a criteria *(Refer Graph 7.6)*.

The above box plot indicated that component 4 (sanitation) was more important for Trust and Private hospitals because of they have large median value. The Government hospitals have lower median value then trust and private hospitals. It means patient choose trust and private hospital because of good sanitation in the hospital compared to Government hospitals.

As the mean score of private hospital was lower (37.76) factor analysis was made to find out the reasons for lower mean value of private hospital.

Graph 7.6: Hospitals-Wise Box Plot for Component 4 for Selected Patients' Reasons for Selection of the Type of Hospitals

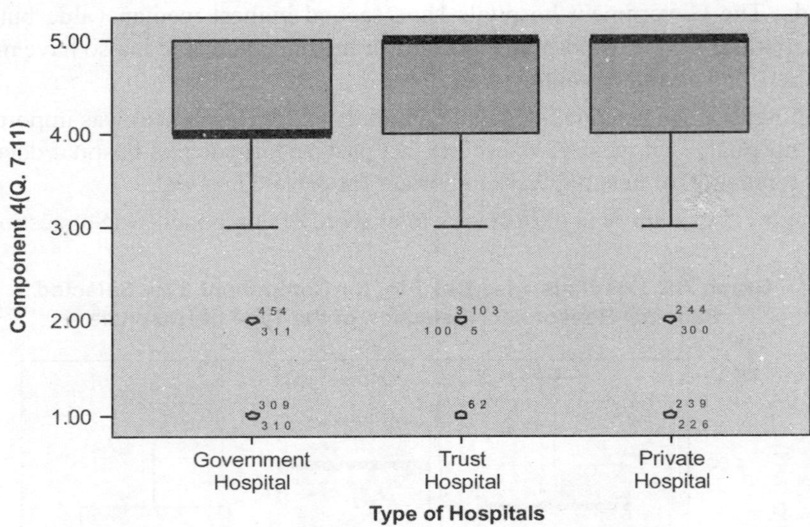

Factor Analysis for Private Hospital for Patients' Reasons for Selection of Private Hospitals

In case of reasons for selection of private hospitals the results showed that the KMO measure of sampling adequacy was 0.588622, which indicated that the present data were suitable for factor analysis. Similarly, Bartlett's test of sphericity (0.00) was significant ($p<.005$), indicating sufficient correlation exist between the criteria to proceed with the analysis.

Table 7.27: Total Variance Explained for Selected Patients' Responses for Selection of Private Hospitals

Component	Initial Eigenvalues			Extraction Sums of Squared Loadings			Rotation Sums of Squared Loadings		
	Total	Percentages of Variance	Cumulative per cent	Total	Percentages of Variance	Cumulative per cent	Total	Percentages of Variance	Cumulative per cent
01	2.52089	22.917	22.9172	2.520892	22.9172	22.9172	2.326036	21.14578	21.14578
02	1.65781	15.071	37.9882	1.657807	15.07097	37.98817	1.545084	14.04622	35.192
03	1.35914	12.356	50.344	1.359143	12.35584	50.34401	1.480005	13.45459	48.64659
04	1.25874	11.443	61.7871	1.258736	11.44306	61.78707	1.445452	13.14048	61.78707

From Table 7.27 it becomes clear that total four number of component can be extracted as they have Initial Eigen values more than 1 and it explain 61 per cent variation from data.

Table 7.28: Communalities and Rotated Component Matrix for Selected Patients' Reasons for Selection of Private Hospitals

Sl. No.	Selected Criteria	Communalities	Rotated Component			
			1	2	3	4
01	Own Decision	0.711268	0.16124	–0.059	0.82561	–0.01097
02	Relatives Suggested	0.736019	–0.2517	0.7105	–0.0788	0.402085
03	Friends Suggested	0.635299	0.09312	0.7891	–0.0375	–0.05072
04	Suggested by Family Doctor	0.706506	0.10405	0.016	–0.8258	–0.1161
05	Past performance of Hospital/Doctor	0.720398	0.79095	–0.186	0.05049	0.240479
06	Only in this Hospital such kind of facility is available	0.506907	0.53309	0.3819	–0.0802	–0.26542
07	Overall Reputation of Hospital	0.718039	0.83015	–0.075	0.12222	0.090913
08	Hospital Located Nearby	0.47978	0.13937	–0.06	0.15826	0.657046
09	Hospital is economical	0.573662	0.27732	0.2146	–0.0105	0.671253
10	Accessibility of Medicine and Test Facilities	0.521571	0.61915	0.2184	–0.0702	0.292549
11	Sanitation in the Hospital	0.487129	0.37227	0.3613	0.23409	–0.40397

All the extracted communalities were acceptable and all criteria were fit for the factor solution as their extraction values were large enough.

Table 7.28 indicated that component 1 is highly correlated with criteria 5, 6, 7 and 10 (Past performance of Hospital/Doctor, Only in this Hospital such kind of facility is available, Overall Reputation of Hospital, Accessibility of Medicine and Test Facilities).

Component 2 was highly correlated with criteria 2 and 3 (Relatives Suggested, Friends Suggested). Component 3 was highly correlated with only criteria 1 (Own Decision). And component 4 was highly correlated with criteria 8 and 9 (Hospital Located Nearby, Hospital is economical).

Table 7.29: Component-wise Mean Value for Selected Patients' Reasons for Selection of Private Hospitals

Component	Mean Value	Selected Factors	Selected Criteria
01	16.052	Performance	Past performance of Hospital/Doctor
			Only in this Hospital such kind of facility is available
			Overall Reputation of Hospital
			Accessibility of Medicine and Test Facilities
02	6.476	Suggestion	Relatives Suggested
			Friends Suggested
03	4.046		Own Decision
04	7.338	Affordability	Hospital Located Nearby
			Hospital is economical

From Table 7.29 it becomes clear that component 1(performance) has high mean value of 16.05. Other components 4, 2, and 3 have lower mean values i.e., 7.34, 6.48, and 4.05 respectively. It means that component 1 (Past performance of Hospital/ Doctor, Only in this Hospital such kind of facility is available, Overall Reputation of Hospital, and Accessibility of Medicine and Test Facilities) was the important reason for selection of private hospitals but component 4 (Hospital Located Nearby, Hospital is economical), component 2 (Relatives Suggested, Friends Suggested), and component 3 (Own Decision) has lower mean value and these factors were responsible for lower mean value of private hospitals.

ONE WAY ANNOVA AND FACTOR ANALYSIS FOR MEDICAL, PARAMEDICAL, AND ADMINISTRATIVE STAFF SERVICES AS WELL AS ENVIRONMENT (PHYSICAL FACILITIES) OF THE HOSPITALS

One way ANNOVA and Factor analysis were applied for analyzing Medical, Paramedical, Administrative Staff, and Environment (Physical facilities) of the Hospitals.

ONE WAY ANNOVA FOR MEDICAL SERVICES CRITERIA

Hypothesis: 19

Mean of patients' view about selected type of hospitals is equal in terms of medical services and an alternative hypothesis is at least one mean is different from other.

Table 7.30: Descriptive Statistics for Medical Services Criteria for All the Three Type of Hospitals

Type of Hospitals	N	Mean	SD	SE
GHS	200	70.58	5.962496	0.421612
THs	200	75.03	6.989518	0.494234
PHs	100	74.92	7.835016	0.783502
Total	500	73.228	7.108099	0.317884

Table 7.30 indicated that highest mean value of 75.03 belongs to Trust hospital. The Private hospital has second highest mean value of 74.92, and Government hospital has lower mean value of 70.58.

Test of Homogeneity of Variances

Table 7.31: Test of Homogeneity of Variances for Medical Services Criteria for All The Three Type of Hospitals

Levene's Statistic	df1	df2	Sig.
1.541867	2	497	0.215003

Table 7.31 indicated that Levene's P value exceed 0.05 (P-value > 0.05) that means variance of all type of hospitals are equal.

Table 7.32: ANOVA for Medical Services for All the Three Type of Hospitals

Particulars	Sum of Squares	Df	Mean Square	F	Sig.
Between Groups	2338.108	2	1169.054	25.401	0.00
Within Groups	22873.900	497	46.02394		
Total	25212.01	499			

From Table 7.32 it becomes clear that difference within the group found to be higher than difference between the groups. Further, P value is < 0.05 that means it has significant value. So, at least one Type of Hospitals was different from other.

Post-Hoc Test (Tamhane)

Table 7.33: Multiple Comparisons for Medical Services for All the Three Type of Hospitals Through Tamhane Test

Type of Hospitals		Mean Difference	SE	Sig.
GHs	GHs			
	THs	–4.45	0.678409	0.00
	PHs	–4.34	0.830879	0.00
THs	GHs	4.45	0.68	0.00
	THs			
	PHs	0.11	0.83	0.99
PHs	GHs	4.34	0.83	0.00
	THs	–0.11	0.83	0.99
	PHs			

Levene's P value indicated that variances of all type of Hospitals are equal therefore Post Hoc Test was applied. Based on above table one can say that Government hospitals were different from trust and private hospitals and trust and private hospitals were not different from each other.

Post-Hoc test (Tukey HSD)

Table 7.34: Multiple Comparisons for Medical Services for All the Three Type of Hospitals Through Tukey HSD Test

Type of Hospitals	Subset for alpha = .05		
	N	1	2
GHs	200	70.58	
PHS	100		74.92
THs	200		75.03
Sig.		1	0.989188

Private hospitals and trust hospitals make one group and Government hospitals makes one separate group as it was found to be different from private and trust hospitals.

Graph 7.7: Means Plots of Type of Hospitals for Medical Services for All the Three Type of Hospitals

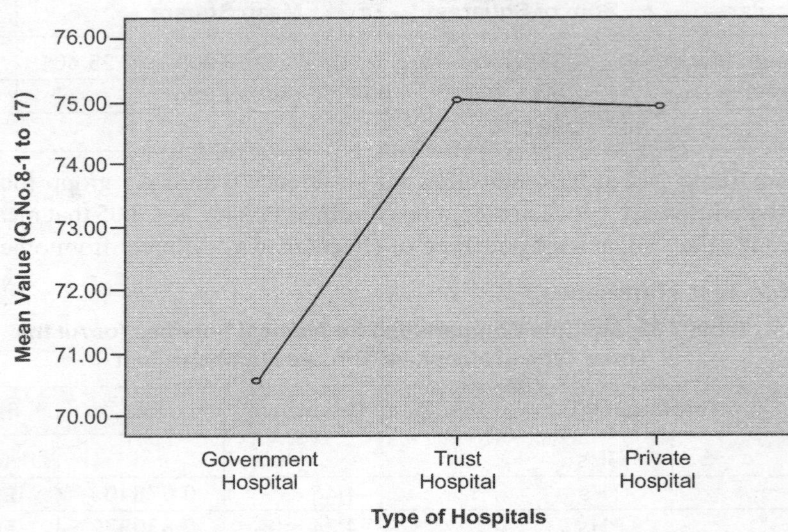

The above means plot (Graph 7.7) indicated that Government hospitals have lower mean value. Trust hospitals have highest mean value and Private hospitals have second highest mean value.

FACTOR ANALYSIS: MEDICAL SERVICES FOR ALL THE THREE TYPE OF HOSPITALS

In case of medical services the results showed the KMO measure of sampling adequacy (0.879182) and Bartlett's test of sphericity (0.00) indicated that data were appropriate for Factor Analysis.

Table 7.35: Total Variance Explained for Medical services for All the Three Type of Hospitals

	Initial Eigen values			Extraction Sums of Squared Loadings			Rotation Sums of Squared Loadings		
Component	Total	Percentages of Variance	Cumulative per cent	Total	Percentages of Variance	Cumulative per cent	Total	Percentages of Variance	Cumulative per cent
01	5.767	33.923	33.923	5.767	33.923	33.923	2.998	17.636	17.636
02	1.631	9.594	43.516	1.631	9.594	43.516	2.589	15.231	32.867
03	1.138	6.697	50.213	1.138	6.697	50.213	2.139	12.584	45.451
04	1.023	6.020	56.233	1.023	6.020	56.233	1.833	10.782	56.233

Extraction Method: Principal Component Analysis

From Table 7.35 one can say that there were four components can be extracted and it extracts 56 per cent variance from data.

Table 7.36: Communalities and Rotated Component Matrix for Medical Services for All the Three Type of Hospitals

Sl. No.	Selected Criteria	Communalities Extraction	Rotated Component			
			1	2	3	4
01	Doctors' Knowledge and Efficiency	0.450273	0.5942	0.153	0.2302	0.1438
02	Doctors' Cooperation to patients	0.634781	0.7498	0.198	0.0965	0.155
03	Doctors' were polite with patients	0.663086	0.7726	0.188	0.017	0.1746
04	Impartial Attitude of Doctors	0.490109	0.6729	0.191	0.0152	0.0281
05	Patients' Felt Comfortable During Doctors Examination	0.549712	0.6225	0.274	0.2917	0.0454
06	Doctors' Experience in Curing Patients	0.560605	0.3679	0.641	0.1171	–0.0316
07	Thorough Checkup by Doctors	0.54321	0.191	0.689	0.1153	0.1391
08	Doctors' Work according to Patients Expectations	0.6928	0.0795	0.14	0.812	0.0862
09	Doctors' Gave Individual Consideration and Confidentiality	0.680895	0.1602	0.292	0.7531	0.0555
10	Doctors' Showed Respect and Support patients	0.477673	0.3288	0.448	0.3963	0.1085
11	Doctors' Makes Good Diagnosis	0.655668	0.1577	0.749	0.1634	0.2064
12	Doctors' Prescribed Good Drugs	0.556846	0.2465	0.664	0.0904	0.2175
13	Doctor' ask for patients Permission for performing Test	0.611574	0.0987	-0.004	0.6638	0.4015
14	Patients' Felt Comfortable asking Questions to Doctors	0.486176	0.0854	0.308	0.1697	0.596
15	Doctors' Honesty in Dealing with patients	0.453895	0.4045	0.25	-0.0826	0.4699
16	Sufficient number of Doctors Remained Present	0.595415	0.2593	0.173	0.0342	0.7052
17	Doctors' Availability in Emergency	0.456923	-0.013	-0.02	0.2618	0.6227

All the extracted communalities were acceptable and all criteria were fit for the factor solution as their extraction values found to be large.

From Table 7.36 it becomes clear that how much different criteria were correlated with four components. The criteria 1 (Doctors' Knowledge and Efficiency), criteria 2 (Doctors' Cooperation to patients), criteria 3 (Doctors' were polite with patients), criteria 4 (Impartial Attitude of Doctors), criteria 5 (Patients' Felt Comfortable during Doctors' Examination) and criteria 14 (Doctors' Prescribed Good Drugs) are more correlated with component 1.

The criterion 6 (Doctors' Experience in Curing Patients), criterion 7 (Thorough Checkup by Doctors), criterion 11 (Doctors' Makes Good Diagnosis), and criterion 12 (Doctors' Prescribed Good Drugs) are more correlated with component 2.

The criteria 8 (Doctors' Work According to Patients Expectations), criterion 9 (Doctors' Give Individual Consideration and Confidentiality) and criterion 13 (Doctors' ask for patients Permission for performing Test) were correlated with component 3. The criterion 16 (Sufficient number of Doctors Remain Present), and criterion 17 (Doctors' Easily Available in Emergency) were more correlated with component 4.

Table 7.37: Component-wise Mean Value for Medical Services' Criteria for All The Three Type of Hospitals

Component	Mean Value	Selected Criteria	Selected Factors
01	26.776	Doctors' Knowledge and Efficiency	Assurance
		Doctors' Cooperation to patients	Responsiveness
		Doctors' were polite with patients	Empathy
		Impartial Attitude of Doctors	Reliability
		Patients' Felt Comfortable During Doctors Examination	Empathy
		Patients' Felt Comfortable asking Questions to Doctors	Responsiveness
02	17.944	Doctors' Experience in Curing Patients	Assurance
		Thorough Checkup by Doctors	Assurance
		Doctors' Makes Good Diagnosis	Reliability
		Doctors' Prescribe Good Drugs	Reliability
03	11.106	Doctors' Work According to Patients Expectations	Empathy
		Doctors' Gave Individual Consideration and Confidentiality,	Empathy
		Doctors' ask for patients Permission for performing Test	Dignity
04	8.52	Sufficient Doctors' Remain Present	Tangibles
		Doctors' Availability in Emergency	Accessibility / Affordability

Table 7.37 represents the mean value of each component. The component 1 having large mean value of 26.77 and it was more correlated with six criteria (Doctors' Knowledge and Efficiency, Doctors' Cooperation to patients, Doctors' were polite with patients, Impartial Attitude of Doctors, Patients' Felt Comfortable During Doctors Examination, Doctors' Prescribed Good Drugs). Component 2 has 17.94 mean values and it was more correlated with four criteria (Doctors' Experience in Curing Patients, Thorough Checkup by Doctors, Doctors' Made Good Diagnosis, Doctors' Prescribed Good Drugs). Component 3 has 11.10 mean value and it was more correlated with

three criteria (Doctors' Work according to Patients Expectations, Doctors' ask for patients Permission for performing Test). Component 4 have low mean value of 8.52 and it was more correlated with two criteria (Sufficient Doctors Remain Present, Doctors' Availability in Emergency).

Importance of Components for Selected Type of Hospitals

The importance of each component to different type of hospitals can be understood with the help of below given box plots. The following box plot explains three type of hospitals' total score of component 1 criteria.

Graph 7.8: Hospitals-wise Box Plot for Component 1 for Medical Services of the Three Type of Hospitals

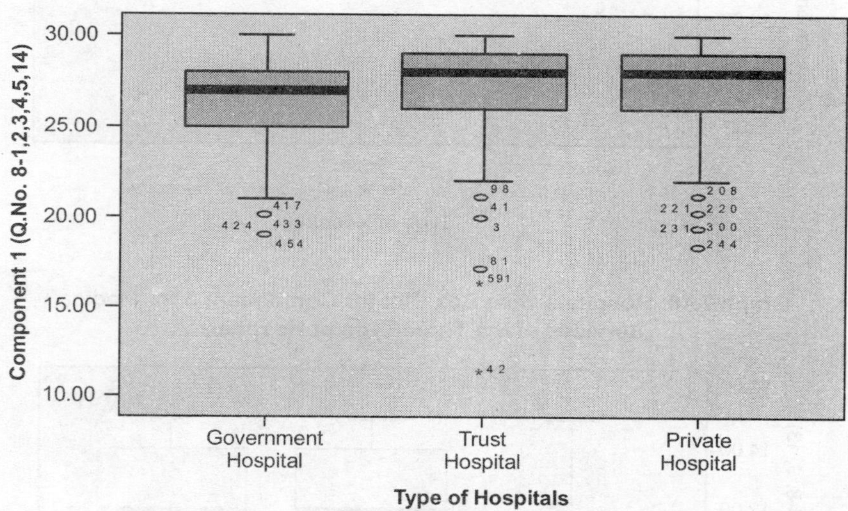

The above box plot (Graph 7.8) indicated that component 1 criteria (Doctor Knowledge and Efficiency, Doctors' Cooperation to patients, Doctors' were polite with patients, Impartial Attitude of Doctors, Patients' Felt Comfortable During Doctors' Examination, Doctors' Prescribed Good Drugs) were more important for private hospital because of large median value and low variation compared to trust and private hospital.

The box plot of Graph 7.10 represent that the component 2 criteria (Doctors' Experience in Curing Patients, Thorough Checkup by Doctors, Doctors' Made Good Diagnosis, Doctors' Prescribe Good Drugs) were also important for private hospitals because it has large median value, low variation and less outliers compared to trust and Government hospitals *(Refer Graph 7.10)*.

From the box plot of Graph 7.11 it becomes clear that component 3 criteria (Doctors' Work According to Patients Expectations, Doctors' asks for patients Permission for performing Test) were important for trust hospitals as it has large median value and low variation then other *(Refer Graph 7.11)*.

Graph 7.9: Hospitals-wise Box Plot for Component 2 for Medical Services of the Three Type of Hospitals

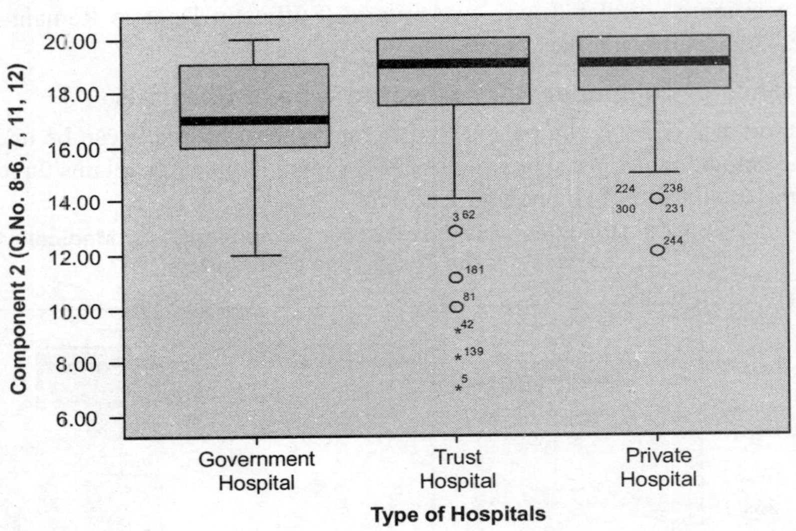

Graph 7.10: Hospitals-wise Box Plot for Component 3 for Medical Services of the Three Type of Hospitals

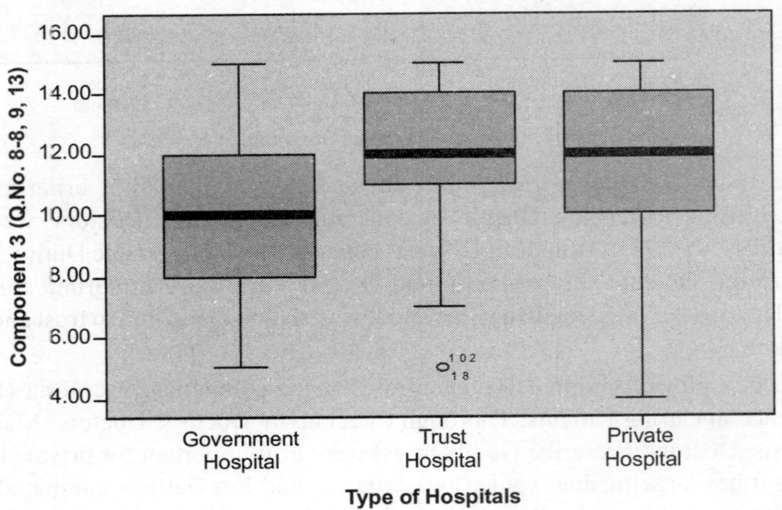

From the box plot of Graph 7.11 it becomes clear that component 4 criteria (Sufficient Doctors Remained Present, Doctors' Availability in Emergency) were important for trust hospitals because of high median value and less outlier.

Graph 7.11: Hospitals-wise Box Plot for Component 4 for Medical Services of the Three Type of Hospitals

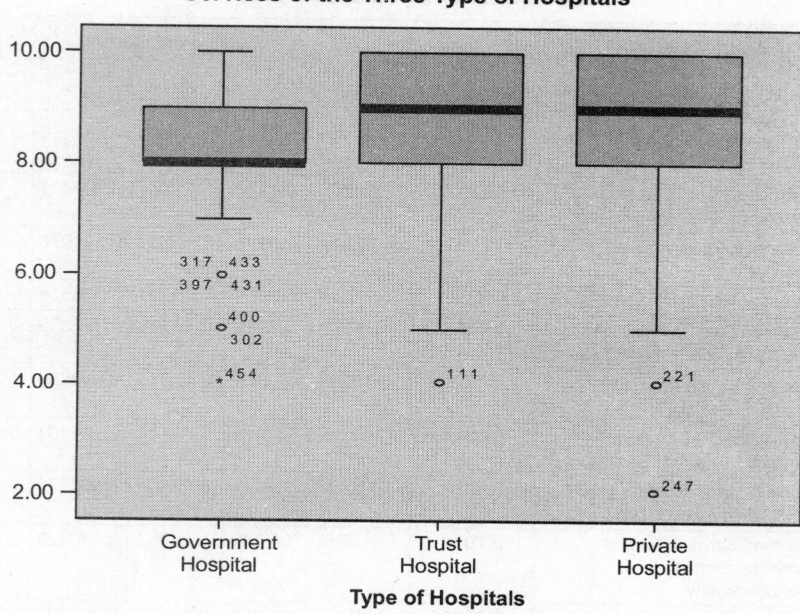

Factor Analysis for Government Hospitals for Medical Services' Criteria

In case of Government hospitals medical services criteria the results showed that the KMO measure of sampling adequacy (0.7755) and Bartlett's test of sphericity (0.00) indicated that data were appropriate for Factor Analysis.

Table 7.38: Total Variance Explained for Government Hospitals for Medical Services

	Initial Eigenvalues			Extraction Sums of Squared Loadings			Rotation Sums of Squared Loadings		
Component	Total	Percentages of Variance	Cumulative per cent	Total	Percentages of Variance	Cumulative per cent	Total	Percentages of Variance	Cumulative per cent
01	4.559	26.820	26.820	4.559	26.820	26.820	2.667	15.688	15.688
02	1.755	10.326	37.146	1.755	10.326	37.146	2.127	12.510	28.198
03	1.440	8.471	45.617	1.440	8.471	45.617	2.112	12.425	40.623
04	1.315	7.734	53.351	1.315	7.734	53.351	1.719	10.113	50.737
05	1.116	6.563	59.914	1.116	6.563	59.914	1.560	9.177	59.914

Extraction Method: Principal Component Analysis.

a Only cases for which Q 2 Type of Hospitals = Government Hospital are used in the analysis phase.

From the Table 7.38 it becomes clear that total five number of components extracted and it explain 59.91 per cent variation from data.

Table 7.39: Communalities and Rotated Component Matrix for Government Hospitals for Medical Services

Sl. No.	Selected Criteria	Communa-lities Extraction	Rotated Component				
			1	2	3	4	5
01	Doctors' Knowledge and Efficiency	0.5995	0.35688	0.1197	0.33038	–0.45916	0.371271
02	Doctors' Cooperation to patients	0.6517	0.77883	0.1552	0.11238	0.023411	0.088716
03	Doctors' were polite with patients	0.7207	0.82627	0.0043	0.18265	0.051078	–0.04428
04	Impartial Attitude of Doctors	0.6932	0.77240	0.1368	–0.0295	0.206526	–0.18531
05	Patients' Felt Comfortable During Doctors Examination	0.4688	0.4262	0.3116	0.36315	0.122339	0.207966
06	Doctors' Experience in Curing Patients	0.563	0.18203	0.191	0.70214	0.009296	–0.01583
07	Thorough Checkup by Doctors	0.6344	0.04794	–0.014	0.78449	0.123101	0.036265
08	Doctors' Work according to Patients Expectations	0.6696	0.04398	0.7827	0.07109	–0.05174	0.217576
09	Doctors' Gave Individual Consideration and Confidentiality	0.7013	0.13615	0.7623	0.28267	0.140323	0.044626
10	Doctors' Showed Respect and Support patients	0.6383	0.27446	0.6311	0.10389	0.265807	–0.28863
11	Doctors' Makes Good Diagnosis	0.5783	–0.0004	0.2554	0.58621	0.401366	–0.09152
12	Doctors' Prescribed Good Drugs	0.5049	0.20855	0.2434	0.41059	0.478847	–0.06512
13	Doctor' ask for patients Permission for performing Test	0.6757	–0.1138	0.4322	–0.1032	0.087265	0.676504
14	Patients' Felt Comfortable asking Questions to Doctors	0.4707	0.0324	0.1619	0.16079	0.624437	0.166339
15	Doctors' Honesty in Dealing with patients	0.4741	0.29698	–0.003	0.26575	0.48503	0.282787
16	Sufficient number of Doctors Remained Present	0.5329	0.44136	–0.024	0.0233	0.52948	0.238006
17	Doctors' Availability in Emergency	0.6084	0.01724	–0.076	0.01655	0.189374	0.752427

It becomes clear from Table 7.39 that all the extracted communalities were acceptable and all criteria were fit for the factor solution as their extraction values were found to be large large.

From the above table it becomes clear that component 1 was (Doctors' Cooperation to patients, Doctors' were polite with patients, Impartial Attitude of Doctors) highly correlated with criteria 2, 3 and 4.

Component 2 (Doctors' Work According to Patients Expectations, Doctors' Gave Individual Consideration and Confidentiality, Doctors' Showed Respect and Support patients) was highly correlated with criteria 8, 9 and 10. Component 3 (Doctors'

Experience in Curing Patients, Thorough Checkup by Doctors, Doctors' Made Good Diagnosis) was highly correlated with criteria 6, 7 and 11.

Component 4 (Patients' Felt Comfortable asking Questions to Doctors, Sufficient Doctors' Remain Present) is highly correlated with criteria 14 and 16. And component 5 (Doctors' ask for patients Permission for performing Test, Doctors' Availability in Emergency) is highly correlated with criteria13 and 17.

Table 7.40: Component-wise Mean value for Government Hospitals for Medical Services

Component	Mean Value	Selected Criteria	Selected Factors
01	13.61	Doctors' Cooperation to patients	Responsiveness
		Doctors' were polite with patients	Empathy
		Impartial Attitude of Doctors	Reliability
02	11.816	Doctors' Work According to Patients Expectations	Empathy
		Doctors' Gave Individual Consideration and Confidentiality	Empathy
		Doctors' Showed Respect and Support patients	Empathy
03	13.416	Doctors' Experience in Curing Patients	Assurance
		Thorough Checkup by Doctors	Assurance
		Doctors' Made Good Diagnosis	Reliability
04	8.534	Patients' Felt Comfortable asking Questions to Doctors	Responsiveness
		Sufficient Doctors Remain Present	Tangibles
05	7.846	Doctors' ask for patients Permission for performing Test	Dignity
		Doctors' Availability in Emergency	Accessibility/
			Affordability

From Table 7.40 it becomes clear that component 1 (Doctors' Cooperation to patients, Doctors' were polite with patients, Impartial Attitude of Doctors) have highest mean value of 13.61. On the other hand component 5 has lowest mean value of 7.85. Government hospitals were weak in criteria related with component 5 (Doctors' ask for patients Permission for performing Test, Doctors' Availability in Emergency) therefore Government hospital needs to put efforts to improve in providing these kind of services.

ONE WAY ANNOVA FOR PARAMEDICAL SERVICES

Hypothesis: 20

Mean of patients' view about selected type of hospitals is equal in terms of paramedical staff services and an alternative hypothesis is at least one mean is different from other.

Table 7.41: Descriptive Statistics for Paramedical Services for All the Three Type of Hospitals

Type of Hospitals	N	Mean	SD	SE
GHs	200	60.45	5.256965	0.371724
THs	200	67.35	7.318834	0.51752
PHs	100	66.87	8.000827	0.800083
Total	500	64.494	7.485856	0.334778

Table 7.41 indicated that trust hospitals has highest mean value of 67.35, Private hospital has 66.87 mean value and Government hospitals has lower mean value of 60.45.

Test of Homogeneity of Variances

Table 7.42: Test of Homogeneity of Variances for Paramedical Services for All the Three Type of Hospitals

Levene's Statistic	df1	df2	Sig.
8.76185	2	497	0.000182

The P-value 0.000182 of leven's test was less then 0.05 indicated that variance of type of hospitals was not equal at least one variance of type of hospitals was different from other type of hospitals.

Analysis of Variance

Table 7.43: ANOVA for Paramedical Services for All the Three Type of Hospitals

Particulars	Sum of Squares	Df	Mean Square	F	Sig.
Between Groups	5466.672	2	2733.336	60.38626	0.00
Within Groups	22496.31	497	45.26421		
Total	27962.98	499			

The P-value 0.00 (P-value > 0.05) indicated that mean of three type of hospitals was not equal at least one mean of type of hospitals was different from other type of hospitals.

Post-Hoc Test (Tamhane)

Table 7.44: Multiple Comparisons for Paramedical Services for All the Three Type of Hospitals Through Tamhane Test

Type of Hospitals		Mean Difference	SE	Sig.
GHs	GHs			
	THs	–6.9	0.637185	0.00
	PHs	–6.42	0.882219	0.00
THs	GHs	6.9	0.637185	0.00
	THs			
	PHs	0.48	0.952869	0.942955
PHs	GHs	6.42	0.882219	0.00
	THs	–0.48	0.952869	0.942955
	PHs			

Table 7.44 indicated that mean of Government hospitals was different from trust and private hospitals, and mean of trust and private hospitals also different from each other.

Post Hoc Test (Tuskey HSD)

Table 7.45: Multiple Comparisons for Paramedical Services for All the Three Type of Hospitals Through Tuskey HSD Test

Type of Hospitals	Subset for alpha = .05		
	N	1	2
GHs	200	60.45	
PHs	100		66.87
THs	200		67.35
Sig.		1	0.810409

From Table 7.45 it becomes clear that Government hospitals make one separate group, and trust and private hospitals make another group.

Graph 7.12: Means Plots for Paramedical Services for All the Three Type of Hospitals

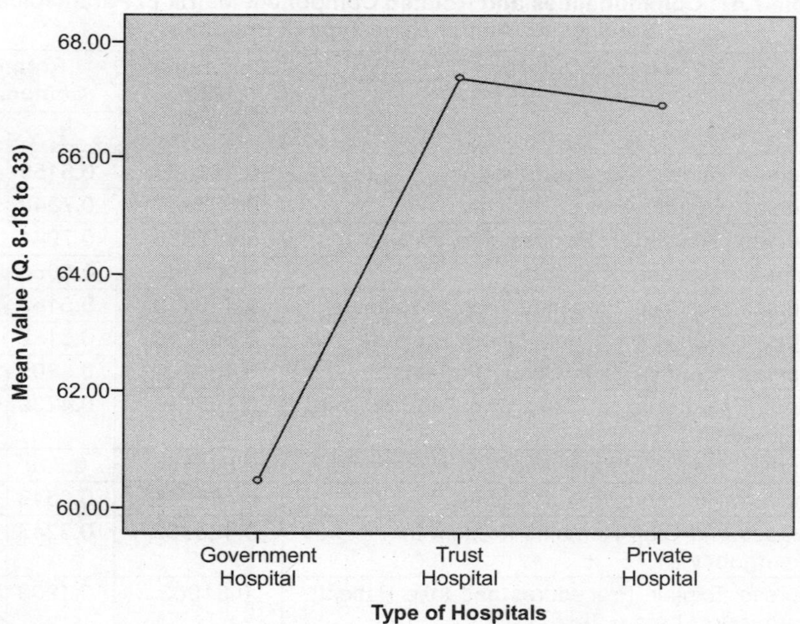

The above means plot (Graph 7.12) indicated that trust hospital have highest mean value, Private hospitals have second highest mean value and Government hospitals have low mean value.

FACTOR ANALYSIS FOR PARAMEDICAL SERVICES

Factor Analysis for Paramedical Services Criteria for All the Three Type of Hospitals is given as below.

In case of paramedical services criteria the results showed that the KMO measure of sampling adequacy (0.906975) and Bartlett's test of sphericity (0.0) which indicated that factor analysis was appropriate.

Table 7.46: Total Variance for Paramedical Services for All the Three Type of Hospitals

Component	Initial Eigenvalues			Extraction Sums of Squared Loadings			Rotation Sums of Squared Loadings		
	Total	% age of Variance	Cumulative per cent	Total	% age of Variance	Cumulative per cent	Total	% age of Variance	Cumulative per cent
01	5.9917	37.45	37.448	5.9917	37.4481	37.448	4.108	25.68	25.677
02	1.4956	9.347	46.796	1.4956	9.34744	46.796	3.379	21.12	46.796

From Table 7.46 it becomes clear that there were two components extracted and they extract 46.79 per cent variation from data.

Table 7.47: Communalities and Rotated Component Matrix of Paramedical Services for All the Three Type of Hospitals

Sl. No.	Selected Criteria	Communalities Extraction	Rotated Component	
			1	2
01	Nurses' Knowledge and Efficiency	0.421065	0.6159	0.204
02	Nurses' Cooperation to Patients	0.553957	0.7348	0.118
03	Nurses' Showed Politeness with Patients	0.642338	0.7944	0.106
04	Impartial Attitude of Nurses	0.41145	0.6063	0.209
05	Nurses' Maintain Proper records of Patients	0.436413	0.5163	0.412
06	Nurses' Handled Patients Query Properly	0.557716	0.3132	0.678
07	Nurses' Experience in Curing Patients	0.480191	0.5809	0.378
08	Good Experience of Those who Perform Test on Patients	0.285717	0.4232	0.326
09	Nurses' Gave Personal Attention to Patients	0.544134	0.319	0.665
10	Nurses' Provided Prompt Service	0.465889	0.0548	0.68
11	Nurses and Staff Remains Present in Emergency	0.425702	0.3243	0.566
12	Nurses' Explain Procedures and take Patient Permission before Test	0.51003	0.1909	0.688
13	Nurses' Explain Rules Regulation in ward	0.317557	0.4814	0.293
14	Nurses' were Kind, Gentle and Sympathetic	0.442409	0.6582	0.096
15	Information Provided to patients for Managing Side Effects	0.546172	0.12	0.729
16	Prompt Service Provided by Sanitation Staff	0.446547	0.619	0.252

As given in Table 7.47 all the extracted communalities were acceptable and all criteria were fit for the factor solution as their extraction values were large.

The component 1 (Nurses' Knowledge and Efficiency, Nurses' Cooperation to Patients, Nurses' Showed Politeness with Patients, Impartial Attitude of Nurses, Nurses' Experience in Curing Patients, Nurses' were Kind, Gentle and Sympathetic, Prompt Service Provided by Sanitation Staff) was highly correlated with criteria 1, 2, 3, 4, 7, 14 and 16. The component 2 (Nurses' Handled Patients Query Properly, Nurses' Gave Personal Attention to Patients, Nurses' Provided Prompt Service, Nurses' and Staff Remained Present in Emergency, Nurses' Explain Procedures and take Patient Permission before Test, Information Provided to patients for Managing Side Effects) was highly correlated with criteria 6, 9, 10, 11, 12 and 15.

Table 7.48: Component-wise Mean Value for Paramedical Services for All the Three Type of Hospitals

Component	Mean Value	Selected Criteria	Selected Factors
01	29.482	Nurses' Knowledge and Efficiency	Assurance
		Nurses' Cooperation to Patients	Responsiveness
		Nurses' Showed Politeness with Patients	Empathy
		Impartial Attitude of Nurses	Reliability
		Nurses' Experience in Curing Patients	Assurance
		Nurses' are Kind, Gentle and Sympathetic	Dignity
		Prompt Service Provided by Sanitation Staff	Responsiveness
02	22.48	Nurses' Handled Patients Query Properly	Assurance
		Nurses' Gave Personal Attention to Patients	Dignity
		Nurses' Provided Prompt Service	Responsiveness
		Nurses' and Staff Remains Present in Emergency	Responsiveness
		Nurses' Explain Procedures and take Patient Permission before Test	Dignity
		Information Provided to patients for Managing Side Effects	Responsiveness

The component 1 (Nurses' Knowledge and Efficiency, Nurses' Cooperation to Patients, Nurses' Showed Politeness with Patients, Impartial Attitude of Nurses, Nurses' Experience in Curing Patients, Nurses' were Kind, Gentle and Sympathetic, Prompt Service Provided by Sanitation Staff) have highest mean value of 29.48. The component 2 (Nurses' Handled Patients Query Properly, Nurses' Gave Personal Attention to Patients, Nurses' Provided Prompt Service, Nurses' and Staff Remained Present in Emergency,

Nurses' Explain Procedures and take Patient Permission before Test, Information Provided to patients for Managing Side Effects) has 22.48 mean value.

Importance of Components for Selected Type of Hospitals

The importance of each component to different type of hospitals can be understood with the help of below given box plots, which explain the three type of hospitals total score of component 1 criteria.

Graph 7.13: Hospitals-wise Box Plot for Component 1 for Paramedical Services of the Three Type of Hospitals

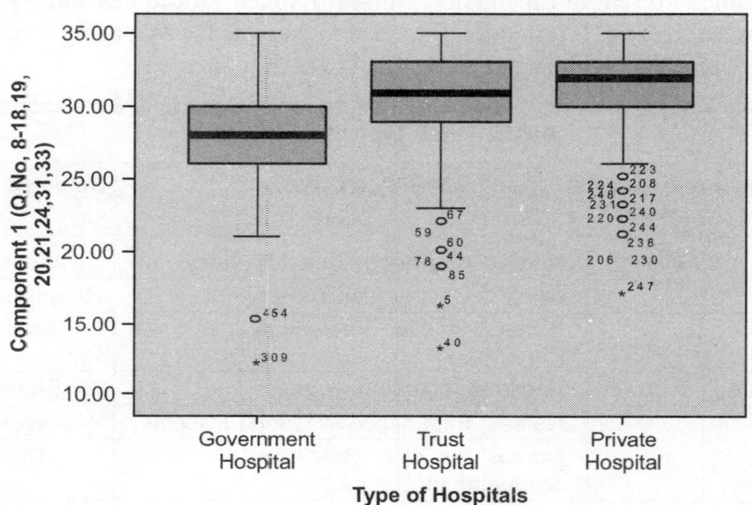

From the above box plot of Graph 7.13 it becomes clear that component 1 (Nurses' Knowledge and Efficiency, Nurses' Cooperation to Patients, Nurses Showed Politeness with Patients, Impartial Attitude of Nurses,

Nurses' Experience in Curing Patients, Nurses' were Kind, Gentle and Sympathetic, Prompt Service Provided by Sanitation Staff) was important for private hospitals because of large median value and low variation then other hospitals *(Refer Graph 7.14)*.

From the box plot of Graph 7.14 it becomes clear that component 2 (Nurses' Handled Patients Query Properly, Nurses' Gave Personal Attention to Patients, Nurses' Provided Prompt Service, Nurses' and Staff Remained Present in Emergency, Nurses' Explain Procedures and take Patient Permission before Test, Information Provided to patients for Managing Side Effects) was important for trust hospitals because of it has large median value and low variation then other hospitals.

As the mean score of Government hospitals was lower (60.45) factor analysis was made to know the reasons for such lower mean value for private hospitals.

Factor Analysis for Government Hospitals for Paramedical Services is given as below.

Graph 7.14: Hospitals-wise Box Plot for Component 2 for Paramedical Services of the Three Type of Hospitals

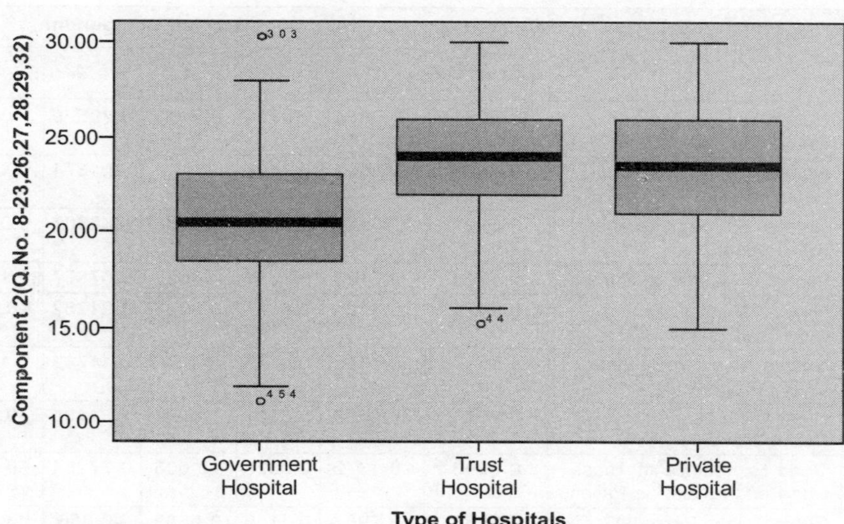

In case of Government hospitals paramedical services, the results showed that the KMO measure of sampling adequacy (0.7189) and Bartlett's test of sphericity (0.00) which indicated that factor analysis was appropriate.

Table 7.49: Total Variance of Government Hospitals for Paramedical Services

Component	Initial Eigenvalues			Extraction Sums of Squared Loadings			Rotation Sums of Squared Loadings		
	Total	% age of Variance	Cumulative per cent	Total	% age of Variance	Cumulative per cent	Total	% age of Variance	Cumulative per cent
01	5.9917	37.45	37.448	5.9917	37.4481	37.448	4.108	25.68	25.677
01	3.444	21.522	21.522	3.444	21.522	21.522	2.581	16.130	16.130
02	2.460	15.373	36.895	2.460	15.373	36.895	2.490	15.561	31.691
03	1.458	9.113	46.008	1.458	9.113	46.008	1.810	11.310	43.002
04	1.394	8.711	54.719	1.394	8.711	54.719	1.478	9.235	52.237
05	1.044	6.528	61.247	1.044	6.528	61.247	1.442	9.010	61.247

Extraction Method: Principal Component Analysis.
a Only cases for which Q 2 Type of Hospitals = Government Hospital are used in the analysis phase.

From Table 7.49 it becomes clear that total five numbers of components were extracted and it explains 61 per cent variation from data.

Table 7.50: Communalities and Rotated Component Matrix of Government Hospitals for Paramedical Services

Sl. No.	Selected Criteria	Communa-lities Extraction	Rotated Component				
			1	2	3	4	5
01	Nurses' Knowledge and Efficiency	0.5264	0.0854	0.6884	0.0179	0.20529	–0.052
02	Nurses' Cooperation to Patients'	0.6472	–0.009	0.7696	0.125	–0.1874	0.064
03	Nurses' Showed Politeness with Patients	0.5899	–0.04	0.7151	0.2756	–0.0307	0.00273
04	Impartial Attitude of Nurses	0.5718	0.0723	0.7391	0.0652	0.07677	0.10092
05	Nurses' Maintain Proper records of Patients	0.4474	0.3183	0.3647	0.3623	0.21282	–0.1912
06	Nurses' Handled Patients Query Properly	0.5587	0.7182	0.1175	–0.0579	0.11742	0.10897
07	Nurses' Experience in Curing Patients	0.7075	0.2278	0.3107	0.588	–0.4435	–0.1287
08	Good Experience of Those who Perform Test on Patients	0.6393	0.1372	0.0635	–0.006	0.77264	–0.1394
09	Nurses' Gave Personal Attention to Patients	0.6558	0.7983	0.1159	0.0309	–0.056	0.03154
10	Nurses' Provided Prompt Service	0.6668	0.4626	0.1323	–0.2307	–0.2391	0.56996
11	Nurses' and Staff Remains Present in Emergency	0.7336	0.1862	–0.042	0.2502	–0.0437	0.79538
12	Nurses' Explain Procedures and take Patient Permission before Test	0.5002	0.6212	–0.067	–0.0219	0.32971	0.02293
13	Nurses' Explain Rules Regulation in ward	0.6899	0.0402	0.1819	0.1916	0.56143	0.55072
14	Nurses' are Kind, Gentle and Sympathetic	0.7106	–0.136	0.0616	0.7873	0.20793	0.1593
15	Information Provided to patients for Managing Side Effects	0.6381	0.766	–0.065	0.074	–0.0772	0.18904
16	Prompt Service Provided by Sanitation Staff	0.5164	0.0002	0.2009	0.6737	–0.0735	0.12954

All the extracted communalities as given in the above table were acceptable and all criteria were fit for the factor solution as their extraction values were large.

From Table 7.50 it becomes clear that component 1 (Nurses' Handled Patients Query Properly, Nurses' Gave Personal Attention to Patients, Nurses' Explain Procedures and take Patient Permission before Test, Information Provided to patients for Managing Side Effects,) was highly correlated with criteria number 6, 9, 12 and 15. Component 2 (Nurses' Knowledge and Efficiency, Nurses' Cooperation to Patients, Nurses' Showed Politeness with Patients, Impartial Attitude of Nurses) was highly correlated with criteria 1, 2, 3 and 4. Component 3 (Nurses' Experience in Curing Patients, Nurses' were Kind, Gentle and Sympathetic, Prompt Service Provided by Sanitation Staff) was highly correlated with criteria 7, 14 and 16.

Component 4 (Good Experience of Those who Perform Test on Patients, Nurses' Explain Rules Regulation in ward) is highly correlated with criteria number 8 and 13. Component 5 (Nurses' Provided Prompt Service, Nurses' and Staff Remained Present in Emergency) was highly correlated with criteria 10 and 11.

Table 7.51: Component wise Mean value for Government Hospitals for Paramedical Services

Component	Mean Value	Selected Criteria	Selected Factors
01	15.112	Nurses' Handled Patients Query Properly	Assurance
		Nurses' Gave Personal Attention to Patients	Dignity
		Nurses' Explain Procedures and take Patient Permission before Test	Dignity
		Information Provided to patients for Managing Side Effects	Responsiveness
02	16.954	Nurses' Knowledge and Efficiency	Assurance
		Nurses' Cooperation to Patients	Responsiveness
		Nurses' Showed Politeness with Patients	Empathy
		Impartial Attitude of Nurses	Reliability
03	12.528	Nurses' Experience in Curing Patients	Assurance
		Nurses' were Kind, Gentle and Sympathetic	Dignity
		Prompt Service Provided by Sanitation Staff	Responsiveness
04	4.194	Good Experience of Those who Perform Test on Patients	Assurance
05	7.368	Nurses' Provide Prompt Service	Responsiveness
		Nurses' and Staff Remains Present in Emergency	Responsiveness

From Table 7.51 it becomes clear that component 2 (Nurses' Knowledge and Efficiency, Nurses' Cooperation to Patients, Nurses' Showed Politeness with Patients, Impartial Attitude of Nurses) have highest mean value of 16.95. Component 4 (Good Experience of Those who Perform Test on Patients) have lowest mean value it 4.19, and Component 5 (Nurses' Provided Prompt Service, Nurses' and Staff Remained Present in Emergency) have second lowest mean value. Government hospitals were weak in component 4 and component 5 and therefore, Government hospitals should improve its service in terms of criteria namely, 'Nurses Provide Prompt Service' and 'Nurses and Staff Remains Present in Emergency'.

ONE WAY ANNOVA FOR ADMINISTRATIVE SERVICES

Analysis of Variance: Selected Patients' Responses for Administrative Services

Hypothesis: 21

Mean of patients' response about selected type of hospital is equal in terms of Administrative services of hospital and an alternative hypothesis is at least one mean is different from other.

Table 7.52: Descriptive Statistics for Administrative Services for All the Three Type of Hospitals

Type of Hospitals	N	Mean	SD	SE
GHs	200	45.62	5.00709	0.354055
THs	200	53.67	7.220233	0.510548
PHs	100	52.03	7.707343	0.770734
Total	500	50.122	7.514789	0.336072

Table 7.52 indicated that trust hospitals have large mean value of 53.67. Private hospitals have second highest mean value of 52.03, and Government hospitals have lowest mean value of 45.62.

Test of Homogeneity of Variances

Table 7.53: Test of Homogeneity of Variances for Administrative Services for All the Three Type of Hospitals

Levene's Statistic	df1	df2	Sig.
16.05063	2	497	0.00

P-Value of levene's test statistics was less then 0.05 (0.00 < 0.05) which indicated that variance of type of Hospitals was not equal at least variance of one type of hospitals was different from other type of hospitals.

Analysis of Variance

Table 7.54: ANOVA for Administrative Services for All the Three Type of Hospitals

Particulars	Sum of Squares	Df	Mean Square	F	Sig.
Between Groups	6935.308	2	3467.654	81.12426	0.00
Within Groups	21244.25	497	42.74497		
Total	28179.56	499			

P-Value (0.00 < 0.05) of ANOVA table also indicated that mean values of Type of Hospitals was not equal at least mean of one type of hospitals was different from other type of hospitals.

Post-Hoc Test (Tamhane)

Table 7.55: Multiple Comparisons for Administrative Services for All the Three Type of Hospitals Through Tamhane Test

Type of Hospitals		Mean Difference	SE	Sig.
GHs	GHs			
	THs	–8.05	0.6213	0
	PHs	–6.41	0.848166	0.00
THs	GHs	8.05	0.6213	0
	THs			
	PHs	1.64	0.924495	0.215457
PHs	GHs	6.41	0.848166	0.00
	THs	–1.64	0.924495	0.215457
	PHs			

Table 7.55 indicated that mean of Government hospitals was different from trust and private hospitals. Trust hospitals and private hospitals make one group and Government hospitals make another group.

Post-Hoc Test (Tukey HSD)

Table 7.56: Multiple Comparisons for Administrative Services for All the Three Type of Hospitals Through Tukey HSD Test

Type of Hospitals	Subset for alpha = .05		
	N	1	2
GHs	200	60.45	
GHs	200	45.62	
PHs	100		52.03
THs	200		53.67
Sig.		1	0.076974

From Table 7.56 it becomes clear that Government hospitals make one separate group and private and trust hospitals makes one group.

The means plot of Graph 7.15 indicated that Government hospitals have lowest mean value. Trust hospitals have highest mean value and private hospitals have second highest mean value.

FACTOR ANALYSIS FOR ADMINISTRATIVE SERVICES

Factor Analysis for Administrative Services for All the Three Type of Hospitals is given as below:

In case administrative services, the behaviour of the staff showed the result that the KMO measure of sampling adequacy (0.906028) and Bartlett's test of sphericity (0.0) indicated that factor analysis was appropriate.

Graph 7.15: Means Plots of Administrative Services for All the Three Type of Hospitals

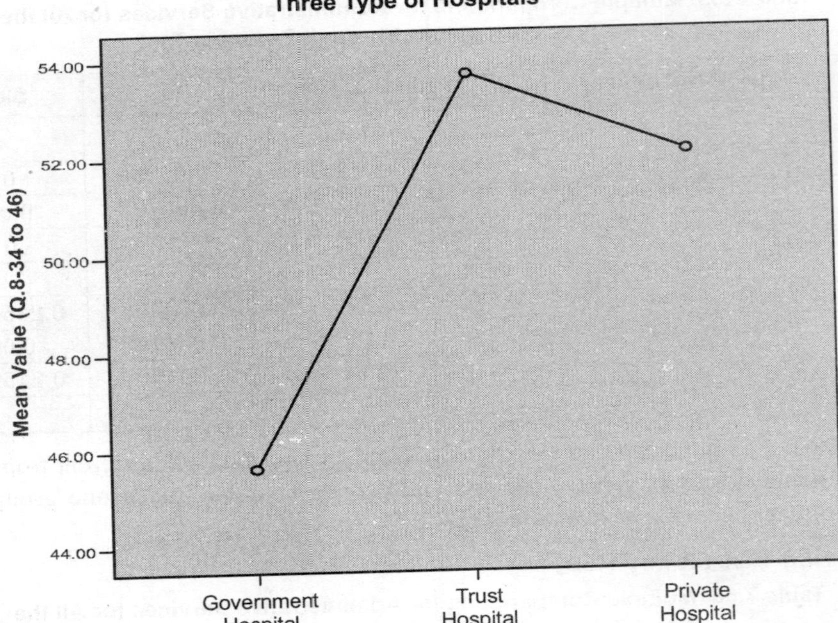

Table 7.57: Total Variance for Administrative Services for All the Three Type of Hospitals

Com-ponent	Initial Eigenvalues			Extraction Sums of Squared Loadings			Rotation Sums of Squared Loadings		
	Total	% age of Var-iance	Cumu-lative per cent	Total	% age of Var-iance	Cumu-lative per cent	Total	% age of Var-iance	Cumu-lative per cent
01	5.8798	45.23	45.229	5.8798	45.2293	45.229	3.974	30.57	30.571
02	1.4301	11	56.23	1.4301	11.001	56.23	3.336	25.66	56.23

Table 7.57 indicates that there were two components extracted and it extracts 56.23 per cent variation from data.

All the extracted communalities were acceptable and all criteria were fit for the factor solution as their extraction values were large.

Table 7.58 indicated that component 1 (Less Waiting Time For Consultation and Treatment, Less Waiting Time for Test, Simple Checking Procedure, Speed, Ease of Admission and Discharge form Hospital, Convenient Office Hours, Patients' were Treated With Dignity and Privacy, Good Concern for Patients' Family and Visitor) was highly correlated with criteria number 1 to 5, 11 and 12. Component 2 (Adm. Staff Gives Prompt Services, Good Grievance handling System, Adm. Staff Welcome

Table 7.58: Communalities and Rotated Component Matrix for Administrative Services for All the Three Type of Hospitals

Sl.	Selected Criteria	Communalities Extraction	Rotated Component	
			1	2
01	Less Waiting Time For Consultation and Treatment	0.399701	0.564	0.286
02	Less Waiting Time for Test	0.416938	0.5809	0.282
03	Simple Checking Procedure	0.623508	0.7639	0.2
04	Speed, Ease of Admission and Discharge form Hospital	0.561188	0.7347	0.146
05	Convenient Office Hours	0.514329	0.6848	0.213
06	Adm. Staff Gives Prompt Services	0.5843	0.3237	0.692
07	No Overcrowding in Hospital	0.427925	0.4342	0.489
08	Good Grievance handling System	0.770759	0.2323	0.847
09	Adm. Staff Welcome and Implement Suggestion	0.783967	0.2137	0.859
10	Adm. Gives Personal Attention To Patient	0.708765	0.1988	0.818
11	Patients' were Treated With Dignity and Privacy	0.461669	0.5729	0.365
12	Good Concern for Patients' Family and Visitor	0.507402	0.6620	0.263
13	Simple Billing Procedures	0.549492	0.72610	0.149

and Implement Suggestion, Adm. Staff Welcome and Implement Suggestion, Adm. Gives Personal Attention To Patient) is highly correlated with criteria number 6, 8, 9 and 10.

Table 7.59: Component wise Mean Value for Administrative Services for All the Three Type of Hospitals

Component	Mean Value	Selected Criteria	Selected Factors
01	32.448	Less Waiting Time For Consultation and Treatment	Responsiveness
		Less Waiting Time for Test	Responsiveness
		Simple Checking Procedure	Empathy
		Speed, Ease of Admission and Discharge form Hospital	Responsiveness
		Convenient Office Hours	Responsiveness
		Patients' were Treated With Dignity and Privacy	Dignity

...(Contd.)

...(*Contd.*)

Component	Mean Value	Selected Criteria	Selected Factors
		Good Concern for Patients' Family and Visitor	Empathy
		Simple Billing Procedures	Empathy
02	13.712	Adm. Staff Gives Prompt Services	Responsiveness
		Good Grievance handling System	Responsiveness
		Adm. Staff Welcome and Implement Suggestion	Dignity
		Adm. Gives Personal Attention To Patient	Dignity

From Table 7.59 it becomes clear that, component 1 (Less Waiting Time For Consultation and Treatment, Less Waiting Time for Test, Simple Checking Procedure, Speed, Ease of Admission and Discharge form Hospital, Convenient Office Hours, Patients' were Treated With Dignity and Privacy, Good Concern for Patients' Family and Visitor) have high mean value of 32.44 and component 2 (Adm. Staff Gives Prompt Services, Good Grievance handling System, Adm. Staff Welcome and Implement Suggestion, Adm. Staff Welcome and Implement Suggestion, Adm. Gives Personal Attention To Patient) have lowest mean value of 13.71.

Importance of Components for Selected Type of Hospitals

The importance of each component to different type of hospitals can be understood with the help of below given box plots. The following box plot explains three type of hospitals total score of component 1 criteria. *(Refer Graph 7.16)*

From the box plot of Graph 7.17 it becomes clear that component 1 (Less Waiting Time For Consultation and Treatment, Less Waiting Time for Test, Simple Checking Procedure, Speed, Ease of Admission and Discharge form Hospital, Convenient Office Hours, Patient Treated With Dignity and Privacy, Good Concern for Patient Family and Visitor) was important for trust hospitals because of large median value and low variation then private hospitals.

The box plot indicated that component 2 was important for trust hospitals because of high median value (Graph 7.17.

As the mean score of Government hospitals was lower (45.62) factor analysis was made to find out the reasons for such lower mean value for Government hospitals.

Factor Analysis for Government Hospitals for Administrative Services is given as below:

In case of Government hospitals administrative services the results showed the KMO measure of sampling adequacy (0.7603) and Bartlett's test of sphericity (0.0) which indicated that factor analysis was appropriate.

Graph 7.16: Hospitals-wise Box Plot for Component 1 for Administrative Services of the Three Type of Hospitals

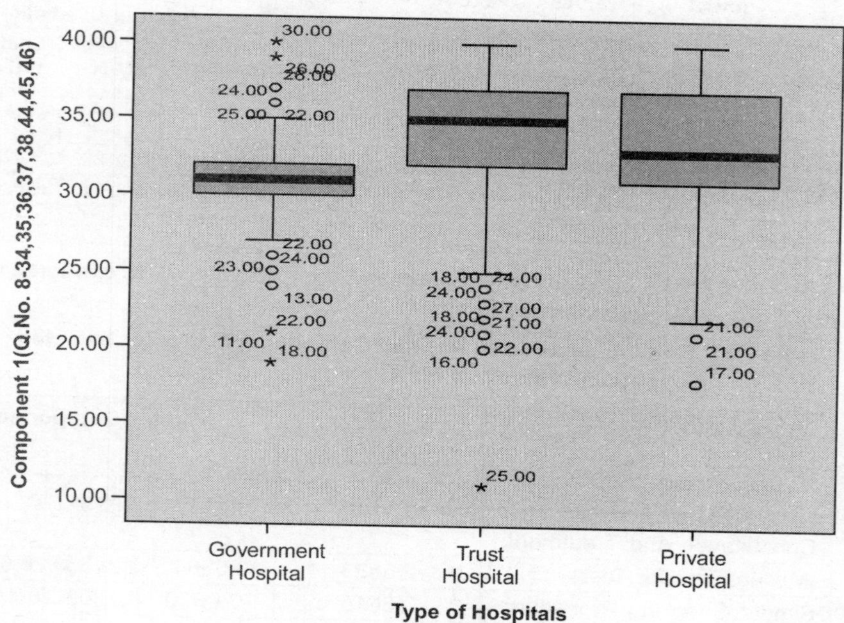

Graph 7.17: Hospitals-wise Box Plot for Component 2 for Administrative Services

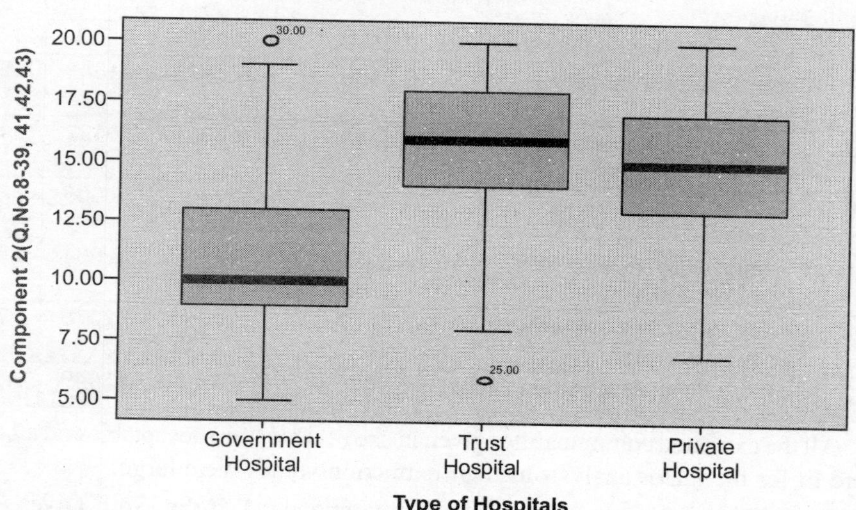

Table 7.60: Total Variance for Government Hospitals for Administrative Services

Component	Initial Eigenvalues			Extraction Sums of Squared Loadings			Rotation Sums of Squared Loadings		
	Total	% age of Variance	Cumulative per cent	Total	% age of Variance	Cumulative per cent	Total	% age of Variance	Cumulative per cent
01	3.4924	26.865	26.865	3.49239	26.8645	26.86452	2.733735	21.02873	21.02873
02	1.9244	14.803	41.668	1.9244	14.8031	41.66763	2.446305	18.81773	39.84646
03	1.4936	11.489	53.157	1.49359	11.4891	53.15678	1.730341	13.31032	53.15678

From Table 7.60 it becomes clear that total 3 components can be extracted and it explains 53 per cent variation from data.

Table 7.61: Communalities and Rotated Component Matrix for Selected Government Hospitals for Administrative Services

Sl.	Selected Criteria	Communalities Extraction	Rotated Component 1	2	3
01	Less Waiting Time For Consultation and Treatment	0.4186	0.1972	0.6152	-0.0346
02	Waiting Time for Test	0.5583	0.0304	0.7453	0.0440
03	Simple Checking Procedure	0.5615	–0.0670	0.7308	0.15140
04	Speed, Ease of Admission and Discharge form Hospital	0.4894	0.1213	0.6602	0.1970
05	Convenient Office Hours	0.3736	0.3180	0.5135	0.0940
06	Adm. Staff Gives Prompt Services	0.4986	0.6752	0.1894	–0.0830
07	No Overcrowding in Hospital	0.3559	0.4039	0.291	–0.3289
08	Good Grievance handling System	0.6456	0.7885	0.1542	0.0029
09	Adm. Staff Welcome and Implement Suggestion	0.7219	0.8383	0.0122	0.1376
10	Gives Personal Attention To Patient	0.6893	0.7736	–0.005	0.3015
11	Patients' were Treated With Dignity and Privacy,	0.5672	0.1763	–0.064	0.7295
12	Good Concern for Patients' Family and Visitor	0.5627	0.0231	0.2078	0.7204
13	Simple Billing Procedures	0.4676	–0.0030	0.2949	0.6169

All the extracted communalities given in above table were acceptable and all criteria were fit for the factor analysis as their extraction values were large.

From Table 7.61 it becomes clear that component 1 (Adm. Staff Gives Prompt Services, No Overcrowding in Hospital, Good Grievance handling System, Adm. Staff Welcome and Implement Suggestion, Adm. Gives Personal Attention To Patients) was highly correlated with criteria 6 to 10. Component 2 (Less Waiting Time For Consultation and Treatment, Less Waiting Time for Test, Simple Checking Procedure, Speed, Ease of Admission and Discharge form Hospital, Convenient Office Hours) was highly correlated with criteria 1 to 5, and component 3 (Patients' were Treated With Dignity and Privacy, Good Concern for Patient Family and Visitor, Simple Billing Procedures) was highly correlated with criteria 11 to 13.

Table 7.62: Component wise Mean value for Selected Government Hospitals for Administrative Services

Component	Mean Value	Selected Criteria	Selected Factors
01	17.674	Adm. Staff Gives Prompt Services	Responsiveness
		No Overcrowding in Hospital	Responsiveness
		Good Grievance handling System	Responsiveness
		Adm. Staff Welcome and Implement Suggestion	Dignity
		Adm. Gives Personal Attention To Patient	Dignity
02	20.038	Less Waiting Time For Consultation and Treatment	Responsiveness
		Less Waiting Time for Test	Responsiveness
		Simple Checking Procedure	Empathy
		Speed, Ease of Admission and Discharge form Hospital	Responsiveness
		Convenient Office Hours	Responsiveness
03	12.41	Patients' were Treated With Dignity and Privacy	Dignity
		Good Concern for Patients' Family and Visitor	Empathy
		Simple Billing Procedures	Empathy

Table 7.62 indicated that component 2 (Less Waiting Time For Consultation and Treatment, Less Waiting Time for Test, Simple Checking Procedure, Speed, Ease of Admission and Discharge form Hospital, Convenient Office Hours) have highest mean value of 20.04. Component 3 (Patient Treated with Dignity and Privacy, Good Concern for Patients' Family and Visitor, Simple Billing Procedures) have lowest mean value of 12.41. That means Government hospitals service was weaker for component 3 criteria. So, Government hospitals should improve its service in terms of criteria namely, 'Patients' were Treated with Dignity and Privacy', 'Good Concern for Patient Family and Visitor' and 'Simple Billing Procedures'.

ONE WAY ANNOVA FOR ENVIRONMENT (PHYSICAL FACILITIES) OF SELECTED TYPE OF HOSPITALS

Analysis of Variance: Selected Patients' Responses for Environment (Physical facilities) of the Three Type of Hospitals.

Hypothesis: 22

Mean of patients' responses about selected type of hospital is equal in terms of Environment (Physical facilities) related criterion of the hospitals and an alternative hypothesis is at least one mean is different from other.

Table 7.63: Descriptive Statistics for Environment (Physical facilities) for All the Three Type of Hospitals

Type of Hospitals	N	Mean	SD	SE
GHs	200	75.855	3.666222	0.259241
THs	200	77.825	6.037103	0.426888
PHs	100	71.20	8.168676	0.816868
Total	500	75.712	6.245885	0.279324

From the above table it becomes clear that trust hospitals have highest mean value of 77.82. Government hospitals have second highest mean value of 75.85 and private hospitals have lowest mean value of 71.20.

Test of Homogeneity of Variances

Table 7.64: Test of Homogeneity of Variances for Environment (Physical facilities) for All the Three Type of Hospitals

Levene's Statistic	df1	df2	Sig.
27.04804	2	497	0.00

P-Value of levene's test statistics as given in the above table was less then 0.05 (0.00 < 0.05) which represent that variance of type of hospitals was not equal at least variance of one type of hospitals was different from other type of hospitals.

Analysis of Variance

Table 7.65: ANOVA for Environment (Physical facilities) for All the Three Type of Hospitals

Particulars	Sum of Squares	Df	Mean Square	F	Sig.
Between Groups	2932.858	2	1466.429	44.08067	0.00
Within Groups	16533.67	497	33.26694		
Total	19466.53	499			

The P-Value (0.00 < 0.05) of ANOVA given in above table indicated that mean of Type of Hospitals was not equal at least mean of one Type of Hospitals was different from other type of hospitals.

Post-Hoc Test (Tamhane)

Table 7.66: Multiple Comparisons for Environment (Physical facilities) for All the Three Type of Hospitals Through Tamhane Test

Type of Hospitals		Mean Difference	SE	Sig.
GHs	GHs			
	THs	–1.97	0.499439	0.000293
	PHs	4.655	0.857017	0.00
THs	GHs	1.97	0.499439	0.000293
	THs			
	PHs	6.625	0.921686	0.00
PHs	GHs	–4.655	0.857017	0.00
	THs	–6.625	0.921686	0.00
	PHs			

From the above table it becomes clear that Government hospitals were different from trust and private hospitals. Trust hospitals were different from Government and private hospitals and private hospitals were different from Government and trust hospitals.

Post-Hoc Test (Tukey HSD)

Table 7.67: Multiple Comparisons for Environment (Physical Facilities) for All the Three Type of Hospitals Through Tukey HSD Test

Type of Hospitals	Subset for alpha = .05			
	N	1	2	3
PHs	100	71.2		
GHs	200		75.855	
THs	200		77.825	
Sig.		1	1	1

From the above table it becomes clear that private hospitals make one group, Government hospitals make another group and trust hospitals make one more group.

The means plot of Graph 7.18 indicated that trust hospitals have high mean value. Government hospitals have second highest mean value and private hospitals have lowest mean value and each make different group.

FACTOR ANALYSIS FOR ENVIRONMENT (PHYSICAL FACILITIES)

Factor Analysis for Environment (Physical facilities) for all Three Types of Hospitals.

In case of responses of patients for environment (physical facilities) the results showed the value for KMO measure of sampling adequacy (0.850) and Bartlett's test of sphericity (0.0) which indicated that factor analysis was appropriate.

Graph 7.18: Means Plots Environment (Physical facilities) for All the Three Type of Hospitals

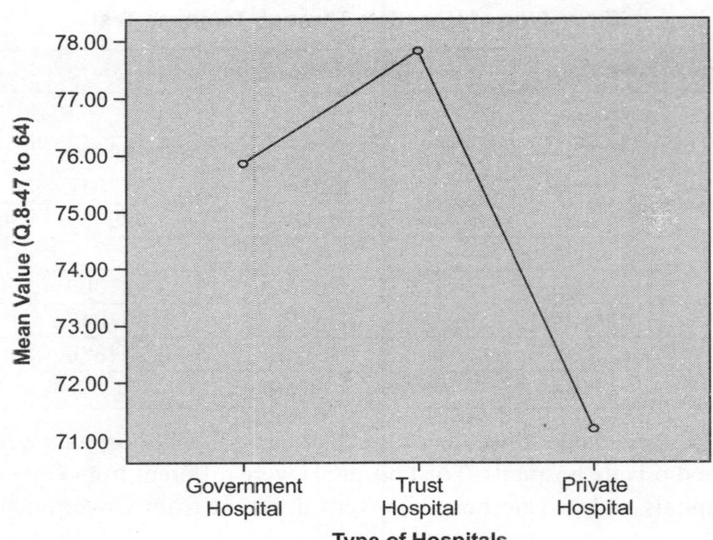

Table 7.68: Total Variance for Environment (Physical facilities) for All the Three Type of Hospitals

Component	Initial Eigenvalues			Extraction Sums of Squared Loadings			Rotation Sums of Squared Loadings		
	Total	% age of Variance	Cumulative per cent	Total	% age of Variance	Cumulative per cent	Total	% age of Variance	Cumulative per cent
01	5.318	29.544	29.544	5.318	29.544	29.544	3.265	18.136	18.136
02	2.452	13.625	43.169	2.452	13.625	43.169	3.118	17.324	35.460
03	1.299	7.218	50.387	1.299	7.218	50.387	2.359	13.103	48.564
04	1.200	6.669	57.056	1.200	6.669	57.056	1.529	8.492	57.056

From the above table it becomes clear that four components can be extracted and they extract 57.056 per cent variation from data.

All the extracted communalities given in the above table were acceptable and all criteria were fit for the factor solution as their extraction values were large.

Table 7.69 indicated the correlation between component and criteria. Component 1 (Comfort in Examination and waiting Room, Natural Light or Illumination in Hospital, Sufficient Number of Dust Bins and Spittoons, No Flies and Mosquitoes in Hospital, Pleasing and Appealing Room of Hospital, Staff Neat in Appearance) was highly correlated with criteria 3, 4, 5, 6, 9, and 11.

Table 7.69: Communalities and Rotated Component Matrix for Environment (Physical facilities) for All the Three Type of Hospitals

Sl. No.	Selected Criteria	Communa-lities Extraction	Rotated Component			
			1	2	3	4
01	Well Equipped Units	0.466	0.233	0.621	–0.126	0.098
02	Proper Sitting and Bedding Arrangements	0.513	0.384	0.519	–0.199	0.237
03	Comfort in Examination and waiting Room	0.595	0.625	0.384	–0.112	0.213
04	Natural Light or Illumination in Hospital	0.514	0.691	0.171	–0.003	0.088
05	Sufficient Number of Dust Bins and Spittoons	0.533	0.714	0.154	0.003	0.007
06	No Flies and Mosquitoes in Hospital	0.558	0.676	–0.124	–0.096	–0.276
07	Adequate parking Arrangements	0.603	0.219	0.434	0.202	0.571
08	Clean Surroundings of Hospitals	0.588	0.483	0.405	–0.139	0.413
09	Pleasing and Appealing Room of Hospital	0.571	0.564	0.477	–0.067	0.146
10	Good Food Served by Hospital	0.665	0.010	–0.103	–0.248	0.770
11	Staff Neat in Appearance	0.493	0.633	0.249	0.052	0.165
12	Inside and Out side Noise kept Minimum	0.448	0.196	0.619	–0.156	0.042
13	Wards Well Decorated and Ventilated	0.430	0.399	0.512	–0.050	-0.074
14	Music Facilities should be provided	0.503	0.010	0.698	0.123	0.028
15	Quick Payment Arrangements	0.627	0.120	0.590	0.374	–0.352
16	Costs were Adequate or Affordable	0.808	–0.080	–0.137	0.880	0.093
17	Drugs Easily Obtained in Hospital	0.628	0.024	0.221	0.731	–0.211
18	Distance to Healthcare is Adequate	0.729	–0.096	–0.216	0.814	–0.100

Extraction Method: Principal Component Analysis. Rotation Method: Varimax with Kaiser Normalization.

a Rotation converged in 7 iterations.

Component 2 (Well Equipped Units, Proper Sitting and Bedding Arrangements, Inside and Out side Noise kept Minimum, Wards Well Decorated and Ventilated, Music Facilities should be provided, Quick Payment Arrangements) was highly correlated with criteria 1, 2, and 12 to 15. Component 3 (Costs were Adequate or Affordable, Drugs Easily Obtained in Hospital, Distance to Healthcare is Adequate) was highly correlated with criteria 16, 17, and 18, and component 4 (Adequate parking Arrangements, Good Food Served by Hospital) was highly correlated with criteria 7 and 10.

Table 7.70: Component Wise Mean Value for Environment (Physical facilities) for All the Three Type of Hospitals

Component	Mean Value	Selected Criteria	Selected Factors
01	29.12	Comfort in Examination and waiting Room	Tangibles
		Natural Light or Illumination in Hospital	Tangibles
		Sufficient Number of Dust Bins and Spittoons	Tangibles
		Pleasing and Appealing Room of Hospital	Tangibles
		Good Food Served by Hospital	Tangibles
		Staff Neat in Appearance	Tangibles
02	12.788	Well Equipped Units	Tangibles
		Proper Sitting and Bedding Arrangements	Tangibles
		Inside and Out side Noise kept Minimum	Tangibles
		Wards Well Decorated and Ventilated	Tangibles
		Music Facilities should be provided	Tangibles
		Quick Payment Arrangements	Accessibility/ Affordability
03	12.166	Costs were Adequate or Affordable	Accessibility/ Affordability
		Drugs Easily Obtained in Hospital	Accessibility/ Affordability
		Distance to Healthcare is Adequate	Accessibility/ Affordability
04	4.422	Adequate parking Arrangements	Tangibles
		Good Food Served by Hospital	Tangibles

From Table 7.70 it becomes clear that component 1 (Comfort in Examination and waiting Room, Natural Light or Illumination in Hospital, Sufficient Number of Dust Bins and Spittoons, No Flies and Mosquitoes in Hospital, Pleasing and Appealing Room of Hospital, Staff Neat in Appearance) has highest mean value of 29.12 and it extract total 6 criteria. Component 2 (Well Equipped Units, Proper Sitting and Bedding Arrangements, Inside and Out side Noise kept Minimum, Wards Well Decorated and Ventilated, Music Facilities should be provided, Quick Payment Arrangements) has second highest mean value of 12.78.

Component 3 (Costs were Adequate or Affordable, Drugs Easily Obtained in Hospital, Distance to Healthcare is Adequate) has 12.16 mean value and component 4 (Adequate parking Arrangements, Good Food Served by Hospital) has lowest mean value of 4.42.

Importance of Components for Selected Type of Hospitals

The importance of each component to different Type of Hospitals can be understood with the help of below given box plots. The following box plot explains Type of Hospitals total score of component 1 criteria.

Graph 7.19: Hospitals-wise Box Plot for Component 1 for Environment (Physical facilities) of the Three Type of Hospitals

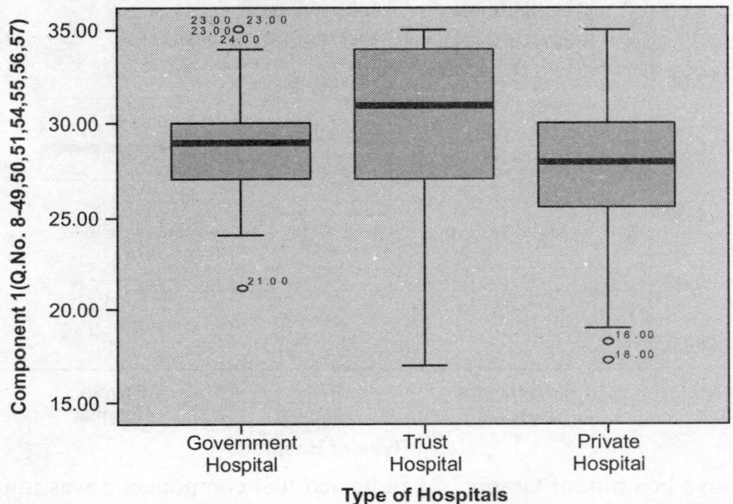

The above box plot of Graph 7.19 indicated that component 1 was important for Trust hospital because of it has highest median value. Though Government hospitals have second highest mean value with less variation but it has many outliers.

Graph 7.20: Hospitals-wise Box Plot for Component 2 for Environment (Physical facilities) of the Three Type of Hospitals

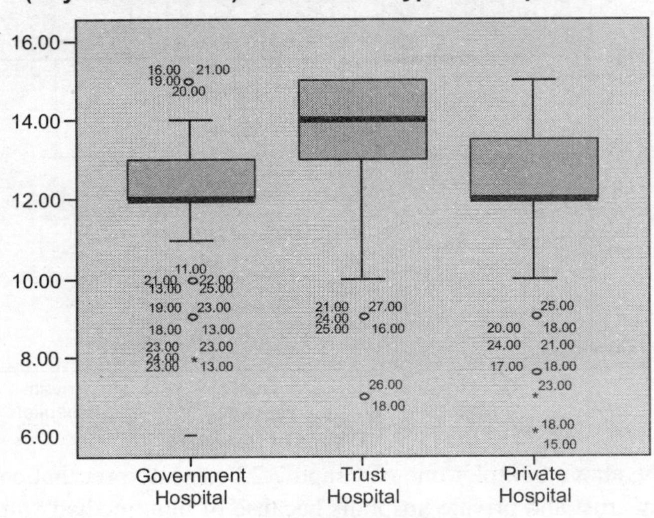

From the above box plot of Graph 7.20 it becomes clear that component 2 was important for trust hospitals because of large mean value and less outlier.

Graph 7.21: Hospitals-wise Box Plot for Component 3 for Environment (Physical facilities) of the Three Type of Hospitals

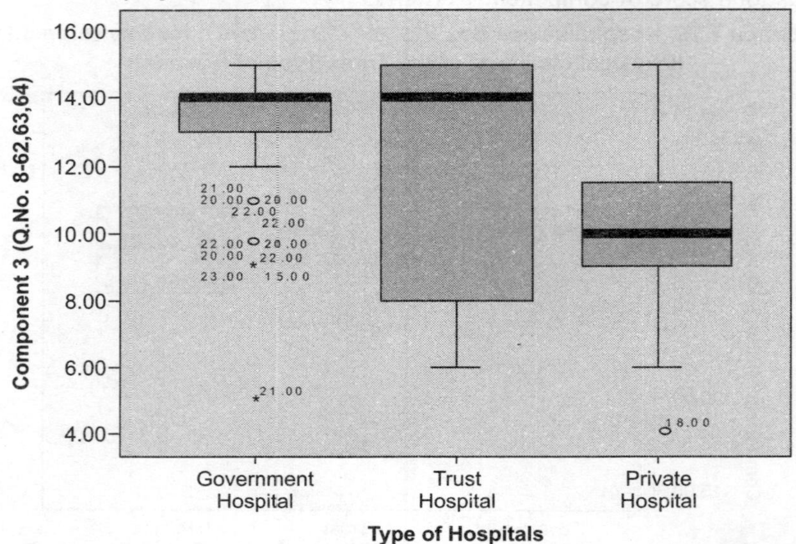

The above box plot of Graph 7.21 indicated that component 3 was important for Government hospitals because of large median value and very low variation.

Graph 7.22: Hospitals wise Box Plot for Component 4 for Environment (Physical facilities) of the Three Type of Hospitals

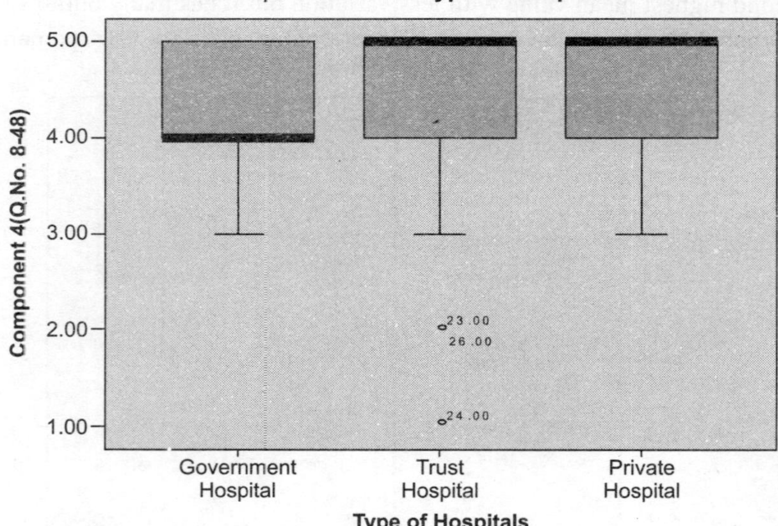

From the above box plot one of Graph 7.22 can interpret that component 4 was important for trust and private hospitals because of high median value. As the mean score of private hospitals were lower (71.20) factor analysis was made to find out the reasons for lower mean value for private hospitals.

Factor Analysis for Selected Type of Private Hospitals for Environment (Physical facilities) is given below.

In case responses of patients of private hospitals for environment (physical facilities) the results showed the value for KMO measure of sampling adequacy (0.8063) and Bartlett's test of sphericity (0.0) which indicated that factor analysis was appropriate.

Table 7.71: Total Variance of Selected Private Hospitals for Environment (Physical facilities)

Component	Initial Eigenvalues			Extraction Sums of Squared Loadings			Rotation Sums of Squared Loadings		
	Total	% age of Variance	Cumulative per cent	Total	% age of Variance	Cumulative per cent	Total	%age of Variance	Cumulative per cent
01	6.3171	35.095	35.095	6.31708	35.0949	35.0949	3.694617	20.52565	20.52565
02	1.6391	9.1063	44.201	1.63913	9.10629	44.20118	2.676086	14.86715	35.3928
03	1.478	8.2112	52.412	1.47802	8.21123	52.41241	2.628004	14.60002	49.99282
04	1.3233	7.3517	59.764	1.32331	7.35174	59.76415	1.516347	8.42415	58.41697
05	1.1602	6.4453	66.209	1.16015	6.44528	66.20942	1.402642	7.792457	66.20942

The above table indicated that there were 5 components extracted and it explains 66per cent variation from data.

Table 7.72: Communalities and Rotated Component Matrix for Selected Private Hospitals for Environment (Physical facilities)

Sl. No.	Selected Criteria	Communalities Extraction	Rotated Component				
			1	2	3	4	5
01	Well Equipped Units	0.6585	0.0662	0.6094	0.3952	-0.3317	0.12889
02	Proper Sitting and Bedding Arrangements	0.7114	0.3122	0.2024	0.6754	0.00142	0.34173
03	Comfort in Examination and waiting Room	0.6562	0.5010	0.1888	0.5245	-0.0726	0.2986
04	Natural Light or Illumination in Hospital	0.622	0.4251	0.1427	0.644	-0.0771	-0.0156
05	Sufficient Number of Dust Bins and Spittoons	0.7591	0.7975	0.2004	-0.0304	-0.2857	0.01895
06	No Flies and Mosquitoes in Hospital	0.5896	0.707	-0.112	0.1653	0.21056	-0.0741
07	Adequate parking Arrangements	0.7454	0.611	0.4821	-0.1462	0.00094	0.34402
08	Clean Surroundings of Hospitals	0.6265	0.6458	0.3119	0.3308	0.00278	-0.0515
09	Pleasing and Appealing Room of Hospital	0.552	0.5336	0.361	0.2856	0.07979	0.22168

...(Contd.)

...(Contd.)

Sl. No.	Selected Criteria	Communa-lities Extraction	Rotated Component				
			1	2	3	4	5
10	Good Food Served by Hospital	0.7432	0.0726	0.0453	-0.0501	0.01407	-0.8562
11	Staff Neat in Appearance	0.6544	0.6193	0.2365	0.3553	0.23418	-0.1839
12	Inside and Out side Noise kept Minimum	0.5397	0.6013	0.0385	0.4035	0.09167	0.07387
13	Wards Well Decorated and Ventilated	0.6259	0.3273	0.5703	0.1585	0.04872	0.40743
14	Music Facilities should be provided	0.6135	0.0459	0.7602	0.1687	0.03308	-0.0629
15	Quick Payment Arrangements	0.8078	0.2306	0.816	0.1499	0.23263	-0.1106
16	Costs were Adequate or Affordable	0.6195	-0.0790	0.0360	0.3517	0.68165	-0.1535
17	Drugs Easily Obtained in Hospital	0.6605	0.0708	0.2390	0.7511	0.1595	-0.0938
18	Distance to Healthcare is Adequate	0.7326	0.1612	0.0912	-0.1725	0.80725	0.12999

All the extracted communalities were acceptable and all criteria were fit for the factor solution as their extraction values are large.

From Table 7.72 it becomes clear that component 1 (Sufficient Number of Dust Bins and Spittoons, No Flies and Mosquitoes in Hospital, Adequate parking Arrangements, Clean Surroundings of Hospitals, Pleasing and Appealing Room of Hospital, Staff Neat in Appearance, Inside and Out side Noise kept Minimum) was highly correlated with criteria number 5 to 9, 11 and 12. Component 2 (Well Equipped Units, Wards Well Decorated and Ventilated, Music Facilities should be provided, Quick Payment Arrangements) was highly correlated with criteria number 1, 13, 14, and 15.

Component 3 (Proper Sitting and Bedding Arrangements, Natural Light or Illumination in Hospital, Drugs Easily Obtained in Hospital) was highly correlated with criteria number 2, 4, and 17. Component 4 (Costs were Adequate or Affordable, Distance to Healthcare is Adequate) was highly correlated with criteria number 16 and 18.

Table 7.73: Component wise Mean value for Selected Private Hospitals for Environment (Physical facilities)

Component	Mean Value	Selected Criteria	Selected Factors
01	30.032	Sufficient Number of Dust Bins and Spittoons	Tangibles
		No Flies and Mosquitoes in Hospital	Tangibles
		Adequate parking Arrangements	Tangibles
		Clean Surroundings of Hospitals	Tangibles
		Pleasing and Appealing Room of Hospital	Tangibles

...(Contd.)

...(Contd.)

Component	Mean Value	Selected Criteria	Selected Factors
		Staff Neat in Appearance	Tangibles
		Inside and Out side Noise kept Minimum	Tangibles
02	17.366	Well Equipped Units	Tangibles
		Wards Well Decorated and Ventilated	Tangibles
		Music Facilities should be provided	Tangibles
		Quick Payment Arrangements	Accessibility/ Affordability
03	13.212	Proper Sitting and Bedding Arrangements	Tangibles
		Wards Well Decorated and Ventilated	Tangibles
		Drugs Easily Obtained in Hospital	Accessibility/ Affordability
04	7.778	Costs were Adequate or Affordable	Accessibility/ Affordability
		Distance to Healthcare is Adequate	Accessibility/ Affordability

From Table 7.73 it becomes clear that component 1 (Sufficient Number of Dust Bins and Spittoons, No Flies and Mosquitoes in Hospital, Adequate parking Arrangements, Clean Surroundings of Hospitals, Pleasing and Appealing Room of Hospital, Staff Neat in Appearance, Inside and Out side Noise kept Minimum) have highest mean value of 30.03. Component 4 (Costs were Adequate or Affordable, Distance to Healthcare is Adequate) have lowest mean value of 7.78. It means private hospitals were weak in component 4. So, there was a need for private hospitals to improve its service and make it affordable by charging adequate price and making arrangement for patients for accessibility of hospital services.

SUMMARY OF FACTOR LOADING SCORE FOR MEDICAL, PARAMEDICAL, AND ADMINISTRATIVE STAFF SERVICES AND ENVIRONMENT OF SELECTED TYPE OF HOSPITALS

Summary of factor analysis for medical services, paramedical services, administrative services, and environment (physical facilities) of the hospital is summarized in the table number 6.74 to 6.77.

Table 7.74: Criteria and Factor-wise Factor Loading for Medical Services

Sl. No.	Selected Criteria	Tangible	Reliability	Responsiveness	Assurance	Empathy	Dignity	Accessibility/ Affordability
01	Doctors' Knowledge and Efficiency	–	–	–	0.5942	–	–	–
02	Doctors' Cooperation to patients	–	–	0.7498	–	–	–	–

...(Contd.)

...(Contd.)

Sl. No.	Selected Criteria	Tangible	Reliability	Responsiveness	Assurance	Empathy	Dignity	Accessibility/ Affordability
03	Doctors' were polite with patients	–	–	–	–	0.7726	–	–
04	Impartial Attitude of Doctors	–	0.6729	–	–	–	–	–
05	Patients' Felt Comfortable During Doctors Examination	–	–	–	–	0.6225	–	–
06	Doctors' Experience in Curing Patients	–	–	–	0.641	–	–	–
07	Thorough Checkup by Doctors	–	–	–	0.689	–	–	–
08	Doctors' Work according to Patients Expectations	–	–	–	–	0.812	–	–
09	Doctors' Gave Individual Consideration and Confidentiality	–	–	–	–	0.7531	–	–
10	Doctors' Showed Respect and Support patients	–	–	–	–	0.3963	–	–
11	Doctors' Makes Good Diagnosis	–	0.749	–	–	–	–	–
12	Doctors' Prescribed Good Drugs	–	0.664	–	–	–	–	–
13	Doctor' ask for patients Permission for performing Test	–	–	–	–	–	0.6638	–
14	Patients' Felt Comfortable asking Questions to Doctors	–	–	0.0854	–	–	–	–
15	Doctors' Honesty in Dealing with patients	–	–	–	–	0.4699	–	–
16	Sufficient number of Doctors Remained Present	0.7052	–	–	–	–	–	–
17	Doctors' Availability in Emergency	–	–	–	–	–	–	0.6227

Table 7.74 provides details about factor loading score for all 17 criteria related with medical services. Out of total 17 criteria 15 criteria can be considered as important as their score is more than 0.5.

Table 7.75: Criteria and Factor-wise Factor Loading for Paramedical Services

Sl. No.	Selected Criteria	Tangible	Reliability	Responsiveness	Assurance	Empathy	Dignity	Accessibility/ Affordability
		Factor Loading Score						
01	Nurses' Knowledge and Efficiency	–	–	–	0.6159	–	–	–
02	Nurses' Cooperation to Patients	–	–	0.7348	–	–	–	–
03	Nurses' Showed Politeness with Patients	–	–	–	–	0.7944	–	–

...(Contd.)

...(Contd.)

Sl. No.	Selected Criteria	Tangible	Reliability	Responsiveness	Assurance	Empathy	Dignity	Accessibility/ Affordability
		Factor Loading Score						
04	Impartial Attitude of Nurses	–	0.6063	–	–	–	–	–
05	Nurses' Maintain Proper records of Patients	–	0.5163	–	–	–	–	–
06	Nurses' Handled Patients Query Properly	–	–	–	0.678	–	–	–
07	Nurses' Experience in Curing Patients	–	–	–	0.5809	–	–	–
08	Good Experience of Those who Perform Test on Patients	–	–	–	0.4232	–	–	–
09	Nurses' Gave Personal Attention to Patients	–	–	–	–	–	0.665	–
10	Nurses' Provided Prompt Service	–	–	0.680	–	–	–	–
11	Nurses' and Staff Remained Present in Emergency	–	–	0.566	–	–	–	–
12	Nurses' Explain Procedures and take Patient Permission before Test	–	–	–	–	–	0.688	–
13	Nurses' Explain Rules Regulation in ward	–	–	–	–	–	0.4814	–
14	Nurses' were Kind, Gentle and Sympathetic	–	–	–	–	–	0.6582	–
15	Information Provided to patients for Managing Side Effects	–	–	0.729	–	–	–	–
16	Prompt Service Provided by Sanitation Staff	–	–	0.619	–	–	–	–

Table 7.75 provides details about factor loading score for all 16 criteria related with Paramedical services. Out of total 16 criteria 13 criteria can be considered as important as their score is more than 0.5.

Table 7.76: Criteria and Factor-wise Factor Loading for Administrative Services

Sl. No.	Selected Criteria	Tangible	Reliability	Responsiveness	Assurance	Empathy	Dignity	Accessibility/ Affordability
		Factor Loading Score						
01	Less Waiting Time For Consultation and Treatment	–	–	0.564	–	–	–	–
02	Less Waiting Time for Test	–	–	0.5809	–	–	–	–
03	Simple Checking Procedure	–	–	–	–	0.7639	–	–
04	Speed, Ease of Admission and Discharge form Hospital	–	–	0.7347	–	–	–	–
05	Convenient Office Hours	–	–	0.6848	–	–	–	–
06	Adm. Staff Gives Prompt Services	–	–	0.692	–	–	–	–

...(Contd.)

...(Contd.)

Sl. No.	Selected Criteria	Tangible	Reliability	Responsiveness	Assurance	Empathy	Dignity	Accessibility/ Affordability
		Factor Loading Score						
07	No Overcrowding in Hospital	–	–	0.489	–	–	–	–
08	Good Grievance handling System	–	–	0.847	–	–	–	–
09	Adm. Staff Welcome and Implement Suggestion	–	–	–	–	–	0.859	–
10	Adm. Gives Personal Attention To Patient	–	–	–	–	–	0.818	–
11	Patients' were Treated With Dignity and Privacy	–	–	–	–	–	0.5729	–
12	Good Concern for Patient Family and Visitor	–	–	–	–	0.662	–	–
13	Simple Billing Procedures	–	–	–	–	0.7261	–	–

Table 2.76 provides details about factor loading score for all 13 criteria related with Administrative services. Out of total 13 criteria 12 criteria can be considered as important as their score is more than 0.5.

Table 7.77: Criteria and Factor-wise Factor Loading for Environment (Physical Facilities)

Sl. No.	Selected Criteria	Tangible	Reliability	Responsiveness	Assurance	Empathy	Dignity	Accessibility/ Affordability
		Factor Loading Score						
01	Well Equipped Units	0.621						
02	Proper Sitting and Bedding Arrangements	0.519	–	–	–	–	–	–
03	Comfort in Examination and waiting Room	0.625	–	–	–	–	–	–
04	Natural Light or Illumination in Hospital	0.691	–	–	–	–	–	–
05	Sufficient Number of Dust Bins and Spittoons	0.714	–	–	–	–	–	–
06	No Flies and Mosquitoes in Hospital	0.676	–	–	–	–	–	–
07	Adequate parking Arrangements	0.571	–	–	–	–	–	–
08	Clean Surroundings of Hospitals	0.483	–	–	–	–	–	–
09	Pleasing and Appealing Room of Hospital	0.564	–	–	–	–	–	–
10	Good Food Served by Hospital	0.770	–	–	–	–	–	–
11	Staff Neat in Appearance	0.633	–	–	–	–	–	–
12	Inside and Out side Noise kept Minimum	0.619	–	–	–	–	–	–
13	Wards Well Decorated and Ventilated	0.512	–	–	–	–	–	–

...(Contd.)

...(Contd.)

Sl. No.	Selected Criteria	Tan-gible	Relia-bility	Resp-onsive ness	Assu-rance	Emp-athy	Dig-nity	Access-ibility/ Afford ability
		Factor Loading Score						
14	Music Facilities should be provided	0.698	–	–	–	–	–	–
15	Quick Payment Arrangements		–	–	–	–	–	0.590
16	Costs were Adequate or Affordable		–	–	–	–	–	0.880
17	Drugs Easily Obtained in Hospital		–	–	–	–	–	0.731
18	Distance to Healthcare is Adequate		–	–	–	–	–	0.814

Table 7.77 provides details about factor loading score for all 18 criteria related with Environment (physical Facilities) Performance. Out of total 18 criteria 17 criteria can be considered as important as their score is more than 0.5. So, total 57 criteria have factor loading score more than 0.5 out of total 64 criteria used to measure patient satisfaction.

ONE WAY ANNOVA AND FACTOR ANALYSIS FOR ANALYZING INTANGIBLE SERVICE CHARACTERISTICS

ONE WAY ANNOVA FOR TANGIBLE SERVICE CHARACTERISTICS

Analysis of Variance: Selected Patients' Responses for Tangibles

Hypothesis: 23

Mean of patients' responses about selected type of hospitals is equal in terms of tangible facilities of hospitals and an alternative hypothesis is at least one mean is different from other.

Table 7.78: Descriptive Statistics for Tangibles for All the Three Type of Hospitals

Type of Hospitals	N	Mean	SD	SE
GHs	200	62.3700	3.16912	0.22409
THs	200	65.4150	7.57228	0.53544
PHs	100	61.3300	7.11245	0.71125
Total	500	63.3800	6.31025	0.28220

The above table indicated the descriptive statistics of Type of Hospitals. The Trust hospital has highest mean value 65.41. Second highest mean value is 62.37of Government hospitals, and private hospitals have lower mean value of 61.33.

Table 7.79: Test of Homogeneity of Variances for Tangible Facilities for All the Three Type of Hospitals

Levene's Statistic	df1	df2	Sig.
43.611	2	497	0.000

Levene's test of homogeneity of variance through which verification can be done about the equality of variance of all group of hospital. Results of Levene's test showed the significant value (0.00) which was less then 0.05. It means that our null hypothesis has been rejected as significant value does not exceed 0.05. It means variance of all groups is not equal.

Table 7.80: ANOVA for Tangible Facilities for All the Three Type of Hospitals

Particulars	Sum of Squares	Df	Mean Square	F	Sig.
Between Groups	1452.515	2	726.258	19.598	0.000
Within Groups	18417.285	497	37.057		
Total	19869.800	499			

The variation between the groups of all the type of hospitals was 1452 and within groups is 18417. The variation within groups was higher then variation between groups of type of hospitals. According to null hypotheses variance of all groups is equal and our alternative hypotheses states that at least one variance is differ from other. As null hypotheses is rejected because of our significance value (0.00) is < 0.05 that means at least one type of Hospitals is different from the other type of hospitals.

Post-Hoc test (Tamhane)

Table 7.81: Multiple Comparisons for Tangible facilities for All the Three Type of Hospitals through Tamhane Test

Type of Hospitals		Mean Difference	SE	Sig.
GHs	GHs			
	THs	–3.04500	0.58044	0.000
	PHs	1.04000	0.74571	0.419
THs	GHs	3.04500	0.58044	0.000
	THs			
	PHs	4.08500	0.89026	0.000
PHs	GHs	–1.04000	0.74571	0.419
	THs	–4.08500	0.89026	0.000
	PHs			

Based on the test of homogeneity of variance it becomes clear that variance of all three type of hospitals was not equal it means at least one variance was different from other. The ANOVA test also indicated that mean of three types of hospitals were not equal. Therefore, Post-Hog test was applied assuming unequal variance. The findings suggest that Government hospitals were different from trust hospitals; trust hospitals were different from Government and private hospitals. The private hospitals were also different from trust hospitals because of significant value of all type of hospitals was < 0.05.

The insignificant value 0.419 indicated that Government hospitals and private hospitals make one group and trust hospitals were making another group.

Post-Hoc test (Tukey HSD)

Table 7.82: Multiple Comparisons for Tangible facilities for All the Three Type of Hospitals Through Tukey HSD Test

Type of Hospitals	Subset for alpha = .05		
	N	1	2
PHs	100	61.3300	
GHs	200	62.3700	
THs	200		65.4150
Sig.		0.302	1.000

(Means for groups in homogeneous subsets are displayed.
a Uses Harmonic Mean Sample Size = 150.000.
b The group sizes are unequal. The harmonic mean of the group sizes is used. Type I error levels are not guaranteed).

From Table 7.82 it becomes evident that private hospitals and Government hospitals makes one group and trust hospitals make another group. The same thing is graphically plotted in the following Means Plot graph (Graph 7.23) which displays how the three types of hospitals differ.

Graph 7.23: Means Plots for Tangible facilities for All the Three Type of Hospitals

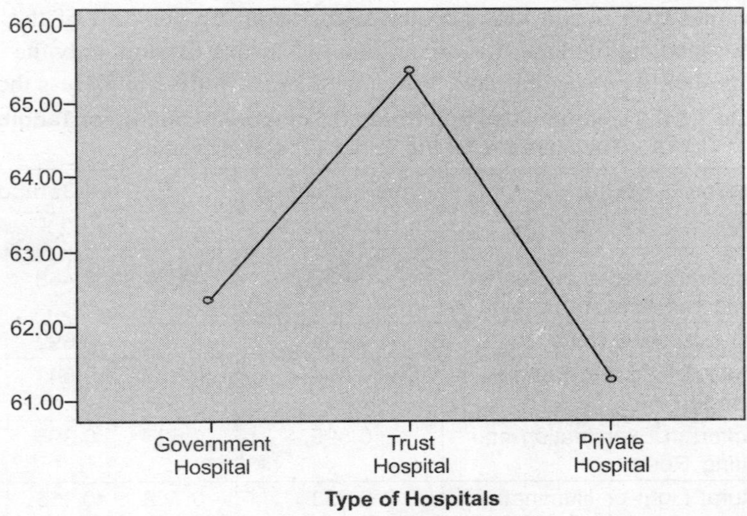

Graph 7.23 indicated different type of hospitals with their mean value. The trust hospitals have large mean value of 65.41, second largest value of 62.37 belongs to Government hospitals and private hospitals have lowest mean value of 61.33. Based on Means plot it becomes clear that at least one mean is different from three type of hospitals.

FACTOR ANALYSIS FOR TANGIBLE FACILITIES

Factor Analysis for Tangible Facilities for All Three Types of Hospitals is given as below:

In case of responses of patients for tangible facilities the results showed the value for KMO measure of sampling adequacy was 0.89, which indicated that the present data were suitable for factor analysis. Similarly, Bartlett's test of sphericity was significant ($p<.005$), indicated sufficient correlation exist between the criteria to proceed with the analysis.

Table 7.83: Total Variance for Tangible Criteria for All the Three Type of Hospitals

Component	Initial Eigenvalues			Extraction Sums of Squared Loadings			Rotation Sums of Squared Loadings		
	Total	% age of Variance	Cumulative per cent	Total	% age of Variance	Cumulative per cent	Total	% age of Variance	Cumulative per cent
01	5.137	34.249	34.249	5.137	34.249	34.249	3.269	21.792	21.792
02	1.298	8.651	42.899	1.298	8.651	42.899	2.897	19.311	41.103
03	1.152	7.682	50.581	1.152	7.682	50.581	1.422	9.479	50.581

Extraction Method: Principal Component Analysis.

As given in the above table the first three components in the initial solution have an Eigenvalues over 1 and they accounted for about 57 per cent of the observed variation for the tangible facilities. According to Kaiser Criterion, only the first three components should be used because subsequent Eigenvalues are all less then 1.

Table 7.84: Communalities and Rotated Component Matrix for Tangible Facilities for All the Three Type of Hospitals

Sl. No.	Selected Criteria	Communalities Extraction	Rotated Component		
			1	2	3
01	Sufficient number of Doctors Remained Present	0.252	0.062	0.468	–0.172
02	Well Equipped Units	0.434	0.258	0.592	0.131
03	Proper Sitting and Bedding Arrangements	0.506	0.392	0.541	0.244
04	Comfort in Examination and waiting Room	0.595	0.627	0.395	0.214
05	Natural Light or Illumination in Hospital	0.538	0.709	0.116	0.147
06	Sufficient Number of Dust Bins and Spittoons	0.531	0.715	0.141	–0.002
07	No Flies and Mosquitoes in Hospital	0.541	0.657	–0.062	–0.324
08	Adequate parking Arrangements	0.481	0.166	0.513	0.436

Contd.

...(Contd.)

Sl. No.	Selected Criteria	Communalities Extraction	Rotated Component		
			1	2	3
09	Clean Surroundings of Hospitals	0.587	0.478	0.433	0.414
10	Pleasing and Appealing Room of Hospital	0.574	0.568	0.482	0.139
11	Good Food Served by Hospital	0.746	0.027	–0.124	0.854
12	Staff Neat in Appearance	0.476	0.623	0.246	0.164
13	Inside and Out side Noise kept Minimum	0.431	0.215	0.617	0.062
14	Wards Well Decorated and Ventilated	0.387	0.437	0.442	–0.018
15	Music Facilities should be provided	0.509	0.001	0.712	–0.038

Extraction Method: Principal Component Analysis. Rotation Method: Varimax with Kaiser Normalization.
a Rotation converged in 5 iterations.

All the extracted communalities shown in the above table were acceptable and all criteria were fit for the factor solution as their extraction values were large.

Factor loadings were used to measure correlation between various criteria and the factors. A factor loading close to 1 indicated a strong correlation between criteria and the factors, while a factor loading closer to zero indicates weak correlation. The factors were rotated with the use of Varimax with Kaiser Normalization rotation method. Principle Component Analysis (PCA) method was used for factor extraction and considered only those factors for interpretation purpose whose values are greater then 0.5.

From Table 7.84 it becomes clear that how the criteria were correlated with four components. The criteria 4 (Comfort in Examination and waiting Room), criteria 5 (Natural Light or Illumination in Hospital), criteria 6 (Sufficient Number of Dust Bins and Spittoons), criteria 7 (No Flies and Mosquitoes in Hospital), criteria 10 (Pleasing and Appealing Room of Hospital), and criteria 12 (Staff Neat in Appearance) were more correlated with component 1. The criteria 2 (Well Equipped Units), criteria 3 (Proper Sitting and Bedding Arrangements), criteria 8 (Adequate parking Arrangements), criteria 13 (Inside and Out side Noise kept Minimum), and criteria 15 (Music Facilities should be provided), were more correlated with component 2. The criteria 11 (Good Food Served by Hospital) was correlated with component 3.

Table 7.85 indicated component wise mean value. The component 1 has higher mean value of 25.86 and it more correlated with six criteria (Comfort in Examination and waiting Room, Natural Light or Illumination in Hospital, Sufficient Number of Dust Bins and Spittoons, No Flies and Mosquitoes in Hospital, Pleasing and Appealing Room of Hospital, and Staff Neat in Appearance). Component 2 have second highest mean value of 21.60 and it more related with five criteria (Well Equipped Units, Proper Sitting and Bedding Arrangements, Adequate parking Arrangements, Inside and Out

Table 7.85: Component wise Mean Value for Tangible Factor for All Type of Hospitals

Sl. No.	Compo-nent	Mean Value	Selected Criteria	Selected Factors
01	01	25.8680	Comfort in Examination and waiting Room	Environment (Physical Facilities)
02			Natural Light or Illumination in Hospital	"
03			Sufficient Number of Dust Bins and Spittoons	"
04			No Flies and Mosquitoes in Hospital	"
05			Pleasing and Appealing Room of Hospital	"
06			Staff Neat in Appearance	"
07	02	21.6020	Well Equipped Units	"
08			Proper Sitting and Bedding Arrangements	"
09			Adequate parking Arrangements	"
10			Inside and Out side Noise kept Minimum	"
11			Music Facilities should be provided	"
12	03	3.05	Good Food Served by Hospital	"

side Noise kept Minimum, Music Facilities should be provided). Component 3 has lowest mean value and it correlated with one criterion (Good Food Served by Hospital). So out of total 15 tangible criteria 12 criteria found more important for determining patients' satisfaction in the hospitals and all these criteria were groped as Environment (Physical Factors).

Box plot of Graph 7.24 explains type of hospitals and total score of component 1 (Environment).

From the box plot of Graph 7.24 it becomes clear that group of criteria of component 1 (Environment) were important for trust hospitals because of large median value and lower variation compared to Government and private hospitals.

So patients prefer trust hospitals considering certain viz., Comfort in Examination and waiting Room; Natural Light or Illumination in Hospital; Sufficient Number of Dust Bins and Spittoons; No Flies and Mosquitoes in Hospital; Pleasing and Appealing Room of Hospital and Staff Neat in Appearance. The private hospitals have second highest median value for the same criteria but Government hospitals have lowest median value for these criteria.

Following Box plot of Graph 7.25 explain three type of hospitals and total score of component 2 (Environment) as a criteria.

Graph 7.24: Hospitals-wise Box Plot for Component 1 for Tangible Facilities of the Three Type of Hospitals

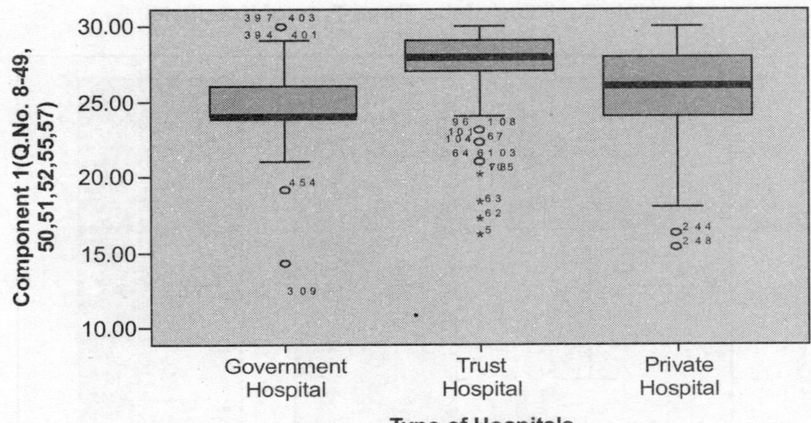

Graph 7.25: Hospitals-wise Box Plot for Component 2 for Tangible Facilities of the Three Type of Hospitals

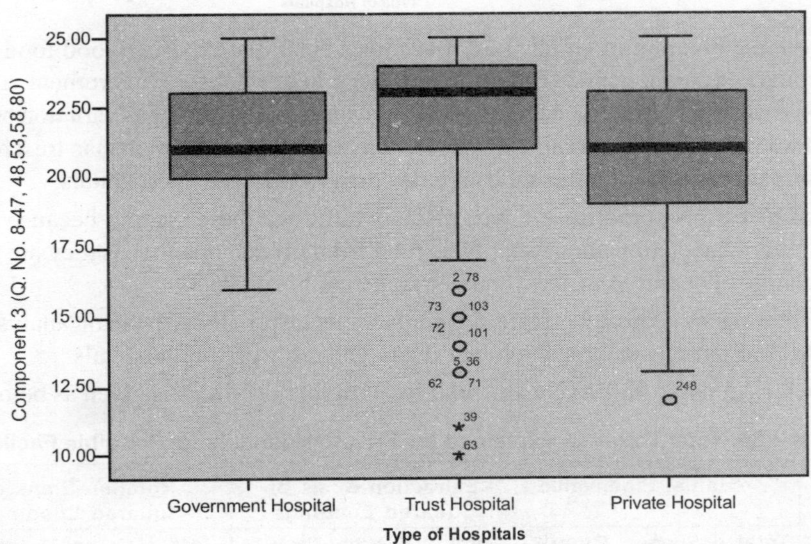

From the above box plot of Graph 7.25 it becomes clear that group of criteria of component 2 (Environment) were important for trust hospitals because of large median value and lower variation compared to Government and private hospitals. So patients preferred trust hospital considering certain criteria viz., Well Equipped Units; Proper Sitting and Bedding Arrangements; Adequate parking Arrangements; Inside and Out side Noise kept Minimum; and Music Facilities should be provided. The median value of private hospitals and Government hospitals were almost similar for these criteria.

Graph 6.26 explains type of hospitals and total score of component 2 (Environment).

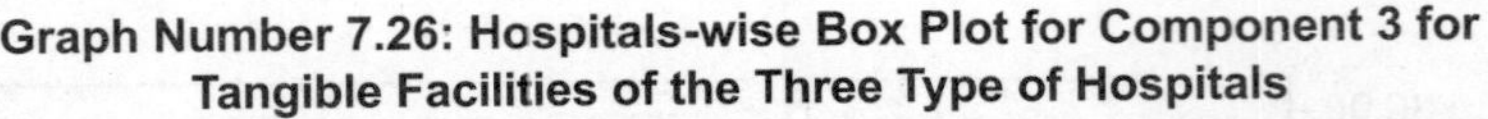

Graph Number 7.26: Hospitals-wise Box Plot for Component 3 for Tangible Facilities of the Three Type of Hospitals

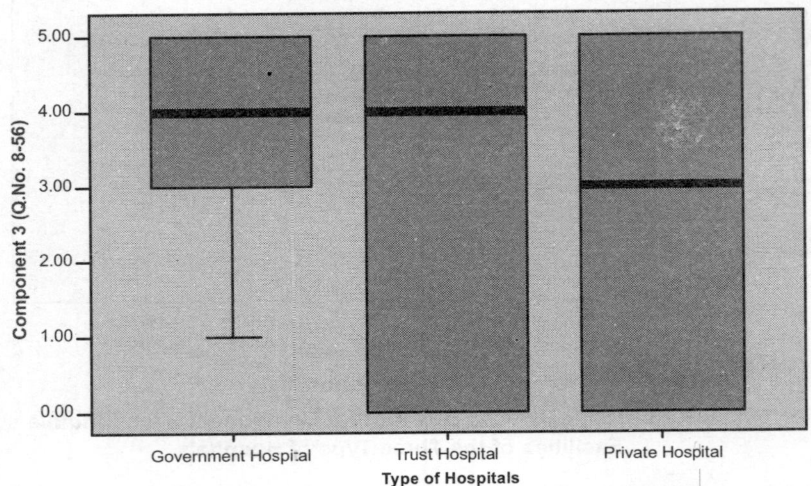

From the box plot of Graph 7.26 it becomes clear that criteria (Good food served by hospital) of component 2 (Environment) were important for Government and trust hospitals because of large median value then private hospital. So far as variation between criteria was concerned Government hospitals have minimum variation than trust hospital because patients were getting food free of cost in Government hospitals.

The private hospital have lower median value for these criteria because people have higher expectation about quality of food from private hospital as they are paying more charges compared to Government and trust hospitals.

As the mean score of private hospitals were lower (61.33) factor analysis was made to find out reasons for the lower mean value for private hospitals.

Factor Analysis for Private Hospital for Tangible Facilities is given as below:

Table 7.86: Total Variance Explained for Private Hospitals for Tangible Facilities

	Initial Eigenvalues			Extraction Sums of Squared Loadings			Rotation Sums of Squared Loadings		
Component	Total	% age of Variance	Cumulative per cent	Total	% age of Variance	Cumulative per cent	Total	% age of Variance	Cumulative per cent
01	5.823	38.822	38.822	5.823	38.822	38.822	4.170	27.803	27.803
02	1.427	9.514	48.336	1.427	9.514	48.336	2.269	15.128	42.931
03	1.281	8.537	56.874	1.281	8.537	56.874	2.091	13.942	56.874

In case of responses of private hospitals patients for tangible facilities the results showed the value for KMO measure of sampling adequacy (0.838) and Bartlett's test of sphericity (0.00-significant) which indicated that factor analysis was appropriate.

From Table 7.86 it becomes clear that total 3 component can be extracted whose Eigen value is more than 1 and it explains 56.87 per cent variation from data.

Table 7.87: Communalities and Rotated Component Matrix for Selected Private Hospitals for Tangible Facilities

Sl. No.	Selected Criteria	Communalities Extraction	Rotated Component		
			1	2	3
01	Sufficient number of Doctors Remained Present	0.653	0.213	0.752	-0.204
02	Well Equipped Units	0.631	0.090	0.663	0.428
03	Proper Sitting and Bedding Arrangements	0.550	0.479	0.265	0.500
04	Comfort in Examination and waiting Room	0.602	0.559	0.315	0.435
05	Natural Light or Illumination in Hospital	0.470	0.568	0.330	0.195
06	Sufficient Number of Dust Bins and Spittoons	0.496	0.664	0.068	0.225
07	No Flies and Mosquitoes in Hospital	0.567	0.746	-0.066	-0.080
08	Adequate parking Arrangements	0.486	0.448	0.239	0.478
09	Clean Surroundings of Hospitals	0.636	0.690	0.383	0.114
10	Pleasing and Appealing Room of Hospital	0.551	0.585	0.267	0.372
11	Good Food Served by Hospital	0.549	0.136	0.180	-0.706
12	Staff Neat in Appearance	0.648	0.756	0.269	-0.062
13	Inside and Out side Noise kept Minimum	0.554	0.729	0.024	0.152
14	Wards Well Decorated and Ventilated	0.588	0.329	0.271	0.637
15	Music Facilities should be provided	0.550	0.085	0.722	0.145

Extraction Method: Principal Component Analysis. Rotation Method: Varimax with Kaiser Normalization.

(a) Rotation converged in 6 iterations.

(b) Only cases for which Q 2 Type of Hospitals = Private Hospital are used in the analysis phase.

Extraction Method: Principal Component Analysis.

(a) Only cases for which Q 2 Type of Hospitals = Private Hospital are used in the analysis phase.

From Table 7.87 it becomes clear that all the extracted communalities were acceptable and all criteria were fit for the factor solution as their extraction values were large.

The above table indicates that component 1wais highly correlated with criterion 4 (Comfort in Examination and waiting Room), criterion 5 (Natural Light or Illumination in Hospital), criterion 6 (Sufficient Number of Dust Bins and Spittoons), criterion 7 (No Flies and Mosquitoes in Hospital) criterion 9 (Clean Surroundings of Hospitals), criterion 10 (Pleasing and Appealing Room of Hospital), criterion 12 (Staff Neat in Appearance), and criterion 13 (Inside and Out side Noise kept Minimum). Component 2 was highly correlated with criterion 1 (Sufficient number of Doctors Remained Present), criterion 2 (Well Equipped Units), and criterion 15 (Music Facilities should be provided). Component 3 was highly correlated with only criterion 3 (Proper Sitting and Bedding Arrangements), and criterion 14 (Wards Well Decorated and Ventilated).

Table 7.88: Component wise Mean value for Selected Private Hospitals for Tangible Facilities

Sl. No.	Compo-nent	Mean Value	Selected Criteria	Selected Factors
01	01	34.3240	Comfort in Examination and waiting Room	Environment (physical facilities)
02			Natural Light or Illumination in Hospital	"
03			Sufficient Number of Dust Bins and Spittoons	"
04			No Flies and Mosquitoes in Hospital	"
05			Clean Surroundings of Hospitals	"
06			Pleasing and Appealing Room of Hospital	"
07			Staff Neat in Appearance	"
08			Inside and Out side Noise kept Minimum	"
09	02	12.8440	Sufficient Doctors Remain Present	Medical Services
10			Well Equipped Units	Environment (physical facilities)
11			Music Facilities should be provided	"
12	03	8.6980	Proper Sitting and Bedding Arrangements	"
			Wards Well Decorated and Ventilated	"

From Table 7.88 it becomes clear that component 1(Environment) have high mean value of 34.32. Components 2 have second highest mean value of 12.84. It means that component 1 (Comfort in Examination and waiting Room; Natural Light or Illumination in Hospital; Sufficient Number of Dust Bins and Spittoons; No Flies and Mosquitoes in Hospital; Clean Surroundings of Hospitals; Pleasing and Appealing Room of Hospital; Staff Neat in Appearance; Inside and Out side Noise kept Minimum) was important tangible criteria for evaluating private hospital services but, component 3 (Proper Sitting and Bedding Arrangements, Wards Well Decorated and Ventilated) have lower mean value and these factors were responsible for lower mean value of private hospital.

ONE WAY ANNOVA FOR RELIABILITY CRITERION

Analysis of Variance: Selected Patients' Responses for Reliability Criterion.

Hypothesis: 24

Mean of patients' responses about selected type of hospital is equal in terms of Reliability criterion of hospital and an alternative hypothesis is at least one mean is different from other.

Table 7.89: Descriptive Statistics for Reliability Criterion for All the Three Type of Hospitals

Type of Hospitals	N	Mean	SD	SE
GHs	200	21.3500	1.88288	0.13314
THs	200	22.7250	2.42047	0.17115
PHs	100	22.3700	2.80568	0.28057
Total	500	22.1040	2.38927	0.10685

From Table 7.89 it becomes clear that trust hospitals have highest mean value of 22.72. Private hospitals has second highest mean value of 22.37 and Government hospitals has lowest mean value of 21.35.

Test of Homogeneity of Variances

Table 7.90: Test of Homogeneity of Variances for Reliability Criterion for All the Three Type of Hospitals

Levene Statistic	df1	df2	Sig.
7.456	2	497	0.001

P-Value of levene's test statistics as given in Table 7.90 found to be less then 0.05 (0.00 < 0.05) which represent that variance of type of hospitals was not equal at least variance of one type of hospitals was different from other type of hospitals.

Analysis of Variance

Table 7.91: ANOVA for Reliability Criterion for All the Three Type of Hospitals

Particulars	Sum of Squares	df	Mean Square	F	Sig.
Between Groups	197.907	2	98.953	18.554	0.000
Within Groups	2650.685	497	5.333		
Total	2848.592	499			

The P-Value (0.00 < 0.05) of ANOVA as given Table 7.91 indicated that mean of type of hospitals was not equal at least mean of one type of hospitals was different from other type of hospitals.

Post-Hoc test (Tamhane)

Table 7.92: Multiple Comparisons for Reliability Criterion for All the Three Type of Hospitals Through Tamhane Test

Type of Hospitals		Mean Difference	SE	Sig.
GHs	GHs			
	THs	-1.37500	.21684	0.000
	PHs	-1.02000	.31055	0.004
THs	GHs	1.37500	.21684	0.000
	THs			
	PHs	0.35500	.32865	0.629
PHs	GHs	1.02000	.31055	0.004
	THs	-.35500	.32865	0.629
	PHs			

Based on the test of homogeneity of variance it becomes clear that variance of all three type of hospitals was not equal that means at least one variance is different from other. The ANOVA test also indicated that mean of three types of hospitals was not equal and at least one mean was different from other. Therefore, Post-Hog test was applied assuming unequal variance, and findings suggested that Government hospitals were different from trust hospitals and private hospitals.

Trust hospitals were different from Government hospitals but, value 0.629 indicated that trust hospitals were not different than private hospitals. The private hospitals were different from Government hospitals because of significant value. The insignificant value of 0.629 indicated that private and trust hospitals makes one group and Government hospitals were making another group.

Post-Hoc test (Tukey HSD)

Table 7.93: Multiple Comparisons for Tangible Facilities for All the Three Type of Hospitals Through Tukey HSD Test

Type of Hospitals	N	Subset for alpha = .05	
		1	2
GHs	200	21.3500	
PHs	100		22.3700
THs	200		22.7250
Sig.	1.000	0.378	

Means for groups in homogeneous subsets are displayed.

(a) Uses Harmonic Mean Sample Size = 150.000.

(b) The group sizes are unequal. The harmonic mean of the group sizes is used. Type I error levels are not guaranteed.

From Table 7.93 it becomes clear that private hospitals and trust hospitals makes one group and Government hospitals make another group. The same thing is graphically plotted in the Plot Graph 7.27.

Graph 7.27: Means Plots of the Three Type of Hospitals for Reliability Criterion

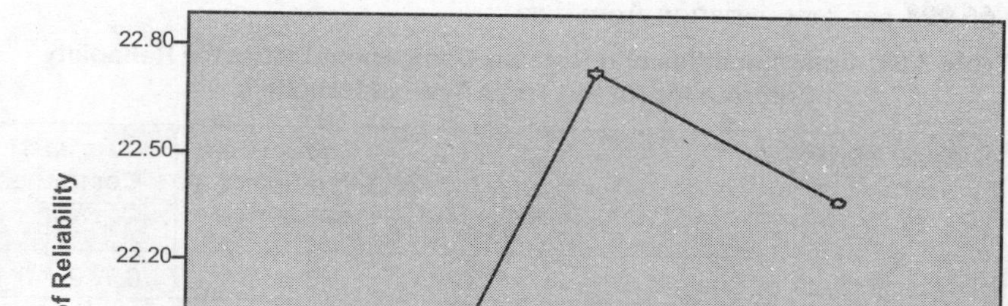

Graph 7.27 indicated different type of hospitals with their mean value. The trust hospital have large mean value of 22.72, second largest value of 22.37 belongs to private hospitals and Government hospitals have lowest mean value of 21.35. Based on Means plot it becomes clear that at least one mean (Government Hospitals) was different from three type of hospitals.

FACTOR ANALYSIS FOR RELIABILITY CRITERION

Factor Analysis for Reliability Criterion for All the Three Type of hospital is given as below:

In case of responses of patients for reliability of the hospital services the results showed the value of KMO measure of sampling adequacy (0.678) and Bartlett's test of sphericity (0.0) which indicated that factor analysis was appropriate.

Table 7.94: Total Variance for Reliability Criterion for All the Three Type of Hospitals

	Initial Eigenvalues			Extraction Sums of Squared Loadings			Rotation Sums of Squared Loadings		
Component	Total	% age of Variance	Cumulative per cent	Total	% age of Variance	Cumulative per cent	Total	% age of Variance	Cumulative per cent
01	2.349	46.981	46.981	2.349	46.981	46.981	1.728	34.553	34.553
02	1.001	20.017	66.998	1.001	20.017	66.998	1.622	32.445	66.998

Extraction Method: Principal Component Analysis.

From Table 7.94 it becomes clear that two components can be extracted and they extract 66.998 per cent variation from data.

Table 7.95: Communalities and Rotated Component Matrix for Reliability Criterion for All the Three Type of Hospitals

Sr.	Selected Criteria	Communa-lities Extraction	Rotated Component	
			1	2
01	Impartial Attitude of Doctors	0.538	0.710	0.183
02	Doctors' Made Good Diagnosis	0.807	0.131	0.889
03	Doctors' Prescribed Good Drugs	0.788	0.246	0.853
04	Impartial Attitude of Nurses	0.746	0.862	0.059
05	Nurses' Maintain Proper records of Patients	0.471	0.635	0.260

Extraction Method: Principal Component Analysis. Rotation Method: Varimax with Kaiser Normalization.
a Rotation converged in 3 iterations.

All the extracted communalities given in Table 7.95 were acceptable and all criteria were fit for the factor solution as their extraction values were large.

Table 7.95 indicated the correlation between Criteria and factors. Component 1 (Impartial Attitude of Doctors, Impartial Attitude of Nurses, Nurses' Maintain Proper records of Patients) was highly correlated with criteria number 1, 4, and. Component 2 (Doctors' Made Good Diagnosis, Doctors' Prescribed Good Drugs) was highly correlated with criteria 1, 2, and 12 to 15.

Table 7.96: Component wise Mean Value for Reliability Criterion for All the Three Type of Hospitals

Sl. No.	Compo-nent	Mean Value	Selected Criteria	Selected Factors
01	01	13.0460	Impartial Attitude of Doctors	Medical Services
02			Impartial Attitude of Nurses	Paramedical Services
03			Nurses' Maintain Proper records of Patients	Paramedical Services
04	02	9.0580	Doctors' Made Good Diagnosis	Medical Services
05			Doctors' Prescribed Good Drugs	Medical Services

From Table 7.96 it becomes clear that component 1 (Impartial Attitude of Doctors, Impartial Attitude of Nurses, Nurses' Maintain Proper records of Patients) has highest mean value of 13.046 and it extract total 6 criteria. Component 2 (Doctors Makes Good Diagnosis, Doctors' Prescribed Good Drugs) has second highest mean value of 9.058, and has extracted two criteria.

The box plot of Graph 7.28 indicated that component 1 was important for trust hospitals because of it have highest median value and lower variation compared to Government and private hospitals. The difference between mean value of trust and private hospitals was not much.

Graph 7.28: Hospitals-wise Box Plot for Component 1 for Reliability Criterion of the Three Type of Hospitals

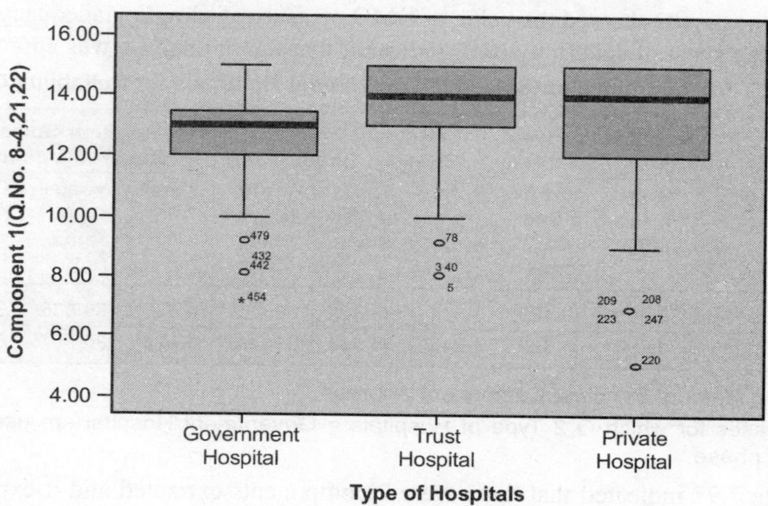

Graph 7.29: Hospitals-wise Box Plot for Component 2 for Reliability Criterion of the Three Type of Hospitals

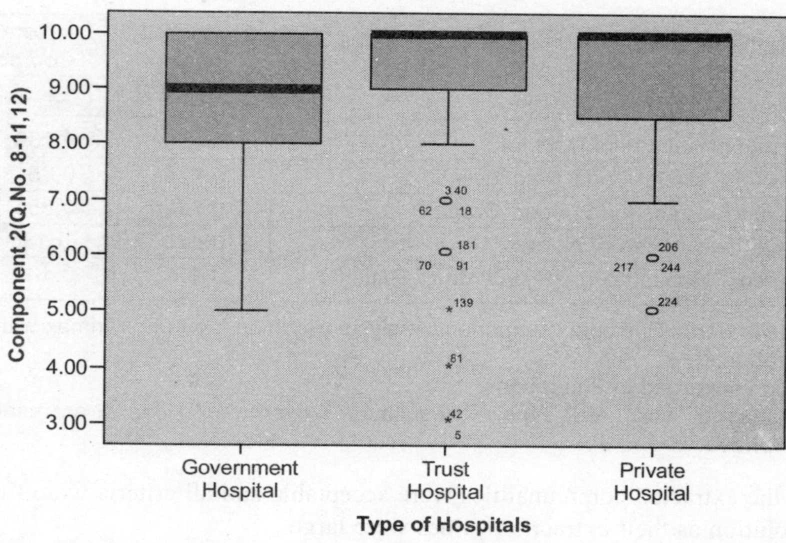

From the box plot of Graph 7.29 it becomes clear that component 2 was important for trust as well as private hospitals because of both have large mean value and less outlier compared to Government hospitals. As the mean score of Government hospital was lower (21.35) factor analysis was made to find out reasons for lower mean value for private hospitals.

Factor Analysis for Government Hospitals for Reliability Criterion

In case of responses of Government hospitals patients for reliability of the hospital services the results showed the value of KMO measure of sampling adequacy (0.533) and Bartlett's test of sphericity (0.0) indicated that factor analysis was appropriate.

Table 7.97: Total Variance for Selected Government Hospitals for Reliability Criterion

Component	Initial Eigenvalues			Extraction Sums of Squared Loadings			Rotation Sums of Squared Loadings		
	Total	% age of Variance	Cumulative per cent	Total	% age of Variance	Cumulative per cent	Total	% age of Variance	Cumulative per cent
01	1.824	36.489	36.489	1.824	36.489	36.489	1.542	30.836	30.836
02	1.245	24.904	61.392	1.245	24.904	61.392	1.528	30.557	61.392

Extraction Method: Principal Component Analysis.
a Only cases for which Q 2 Type of Hospitals = Government Hospital are used in the analysis phase.

Table 7.97 indicated that there were 2 components extracted and it explains 66 per cent variation from data.

Table 7.98: Communalities and Rotated Component Matrix for Selected Government Hospital for Reliability Criterion

Sl.	Selected Criteria	Communalities Extraction	Rotated Component	
			1	2
01	Impartial Attitude of Doctors	0.458	0.239	0.633
02	Doctors' Made Good Diagnosis	0.725	0.851	-0.022
03	Doctors' Prescribed' Good Drugs	0.768	0.851	0.209
04	Impartial Attitude of Nurses	0.640	-0.138	0.788
05	Nurses' Maintain Proper records of Patients	0.479	0.130	0.680

Extraction Method: Principal Component Analysis. Rotation Method: Varimax with Kaiser Normalization.
a Rotation converged in 3 iterations.
b Only cases for which Q 2 Type of Hospitals = Government Hospital are used in the analysis phase.

All the extracted communalities were acceptable and all criteria were fit for the factor solution as their extraction values were large.

From Table 7.98 it becomes clear that component 1 (Doctors' Made Good Diagnosis, Doctors' Prescribed Good Drugs) was highly correlated with criteria 2, and 3. Component 2 (Impartial Attitude of Doctors, Impartial Attitude of Nurses, Nurses' Maintain Proper records of Patients) was highly correlated with criteria 1, 4, and 5.

Table 7.99: Component wise Mean value for Selected Government Hospital for Reliability Criterion

Sl. No.	Component	Mean Value	Selected Criteria	Selected Factors
01	01	9.0580	Doctors' Made Good Diagnosis	Medical Services
02			Doctors' Prescribed Good Drugs	Medical Services
03	02	13.0460	Impartial Attitude of Doctors	Medical Services
04			Impartial Attitude of Nurses	Paramedical Services
05			Nurses' Maintain Proper records of Patients	Paramedical Services

From Table 7.99 it becomes clear that component 2 (Impartial Attitude of Doctors, Impartial Attitude of Nurses, Nurses' Maintain Proper records of Patients) have highest mean value of 13.046. Component 1 (Doctors Makes Good Diagnosis, Doctors' Prescribed Good Drugs) have lowest mean value of 7.78. It means Government hospitals were poor in performance in component 1 criteria. So, there was a need for Government hospitals to improve its service in terms of 'Doctors' makes Good diagnoses and 'Doctors' Prescribe Good Drugs'.

ONE WAY ANNOVA FOR RESPONSIVENESS CRITERION

Analysis of Variance: Selected Patients Responses for Responsiveness Criterion.

Hypothesis: 25

Mean of patients' responses about selected type of hospital is equal in terms of Responsiveness criterion of hospital and an alternative hypothesis is at least one mean is different from other.

Table 7.100: Descriptive Statistics for Responsiveness Criterion for All the Three Type of Hospitals

Type of Hospitals	N	Mean	SD	SE
GHs	200	50.8000	4.78797	0.33856
THs	200	57.7200	5.75825	0.40717
PHs	100	57.3300	6.61045	0.66105
Total	500	54.8740	6.49172	0.29032

From Table 7.100 it becomes clear that trust hospitals have highest mean value of 57.72. Private hospitals have second highest mean value of 57.33 and Government hospitals have lowest mean value of 50.80.

Test of Homogeneity of Variances

Table 7.101: Test of Homogeneity of Variances for Responsiveness Criterion for All the Three Type of Hospitals

Levene's Statistic	df1	df2	Sig.
5.701	2	497	0.004

P-Value of levene's test statistics as given in Table 7.101 was less then 0.05 (0.004 < 0.05) which represent that variance of type of hospitals was not equal at least variance of one type of hospitals was different from other type of hospitals.

Analysis of Variance

Table 7.102: ANOVA for Responsiveness Criterion for All the Three Type of Hospitals

Particulars	Sum of Squares	Df	Mean Square	F	Sig.
Between Groups	5542.632	2	2771.316	88.939	0.000
Within Groups	15486.430	497	31.160		
Total	21029.062	499			

The P-Value (0.00 < 0.05) of ANOVA as given Table 7.102 indicated that mean value of type of hospitals was not equal, at least mean of one type of hospitals was different from other type of hospitals.

Post-Hoc test (Tamhane)

Table 7.103: Multiple Comparisons for Responsiveness Criterion for All the Three Type of Hospitals Through Tamhane Test

Type of Hospitals		Mean Difference	SE	Sig.
GHs	GHs			
	THs	-6.92000	.52954	.000
	PHs	-6.53000	.74270	.000
THs	GHs	6.92000	.52954	.000
	THs			
	PHs	.39000	.77638	.943
PHs	GHs	6.53000	.74270	.000
	THs	-.39000	.77638	.943
	PHs			

Table 7.103 indicated that mean of Government hospitals were different from trust and private hospitals, mean of trust hospitals was different than private hospitals and private hospitals mean was also different from trust hospitals. Thus, Government hospitals make one group and trust and private hospitals makes another group.

Post-Hoc test (Tukey HSD)

From the Table 7.104 it becomes clear that private and trust hospitals make one group, Government hospitals make another group.

The means plot of Graph 7.30 indicated that trust hospital have high mean value. Private hospitals have second highest mean value and Government hospitals have lowest mean value. Private hospitals and Trust hospitals make one group and Government hospitals make another group.

Table 7.104: Multiple Comparisons for Responsiveness Criterion for All the Three Type of Hospitals Through Tukey HSD Test

Type of Hospitals	Subset for alpha = .05		
	N	1	2
GHs	200	50.8000	
PHs	100	57.3300	
THs	200	57.7200	
Sig.	1.000	0.817	

Means for groups in homogeneous subsets are displayed.
a Uses Harmonic Mean Sample Size = 150.000.
b The group sizes are unequal. The harmonic mean of the group sizes is used. Type I error levels are not guaranteed.

Graph 7.30: Means Plots of the Three Type of Hospitals for Responsiveness Criterion

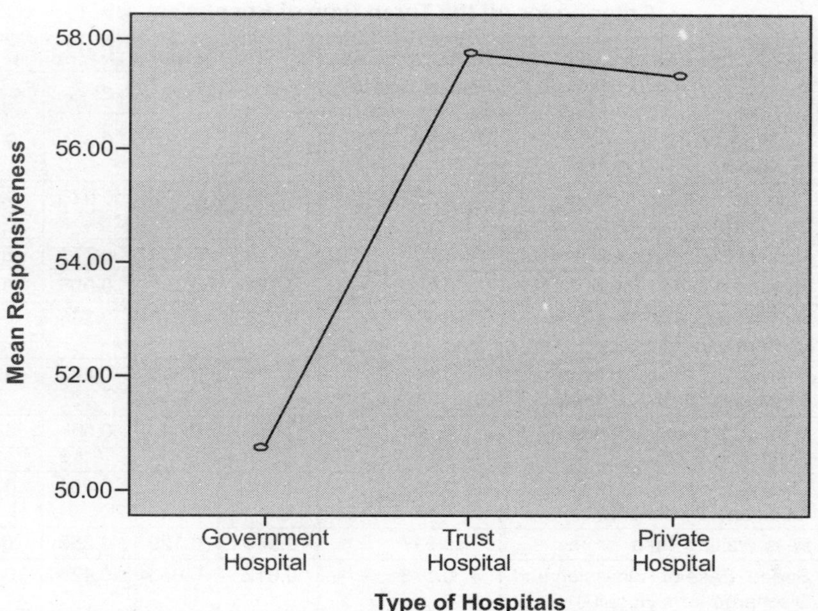

FACTOR ANALYSIS FOR RESPONSIVENESS CRITERION

Factor analysis for Responsiveness Criterion for All the Three Type of Hospitals is given as below.

In case of responses of patients for responsiveness of hospital staff members, the results showed the value of KMO measure of sampling adequacy (0.856) and Bartlett's test of sphericity (0.0) which indicated that factor analysis was appropriate.

Table 7.105: Total Variance for Responsiveness Criterion for All the Three Type of Hospitals

Component	Initial Eigenvalues			Extraction Sums of Squared Loadings			Rotation Sums of Squared Loadings		
	Total	% age of Variance	Cumulative per cent	Total	% age of Variance	Cumulative per cent	Total	% age of Variance	Cumulative per cent
01	4.645	33.182	33.182	4.645	33.182	33.182	2.888	20.626	20.626
02	1.374	9.812	42.994	1.374	9.812	42.994	2.384	17.028	37.653
03	1.199	8.567	51.560	1.199	8 567	51.560	1.758	12.560	50.214
04	1.018	7.272	58.833	1.018	7.272	58.833	1.207	8.619	58.833

Extraction Method: Principal Component Analysis.

From the above table it becomes clear that four components can be extracted and they extract 58.833 per cent variation from data.

Table 7.106: Communalities and Rotated Component Matrix for Responsiveness Criterion for All the Three Type of Hospitals

Sl. No.	Selected Criteria	Communalities Extraction	Rotated Component			
			1	2	3	4
01	Doctors' Cooperation to patients	0.640	0.178	-0.107	0.621	0.459
02	Patients' Felt Comfortable asking Questions to Doctors	0.782	0.065	0.153	0.028	0.868
03	Nurses' Cooperation to Patients	0.664	0.119	0.194	0.777	-0.087
04	Nurses Provide Prompt Service	0.605	0.124	0.766	0.053	-0.003
05	Nurses' and Staff Remains Present in Emergency	0.625	0.088	0.668	0.386	-0.151
06	Information Provided to patients for Managing Side Effects	0.442	0.178	0.543	0.183	0.288
07	Prompt Service Provided by Sanitation Staff	0.506	0.057	0.417	0.568	0.078
08	Less Waiting Time For Consultation and Treatment	0.519	0.707	0.125	0.054	0.027
09	Less Waiting Time for Test	0.517	0.660	0.129	0.255	-0.015
10	Speed, Ease of Admission and Discharge form Hospital	0.578	0.612	0.053	0.429	0.129
11	Convenient Office Hours	0.552	0.732	0.125	0.030	0.003
12	Adm. Staff Gives Prompt Services	0.605	0.489	0.574	0.073	0.177
13	No Overcrowding in Hospital	0.532	0.678	0.230	0.004	0.141
14	Good Grievance handling System	0.668	0.486	0.614	-0.038	0.232

Extraction Method: Principal Component Analysis. Rotation Method: Varimax with Kaiser Normalization.

a Rotation converged in 9 iterations.

All the extracted communalities given in the Table 7.106 were acceptable and all criteria were fit for the factor solution as their extraction values were large.

Table 7.106 indicated the correlation between criteria and factor. Component 1 (Less Waiting Time For Consultation and Treatment, Less Waiting Time for Test, Speed, Ease of Admission and Discharge form Hospital, Convenient Office Hours, No Overcrowding in Hospital) was highly correlated with criteria number 8 to 11, and 13. Component 2 (Nurses' Provided Prompt Service, Nurses' and Staff Remained Present in Emergency, Information Provided to patients for Managing Side Effects, Adm. Staff Gives Prompt Services, Good Grievance handling System) was highly correlated with criteria number 4, 5, 6, 12 and 14. Component 3 (Doctors' Cooperation to patients, Nurses' Cooperation to Patients, Prompt Service Provided by Sanitation Staff) was highly correlated with criteria number 1, 3, and 7, and component 4 (Patients' Felt Comfortable asking Questions to Doctors) was highly correlated with criteria number 2.

Table 7.107: Component wise Mean Value for Responsiveness Criterion for All the Three Type of Hospitals

Sl. No.	Component	Mean Value	Selected Criteria	Selected Factors
01	01	19.9040	Less Waiting Time For Consultation and Treatment	Administration
02			Less Waiting Time for Test	Administration
03			Speed, Ease of Admission and Discharge form Hospital	Administration
04			Convenient Office Hours	Administration
05			No Overcrowding in Hospital	Administration
06	02	17.9060	Nurses' Provide Prompt Service	Paramedical
07			Nurses' and Staff Remains Present in Emergency	Paramedical
08			Information Provided to patients for Managing Side Effects	Paramedical
09			Adm. Staff Gives Prompt Services	Administration
10			Good Grievance handling System	Administration
11	003	12.8000	Doctors' Cooperation to patients	Medical
12			Nurses Cooperation to Patients	Paramedical
13			Prompt Service Provided by Sanitation Staff	Paramedical
14	4	4.2640	Felt Comfortable asking Questions to Doctors	Medical

From Table 7.107 it becomes clear that component 1 (Less Waiting Time For Consultation and Treatment; Less Waiting Time for Test; Speed, Ease of Admission and Discharge form Hospital; Convenient Office Hours; No Overcrowding in Hospital) has highest mean value of 19.9040 and it extracts total 5 criteria. Component 2 (Nurses Provide Prompt Service, Nurses' and Staff Remains Present in Emergency; Information Provided to patients for Managing Side Effects; Adm. Staff Gives Prompt Services, Good Grievance handling System) has second highest mean value of 17.9060. Component

3 (Doctors' Cooperation to patients; Nurses' Cooperation to Patients; Prompt Service Provided by Sanitation Staff) has mean value of 12.8000, and component 4 (Patients' Felt Comfortable asking Questions to Doctors) has lowest mean value it is 4.2640.

Importance of Components for Selected Type of Hospitals

The importance of each component to different type of hospitals can be understood with the help of below given box plots. The following box plot explains three type of hospitals total score of component 1 criteria.

Graph 7.31: Hospitals-wise Box Plot for Component 1 for Responsiveness Criterion of the Three Type of Hospitals

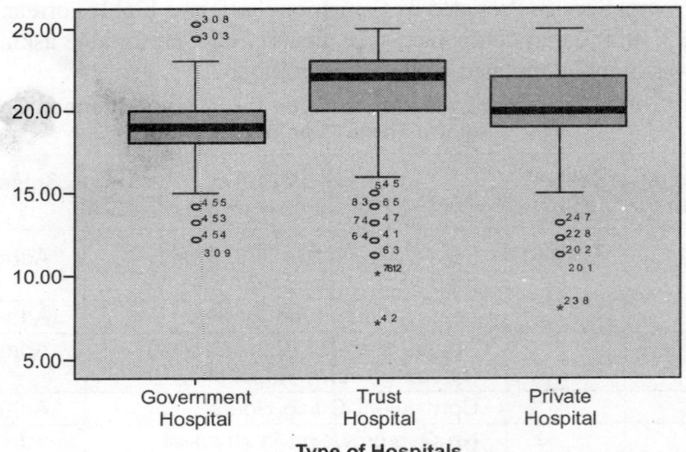

The above box plot of Graph 7.31 indicated that component 1 was important for trust hospitals because of second highest median value and lower variation.

Graph 7.32: Hospitals-wise Box Plot for Component 2 for Responsiveness Criterion of the Three Type of Hospitals

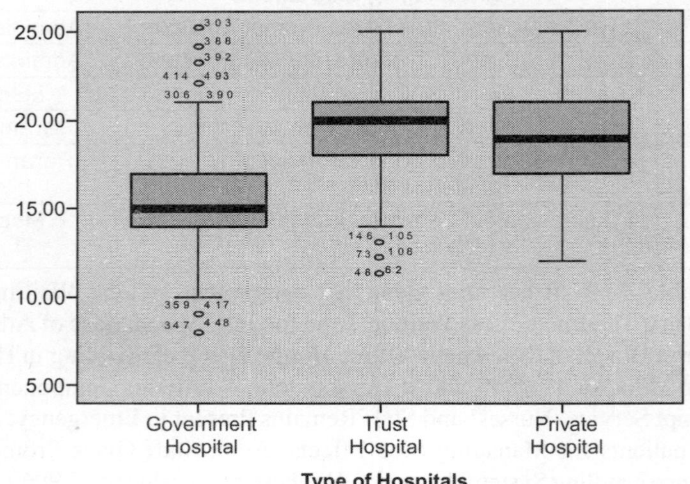

From the above box plot of Graph 7.32 it becomes clear that component 2 was important for trust hospitals because of large median value and less outlier.

Graph 7.33: Hospitals-wise Box Plot for Component 3 for Responsiveness Criterion of the Three Type of Hospitals

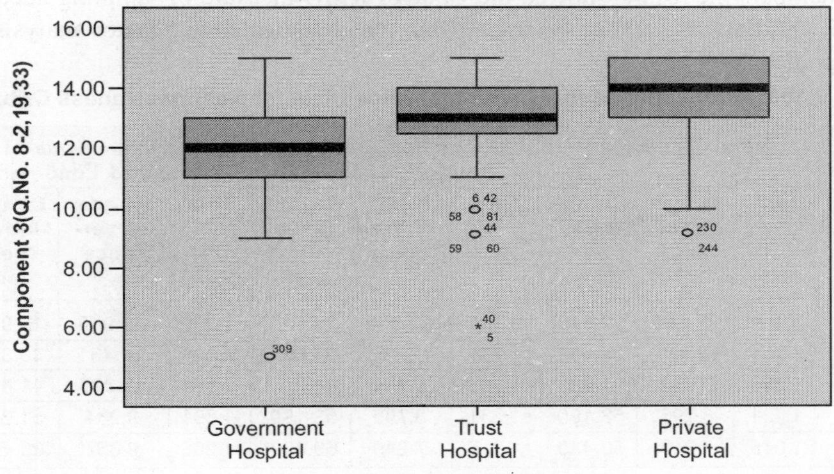

The above box plot of Graph 7.33 indicated that component 3 was important for private hospital because of large median value and very low variation.

Graph 7.34: Hospitals-wise Box Plot for Component 4 for Responsiveness Criterion of the Three Type of Hospitals

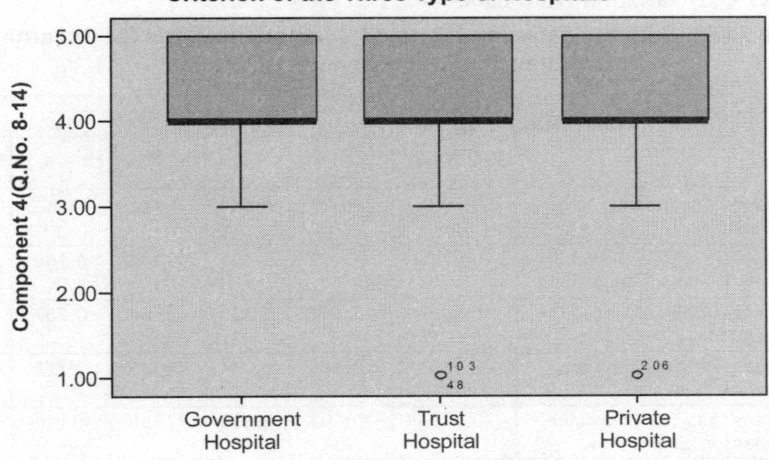

From the above box plot of Graph 7.34 it becomes clear that component 4 was equally important for all three type of hospitals because all have almost similar median value.

As the mean score of Government hospitals was lower (50.80) factor analysis was made to find out the reasons foe lower mean value for private hospitals.

Factor Analysis for Selected Government Hospitals for Responsiveness Criterion

In case of responses of Government hospitals patients for responsiveness of hospital staff members the results showed the value of KMO measure of sampling adequacy (0.705) and Bartlett's test of sphericity (0.0) which indicated that factor analysis was appropriate.

Table 7.108: Total Variance for Government Hospitals for Responsiveness Criterion

Com-ponent	Initial Eigenvalues			Extraction Sums of Squared Loadings			Rotation Sums of Squared Loadings		
	Total	% age of Var-iance	Cumu-lative per cent	Total	% age of Var-iance	Cumu-lative per cent	Total	% age of Var-iance	Cumu-lative per cent
01	3.151	22.510	22.510	3.151	22.510	22.510	2.229	15.919	15.919
02	1.701	12.151	34.661	1.701	12.151	34.661	2.020	14.431	30.350
03	1.363	9.734	44.395	1.363	9.734	44.395	1.554	11.098	41.448
04	1.231	8.795	53.190	1.231	8.795	53.190	1.391	9.934	51.382
05	1.015	7.249	60.439	1.015	7.249	60.439	1.268	9.057	60.439

Extraction Method: Principal Component Analysis.
a Only cases for which Q 2 Type of Hospitals = Government Hospital are used in the analysis phase.

Table 7.108 indicated that there were 5 components extracted and it explains 60.439 per cent variation from data.

Table 7.109: Communalities and Rotated Component Matrix for Government Hospitals for Responsiveness Criterion

Sl. No.	Selected Criteria	Communa-lities Extraction	Rotated Component				
			1	2	3	4	5
01	Doctors' Cooperation to patients	0.693	0.076	0.054	0.471	-0.062	0.678
02	Patients' Felt Comfortable asking Questions to Doctors	0.671	-0.025	0.131	-0.345	0.109	0.723
03	Nurses' Cooperation to Patients	0.506	-0.036	0.222	0.624	0.257	-0.018
04	Nurses' Provided Prompt Service	0.485	0.669	0.064	0.035	0.172	0.039
05	Nurses' and Staff Remains Present in Emergency	0.675	0.693	0.095	0.180	-0.293	-0.260
06	Information Provided to patients for Managing Side Effects	0.598	0.747	0.027	0.039	0.070	0.182
07	Prompt Service Provided by Sanitation Staff	0.485	0.050	-0.033	0.693	-0.025	-0.033
08	Less Waiting Time For Consultation and Treatment	0.525	0.212	0.649	0.072	0.049	0.226

...(Contd.)

...(Contd.)

Sl. No.	Selected Criteria	Communa-lities Extraction	Rotated Component				
			1	2	3	4	5
09	Less Waiting Time for Test	0.678	-0.091	0.775	0.168	0.114	0.164
10	Speed, Ease of Admission and Discharge form Hospital	0.508	0.218	0.524	0.427	-0.019	0.052
11	Convenient Office Hours	0.714	0.133	0.755	-0.185	0.089	-0.291
12	Adm. Staff Gives Prompt Services	0.571	0.611	0.202	-0.088	0.379	-0.075
13	No Overcrowding in Hospital	0.692	0.060	0.056	0.202	0.798	0.091
14	Good Grievance handling System	0.661	0.487	0.160	-0.098	0.620	-0.062

Extraction Method: Principal Component Analysis. Rotation Method: Varimax with Kaiser Normalization.
a Rotation converged in 7 iterations.
b Only cases for which Q 2 Type of Hospitals = Government Hospital are used in the analysis phase.

All the extracted communalities were acceptable and all criteria were fit for the factor solution as their extraction values were large.

From Table 7.109 it becomes clear that component 1 (Nurses' Provided Prompt Service, Nurses' and Staff Remained Present in Emergency, Information Provided to patients for Managing Side Effects, Adm. Staff Gives Prompt Services) was highly correlated with criteria number 4, 5, 6, and 12.

Component 2 (Less Waiting Time For Consultation and Treatment, Less Waiting Time for Test, Speed, Ease of Admission and Discharge form Hospital, Convenient Office Hours) was highly correlated with criteria number 8 to 11. Component 3 (Nurses' Cooperation to Patients, Prompt Service Provided by Sanitation Staff) is highly correlated with criteria number 3, and 7. Component 4 (No Overcrowding in Hospital, Good Grievance handling System) was highly correlated with criteria number 13 and 14. Component 5 (Doctors Cooperation to patients, Felt Comfortable asking Questions to Doctors) was highly correlated with criteria number 1 and 2.

Table 7.110: Component-wise Mean value for Selected Government Hospitals for Responsiveness Criterion

Sl. No.	Compo-nent	Mean Value	Selected Criteria	Selected Factors
01	1	14.4940	Nurses' Provide Prompt Service	Paramedical
02			Nurses' and Staff Remains Present in Emergency	Paramedical
03			Information Provided to patients for Managing Side Effects	Paramedical
04			Adm. Staff Gives Prompt Services	Administration
05	2	15.9420	Less Waiting Time For Consultation and Treatment	Administration

...(Contd.)

...(Contd.)

Sl. No.	Component	Mean Value	Selected Criteria	Selected Factors
06			Less Waiting Time for Test	Administration
07			Speed, Ease of Admission and Discharge form Hospital	Administration
08			Convenient Office Hours	Administration
09	3	8.2640	Nurses' Cooperation to Patients	Paramedical
10			Prompt Service Provided by Sanitation Staff	Paramedical;
11	4	7.3740	No Overcrowding in Hospital	Administration
12			Good Grievance handling System	Administration
13	5	8.8000	Doctors' Cooperation to patients	Medical
14			Patients' Felt Comfortable asking Questions to Doctors	Medical

From Table 7.110 it becomes clear that component 2 (Less Waiting Time For Consultation and Treatment, Less Waiting Time for Test, Speed, Ease of Admission and Discharge form Hospital, Convenient Office Hours) have highest mean value of 15.9420. Component 4 (No Overcrowding in Hospital, Good Grievance handling System) have lowest mean value of 7.3740. Component 3 (Nurses' Cooperation to Patients, Prompt Service Provided by Sanitation Staff) have mean value of 8.2640 and component 5 have (Doctors' Cooperation to patients, Patients' Felt Comfortable asking Questions to Doctors) have mean value of 8.800 and both the mean value can also be considered as low. It means Government hospitals are weak in component number 3, 4, and 5. So, there was a need for Government hospitals to improve its service by of ensuring that there should be no overcrowding in the hospital; the grievance and complaints of the patients should be handled properly; better cooperation and prompt services from nursing staff cooperation from doctors to patients; and environment in which patients feel comfortable to ask questions to doctors.

ONE WAYANNOVA FOR ASSURANCE CRITERION

Analysis of variance: Selected Patients' Responses for Assurance Criterion.

Hypothesis: 26

Mean of patients' responses about selected type of hospital is equal in terms of Assurance criterion of hospitals and an alternative hypothesis is at least one mean is different from other.

Table 7.111: Descriptive Statistics for Assurance Criterion for All the Three Type of Hospitals

Type of Hospitals	N	Mean	SD	SE
GHs	200	28.7850	2.01721	0.14264
THs	200	30.4350	3.30612	0.23378
PHs	100	30.5500	3.10221	0.31022
Total	500	29.7980	2.92888	0.13098

From Table 7.111 it becomes clear that private hospital having highest mean value of 30.55. trust hospital has second highest mean value of 30.43 and Government hospitals has lowest mean value of 28.78.

Test of Homogeneity of Variances

Table 7.112: Test of Homogeneity of Variances for Assurance Criterion for All the Three Type of Hospitals

Levene Statistic	df1	df2	Sig.
19.708	2	497	0.000

P-Value of levene's test statistics as given in the above Table 7.112 was found to be less then 0.05 (0.00 < 0.05) which wais different from other type of hospitals.

Analysis of Variance

Table 7.113: ANOVA for Assurance Criterion for All the Three Type of Hospitals

Particulars	Sum of Squares	df	Mean Square	F	Sig.
Between Groups	342.938	2	171.469	21.642	0.000
Within Groups	3937.660	497	7.923		
Total	4280.598	499			

The P-Value (0.00 < 0.05) of ANOVA as given in Table 7.113 indicated that mean of type of hospitals was not equal at least mean of one type of hospitals was different from other type of hospitals.

Post-Hoc test (Tamhane)

Table 7.114: Multiple Comparisons for Assurance Criterion for All the Three Type of Hospitals Through Tamhane Test

Type of Hospitals			Mean Difference	SE	Sig.
GHs	GHs				
	THs	-1.65000	.27386	0.000	
	PHs	-1.76500	.34144	0.000	
THs	GHs	1.65000	.27386	0.000	
	THs	-.11500	.38844	0.987	
	PHs				
PHs	GHs	1.76500	.34144	0.000	
	THs	.11500	.38844	0.987	
	PHs				

From Table 7.114 it becomes clear that Government hospitals were different from trust and private hospitals. Trust hospitals were different from Government hospitals but insignificant value (0.987) indicated that trust hospitals were not different than private hospitals. Similarly, private hospitals were different from Government hospitals but do not different than trust hospitals.

Post Hoc test (Tukey HSD)

Table Number 7.115: Multiple Comparisons for Assurance Criterion for All the Three Type of Hospitals Through Tukey HSD Test

Type of Hospitals	Subset for alpha = .05		
	N	1	2
GHs	200	28.7850	
THs	200		30.4350
PHs	100		30.5500
Sig.	1.000		.933

Means for groups in homogeneous subsets are displayed.
a Uses Harmonic Mean Sample Size = 150.000.
b The group sizes are unequal. The harmonic mean of the group sizes is used. Type I error levels are not guaranteed.

From Table 7.115 it becomes clear that private hospitals and trust hospitals makes one group, Government hospitals make another group.

Graph 7.35: Means Plots of All the Three Type of Hospitals for Assurance Criterion

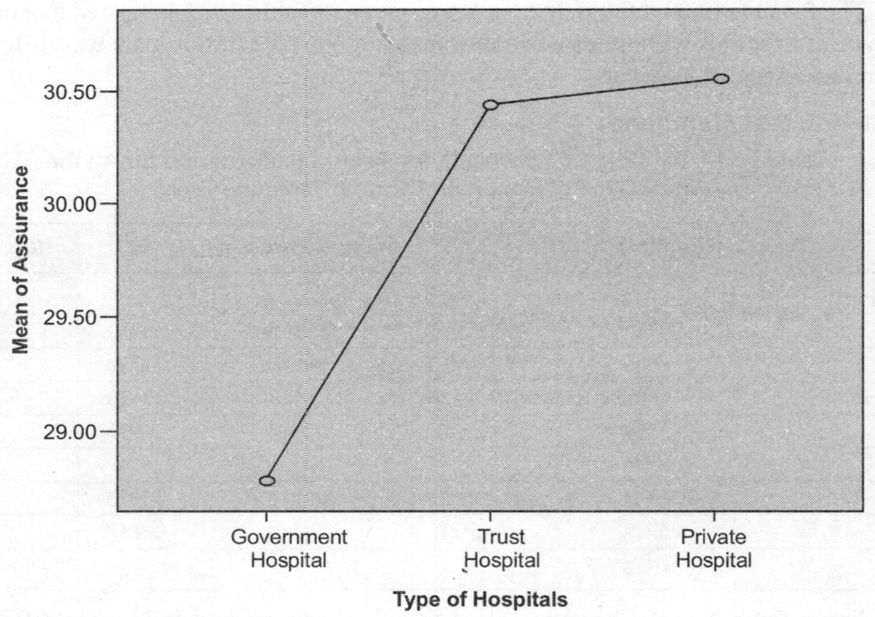

Above means plot of Graph 7.35 indicated that private hospitals have high mean value. Trust hospital have second highest mean value and Government hospitals have lowest mean value and each make different group.

FACTOR ANALYSIS FOR ASSURANCE CRITERION

Factor analysis for Assurance Criteria for All the Three Type Of Hospitals is given as below.

In case of responses of patients' for assurance of hospital services the results showed the value of KMO measure of sampling adequacy (0.746) and Bartlett's test of sphericity (0.0) which indicated that factor analysis was appropriate.

Table 7.116: Total Variance for Assurance Criterion for All the Three Type of Hospitals

Component	Initial Eigenvalues			Extraction Sums of Squared Loadings			Rotation Sums of Squared Loadings		
	Total	% age of Variance	Cumulative per cent	Total	% age of Variance	Cumulative per cent	Total	% age of Variance	Cumulative per cent
01	2.623	37.466	37.466	2.623	37.466	37.466	2.101	30.007	30.007
02	1.348	19.253	56.720	1.348	19.253	56.720	1.870	26.712	56.720

Extraction Method: Principal Component Analysis.

From Table 7.116 it becomes clear that two components can be extracted and they extract 56.720 per cent variation from data.

Table 7.117: Communalities and Rotated Component Matrix for Assurance Criterion for All the Three Type of Hospitals

Sl. No.	Selected Criteria	Communalities Extraction	Rotated Component	
			1	2
01	Doctors' Knowledge and Efficiency	0.465	0.217	0.647
02	Doctors' Experience in Curing Patients	0.732	0.015	0.856
03	Thorough Checkup by Doctors	0.645	0.147	0.790
04	Nurses' Knowledge and Efficiency	0.519	0.720	0.003
05	Nurses' Handled Patients Quarry Properly	0.556	0.736	0.122
06	Nurses' Experience in Curing Patients	0.554	0.731	0.141
07	Good Experience of Those who Perform Test on Patients	0.498	0.661	0.247

Extraction Method: Principal Component Analysis. Rotation Method: Varimax with Kaiser Normalization.
a Rotation converged in 3 iterations.

All the extracted communalities given in Table 7.117 were acceptable and all criteria were fit for the factor solution as their extraction values were large.

Table 7.117 indicated the correlation between criteria and factors. Component 1 (Nurses' Knowledge and Efficiency, Nurses' Handled Patients Quarry Properly, Nurses' Experience in Curing Patients, Good Experience of Those who Perform Test on Patients) was highly correlated with criteria , 4, 5, 6, and 7. Component 2 (Doctors'

Knowledge and Efficiency, Doctors' Experience in Curing Patients, Thorough Checkup by Doctors) was highly correlated with criteria 1, 2, and 3.

Table 7.118: Component-wise Mean Value for Assurance Criterion for All the Three Type of Hospitals

Sl. No.	Compo-nent	Mean Value	Selected Criteria	Selected Factors
01	1	16.3560	Nurses' Knowledge and Efficiency	Paramedical
02			Nurses' Handled Patients Quarry Properly	Paramedical
03			Nurses' Experience in Curing Patients	Paramedical
04			Good Experience of Those who Perform Test on Patients	Paramedical
05	2	13.4420	Doctors' Knowledge and Efficiency	Medical
06			Doctors' Experience in Curing Patients	Medical
07			Thorough Checkup by Doctors	Medical

From Table 7.118 it becomes clear that component 1 (Nurses' Knowledge and Efficiency, Nurses' Handled Patients Quarry Properly, Nurse's Experience in Curing Patients, Good Experience of Those who Perform Test on Patients) has highest mean value of 16.3560 and it extract total 6 criteria. Component 2 (Doctors' Knowledge and Efficiency, Doctors' Experience in Curing Patients, Thorough Checkup by Doctors) has second highest mean value of 13.4420.

Importance of Components for Selected Type of Hospitals

Graph 7.36: Hospitals-wise Box Plot for Component 1 for Assurance Criterion of the Three Type of Hospitals

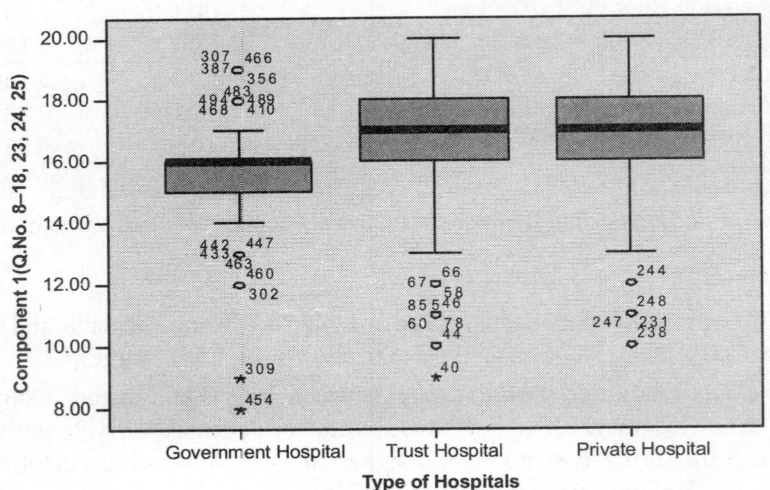

The importance of each component to different type of hospitals can be understood with the help of given box plots of Graph 7.36. The following box plot explains three type of hospitals total score of component 1 (Paramedical).

The box plot of Graph 7.36 indicated that component 1 was important for private and trust hospitals because it has highest median value and lower variation.

Graph 7.37: Hospitals-wise Box Plot for Component 2 for Assurance Criterion of the Three Type of Hospitals

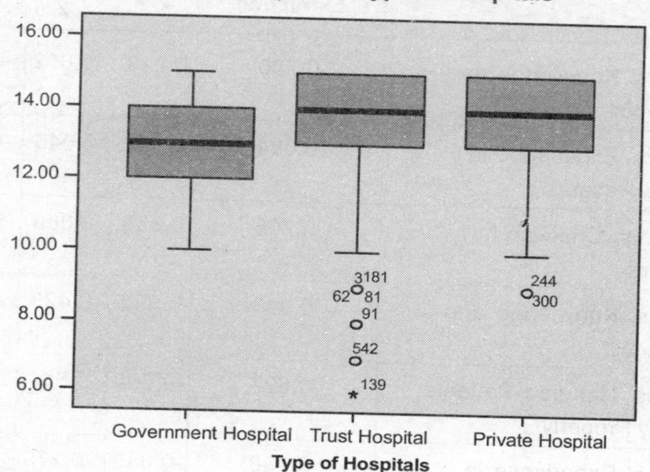

From the above box plot of Graph 7.37 becomes clear that component 2 was important for trust and private hospitals because it has large mean value and less outlier.

As the mean score of Government hospitals was found to be lower (28.78) factor analysis was made to find out the reasons for lower mean value of Government hospitals.

Factor Analysis for Government Hospitals for Assurance Criterion is given below:

In case of responses of Government hospitals patients' for assurance of hospital services, the results showed the value of KMO measure of sampling adequacy (0.512) and Bartlett's test of sphericity (0.0) indicated that factor analysis was appropriate.

Table 7.119: Total Variance for Government Hospitals for Assurance Criterion

Component	Initial Eigenvalues			Extraction Sums of Squared Loadings			Rotation Sums of Squared Loadings		
	Total	% age of Variance	Cumulative per cent	Total	% age of Variance	Cumulative per cent	Total	% age of Variance	Cumulative per cent
01	1.596	22.806	22.806	1.596	22.806	22.806	1.490	21.290	21.290
02	1.352	19.316	42.122	1.352	19.316	42.122	1.261	18.019	39.309
03	1.105	15.790	57.912	1.105	15.790	57.912	1.198	17.115	56.425
04	1.001	14.299	72.211	1.001	14.299	72.211	1.105	15.786	72.211

Extraction Method: Principal Component Analysis.

(a) Only cases for which Q 2 Type of Hospitals = Government Hospital are used in the analysis phase.

Table 7.119 indicated that there were 4 components extracted and it explains 72 per cent variation from data.

Table 7.120: Communalities and Rotated Component Matrix for Selected Government Hospitals for Assurance Criterion

Sl. No.	Selected Criteria	Communalities Extraction	Rotated Component			
			1	2	3	4
01	Doctors' Knowledge and Efficiency	0.786	0.228	-0.092	-0.043	0.851
02	Doctors' Experience in Curing Patients	0.684	0.801	0.046	-0.084	0.181
03	Thorough Checkup by Doctors	0.706	0.833	0.069	0.076	-0.034
04	Nurses' Knowledge and Efficiency	0.643	0.055	0.423	0.670	-0.112
05	Nurses' Handled Patients Quarry Properly	0.697	-0.269	0.514	0.198	0.567
06	Nurses' Experience in Curing Patients	0.780	-0.045	-0.279	0.829	0.112
07	Good Experience of Those who Perform Test on Patients	0.758	0.158	0.852	-0.087	-0.024

Extraction Method: Principal Component Analysis. Rotation Method: Varimax with Kaiser Normalization.

(a) Rotation converged in 7 iterations.

(b) Only cases for which Q 2 Type of Hospitals = Government Hospital are used in the analysis phase.

All the extracted communalities were acceptable and all criteria were fit for the factor solution as their extraction values were large.

From the above table it becomes clear that component 1 (Doctors' Experience in Curing Patients, Thorough Checkup by Doctors) was highly correlated with criteria 2 and 3. Component 2 (Good Experience of Those who Perform Test on Patients) was highly correlated with criterion 7. Component 3 (Nurses' Knowledge and Efficiency, Nurses' Experience in Curing Patients) was highly correlated with criteria 4, and 6. Component 4 (Doctors' Knowledge and Efficiency, Nurses' Handled Patients Quarry Properly) was highly correlated with criteria 1 and 5.

Table 7.121: Component wise Mean value for Selected Government Hospitals for Assurance Criterion

Sl. No.	Compo-nent	Mean Value	Selected Criteria	Selected Factors
01	1	8.8860	Doctors' Experience in Curing Patients	Medical
02			Thorough Checkup by Doctors	Medical
03	2	4.1940	Good Experience of Those who Perform Test on Patients	Paramedical
04	3	8.1680	Nurses' Knowledge and Efficiency	Paramedical
05			Nurses' Experience in Curing Patients	Paramedical
06	4	8.5500	Doctor' Knowledge and Efficiency	Medical
07			Nurses' Handled Patients Quarry Properly	Paramedical

From Table 7.121 it becomes clear that component 1 (Doctors' Experience in Curing Patients, Thorough Checkup by Doctors) have highest mean value of 8.8860. Component 2 (Good Experience of Those who Perform Test on Patients) have lowest mean value of 4.1940. It means Government hospitals were found to be weak in component 2. So, Government hospitals need to improve its service in terms of providing better service by staff who perform various test on patients.

ONE WAYANNOVA FOR EMPATHY CRITERION

Analysis of variance: Selected Patients' Responses for Empathy Criterion

Hypothesis: 46

Mean of patients' responses about selected type of hospital is equal in terms of Empathy criteria of hospitals and an alternative hypothesis is at least one mean is different from other.

Table 7.122: Descriptive Statistics for Empathy Criterion for All the Three Type of Hospitals

Type of Hospitals	N	Mean	SD	SE
GHs	200	40.0400	3.55409	0.25131
THs	200	43.3350	3.99909	0.28278
PHs	100	43.2700	5.17542	0.51754
Total	500	42.0040	4.39393	0.19650

From Table 7.122 it becomes clear that trust hospitals have highest mean value of 33.3350. Private hospitals have second highest mean value of 43.27 and Government hospitals have lowest mean value of 40.04.

Test of Homogeneity of Variances

Table 7.123: Test of Homogeneity of Variances for Empathy Criterion for All the Three Type of Hospitals

Levene Statistic	df1	df2	Sig.
5.451	2	497	0.005

P-Value of levene's test statistics as given in Table 7.123 was less then 0.05 (0.00 < 0.05) which indicate that variance of type of hospitals was not equal, at least variance of one type of hospitals was different from other type of hospitals.

Analysis of Variance

Table 7.124: ANOVA for Empathy Criterion for All the Three Type of Hospitals

Selected Criteria	Sum of Squares	df	Mean Square	F	Sig.
Between Groups	1286.047	2	643.024	38.283	0.000
Within Groups	8347.945	497	16.797		
Total	9633.992	499			

The P-Value (0.00 < 0.05) of ANOVA as given in Table 7.124 indicated that mean of type of hospitals was not equal, at least mean of one type of hospitals is different from other type of hospitals.

Post-Hoc test (Tamhane)

Table 7.125: Multiple Comparisons for Empathy Criterion for All the Three Type of Hospitals Through Tamhane Test

Type of Hospitals		Mean Difference	SE	Sig.
GHs	GHs			
	THs	-3.29500	.37831	0.000
	PHs	-3.23000	.57533	0.000
THs	GHs	3.29500	.37831	0.000
	THs			
	PHs	.06500	.58976	0.999
PHs	GHs	3.23000	.57533	0.000
	THs	-.06500	.58976	0.999
	PHs			

From Table 7.125 it becomes clear that Government hospitals were different from trust and private hospitals. Trust hospitals were different from Government hospitals but the insignificant value (0.999) indicated that trust hospitals were not different than private hospitals. Similarly private hospitals were different from Government hospitals but do not different than trust hospitals.

Post-Hoc test (Tukey HSD)

Table 7.126: Multiple Comparisons for Empathy Criterion for All the Three Type of Hospitals Through Tukey HSD Test

Type of Hospitals	N	Subset for alpha = .05	
		1	2
GHs	200	40.0400	
PHs	100		43.2700
THs	200		43.3350
Sig.		1.000	.990

Means for groups in homogeneous subsets are displayed.

(a) Uses Harmonic Mean Sample Size = 150.000.

(b) The group sizes are unequal. The harmonic mean of the group sizes is used. Type I error levels are not guaranteed.

From Table 7.126 it becomes clear that private hospitals and trust hospitals makes one group, and Government hospitals make another group.

Graph 7.38: Means Plots of Type of Hospitals for Empathy Criterion for All the Three Type of Hospitals

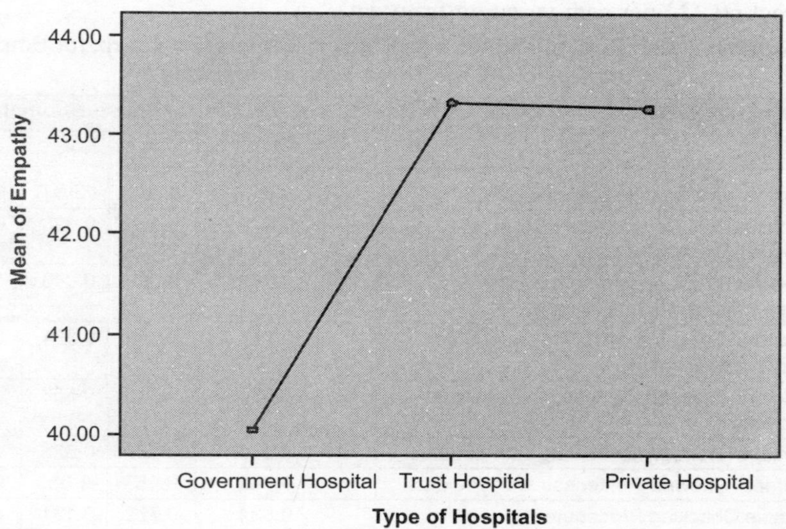

Above means plot of Graph 7.38 indicated that trust hospitals having high mean value. Private hospitals have second highest mean value and Government hospitals have lowest mean value, and private and Trust hospitals makes one group and Government hospitals makes different group.

FACTOR ANALYSIS FOR EMPATHY CRITERION

Factor Analysis for Empathy Criterion for All the Three Type of Selected Hospitals is given as below.

In case of responses of patients' for empathy experienced by them from hospital staff and the results showed the value of KMO measure of sampling adequacy (0.796) and Bartlett's test of sphericity (0.0) which indicated that factor analysis was appropriate.

Table 7.127: Total Variance Explained for Empathy Criterion for All the Three Type of Hospitals

Component	Initial Eigenvalues			Extraction Sums of Squared Loadings			Rotation Sums of Squared Loadings		
	Total	% age of Variance	Cumulative per cent	Total	% age of Variance	Cumulative per cent	Total	% age of Variance	Cumulative per cent
01	3.499	34.985	34.985	3.499	34.985	34.985	2.194	21.939	21.939
02	1.420	14.199	49.184	1.420	14.199	49.184	1.953	19.529	41.469
03	1.114	11.137	60.322	1.114	11.137	60.322	1.885	18.853	60.322

Extraction Method: Principal Component Analysis.

From Table 7.127 it becomes clear that four components can be extracted and they extract 60.322 per cent variation from data.

Table Number 7.128: Communalities and Rotated Component Matrix for Empathy Criterion for All the Three Type of Hospitals

Sl. No.	Selected Criteria	Communalities Extraction	Rotated Component		
			1	2	3
01	Doctors' were polite with patients	0.663	0.141	0.104	0.795
02	Patients' Felt Comfortable During Doctors Examination	0.572	0.054	0.398	0.641
03	Doctors' Work According to Patients Expectations	0.717	0.066	0.843	-0.037
04	Doctors' Gave Individual Consideration and Confidentiality	0.741	0.099	0.834	0.188
05	Doctors' Showed Respect and Support patients	0.550	0.313	0.563	0.368
06	Doctors' Honesty in Dealing with patients	0.510	0.187	0.028	0.689
07	Nurses' Showed Politeness with Patients	0.352	0.453	-0.051	0.379
08	Simple Checking Procedure	0.634	0.772	0.131	0.147
09	Good Concern for Patient Family and Visitor	0.625	0.769	0.083	0.163
10	Simple Billing Procedures	0.667	0.794	0.182	0.051

Extraction Method: Principal Component Analysis. Rotation Method: Varimax with Kaiser Normalization.

(a) Rotation converged in 5 iterations.

All the extracted communalities given in Table 7.128 were acceptable and all Criterion were fit for the factor solution as their extraction values were large.

Table 7.128 indicated the correlation between Criterion and factors. Component 1 (Simple Checking Procedure, Good Concern for Patient Family and Visitor, Simple Billing Procedures) was highly correlated with Criterion 8, 9, and 10. Component 2 (Doctors' Work According to Patients Expectations, Doctors' Gave Individual Consideration and Confidentiality, Doctors' Showed Respect and Support patients) was highly correlated with Criterion 3 to 5. Component 3 (Doctors' were polite with patients, Patients' Felt Comfortable during Doctors' Examination, Doctors' Honesty in Dealing with patients) was highly correlated with Criterion 1, 2, and 6.

Table 7.129: Component wise Mean Value for Empathy Criterion for All the Three Type of Hospitals

Sl. No.	Compo-nent	Mean Value	Selected Criteria	Selected Factors
01	01	12.3540	Simple Checking Procedure	Administration
02			Good Concern for Patient Family and Visitor	Administration
03			Simple Billing Procedures	Administration
04	02	11.8160	Doctors' Work According to Patients Expectations	Medical
05			Doctors' Gave Individual Consideration and Confidentiality	Medical
06			Doctors' Showed Respect and Support patients	Medical
07	03	13.5000	Doctors' were polite with patients	Medical
08			Patients' Felt Comfortable During Doctors Examination	Medical
09			Doctors' Honesty in Dealing with patients	Medical

From Table 7.129 it becomes clear that component 3 (Doctors' were polite with patients, Patients' Felt Comfortable during Doctors' Examination, Doctors' Honesty in Dealing with patients) has highest mean value of 13.50 and it extracted total 3 criterion.

Component 1 (Simple Checking Procedure, Good Concern for Patient Family and Visitor, Simple Billing Procedures) has second highest mean value of 12.35. Component 2 (Doctors' Work According to Patients' Expectations, Doctors' Gave Individual Consideration and Confidentiality, Doctors' Showed Respect and Support patients) has lowest mean value of 11.82.

Importance of Components for Selected Type of Hospitals

The importance of each component to different type of hospitals can be understood with the help of below given box plots. The following box plot of Graph 7.39 explains the type of hospitals total score of component 1 (Administration).

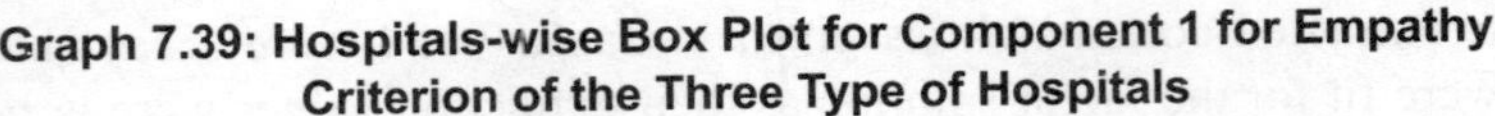

Graph 7.39: Hospitals-wise Box Plot for Component 1 for Empathy Criterion of the Three Type of Hospitals

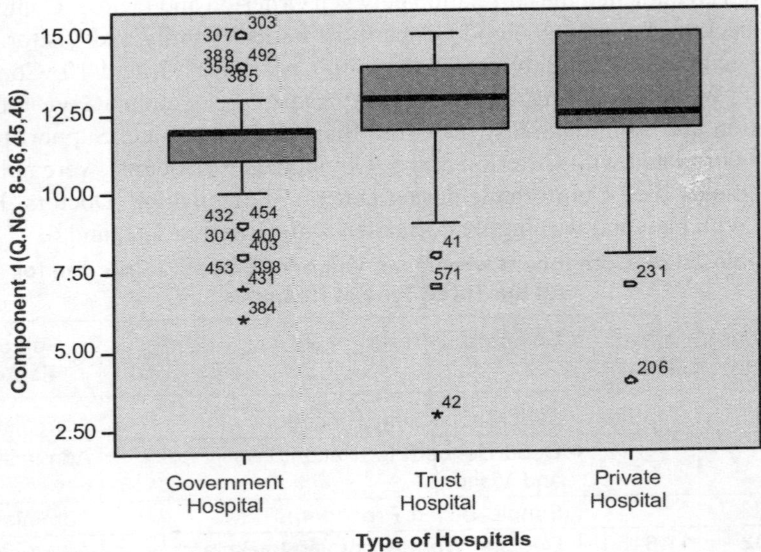

The above box plot of Graph 7.39 indicated that component 1 was important for trust hospitals because of highest median value and lower variation.

Graph 7.40: Hospitals-wise Box Plot for Component 2 for Empathy Criterion of the Three Type of Hospitals

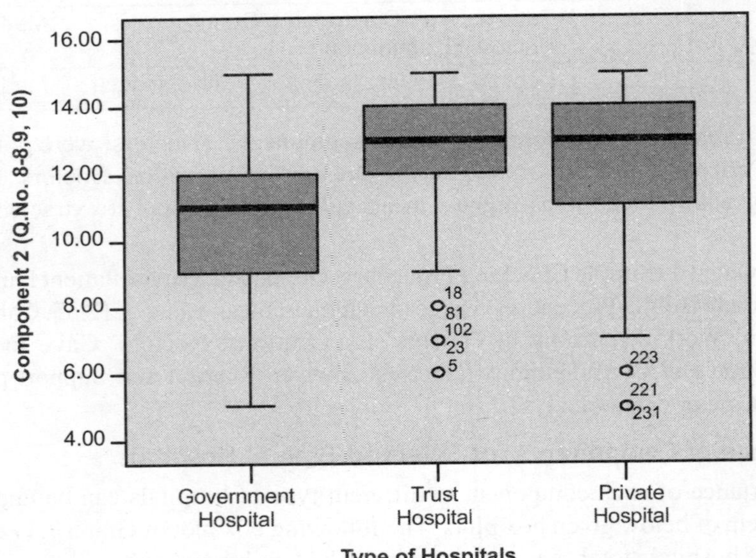

From the above box plot of Graph 7.40 it becomes clear that component 2 was important for trust hospitals because of large mean value and less outlier.

Graph 7.41: Hospitals-wise Box Plot for Component 3 for Empathy Criterion of the Three Type of Hospitals

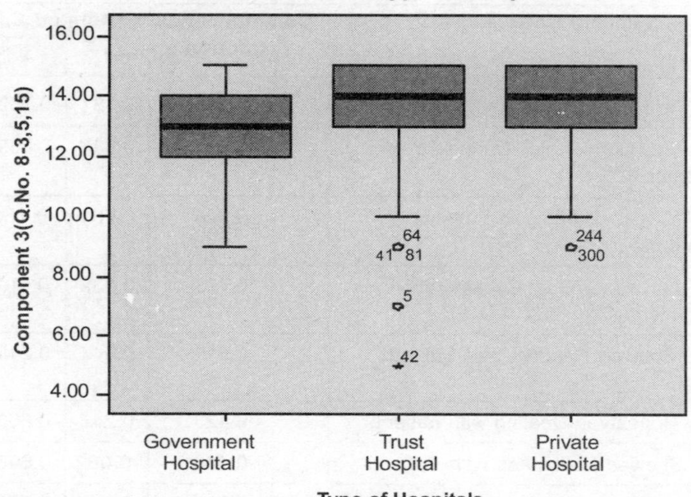

The above box plot of Graph 7.41 indicated that component 3 was important for private hospital because of large median value and low variation and less outlier than trust hospitals.

As the mean score of Government hospitals was lower (40.04), the factor analysis was applied to find out the reasons for lower mean value for Government hospitals.

Factor Analysis for Selected Government Hospitals for Empathy Criterion is given as below.

In case of responses of Government hospitals patients' for empathy experienced by them from hospital staff the results showed the value of KMO measure of sampling adequacy (0.699) and Bartlett's test of sphericity (0.0) which indicated that factor analysis was appropriate.

Table 7.130: Total Variance for Selected Government Hospitals for Empathy Criterion

	Initial Eigenvalues			Extraction Sums of Squared Loadings			Rotation Sums of Squared Loadings		
Component	Total	% age of Variance	Cumulative per cent	Total	% age of Variance	Cumulative per cent	Total	% age of Variance	Cumulative per cent
01	2.667	26.671	26.671	2.667	26.671	26.671	2.179	21.788	21.788
02	1.651	16.514	43.185	1.651	16.514	43.185	1.779	17.790	39.578
03	1.241	12.410	55.595	1.241	12.410	55.595	1.602	16.017	55.595

Extraction Method: Principal Component Analysis.

(a) Only cases for which Q 2 Type of Hospitals = Government Hospital are used in the analysis phase.

Table 7.130 indicated that there were 3 components extracted and it explains 55.59 per cent variation from data.

Table 7.131: Communalities and Rotated Component Matrix for Selected Government Hospitals for Empathy Criterion

Sl. No.	Selected Criteria	Communalities Extraction	Rotated Component		
			1	2	3
01	Doctors' were polite with patients	0.588	0.181	0.732	-0.139
02	Patients' Felt Comfortable During Doctors Examination	0.484	0.586	0.365	-0.084
03	Doctors' Work According to Patients Expectations	0.604	0.761	-0.155	-0.036
04	Doctors' Gave Individual Consideration and Confidentiality	0.723	0.839	0.110	0.080
05	Doctors' Showed Respect and Support patients	0.516	0.647	0.248	0.187
06	Doctors' Honesty in Dealing with patients	0.423	0.247	0.602	-0.018
07	Nurses' Showed Politeness with Patients	0.443	-0.082	0.608	0.258
08	Simple Checking Procedure	0.590	-0.051	0.530	0.554
09	Good Concern for Patient Family and Visitor	0.562	-0.026	0.001	0.749
10	Simple Billing Procedures	0.628	0.174	-0.016	0.773

Extraction Method: Principal Component Analysis. Rotation Method: Varimax with Kaiser Normalization.

(a) Rotation converged in 5 iterations.

(b) Only cases for which Q 2 Type of Hospitals = Government Hospital are used in the analysis phase.

All the extracted communalities were acceptable and all Criterion were fit for the factor solution as their extraction values were large.

From Table 7.131 it becomes clear that component 1 (Patients' Felt Comfortable during Doctors' Examination, Doctors' Work according to Patients' Expectations, Doctors' Gave Individual Consideration and Confidentiality, Doctors' Showed Respect and Support patients) was highly correlated with Criterion 2 to 5. Component 2 (Doctors' were polite with patients, Doctors' Honesty in Dealing with patients, Nurses' Showed Politeness with Patients) was highly correlated with Criterion 1, 6, and 7. Component 3 (Simple Checking Procedure, Good Concern for Patients' Family and Visitor, Simple Billing Procedures) was highly correlated with Criterion 8, 9, and 10.

Table 7.132: Component wise Mean value for Selected Government Hospitals for Empathy Criterion

Sl. No.	Compo-nent	Mean Value	Selected Criteria	Selected Factors
01	01	16.1620	Patients' Felt Comfortable During Doctors Examination	Medical
02			Doctors' Work According to Patients Expectations	Medical
03			Doctors' Gave Individual Consideration and Confidentiality	Medical
04			Doctors' Showed Respect and Support patients	Medical
05	02	13.4880	Doctors' were polite with patients	Medical
06			Doctors' Honesty in Dealing with patients	Medical
07			Nurses' Showed Politeness with Patients	Paramedical
08	03	12.3540	Simple Checking Procedure	Administration
09			Good Concern for Patients' Family and Visitor	Administration
10			Simple Billing Procedures	Administration

From Table 7.132 it becomes clear that component 1 (Patients' Felt Comfortable during Doctors' Examination, Doctors' Work According to Patients' Expectations, Doctors' Gave Individual Consideration and Confidentiality, Doctors' Showed Respect and Support patients) have highest mean value of 16.1620. Component 3 (Simple Checking Procedure, Good Concern for Patients' Family and Visitor, Simple Billing Procedures) have lowest mean value of 12.3540. It means Government hospitals were found to be weak in component 3. So, Government hospitals need to improve its service in terms of simple checking procedures, good concern for patients' family and visitor and simple billing procedures.

ONE WAY ANNOVA FOR DIGNITY CRITERION

Analysis of Variance: Selected Patients' Responses for Dignity Criterion.

Hypothesis: 27

Mean of patients' responses about selected type of hospital is equal in terms of dignity criterion of hospitals and an alternative hypothesis is at least one mean is different from other.

Table 7.133: Descriptive Statistics for Dignity Criterion for All the Three Type of Hospitals

Type of Hospitals	N	Mean	SD	SE
GHs	200	27.4100	3.87518	0.27402
THs	200	33.0550	3.73924	0.26440
PHs	100	31.7900	4.99959	0.49996
Total	500	30.5440	4.82687	0.21586

From Table 7.133 it becomes clear that trust hospitals have highest mean value of 33.05. Private hospitals have second highest mean value of 31.79 and Government hospitals have lowest mean value of 27.41.

Test of Homogeneity of Variances

Table 7.134: Test of Homogeneity of Variances for Dignity Criterion for All the Three Type of Hospitals

Levene Statistic	df1	df2	Sig.
5.735	2	497	0.003

P-Value of levene's test statistics as given in Table 7.134 was found to be less then 0.05 (0.00 < 0.05) which indicate that variance of type of hospitals were not equal, at least variance of one type of hospitals is different from other type of hospitals.

Analysis of Variance

Table 7.135: ANOVA for Dignity Criterion for All the Three Type of Hospitals

Particulars	Sum of Squares	df	Mean Square	F	Sig.
Between Groups	3380.667	2	1690.333	101.887	0.000
Within Groups	8245.365	497	16.590		
Total	11626.032	499			

The P-Value (0.00 < 0.05) of ANOVA table given above indicated that mean of type of hospitals was not equal at least mean of one type of hospitals was different from other type of hospitals.

Post Hoc test (Tamhane)

Table 7.136: Multiple Comparisons for Dignity Criterion for All the Three Type of Hospitals Through Tamhane Test

Type of Hospitals		Mean Difference	SE	Sig.
GHs	GHs			
	THs	-5.64500	0.38078	0.000
	PHs	-4.38000	0.57013	0.000
THs	GHs	5.64500	0.38078	0.000
	THs			
	PHs	1.26500	0.56557	0.078
PHs	GHs	4.38000	0.57013	0.000
	THs	-1.26500	0.56557	0.078
	PHs			

From Table 7.136 it becomes clear that Government hospitals were different from trust and private hospitals. Trust hospitals were different from Government and private hospitals and private hospitals were different from Government and trust hospitals.

Post-Hoc test (Tukey HSD)

Table 7.137: Multiple Comparisons for Dignity Criterion for All the Three Type of Hospitals Through Tukey HSD Test

Type of Hospitals	N	Subset for alpha = .05		
		1	2	3
GHs	200	27.4100		
PHs	100		31.7900	
THs	200			33.0550
Sig.		1.000	1.000	1.000

Means for groups in homogeneous subsets are displayed.

(a) Uses Harmonic Mean Sample Size = 150.000.

(b) The group sizes are unequal. The harmonic mean of the group sizes is used. Type I error levels are not guaranteed.

From Table 7.137 it becomes clear that private hospitals make one group, Government hospitals make another group and trust hospitals make one more group.

Graph 7.42: Means Plots of Type of Hospitals for Dignity Criterion for All the Three Type of Hospitals

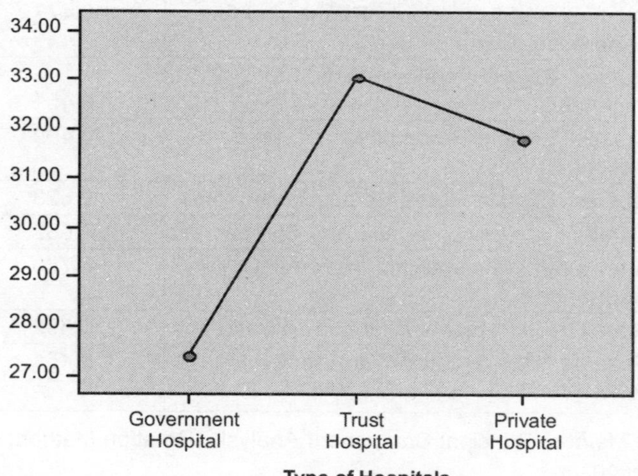

Above means plot of Graph 7.42 indicated that trust hospitals have high mean value. Private hospitals have second highest mean value and Government hospitals have lowest mean value and each make different group.

FACTOR ANALYSIS FOR DIGNITY CRITERION

Factor Analysis for Dignity Criterion for All the Three Type of Hospitals.

In case of responses of patients for dignity maintained by hospital staff, the results showed the value of KMO measure of sampling adequacy (0.785) and Bartlett's test of sphericity (0.0) which indicated that factor analysis was appropriate.

Table 7.138: Total Variance for Dignity Criterion for All the Three Type of Hospitals

Component	Initial Eigenvalues			Extraction Sums of Squared Loadings			Rotation Sums of Squared Loadings		
	Total	% age of Variance	Cumulative per cent	Total	% age of Variance	Cumulative per cent	Total	% age of Variance	Cumulative per cent
01	3.348	41.846	41.846	3.348	41.846	41.846	2.738	34.223	34.223
02	1.308	16.344	58.190	1.308	16.344	58.190	1.917	23.967	58.190

Extraction Method: Principal Component Analysis.

From Table 7.138 it becomes clear that two components can be extracted and they extract 58.19 per cent variation from data.

Table 7.139: Communalities and Rotated Component Matrix for Dignity Criterion for All the Three Type of Hospitals

Sl. No.	Selected Criteria	Communalities Extraction	Rotated Component	
			1	2
01	Doctors' ask for patients Permission for performing Test	0.477	0.687	0.076
02	Nurses' Gave Personal Attention to Patients	0.451	0.555	0.379
03	Nurses' Explain Procedures and take Patient Permission before Test	0.499	0.522	0.476
04	Nurses' Explain Rules Regulation in ward	0.623	0.137	0.778
05	Nurses' were Kind, Gentle and Sympathetic	0.682	-0.027	0.826
06	Adm. Staff Welcome and Implement Suggestion	0.780	0.883	0.005
07	Adm. Gives Personal Attention To Patient	0.692	0.821	0.135
08	Patients' were Treated With Dignity and Privacy	0.451	0.462	0.487

Extraction Method: Principal Component Analysis. Rotation Method: Varimax with Kaiser Normalization.

(a) Rotation converged in 3 iterations.

All the extracted communalities given in Table 7.139 were acceptable and all Criterion were fit for the factor solution as their extraction values were large.

The Table 7.139 indicated the correlation between Criterion and factors. Component 1 (Doctors' ask for patients Permission for performing Test, Nurses' Gave Personal Attention to Patients, Nurses' Explain Procedures and take Patient Permission before Test, Adm. Staff Welcome and Implement Suggestion, Adm. Gives Personal Attention To Patient) was highly correlated with Criterion 1, 2, 3, 6, and 7. Component 2 (Nurses' Explain Rules Regulation in ward, Nurses' were Kind, Gentle and Sympathetic) was highly correlated with Criterion 4, 5.

Table 7.140: Component wise Mean Value for Dignity Criterion of All the Three Type of Hospitals

Sl. No.	Compo-nent	Mean Value	Selected Criteria	Selected Factors
01	01	17.8880	Doctors' ask for patients Permission for performing Test	Medical
02			Nurses' Gave Personal Attention to Patients	Paramedical
03			Nurses' Explain Procedures and take Patient Permission before Test	Paramedical
04			Adm. Staff Welcome and Implement Suggestion	Administration
05			Adm. Gives Personal Attention To Patient	Administration
06	02	8.5040	Nurses' Explain Rules Regulation in ward	Paramedical
07			Nurses' were Kind, Gentle and Sympathetic	Paramedical

From Table 7.140 it becomes clear that component 1 (Doctors' ask for patients' Permission for performing Test, Nurses' Gave Personal Attention to Patients, Nurses' Explain Procedures and take Patient Permission before Test, Adm. Staff Welcome and Implement Suggestion, Adm. Gives Personal Attention To Patient) has highest mean value of 17.888 and it extract total 5 Criterion. Component 2 (Nurses' Explain Rules Regulation in ward, Nurses' were Kind, Gentle and Sympathetic) has lowest mean value of 8.504.

Importance of Components for Selected Type of Hospitals

The importance of each component to different Type of Hospitals can be understood with the help of below given box plots. The following box plot explains type of hospitals total score of component 1 Criterion.

Graph 7.43: Hospitals-wise Box Plot for Component 1 for Dignity Criterion of the Three Type of Hospitals

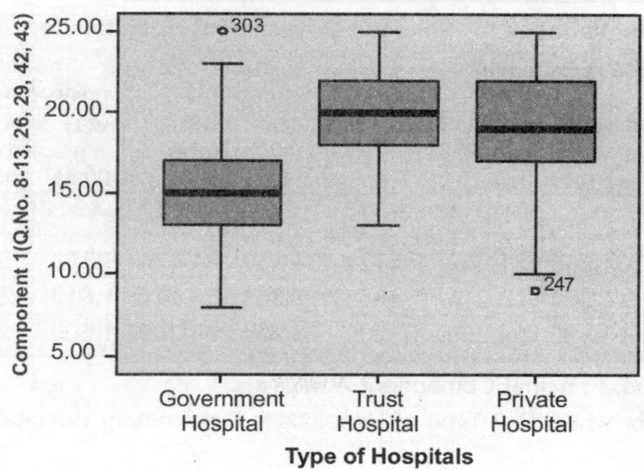

The above box plot of Graph 7.43 indicated that component 1 was important for Trust hospitals because of highest median value and lower variation.

Graph 7.44: Hospitals-wise Box Plot for Component 2 for Dignity Criterion of the Three Type of Hospitals

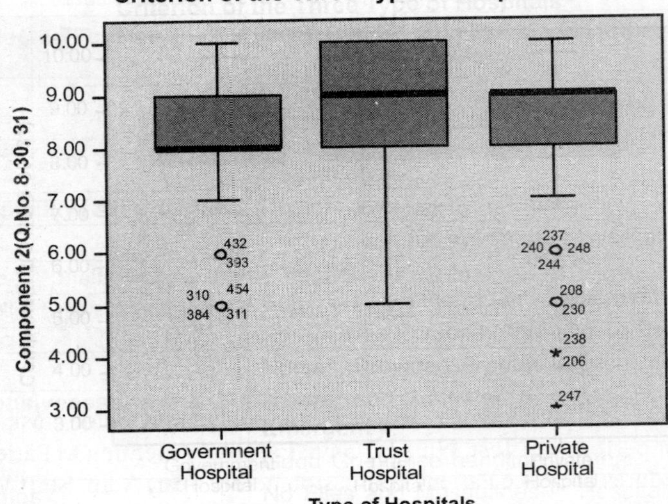

From the above box plot of Graph 7.44 it becomes clear that component 2 was important for private hospital because of large mean value and less variation.

As the mean score of Government hospitals were lower (27.41), the factor analysis was applied to find out the reasons foe lower mean value for Government hospitals.

Factor Analysis for Selected Government Hospitals for Dignity Criterion is given as below.

In case of responses of Government hospitals patients for dignity maintained by hospital staff and the results showed the value of KMO measure of sampling adequacy (0.677) and Bartlett's test of sphericity (0.0) which indicated that factor analysis was appropriate.

Table 7.141: Total Variance for Selected Government Hospitals for Dignity Criterion

Com-ponent	Initial Eigenvalues			Extraction Sums of Squared Loadings			Rotation Sums of Squared Loadings		
	Total	% age of Var-iance	Cumu-lative per cent	Total	% age of Var-iance	Cumu-lative per cent	Total	% age of Var-iance	Cumu-lative per cent
01	2.532	31.650	31.650	2.532	31.650	31.650	1.819	22.733	22.733
02	1.485	18.564	50.214	1.485	18.564	50.214	1.813	22.657	45.391
03	1.120	13.995	64.209	1.120	13.995	64.209	1.505	18.819	64.209

Extraction Method: Principal Component Analysis.

(a) Only cases for which Q 2 Type of Hospitals = Government Hospital are used in the analysis phase.

Table 7.14 indicated that there were 3 components extracted and it explains 64 per cent variation from data.

Table 7.142: Communalities and Rotated Component Matrix for Selected Government Hospitals for Dignity Criterion

Sl. No.	Selected Criteria	Communalities Extraction	Rotated Component		
			1	2	3
01	Doctors' ask for patients Permission for performing Test	0.537	0.685	0.261	-0.005
02	Nurses' Gave Personal Attention to Patients	0.560	0.689	0.291	-0.025
03	Nurses' Explain Procedures and take Patient Permission before Test	0.679	0.815	-0.037	0.113
04	Nurses' Explain Rules Regulation in ward	0.508	0.258	-0.004	0.664
05	Nurses' are Kind, Gentle and Sympathetic	0.660	-0.083	-0.137	0.797
06	Adm. Staff Welcome and Implement Suggestion	0.740	0.312	0.799	-0.063
07	Adm. Gives Personal Attention To Patient	0.794	0.159	0.877	0.028
08	Patients' were Treated With Dignity and Privacy	0.659	-0.122	0.482	0.642

Extraction Method: Principal Component Analysis. Rotation Method: Varimax with Kaiser Normalization.

(a) Rotation converged in 5 iterations.

(b) Only cases for which Q 2 Type of Hospitals = Government Hospital are used in the analysis phase.

All the extracted communalities were acceptable and all Criterion were fit for the factor solution as their extraction values were large.

From Table 7.142 it becomes clear that component 1 (Doctors' ask for patients Permission for performing Test, Nurses' Gave Personal Attention to Patients, Nurses' Explain Procedures and take Patients' Permission before Test) was highly correlated with Criterion number 1 to 3.

Component 2 (Adm. Staff Welcome and Implement Suggestion, Adm. Gives Personal Attention to Patient) was highly correlated with Criterion 6, 7. Component 3 (Nurses' Explain Rules Regulation in ward, Nurses' were Kind, Gentle and Sympathetic, Patients' were Treated with Dignity and Privacy) was highly correlated with Criterion 4, 5, and 8.

Table 7.143: Component wise Mean value for Selected Government Hospitals for Dignity Criterion

Sl. No.	Compo-nent	Mean Value	Selected Criteria	Selected Factors
01	01	11.2140	Doctors' ask for patients Permission for performing Test	Medical
02			Nurses' Gave Personal Attention to Patients	Medical
03			Nurses' Explain Procedures and take Patient Permission before Test	Paramedical
04	02	6.6740	Adm. Staff Welcome and Implement Suggestion	Administration
05			Adm. Gives Personal Attention To Patient	Administration
06	03	12.6560	Nurses' Explain Rules Regulation in ward	Paramedical
07			Nurses' were Kind, Gentle and Sympathetic	Paramedical
08			Patients' were Treated With Dignity and Privacy	Administration

From Table 7.143 it becomes clear that component 3 (Nurses' Explain Rules Regulation in ward, Nurses' were Kind, Gentle and Sympathetic, Patients' were Treated with Dignity and Privacy) have highest mean value of 12.656. Component 2 (Administration Staff Welcome and Implement Suggestion, Administration Staff Gives Personal Attention to Patient) have lowest mean value of 6.674.

It means Government hospitals were found to be weak in component 2. So, Government hospitals need to improve its service with regard to the paramedical staff should Explain Rules Regulation in ward, they should be kind, gentle and sympathetic and should treat patient with dignity and privacy.

ONE WAYANNOVA FOR ACCESSIBILITY/AFFORDABILITY CRITERION

Analysis of Variance: Selected Patients' Responses for Accessibility/Affordability Criterion.

Hypothesis: 28

Mean of patients' responses about selected type of hospital is equal in terms of Accessibility/Affordability Criterion of hospital and an alternative hypothesis is at least one mean is different from other.

Table 7.144: Descriptive Statistics for Accessibility/Affordability Criterion for All the Three Type of Hospitals

Type of Hospitals	N	Mean	SD	SE
GHs	200	21.7500	1.90938	0.13501
THs	200	21.1900	4.06776	0.28763
PHs	100	18.3800	2.93973	0.29397
Total	500	20.8520	3.37058	0.15074

From Table 7.144 it becomes clear that Government hospitals have highest mean value of 21.75. Trust hospitals have second highest mean value of 21.19 and private hospitals have lowest mean value of 18.38.

Test of Homogeneity of Variances

Table 7.145: Test of Homogeneity of Variances for Accessibility/Affordability Criterion for All the Three Type of Hospitals

Levene Statistic	df1	df2	Sig.
176.001	2	497	0.000

P-Value of levene's test statistics as given in Table 7.145 was less then 0.05 type of hospitals is different from other type of hospitals.

Analysis of Variance

Table 7.146: ANOVA for Accessibility/Affordability Criterion for All the Three Type of Hospitals

Particulars	Sum of Squares	df	Mean Square	F	Sig.
Between Groups	795.208	2	397.604	40.545	0.000
Within Groups	4873.840	497	9.807		
Total	5669.048	499			

The P-Value (0.00 < 0.05) of ANOVA table given above indicated that mean of type of hospitals was not equal, at least mean of one type of hospitals was different from other type of hospitals.

Post-Hoc test (Tamhane)

Table 7.147: Multiple Comparisons for Accessibility/Affordability Criterion for All the Three Type of Hospitals Through Tamhane Test

Type of Hospitals		Mean Difference	SE	Sig.
GHs	GHs			
	THs	0.56000	.31774	0.219
	PHs	3.37000	.32349	0.000
THs	GHs	-0.56000	.31774	0.219
	THs			
	PHs	2.81000	.41128	0.000
PHs	GHs	-3.37000	.32349	0.000
	THs	-2.81000	.41128	0.000
	PHs			

From Table 7.147 it becomes clear that Government hospitals were different from Private hospitals but the significant value (0.219) indicated that Government hospitals were not different than trust hospital. Similarly, trust hospitals were not different from Government hospitals but it was different than private hospitals. The private hospitals were different from Government and trust hospitals.

Post-Hoc test (Tukey HSD)

Table 7.148: Multiple Comparisons for Accessibility/Affordability Criterion for All the Three Type of Hospitals Through Tukey HSD Test

Type of Hospitals	N	Subset for alpha = .05	
		1	2
PHs	100	18.3800	
THs	200		21.1900
GHs	200		21.7500
Sig.	1.000	.269	

Means for groups in homogeneous subsets are displayed.

(a) Uses Harmonic Mean Sample Size = 150.000.

(b) The group sizes are unequal. The harmonic mean of the group sizes is used. Type I error levels are not guaranteed.

From Table 7.148 it becomes clear that private hospitals make one group, Government hospitals and trust hospitals makes another group.

Graph 7.45: Means Plots of Type of Hospitals for Accessibility/Affordability Criterion for All the Three Type of Hospitals

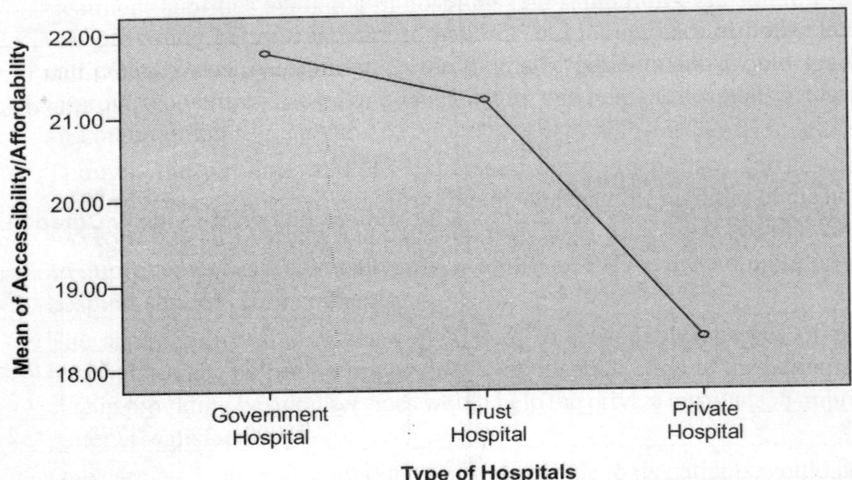

Above means plot of Graph 7.45 indicated that Government hospitals have high mean value. Trust hospital have second highest mean value and private hospitals have lowest mean value.

FACTOR ANALYSIS FOR ACCESSIBILITY/AFFORDABILITY CRITERION

Factor Analysis for Accessibility/Affordability Criterion for All the Three Type of Hospitals is given as below.

In case of responses of patients for accessibility and affordability of hospital services the results showed the value of KMO measure of sampling adequacy (0.696) and Bartlett's test of sphericity (0.0) which indicated that factor analysis was appropriate.

Table 7.149: Total Variance for Accessibility/Affordability Criterion for All the Three Type of Hospitals

Com-ponent	Initial Eigenvalues			Extraction Sums of Squared Loadings			Rotation Sums of Squared Loadings		
	Total	% age of Variance	Cumulative per cent	Total	% age of Variance	Cumulative per cent	Total	% age of Variance	Cumulative per cent
01	2.462	49.232	49.232	2.462	49.232	49.232	1.947	38.940	38.940
02	1.023	20.462	69.693	1.023	20.462	69.693	1.538	30.754	69.693

Extraction Method: Principal Component Analysis.

From Table 7.149 it becomes clear that two components can be extracted and they extract 69.693 per cent variation from data.

Table 7.150: Communalities and Rotated Component Matrix for Accessibility/ Affordability Criterion for All the Three Type of Hospitals

Sl. No.	Selected Criteria	Communalities Extraction	Rotated Component	
			1	2
01	Doctors' Availability in Emergency	0.498	0.259	0.657
02	Quick Payment Arrangements	0.788	-0.006	0.887
03	Costs were Adequate or Affordable	0.806	0.884	0.158
04	Drugs Easily Obtained in Hospital	0.597	0.560	0.533
05	Distance to Healthcare is Adequate	0.795	0.886	0.099

Extraction Method: Principal Component Analysis. Rotation Method: Varimax with Kaiser Normalization.
a Rotation converged in 3 iterations.

All the extracted communnalities given in Table 7.150 were acceptable and all Criterion wee fit for the factor solution as their extraction values were large.

Table 7.150 indicated the correlation between component and Criterion. Component 1 (Costs were Adequate or Affordable, Drugs Easily Obtained in Hospital, Distance to Healthcare is Adequate) was highly correlated with Criterion number 3, 4, and 5. Component 2 (Doctors' Availability in Emergency, Quick Payment Arrangements) was highly correlated with Criterion number 1, 2. *(Refer Table 7.151)*

From Table 7.151 below it becomes clear that component 1 (Costs were Adequate or Affordable, Drugs Easily Obtained in Hospital, Distance to Healthcare is Adequate) has highest mean value of 12.166 and it extracted total 3 Criterion. Component 2 (Doctors' Availability in Emergency, Quick Payment Arrangements) has lowest mean value of 8.686.

Table 7.151: Component wise Mean Value for Accessibility/Affordability Criterion for All the Three Type of Hospitals

Sl. No.	Compo-nent	Mean Value	Selected Criteria	Selected Factors
01	01	12.1660	Costs were Adequate or Affordable	Environment
02			Drugs Easily Obtained in Hospital	Environment
03			Distance to Healthcare is Adequate	Environment
04	02	8.6860	Doctors' Availability in Emergency	Medical
05			Quick Payment Arrangements	Environment

Importance of Components for Selected Type of Hospitals

The importance of each component to different type of hospitals can be understood with the help of below given box plots. The following box plot (Graph 7.46) explains type of hospitals total score of component 1 (Environment) Criterion.

Graph 7.46: Hospitals-wise Box Plot for Component 1 for Accessibility/Affordability Criterion of the Three Type of Hospitals

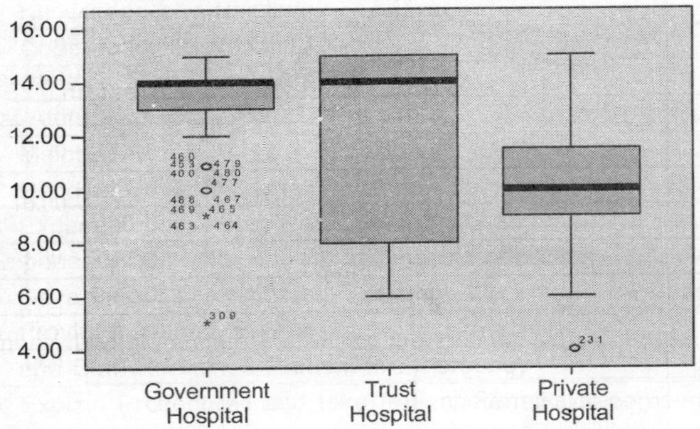

The above box plot (Graph 7.46) indicated that component 1 was important for Government hospitals because of highest median value and lower variation. Trust hospitals have similar median value but it has more variations.

From the box plot of Graph 7.47 it becomes clear that component 2 was important for trust hospitals because of large mean value and less variation.

As the mean score of private hospitals were lower (18.38) factor analysis was made to find out the reasons for lower mean value for private hospitals.

Factor Analysis for Selected Private Hospitals for Accessibility/Affordability Criterion is given as below.

In case of responses of private hospitals patients for accessibility and affordability of hospital services the results showed the value of KMO measure of sampling adequacy

Graph 7.47: Hospitals-wise Box Plot for Component 2 for Accessibility/ Affordability Criterion of the Three Type of Hospitals

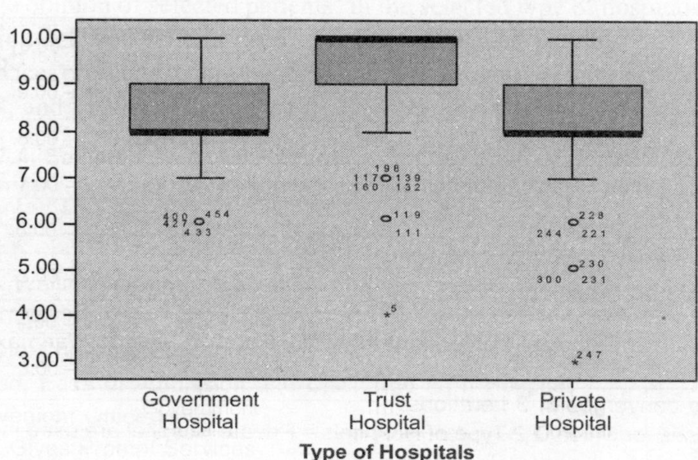

(0.690) and Bartlett's test of sphericity (0.0) which indicated that factor analysis was appropriate.

Table 7.152: Total Variance for Selected Private Hospitals for Accessibility/ Affordability Criterion

Component	Initial Eigenvalues			Extraction Sums of Squared Loadings			Rotation Sums of Squared Loadings		
	Total	% age of Variance	Cumulative per cent	Total	% age of Variance	Cumulative per cent	Total	% age of Variance	Cumulative per cent
01	2.066	41.313	41.313	2.066	41.313	41.313			
02	1.004	20.078	61.391	1.004	20.078	61.391			

Extraction Method: Principal Component Analysis.

(a) Only cases for which Q 2 Type of Hospitals = Private Hospital are used in the analysis phase.

Table 7.152 indicated that there were 2 components extracted and it explains 61.391 per cent variation from data.

All the extracted communalities were acceptable and all Criterion were fit for the factor solution as their extraction values were large.

From Table 7.153 below it becomes clear that component 1 (Doctors' Availability in Emergency, Quick Payment Arrangements, Drugs Easily Obtained in Hospital) was highly correlated with Criterion number 1, 2, and 4. Component 2 (Costs were Adequate or Affordable, Distance to Healthcare is Adequate) was highly correlated with Criterion number 3, and 5.

Table 7.153: Communalities and Rotated Component Matrix for Selected PrivateHospitals for Accessibility/Affordability Criterion

Sl. No.	Selected Criteria	Communa-lities Extraction	Rotated Component	
			1	2
01	Doctors' Availability in Emergency	0.560	0.654	0.363
02	Quick Payment Arrangements	0.614	0.771	0.143
03	Costs were Adequate or Affordable	0.619	0.263	0.741
04	Drugs Easily Obtained in Hospital	0.592	0.769	-0.032
05	Distance to Healthcare is Adequate	0.684	-0.010	0.827

Extraction Method: Principal Component Analysis. Rotation Method: Varimax with Kaiser Normalization.

(a) Rotation converged in 3 iterations.

(b) Only cases for which Q 2 Type of Hospitals = Private Hospital are used in the analysis phase.

Table 7.154: Component-wise Mean Value for Selected Private Hospitals for Accessibility/Affordability Criterion

Sl. No.	Compo-nent	Mean Value	Selected Criteria	Selected Factors
01	01	12.1660	Costs were Adequate or Affordable	Environment
02			Drugs Easily Obtained in Hospital	Environment
03			Distance to Healthcare is Adequate	Environment
04	02	8.6860	Doctors' Availability in Emergency	Medical
05			Quick Payment Arrangements	Environment

From Table 7.154 it becomes clear that component 1 (Doctors' Availability in Emergency, Quick Payment Arrangements, Drugs Easily Obtained in Hospital) have highest mean value of 12.166. Component 2 (Costs were Adequate or Affordable, Distance to Healthcare is Adequate) have lowest mean value of 8.686. It means private hospitals are weak in component 2. So, private hospitals need to improve its service in terms of availability of doctors in emergency and speedy payment arrangement in the hospital.

SUMMARY OF FACTOR LOADING SCORE FOR INTANGIBLE SERVICES CHARACTERISTICS

Summary of factor analysis for tangibles, reliability, responsiveness, assurance, empathy, dignity, and accessibility/affordability Criterion of the hospital is summarized in Table 7.155 to Table 7.161.

Table 7.155: Criterion and Factor wise Factor Loading for Tangible Criterion

Sl. No.	Selected Criteria	Selected Factors			
		Medical Services	Param-edical Serv-ices	Admin-istrative Service	Enviro-nment (Physical) Facilities
		Factor Loading score			
01	Sufficient Doctors Remain Present	0.468	-	-	-
02	Well Equipped Units	-	-	-	0.592
03	Proper Sitting and Bedding Arrangements	-	-	-	0.541
04	Comfort in Examination and waiting Room	-	-	-	0.627
05	Natural Light or Illumination in Hospital	-	-	-	0.709
06	Sufficient Number of Dust Bins and Spittoons	-	-	-	0.715
07	No Flies and Mosquitoes in Hospital	-	-	-	0.657
08	Adequate parking Arrangements	-	-	-	0.513
09	Clean Surroundings of Hospitals	-	-	-	0.478
10	Pleasing and Appealing Room of Hospital	-	-	-	0.568
11	Good Food Served by Hospital	-	-	-	0.854
12	Staff Neat in Appearance	-	-	-	0.623
13	Inside and Out side Noise kept Minimum	-	-	-	0.617
14	Wards Well Decorated and Ventilated	-	-	-	0.442
15	Music Facilities should be provided	-	-	-	0.712

Table 7.155 gives details about factor loading score for all 15 criteria related with tangible criterion of hospital. Out of total 15 Criterion 12 criteria can be considered as important as their score is more than 0.5.

Table 7.156: Criterion and Factor wise Factor Loading for Reliability Criterion

Sl. No.	Selected Criteria	Selected Factors			
		Medical Services	Param-edical Serv-ices	Admini-strative Service	Environ-ment (Physical) Facilities
		Factor Loading score			
01	Impartial Attitude of Doctors	0.710	-	-	-
02	Doctors' Makes Good Diagnosis	0.889	-	-	-
03	Doctors' Prescribed Good Drugs	0.853	-	-	-
04	Impartial Attitude of Nurses	-	0.862	-	-
05	Nurses' Maintain Proper records of Patients	-	0.635	-	-

Table 7.156 gives details about factor loading score for all 5 criteria related with Reliability Criterion of hospital, and all Criteria can be considered as important as their score is more than 0.5.

Table 7.157: Criterion and Factor wise Factor Loading for Responsiveness Criterion

Sl. No.	Selected Criteria	Selected Factors			
		Medical Services	Para-medical Services	Admini-strative Service	Environ-ment (Physical) Facilities
		Factor Loading score			
01	Doctors' Cooperation to patients	0.621	-	-	-
02	Patients' Felt Comfortable asking Questions to Doctors	0.868	-	-	-
03	Nurses' Cooperation to Patients	-	0.777	-	-
04	Nurses' Provide Prompt Service	-	0.766	-	-
05	Nurses' and Staff Remains Present in Emergency	-	0.668	-	-
06	Information Provided to patients for Managing Side Effects	-	0.543	-	-
07	Prompt Service Provided by Sanitation Staff	-	0.568	-	-
08	Less Waiting Time For Consultation and Treatment	-	-	0.707	-
09	Less Waiting Time for Test	-	-	0.660	-
10	Speed, Ease of Admission and Discharge form Hospital	-	-	0.612	-
11	Convenient Office Hours	-	-	0.732	-
12	Adm. Staff Gives Prompt Services	-	-	0.574	-
13	No Overcrowding in Hospital	-	-	0.678	-
14	Good Grievance handling System	-	-	0.614	-

Table 7.157 gives details about factor loading score for all 14 criteria related with Responsiveness of hospital. All criteria can be considered as important as their score is more than 0.5.

Table 7.158: Criterion and Factor wise Factor Loading for Assurance Criterion

Sl. No.	Selected Criteria	Selected Factors			
		Medical Services	Para-medical Services	Admini-strative Service	Environ-ment (Physical) Facilities
		Factor Loading score			
01	Doctors' Knowledge and Efficiency	0.647	-	-	-
02	Doctors' Experience in Curing Patients	0.856	-	-	-
03	Thorough Checkup by Doctors	0.790	-	-	-
04	Nurses' Knowledge and Efficiency	-	0.720	-	-
05	Nurses' Handled Patients Quarry Properly	-	0.736	-	-
06	Nurses' Experience in Curing Patients	-	0.731	-	-
07	Good Experience of Those who Perform Test on Patients	-	0.661	-	-

Table 7.158 gives details about factor loading score for all 7 Criterion related with Assurance Criterion of hospital. All Criterion can be considered as important as their score is more than 0.5.

Table 7.159: Criterion and Factor wise Factor Loading for Empathy Criterion

Sl. No.	Selected Criteria	Selected Factors			
		Medical Services	Para-medical Services	Admini-strative Service	Environ-ment (Physical) Facilities
		Factor Loading score			
01	Doctors' were polite with patients	0.795	-	-	-
02	Patients' Felt Comfortable During Doctors Examination	0.641	-	-	-
03	Doctors' Work According to Patients Expectations	0.843	-	-	-
04	Doctors' Give Individual Consideration and Confidentiality	0.834	-	-	-
05	Doctors' Show Respect and Support patients	0.563	-	-	-
06	Doctors' Honesty in Dealing with patients	0.689	-	-	-
07	Nurses' Showed Politeness with Patients	-	0.453	-	-
08	Simple Checking Procedure	-	-	0.772	-
09	Good Concern for Patients' Family and Visitor	-	-	0.769	-
10	Simple Billing Procedures	-	-	0.794	-

Table 7.159 gives details about factor loading score for all 10 criteria related with Empathy Criterion of hospital. Out of total 10 criteria 9 criteria can be considered as important as their score is more than 0.5.

Table 7.160: Criterion and Factor wise Factor Loading for Dignity Criterion

Sl. No.	Selected Criteria	Selected Factors			
		Medical Services	Para-medical Services	Admini-strative Service	Environ-ment (Physical) Facilities
		Factor Loading score			
01	Doctors' ask for patients Permission for performing Test	0.687	-	-	-
02	Nurses' Gave Personal Attention to Patients	-	0.555	-	-
03	Nurses' Explain Procedures and take Patient Permission before Test	-	0.522	-	-
04	Nurses' Explain Rules Regulation in ward	-	0.778	-	-
05	Nurses' were Kind, Gentle and Sympathetic	-	0.826	-	-
06	Adm. Staff Welcome and Implement Suggestion	-	-	0.883	-
07	Adm. Gives Personal Attention To Patient	-	-	0.821	-
08	Patient Treated With Dignity and Privacy	-	-	0.487	-

Table 7.160 gives details about factor loading score for all 8 criteria related with Dignity expressed by staff of hospital. Out of total 8 criteria 7 criteria can be considered as important as their score is more than 0.5.

Table 7.161: Criterion and Factor wise Factor Loading for Accessibility/ Affordability Criterion

Sl. No.	Selected Criteria	Selected Factors			
		Medical Services	Para-medical Services	Admini-strative Service	Environ-ment (Physical) Facilities
		Factor Loading score			
01	Doctors' Easily Available in Emergency	0.657	-	-	-
02	Quick Payment Arrangements	-	-	-	0.887
03	Costs were Adequate or Affordable	-	-	-	0.884
04	Drugs Easily Obtained in Hospital	-	-	-	0.560
05	Distance to Healthcare is Adequate	-	-	-	0.886

Table 7.161 gives details about factor loading score for all 5 Criterion related with Accessibility/Affordability Criterion of hospital. All criteria can be considered as important as their score is more than 0.5.

So, out of total 64 criteria used to measure patient satisfaction, total 59 criteria have factor loading score more than 0.5.

8

Conclusion and Suggestions of the Research Study

MAJOR FINDINGS OF THE RESEARCH STUDY

The research study demonstrated that such efforts for conducting research could help the hospitals in identifying service characteristics that are considered important by patients. Such findings are more important for hospitals service providers as study showed that reliability, with mean score 4.42, is the most important of other dimensions of service quality followed by assurance, with mean score of 4.26, is second important factor; tangible facilities, with mean score of 4.23, is third important factor; empathy, with mean score of 4.20, is the fourth factor; accessibility and affordability, with mean score of 4.17, is the fifth factor; responsiveness, with mean score 3.92, is sixth factor; and dignity, with mean score of 3.82, is seventh factor.

These results, when considered collectively implies an important message from patients to hospital managers, that is, be reliable by providing consistent services and provide assurance by showing knowledge and courtesy in developing trust and confidence in patients; be positive in providing good tangible facilities; express empathy by caring and giving individualized attention to patients; make the hospital services more accessible and affordable by charging reasonable rates; be responsive by providing prompt services; and treat patients with dignity and respect.

Further, the research study has also identified the important findings and important criteria which need improvement in different types of hospitals.

Table 8.1 gives details about six important criteria which patients' have considered important for Government hospitals for expressing their satisfaction with hospital services availed by them.

Table 8.2 gives details about 21 important criteria which patients' considered as important ones and further improvement in performance of the Government hospitals.

Table 8.1: Summary of Important Criteria for Government Hospitals

Sl. No.	Selected Factors	Important Criteria
01	**Affordability** - Important	Patients' Own Decision Reasons for Selection of Hospital
		Hospital Located Nearby
		Hospital is economical
02	**Accessibility/Affordability**	Costs were Adequate or Affordable
		Drugs Easily Obtained in Hospital
		Distance to Healthcare is Adequate

Table 8.2: Summary of Criteria Needs Improvement for Government Hospitals

Sl. No.	Selected Factors	Important Criteria that Needs Improvement
01	**Dignity**	Doctors' ask for patients Permission for performing Test
		Patients' were Treated With Dignity and Privacy
		Administration Staff Welcome and Implement Suggestion
		Administration Staff Gives Personal Attention to Patient
02	**Accessibility / Affordability**	Doctors' Availability in Emergency
03	**Responsiveness**	Patients' Felt Comfortable asking Questions to Doctors
		Nurses' Provide Prompt Service
		Nurses' and Staff Remains Present in Emergency
		Nurses' Cooperation to Patients
		Prompt Service Provided by Sanitation Staff
		No Overcrowding in Hospital
		Good Grievance handling System
		Doctors' Cooperation to patients
04	**Tangibles**	Sufficient Doctors Remain Present
		Adequate parking Arrangements
		Good Food Served by Hospital
05	**Assurance**	Good Experience of Those who Perform Test on Patients
06	**Empathy**	Good Concern for Patients' Family and Visitor
		Simple Billing Procedures
07	**Reliability**	Doctors' Made Good Diagnosis
		Doctors' Prescribed Good Drugs

Table 8.3: Summary of Important Criteria for Trust Hospitals

Sl. No.	Selected Factors	Important Criteria
01	**Reference /Suggestion -** Important Reasons for Selection of Hospital	Suggested by Relatives
		Suggested by Friends
02	**Sanitation** - Important Reasons for Selection of Hospital	Sanitation of the Hospital
03	**Empathy**	Simple Checking Procedure
		Good Concern for Patient Family and Visitor
		Simple Billing Procedures
04	**Dignity**	Nurses' Gave Personal Attention to Patients
		Nurses' Explain Procedures and take Patient Permission before Test
		Patients' were Treated With Dignity and Privacy
05	**Tangibles**	Sufficient Doctors' Remained Present
		Comfort in Examination and waiting Room
		Natural Light or Illumination in Hospital
		Sufficient Number of Dust Bins and Spittoons
		Pleasing and Appealing Room of Hospital
		Good Food Served by Hospital
		Staff Neat in Appearance
		Well Equipped Units
		Proper Sitting and Bedding Arrangements
		Inside and Out side Noise kept Minimum
		Wards Well Decorated and Ventilated
		Music Facilities should be provided
		Adequate parking Arrangements
		Good Food Served by Hospital
06	**Accessibility /Affordability**	Quick Payment Arrangements
07	**Assurance**	Nurses' Handled Patients Query Properly
08	**Responsiveness**	Information Provided to patients for Managing Side Effects
		Less Waiting Time For Consultation and Treatment
		Less Waiting Time for Test
		Speed, Ease of Admission and Discharge form Hospital
		Convenient Office Hours
		Adm. Staff Gives Prompt Services

Table 8.3 gives details about 31 important criteria which patients' have considered important for trust hospitals to express their satisfaction with hospital services availed by them.

Table 8.4: Summary of Criteria Needs Improvement for Trust Hospitals

Sl. No.	Selected Factors	Important Criteria that Needs Improvement
01	**Empathy**	Doctors' Work According to Patients Expectations
		Doctors' Gave Individual Consideration and Confidentiality
02	**Accessibility / Affordability**	Doctors' Availability in Emergency
03	**Dignity**	Doctors' ask for patients Permission for performing Test
		Adm. Staff Welcome and Implement Suggestion
		Adm. Gives Personal Attention To Patient
04	**Responsiveness**	Nurses' Provided Prompt Service
		Nurses' and Staff Remains Present in Emergency
		Good Grievance handling System
05	**Tangibles**	No Flies and Mosquitoes in Hospital

Table 8.4 gives details about 10 important criteria which patients' have considered important ones and further improvement in performance of the trust hospitals.

Table 8.5: Summary of Important Criteria for Private Hospitals

Sl. No.	Selected Factors	Important Criteria that Needs Improvement
01	**Performance** - Important Reasons for Selection of Hospital	Past performance of Hospital / Doctor
		Overall Reputation of Hospital
		Only in this Hospital such kind of facility is available
02	**Sanitation** - Important Reasons for Selection of Hospital	Sanitation in the Hospital
03	**Assurance**	Doctors' Knowledge and Efficiency
		Thorough Checkup by Doctors
		Nurses' Experience in Curing Patients
04	**Responsiveness**	Doctors' Cooperation to patients
		Patients' Felt Comfortable asking Questions to Doctors
		Nurses' Cooperation to Patients
		Prompt Service Provided by Sanitation Staff

...(Contd.)

...(Contd.)

Sl. No.	Selected Factors	Important Criteria that Needs Improvement
05	**Empathy**	Doctors' were polite with patients
		Nurses' Showed Politeness with Patients
06	**Reliability**	Doctors' Makes Good Diagnosis
		Doctors' Prescribed Good Drugs
		Impartial Attitude of Nurses
07	**Dignity**	Nurses' were Kind, Gentle and Sympathetic
08	**Tangible**	Adequate parking Arrangements
		Good Food Served by Hospital

Table 8.5 gives details about 19 important criteria which patients' have considered important for private hospitals to express their satisfaction with hospital services availed by them.

Table 8.6: Summary of Criteria Needs Improvement for Private Hospitals

Sl. No.	Selected Factors	Important Criteria that Needs Improvement
01	**Affordability -** Important Reasons for Selection of Hospital	Hospital Located Nearby
		Hospital is economical
02	**Accessibility/Affordability**	Costs were Adequate or Affordable
		Distance to Healthcare is Adequate
		Availability of doctors in emergency
		Speedy payment arrangement in the hospital
03	**Reliability**	Impartial Attitude of Doctors
04	**Empathy**	Patients' Felt Comfortable During Doctors Examination
		Simple Checking Procedure
		Simple Billing Procedures
05	**Assurance**	Doctors' Experience in Curing Patients
		Nurses' Knowledge and Efficiency
06	**Responsiveness**	Information Provided to patients for Managing Side Effects
		Speed, Ease of Admission and Discharge form Hospital
07	**Tangibles**	Proper Sitting and Bedding Arrangements
		Wards Well Decorated and Ventilated

Table 8.6 gives details about 16 important criteria which patients' have considered important ones and further improvement in performance of the private hospitals.

IMPLICATIONS OF THE RESEARCH STUDY

The results of this research study indicated that a high degree of variance in selected patients' satisfaction with regard to hospital services that were delivered to them in terms of different characteristics of services. These characteristics were related with quality of care and needs due recognition by all involved in the process of providing healthcare services.

The overall implications of this research study for GHs, THs, and PHs are given as follows:

Implications of Research Study for GHs

- The patients of GHs appeared to be more concerned with the accessibility and affordability of services which included three major criteria, namely, nearby location of hospital; economy, and easy availability of drugs. This provides an understanding to the GHs that nearby location, economy and easy availability of drugs are the criteria which have greater impact on attracting the patients in the hospitals. Hence, with due recognitions to these criteria, the GHs should be able to attract and maintain the regular flow of patients in the GHs.
- But, still variations in GHs patients' responses were observed and patients rated some characteristics of service delivery as poor, which needs improvement because GHs carries adverse implications on ability of GHs to provide satisfactory services to its patients.
- The first characteristic which needs improvement is related with dignity to be maintained by GHs while dealing with patients, which included two criteria, viz., patients should be treated by doctors with dignity by maintaining privacy and convincing patients before performing any kind of test on the patients. Less recognition to these two criteria have an adverse impact on impressions patients have developed in their minds about doctors of GHs. Hence, it gave an understanding that maintaining dignity with patients by ensuring privacy with patients and convincing patients before performing tests on them, would help in developing positive impression for GHs. Further, administrative staff of the GHs would be able to create positive impression in the minds of patients by giving personal attention and by welcoming them and through implementing their good suggestions.
- Other characteristics for which patients of GHs have reported unfavorably are accessibility / availability of doctors in emergency. The non-availability of doctors in emergency causes an adverse impact on level of satisfaction of patients. Hence, the due recognitions in making doctors' availability in emergency at the GHs would help it in improving the level of patients' satisfaction.
- Other characteristics for which patients' of GHs reported unfavorably was responsiveness criterion that affects the patients' positive word of mouth in favour of GHs. The selected criteria viz., the doctors' cooperation and making

patients comfortable while asking questions; easy availability of nurses in emergency; prompt service by nursing and sanitation staff; no overcrowding and good grievance handling system reflects a proper responsiveness of hospital and would be able to create a positive word of mouth amongst the patients' GHs.

- For the tangible facilities, amongst the patients' of the GHs reported adversely in some of the criteria that had a direct impact on level of comfort felt by the patients. The good quality of food; parking arrangements, and regular availability of doctors should certainly increase the level of comfort of patients and would act as key inputs in improving the level of patients' satisfaction.
- The assurance on the experience of people performing tests on the patients causes an impact on trust and confidence of patients on hospital services, hence the due recognition on training of people who perform such tests on patients would help in not only winning their trust and confidence, but would affect the patients' post-behaviour.
- The empathy as experienced by patients of the GHs appeared to be capable of improving the patients' satisfaction by showing good concern for patients' family members and visitors; by developing simple billing procedures, and by removing the complexity in the hospital procedure.
- The responses of patients for reliability criterion of the GHs have an impact not only on patients' future visits in the GHs but also on the patients' intention to recommend GHs to others in future. So, due recognition by doctors in diagnosing the patients' diseases, and in prescribing good drugs would help in strengthening reliability criterion for the GHs amongst the patients.

Implications of Research Study for THs

- The patients' of THs appeared to be more concerned with the references or recommendations made by their friends and relatives for availing hospital services from THs. So, this provides an understanding to the THs that by providing good overall services to patients, the hospital would be able to get more patients based on references provided by its satisfied patients.
- But, still variation in THs patients' responses was observed. Though, compared to GHs, the THs patients showed better responses for criteria viz., empathy, dignity, tangible facilities, accessibility and affordability, assurance and responsiveness of hospital services, but, still variation in trust hospital patients' responses were observed and patients' rated some characteristics of service delivery as poor which needed improvement as it causes an adverse impact on ability of THs to provide satisfactory hospital services to its patients.
- The patients' feedback on empathy criterion experienced by them in case of the THs calls for an improvement in the delivery of patients' satisfaction with regard to maintaining confidentiality, giving individual consideration to patients and putting efforts to meet patients' expectations.

- Due recognition in making doctors' availability in emergency would help the THs in improving patients' satisfaction.
- The research study provided an understanding, based on confirmatory evidence, that maintaining dignity with patients of trust hospitals, with regard to convincing the patients by doctors before applying tests on them; and also giving personal attention on them by welcoming and implementing patients' suggestions by administrative staff, would help in creating positive impression for THs.
- The responsiveness of paramedical service providers in terms of providing prompt services and remaining present in emergency can be helpful to THs in creating a positive word of mouth amongst the patients.
- For the tangible facilities in the trust hospitals, the patients reported unfavourably with regard to presence of flies and mosquitoes in the THs. So due care must be taken by the THs.

Implications of Research Study for PHs

- The patients of PHs appeared to be more concerned with the past performance of hospitals and doctors; reputation of hospital; kind of specific medical treatment facilities available in hospitals and sanitation of hospital. It means that providing better treatment to patients and taking care of house keeping can create a positive opinion in the minds of patients and would gradually improve reputation of hospitals, which in turn will help the hospitals in attracting and maintaining regular flow of patients in PHs.
- Though, the patients of PHS expressed better responses for assurance, responsiveness, empathy, reliability, dignity and tangible facilities of the hospital services, but, still variation in patients' responses were observed that calls for an improvement as it adversely affects ability of PHs in providing satisfactory hospital services to its patients.
- The accessibility of services with regard to reasonable charges of private hospitals can be helpful in improving level of satisfaction of the patients. Due care in providing hospital services would help the private hospitals in improving patients' satisfaction.
- Due care by doctors in showing impartial attitude to its patients would help in developing feeling of reliability about hospital services amongst the patients and it would further lead to recommendation of PHs by patients to others.
- The empathy experienced by patients from the service provider in the PHs appeared to be capable to improve the level of patients' satisfaction with regard to making patients felt comfortable during doctors' examinations; simple checking and billing procedures.
- The assurance on the experience of doctors and paramedical staff and their knowledge and efficiency in performing their duty has positive impact on trust and confidence of patients on hospital services of PHs. Hence, the due

recognition by doctors and nurses in utilizing their experience and in enhancing their knowledge and efficiency would be helpful not only in winning trust of patients but, it would also affect the patients' future intention in visiting hospital again for illness in future ass the case may be.

- The responsiveness of paramedical staff in providing information to patients about side effects of treatment provided; and responsiveness of administrative staff in developing speedy, easy procedure for admission and discharge of patients from PHs, would help the PHs in creating the positive word of mouth in favour of PHs.

CONCLUSIONS

The earlier concept of hospital was giving importance to traditional custodian functions but today the hospital is recognized as a social institution as the today's customers considered to be critical and enthusiastic towards high standard quality of services. The only reason for existence of hospital is patient who needs services which should be reasonably and readily available at all the times, and such patients' needs should become a focal point in the rapidly changing dynamic environment. In such a situation, hospitals should strive for providing maximum satisfaction to patients and show patient-orientation in providing services as it shall provides confidence to them in facing the diseases. To become successful the hospitals', healthcare organizations, should monitor patients' perceptions about the hospital services to improve hospital's performance.

The hospital management should use identified areas of concern and plan its action plan in a right direction. There would not be any scope to improve the hospital services unless such bold steps of measuring patients' satisfaction are perused. Repeating study related with measuring patients' satisfaction will always be useful guide for managerial intervention in the hospitals.

SUGGESTIONS

An attempt has been made by the researcher to list out suggestions that have evolved for the GHs, THs, and PHs as follows:

Suggestions for GHs

- In terms of doctors' behaviour there is a need to make efforts to improve for availability of doctors in emergency and doctors should take patients in to confidence before applying any test in the GHs.
- In case of behaviour of paramedical staff, there exist a need that nurses in should provide prompt service and should remain present in emergency.
- There is a need for GHs to improve various services provided to patients viz., treating patients with dignity and marinating privacy, showing good concern to wards patients' family and visitors' and simplification of billing settlement procedures.

- The doctors of GHs should improve its performance in making diagnosis of patients' illness and prescribe good drugs to patients.
- The GHs should improve its service in terms of ensuring that there should be no overcrowding in the hospital; the grievance and complaints of the patients should be handled properly; better cooperation and prompt services from nursing staff; cooperation from doctors to patients; and free environment in which patients feel comfortable to ask questions to doctors.
- The staff of the GHs' should improve its performance while performing tests on the patients.
- The GHs should improve its service in terms empathy criterion by focusing more on developing simple checking procedures, good concern for patient family and visitor and simple billing procedures.
- The GHs should improve its service in terms of maintaining dignity with patients while dealing with patients by focusing more on the paramedical staff should explain rules regulation in ward, they should be kind, gentle and sympathetic and should treat patient with dignity and privacy.

Suggestions for PHs

- The PHs should try to reduce the charges/fees charged and should also be helpful to its patients by providing regular ambulance facilities or by selecting a location of hospital in the city where people can easily make the approach of PHs.
- There is a need for PHs to make proper sitting and bedding arrangements and make the wards more decorated with proper ventilation. This is because people consider PHs as less economical, compared to GHs and THs.
- The PHs should improve its service in terms of availability of doctors in emergency and speedy payment arrangement in the hospital.
- In terms of reliability of hospital services, the doctors of the PHs should have impartial attitude towards its patients.
- The PHs should show empathy while dealing with its patients by focusing on variables such as; doctors' makes their patients feel comfortable during doctors' examination. PHs should also develop simple checking procedure and simple billing procedures.
- The doctors of the PHs should project their experience in curing patients. There is also need for PHs to appoint knowledgeable and efficient nurses or provide training to nurses for increasing their knowledge and improve their efficiency.
- There is a need for PHs to provide information to patients for managing side effects, and also improve in terms of speed, ease of admission and discharge form PHs.
- The PHs should have proper sitting and bedding arrangements, and wards should be well decorated and ventilated.

Suggestions for THs

- The THS should ensure that there should not be files and mosquitoes in THs.
- There is a need for the THs to ensure that their nursing staff should provide prompt services, nurses and staff remains present in emergency, and should also have good grievance handling system.
- The dignity of the patients should be maintained and there is a need for THs to ensure that their doctors' ask their patient's permission for performing test on them. Further, administration staff of hospital should give personal attention to patients and welcome and implement the patients' suggestion for providing better administrative services to patients.
- The doctors of the THs should remain available during emergency.
- The doctors of the THs should work according to patients' expectations and as far as possible give individual consideration to patients and maintain confidentiality in dealing with patients.

PATIENTS' SUGGESTIONS FOR HOSPITAL SERVICES

An attempt has been made by the researcher to list out suggestions given by the patients' of the GHs, THs, and PHs as follows.

Patients' Suggestions for PHs

- Patients' suggested that the PHs should make provision for adequate lights and fans at waiting place in the hospitals.
- The PHs should prefer larger buildings where more assistant doctors can be accommodated in parity with rush of patients.
- It should charge reasonably with the in house facilities of tests and X-rays in the PHs.
- It should provide in house facilities of food to persons accompanying patients in the PHs.
- An improvement in overall medical treatment and services provided by the nurses is needed in the PHs.
- The PHs should provide information relating to estimated expenses of medical treatment and other charges like lodging/boarding etc before hand to patients.
- A courteous behaviour of staff of hospital with visitors; economic charges; facilities for night halts for persons accompanying the patients should be considered by the PHs.
- The patients' expected that the PHs should ascertain satisfactory services from doctor and its staff while providing treatment as well as such services should be provided at concessional rates with easy payment scheme for needy patients.
- The resident doctors need to overcome the inefficiency and ineffectiveness by following the instructions of the specialist doctors in case of PHs.

- The PHs should charge reasonably for its treatment provided to the patients not covered under medic-claim policy.
- The PHs should have clean and airy ambience with enough sunlight in the hospital.
- The patients need pollution free and noiseless environment of the hospital, so that patients will be free from disturbances in the PHs.
- The patients' of the PHs expect lesser congestion and provision for adequate sunlight and air circulation in the PHs.
- The PHs should ensure that its staff should be well informed through proper communication of instructions to the staff from doctors.
- The patients' found that the PHs should refrain from common pitfalls such as lack of facilities in spite higher charges; long waiting; unwanted treatment in view of ignorance of patients.
- The PHs should provide satisfactory treatment while sanitary conditions should be made satisfactory.
- The request made by patients of the PHs with regard to more persons should be allowed together to visit patients during visiting hours.
- No health related experiments should be made on patients by doctors of the PHs.
- The PHs should always bear in mind that, patients are God and they should be treated with enough care and due respect.
- The patients of the PHs wanted staff to be decent and soft spoken.
- The patients of the PHs expect hospitals to be green and carry pleasant premises.
- The hospital rooms of the PHs should ensure proper air ventilation.
- The patients of the PHs found two difficulties that are disturbance of medical representative and lack of facilities for keeping luggage. So, PHs should predetermine visiting hours for medical representatives and provide adequate facilities for keeping luggage.

Patients Suggestions for THs

- The THs should have liberal monetary terms for patients.
- There is a need for training of the hospital staff for better human relations with patients as well as with visitors in case of the THs.
- The THs should recruit/hire more qualified and efficient resident doctors apart from external doctors.
- The THs should ensure timely checkup and treatment of patients by doctors.
- The frequency of visit of specialist doctors in the THs should be increased,
- As some of the THs are located far from city, so the THs should make arrangement of transportation for its patients.

- Administration of the THs needs improvement.
- The THs should provide instructions to patients in Hindi or vernacular language, so that they can understand it easily.
- The facilities regarding breakfast, lunch and dinner to patient as well as for the relatives of the patients should be provided economically by the THs.
- The THs should provide permission to visit the patient till late in the night as relatives being businessmen, get time only at night.
- There exists need for good parking facility in case of THs.
- The THs should employ adequate number of doctors and other staff so that, the right time treatment will be made available to patient.
- The facilities viz., news papers; lift and liftmen; tea and lunch for the patients and visitors should be provided in the THs.
- The need for change of bed sheets of good quality twice a day for which hospital may charge fees from the patients, should be improved and introduced in case of the THs.
- Sufficient quantity of food should be provided to the patients of the THs.
- Urine pots should be provided separately to the needy patients in the THs.
- Patients suggested for single window concept for providing treatment for all diseases; and also requested for two to three attendants for patient by the THs.
- The THs should make provision for facility of music for relaxation and peace of mind.
- The THs should make provision for separate ways for entry and exit.
- The THs should provide clean bathroom with acid and pheneil and keep pheneil tablets in bathrooms.
- The water cooler of the hospitals should be cleaned frequently in case of the THs.
- Proper arrangement should be made for parking vehicles in the THs.

Patients' Suggestions for GHs

- There exists a need for improvement in attitude of hospital staff of the GHs.
- Patients' and relatives face difficulties in view of negligent approach of nurses and sanitation staff which should be taken care of by the GHs to put the patients at ease.
- There exists excellent method of treatment and chief doctors should be aware about it but, cooperation from nurses, resident doctors and other staff members, in case of the GHs, should be streamlined.
- Patients' stressed on the need for more experienced and specialized doctors in case of the GHs for better treatment and diagnosis of illness of patients.
- An overcrowding in the GHs should be managed properly by administrative staff.

- The patients' of the GHs focused on the need for doing counseling about proper sanitation facilities and especially keeping in view bad habits of patients who make the hospital dirty.

OVERALL SUGGESTIONS

Overall suggestions for improving the performance in marketing and delivering the hospital services, are given as below:

- The hospitals need to develop marketing orientation.
- Marketing departments with well defined goals need to be created in the hospitals' set up to design marketing planning and to succeed in the competitive markets.
- Marketing department should be headed by qualified experienced marketing professional and s/he should be given a fair chance to the head marketing department to interact closely with all divisions of the hospitals.
- Hospitals, to experience better occupancy rate and net revenues, need to understand patient population, availability of physicians and offerings of their competition.
- The hospitals need to realize that doing things differently is more powerful in the market place than doing things better.
- The hospitals should realize that finding patients, identifying what they want, before competitors do is imperative for hospitals and is crucial to their survival.
- Cost effective services need to be provided by developing control on inter-relationship among the factors of planning occupancy, medical decision and expenditures.
- Providing effective hospital services requires considerable human relations skills and the reduction of length of stay of inpatients in the hospitals.
- The hospitals need to develop a well-designed information system to obtain prompt feedback about the performance of facilities and people.
- A follow-up of patients' satisfaction need to be assessed by developing and administering a structured questionnaire at the exit point of service which helps hospitals to realize weakness and loop holes in the system leading to customer dissatisfaction.
- The hospitals need to make efforts to transfer the responsibility of paying the bill from the patient to some faceless entity. Indian insurance bill paved the way for entry of private players have already initiated their efforts to catch the market. Hospital tie-ups with insurance companies will lead the fate in the future. Hence, hospitals need to create integrated system combining services and financing mechanisms.
- The hospitals may promote their services for patients abroad. World-class treatment coupled with low cost compared to advanced countries would contribute to market growth.

- The hospitals should consider healthcare service delivery as an interactive process between hospitals personnel and customer. So, hospitals advertising in particular must concentrate not only on encouraging customer to buy or utilize service but, also on encouraging hospital personnel to interact in a friendly and reassuring manner.
- The health plan packages should be provided by hospitals to family by designing comprehensive health plan packages but not expensive. Health plan packages need to offer various services for the family and corporate employees which may increase the turnover of the hospitals.
- The hospitals should develop a brochure which provide information relating to history of the hospital, description of services, availability of equipment and facilities, doctors, visiting consultants, prices of the diagnostic procedures and surgeries, billing procedures etc. this can avoid misconceptions among the patients about the hospital and its functioning.

Index